Visitor 5

Final Volume

VISITOR

Visitor Vol. 5
Created By Yee-Jung No

Translation - Jennifer Hahm
English Adaption - Jessica Cathryn Feinberg
Layout and Lettering - StarPrint Brokers
Cover Layout - Christopher Tjalsma

Editor - Tim Beedle
Digital Imaging Manager - Chris Buford
Pre-Production Supervisor - Erika Terriquez
Art Director - Anne Marie Horne
Production Manager - Elisabeth Brizzi
Managing Editor - Vy Nguyen
VP of Production - Ron Klamert
Editor-in-Chief - Rob Tokar
Publisher - Mike Kiley
President and C.O.O. - John Parker
C.E.O. and Chief Creative Officer - Stuart Levy

A TOKYOPOP® Manga

TOKYOPOP Inc.
5900 Wilshire Blvd. Suite 2000
Los Angeles, CA 90036

E-mail: info@TOKYOPOP.com
Come visit us online at www.TOKYOPOP.com

ISBN: 978-1-59532-664-5

First TOKYOPOP printing: January 2007
10 9 8 7 6 5 4 3 2 1
Printed in the USA

VISITOR

by
Yee-Jung No

Vol. 5

HAMBURG // LONDON // LOS ANGELES // TOKYO

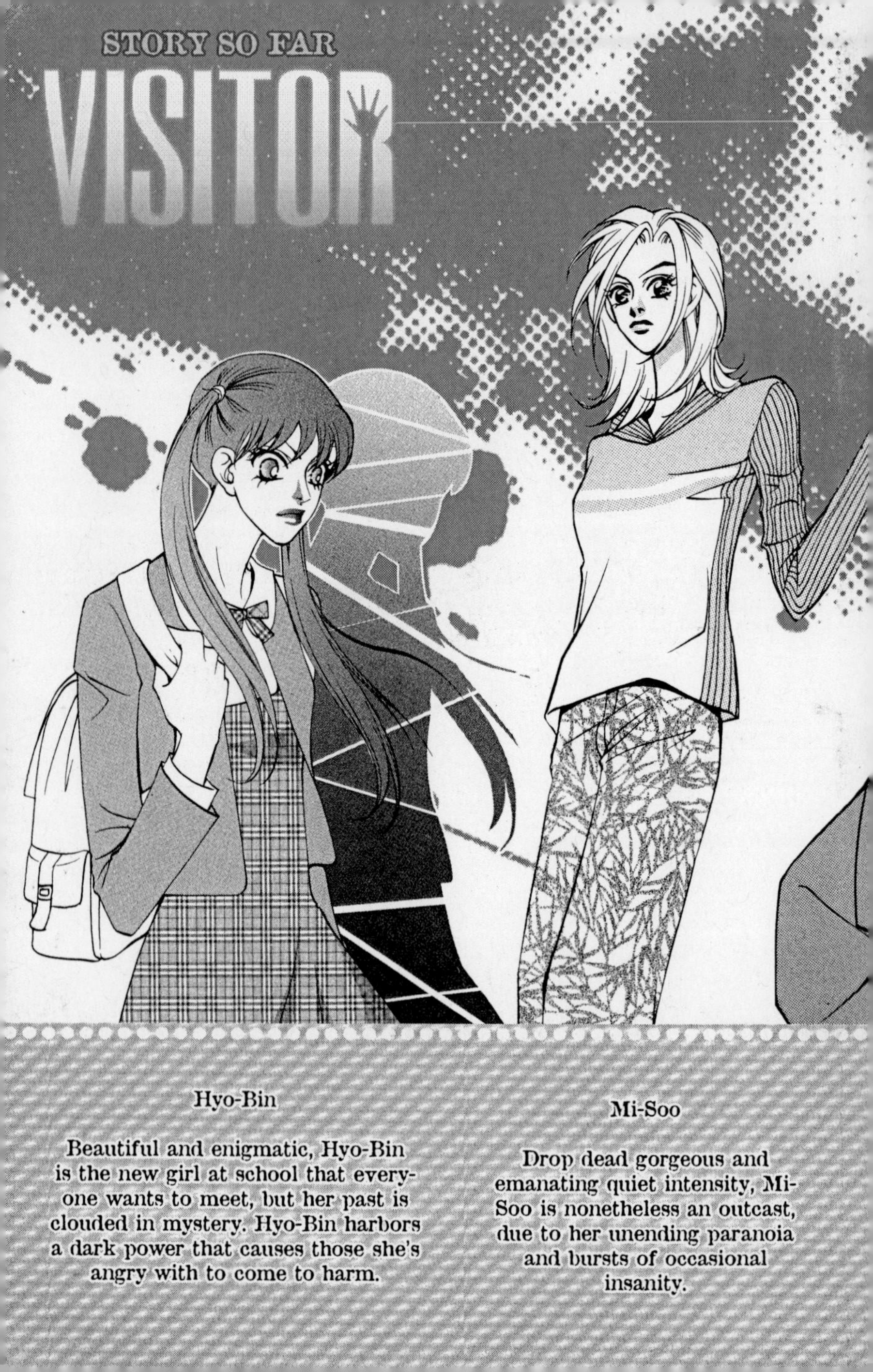
STORY SO FAR
VISITOR

Hyo-Bin

Beautiful and enigmatic, Hyo-Bin is the new girl at school that everyone wants to meet, but her past is clouded in mystery. Hyo-Bin harbors a dark power that causes those she's angry with to come to harm.

Mi-Soo

Drop dead gorgeous and emanating quiet intensity, Mi-Soo is nonetheless an outcast, due to her unending paranoia and bursts of occasional insanity.

Previously in Visitor

High school student Hyo-Bin Na looks as if she should be one of the most popular students at her school. But she isn't popular—she's feared. Hyo-Bin has a very dangerous power. Her anger manifests itself physically, causing the subject of her ire to go down in a bloody display of pain. Hyo-Bin also has nightly visions of death and torture, often inflicted on people she knows. For years, they have been a burden that Hyo-Bin has had to bear.

Hyo-Bin recently made a startling discovery. The dreams may have their foundation in reality. At the core of the mystery is a sister that Hyo-Bin never knew she had: Hyo-Ri. Older than her by a few years, Hyo-Ri died under mysterious and tragic circumstances, and for reasons that are unknown to her, Hyo-Bin can't recall any of it.

Why this memory has been lost to Hyo-Bin and why her parents have never before spoken of her sister are mysteries Hyo-Bin has yet to solve. She also has yet to determine precisely how her power and her dreams tie in to this newfound discovery. However, the pieces have slowly begun falling into place as we enter our final chapter...

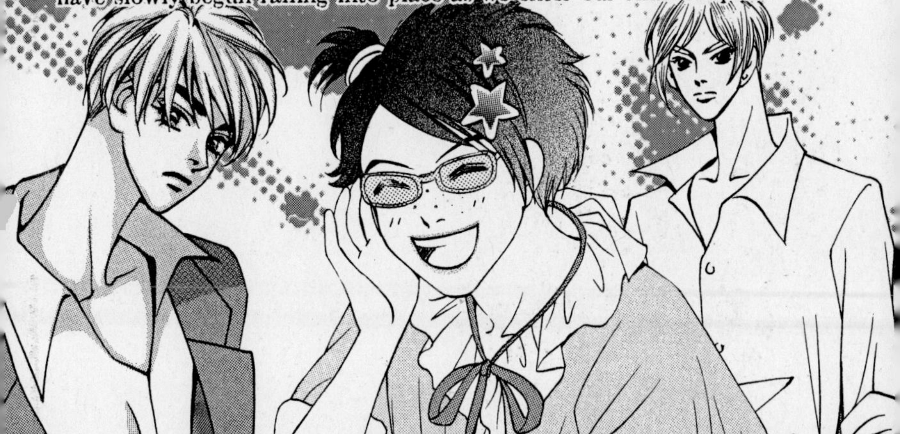

Ji-Hwan

The most popular boy in Hyo-Bin's class. Ji-Hwan has befriended Hyo-Bin, but who knows what his real intentions are? He's very attractive and is rumored to be a player.

Ye-Won

Outgoing to a fault and quite unpopular, when Ye-Won learns that Hyo-Bin wants to avoid making friends, she senses a kindred spirit...or at least a fellow outcast who can be her companion.

Gun-Yang

Boyishly handsome and very popular with the ladies, Gun-Yang is Ji-Hwan's best friend. The two have much in common, but Gun-Yang does not share Ji-Hwan's arrogance. Gun-Yang has a good heart, a rarity among his crowd.

CONTENTS

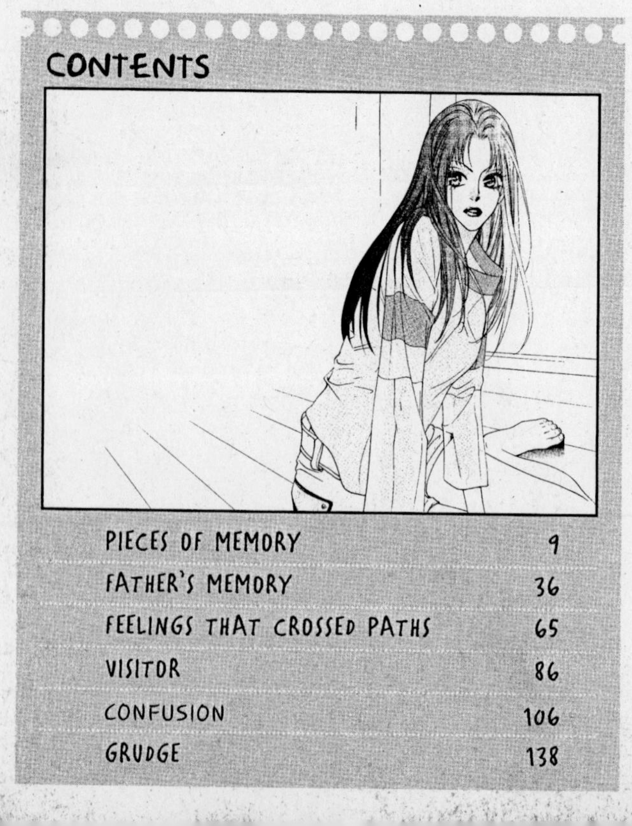

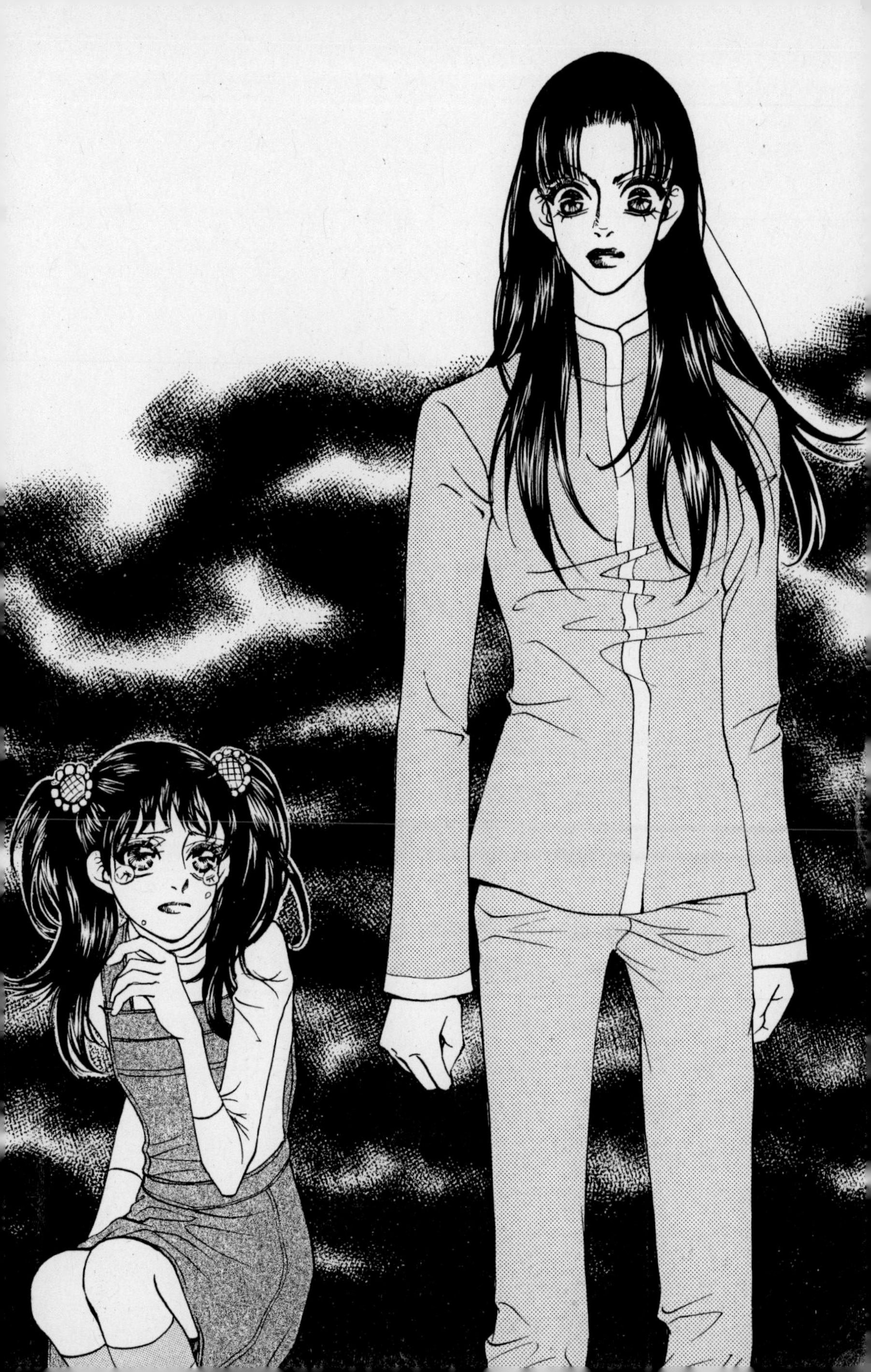

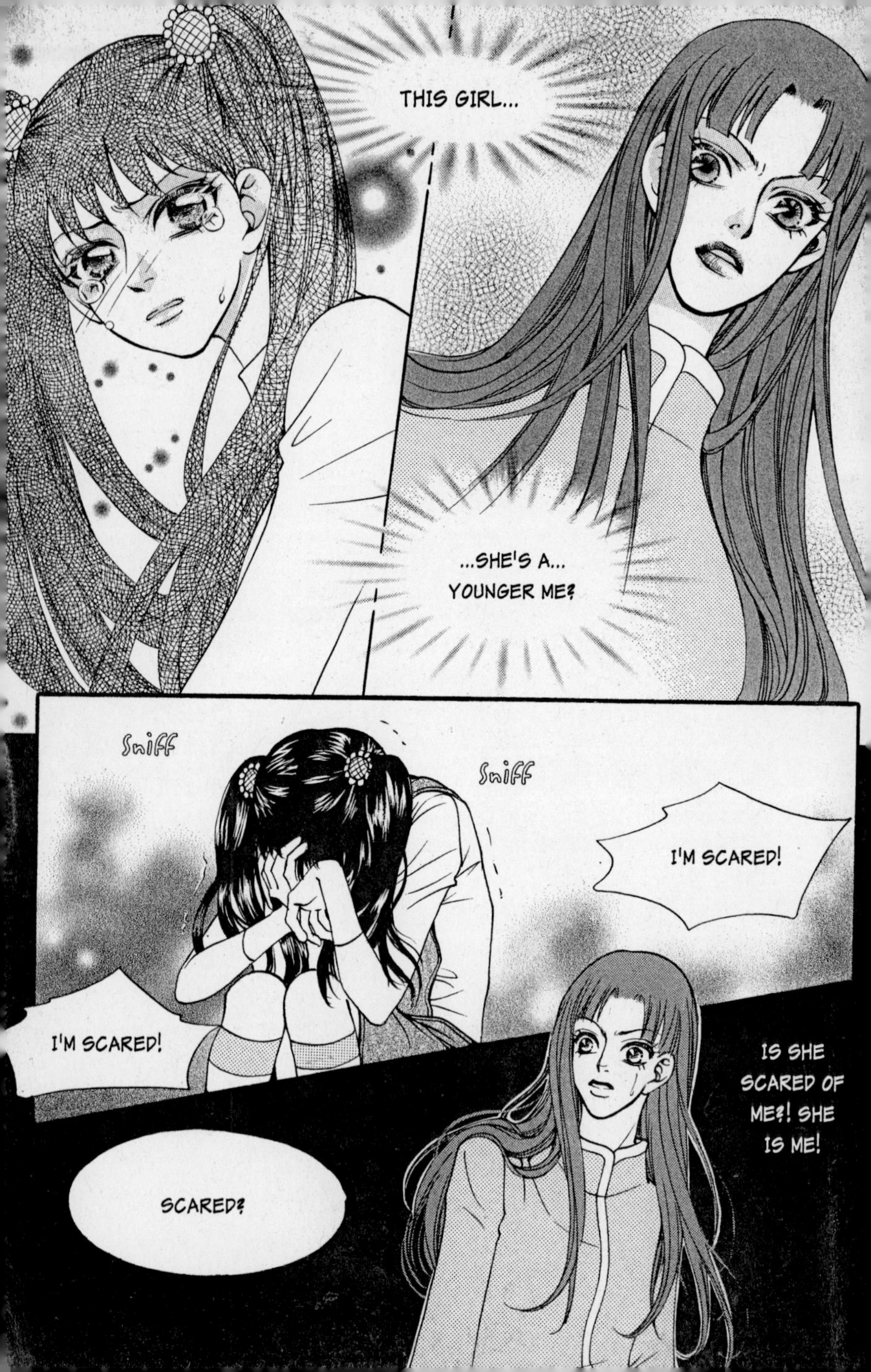
THIS GIRL...
...SHE'S A... YOUNGER ME?
Sniff
Sniff
I'M SCARED!
I'M SCARED!
IS SHE SCARED OF ME?! SHE IS ME!
SCARED?

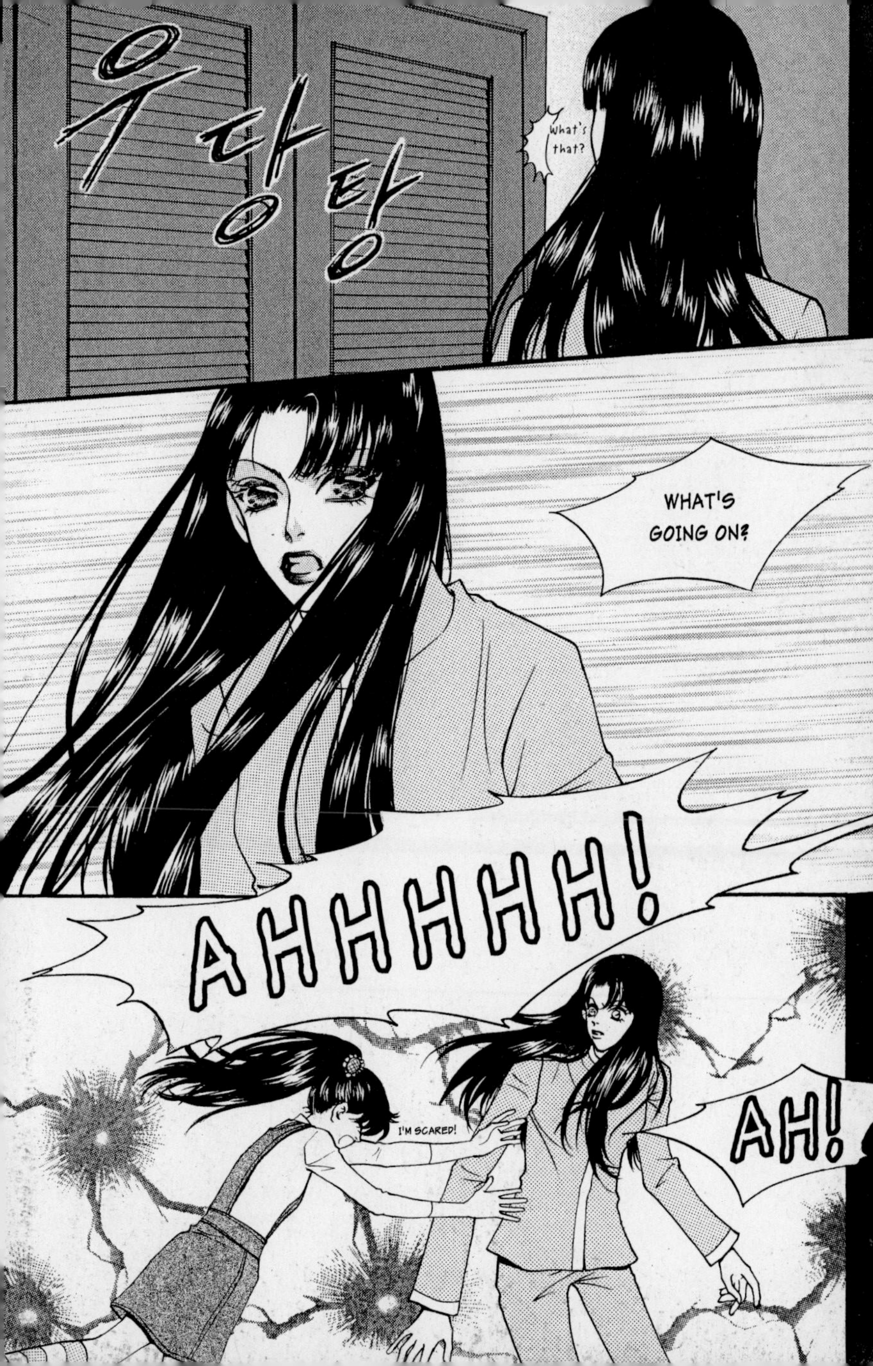

우당탕
What's that?
WHAT'S GOING ON?
AHHHHH!
I'M SCARED!
AH!

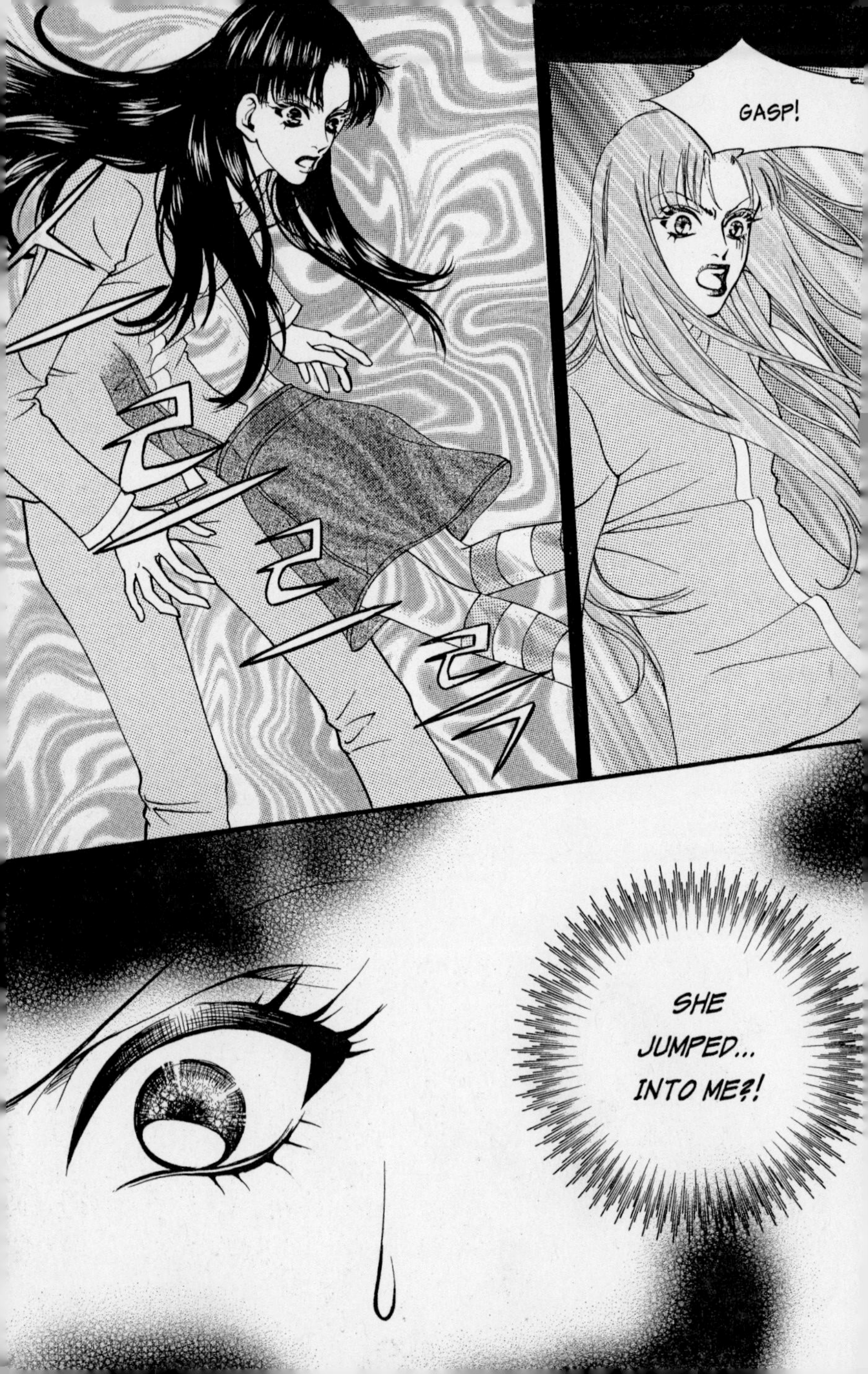
GASP!
SHE JUMPED... INTO ME?!

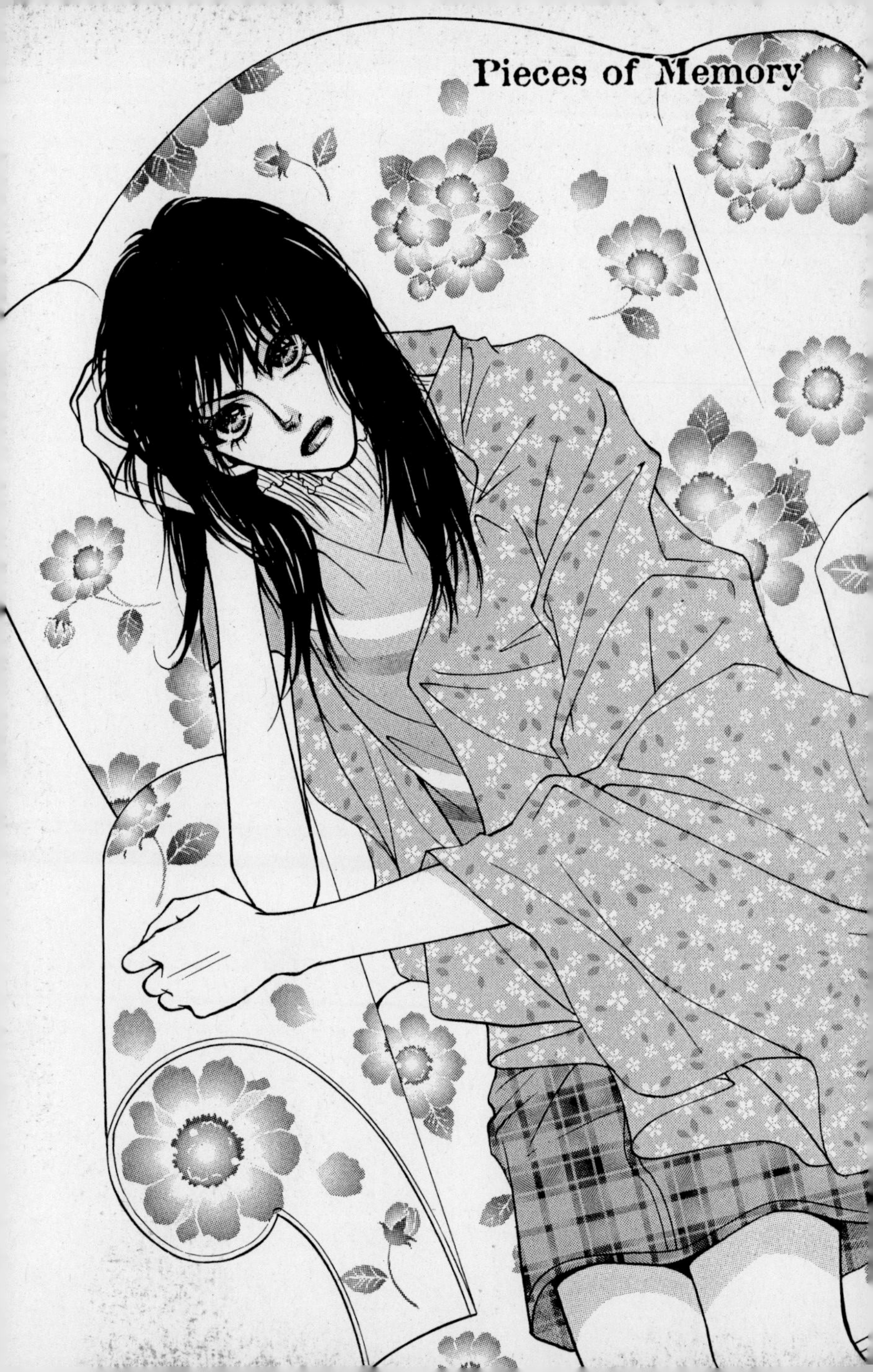
Pieces of Memory

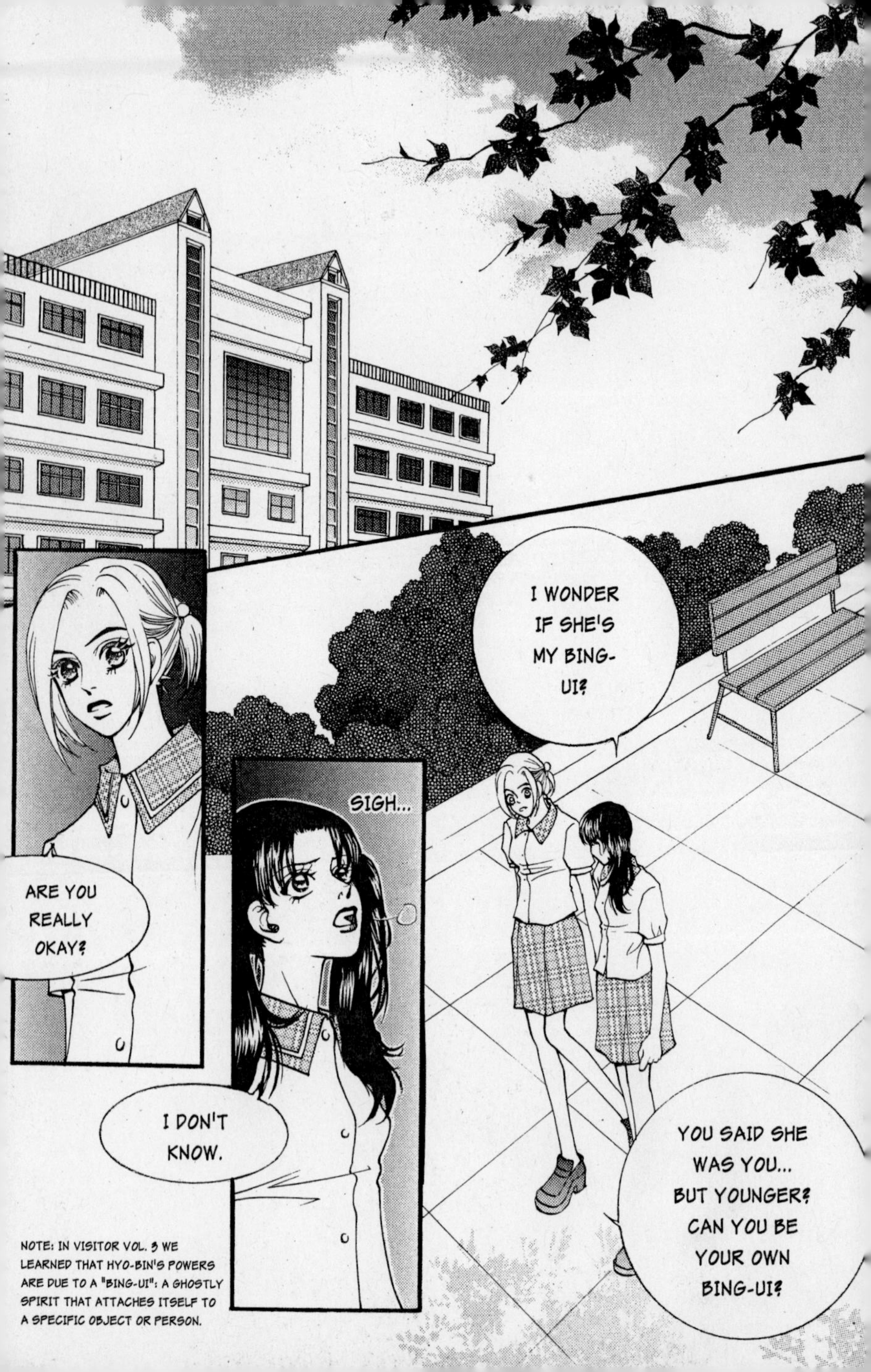
ARE YOU REALLY OKAY?
SIGH...
I DON'T KNOW.
I WONDER IF SHE'S MY BING-UI?
YOU SAID SHE WAS YOU... BUT YOUNGER? CAN YOU BE YOUR OWN BING-UI?

NOTE: IN VISITOR VOL. 3 WE LEARNED THAT HYO-BIN'S POWERS ARE DUE TO A "BING-UI": A GHOSTLY SPIRIT THAT ATTACHES ITSELF TO A SPECIFIC OBJECT OR PERSON.

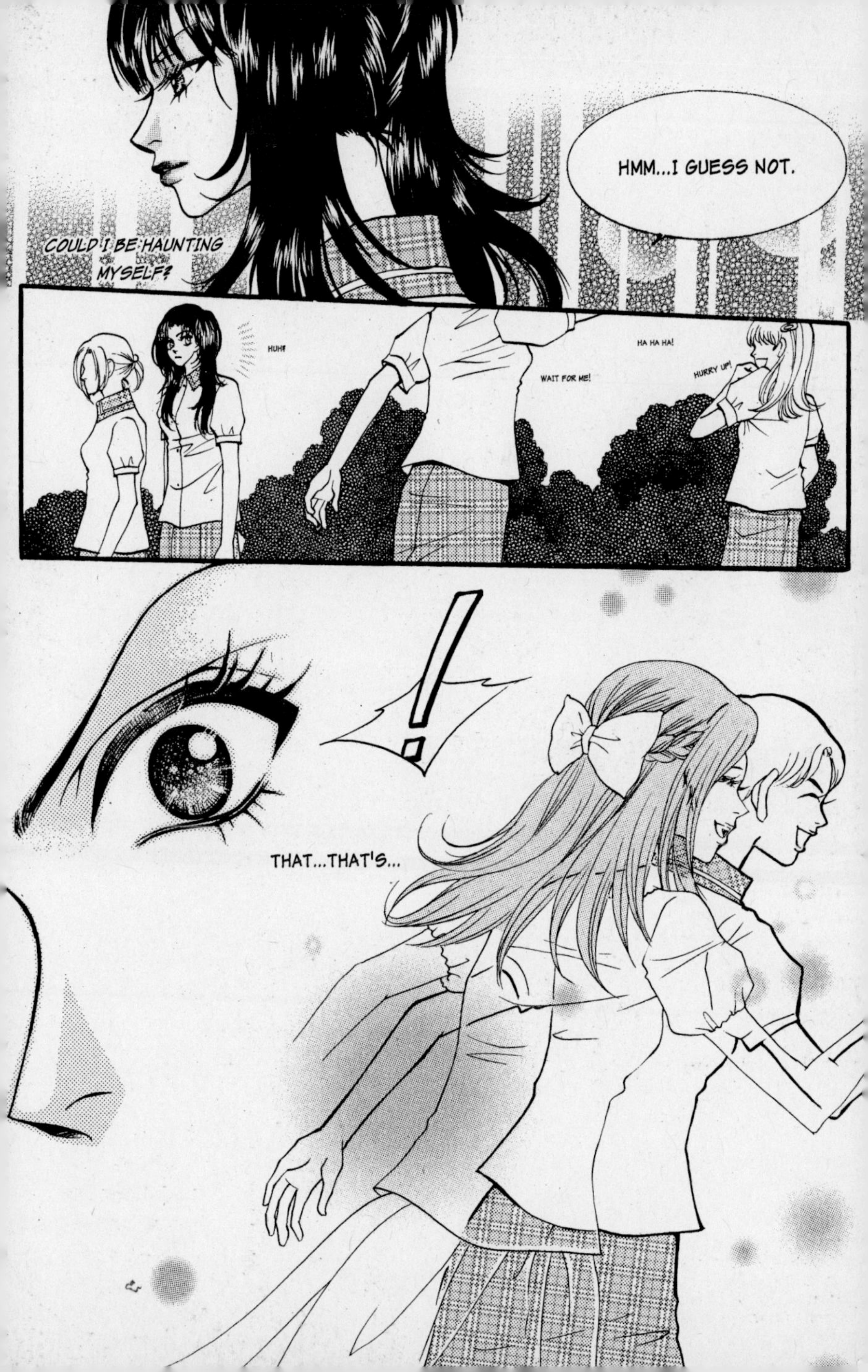
COULD I BE HAUNTING MYSELF?
HMM...I GUESS NOT.
HUH?
WAIT FOR ME!
HA HA HA!
HURRY UP!
!
THAT...THAT'S...

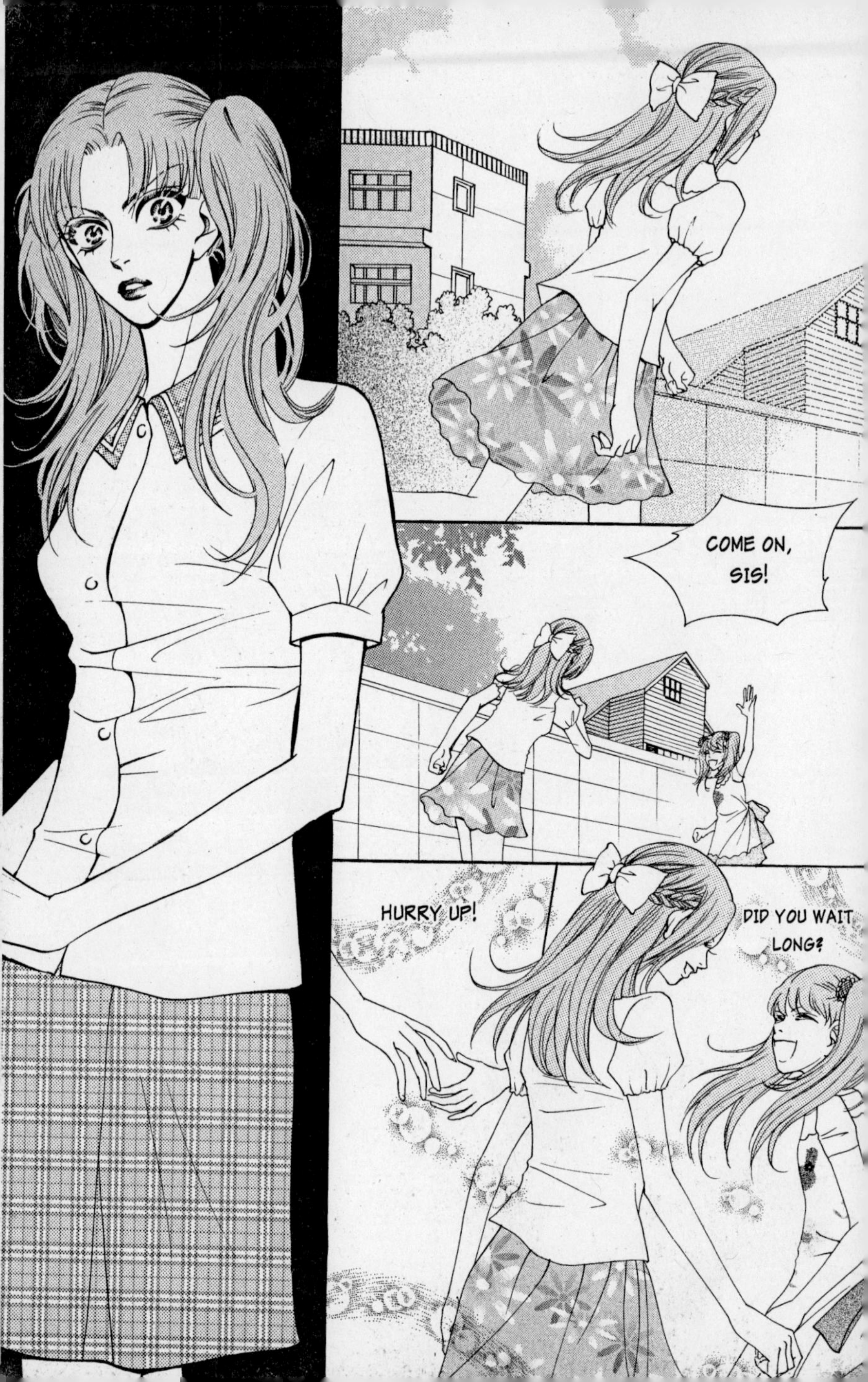
COME ON, SIS!
HURRY UP!
DID YOU WAIT LONG?

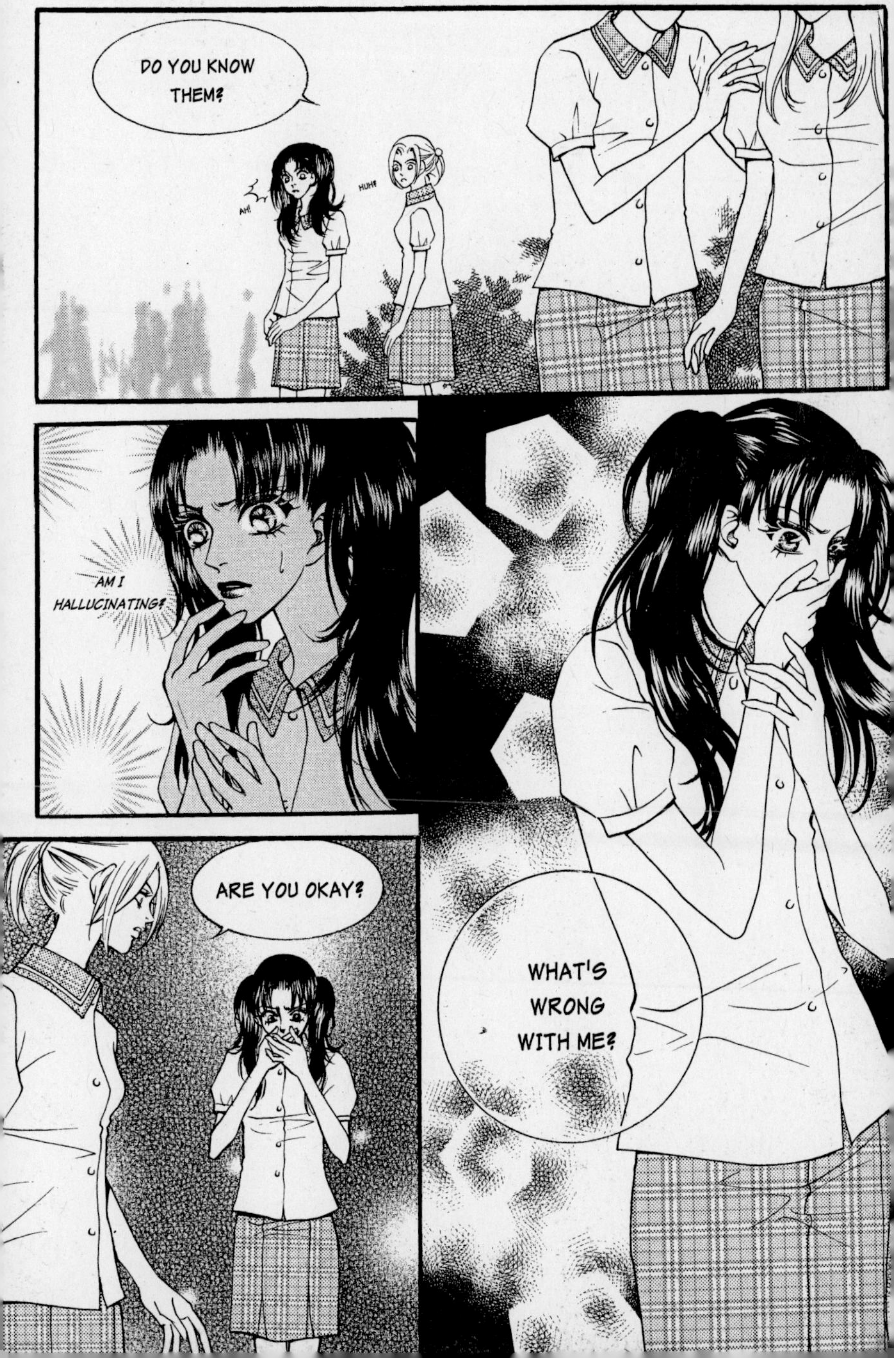
DO YOU KNOW THEM?
AH!
HUH?
AM I HALLUCINATING?
ARE YOU OKAY?
WHAT'S WRONG WITH ME?

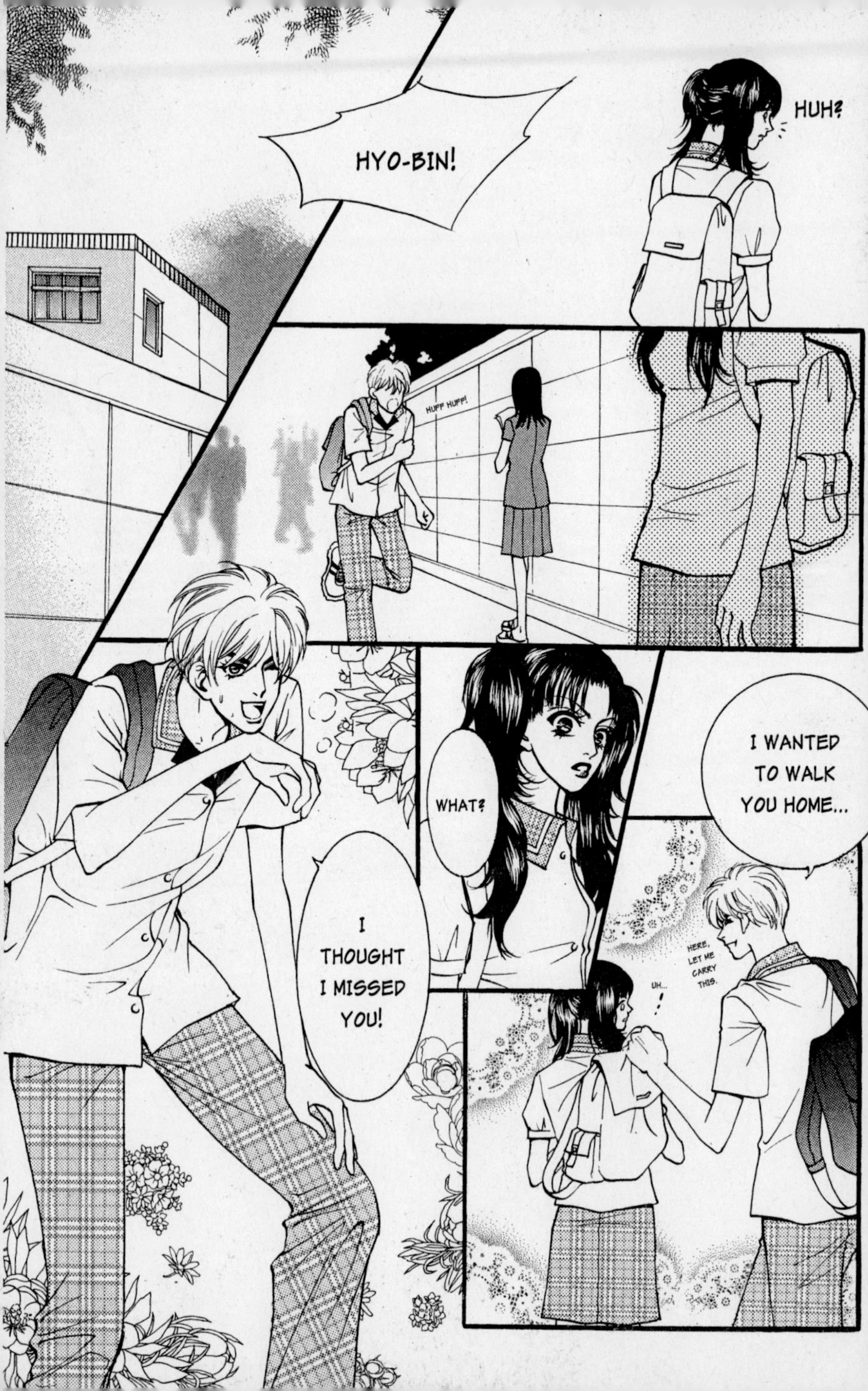
HYO-BIN!
HUH?
HUFF HUFF!
I THOUGHT I MISSED YOU!
WHAT?
I WANTED TO WALK YOU HOME...
UH... !
HERE, LET ME CARRY THIS.

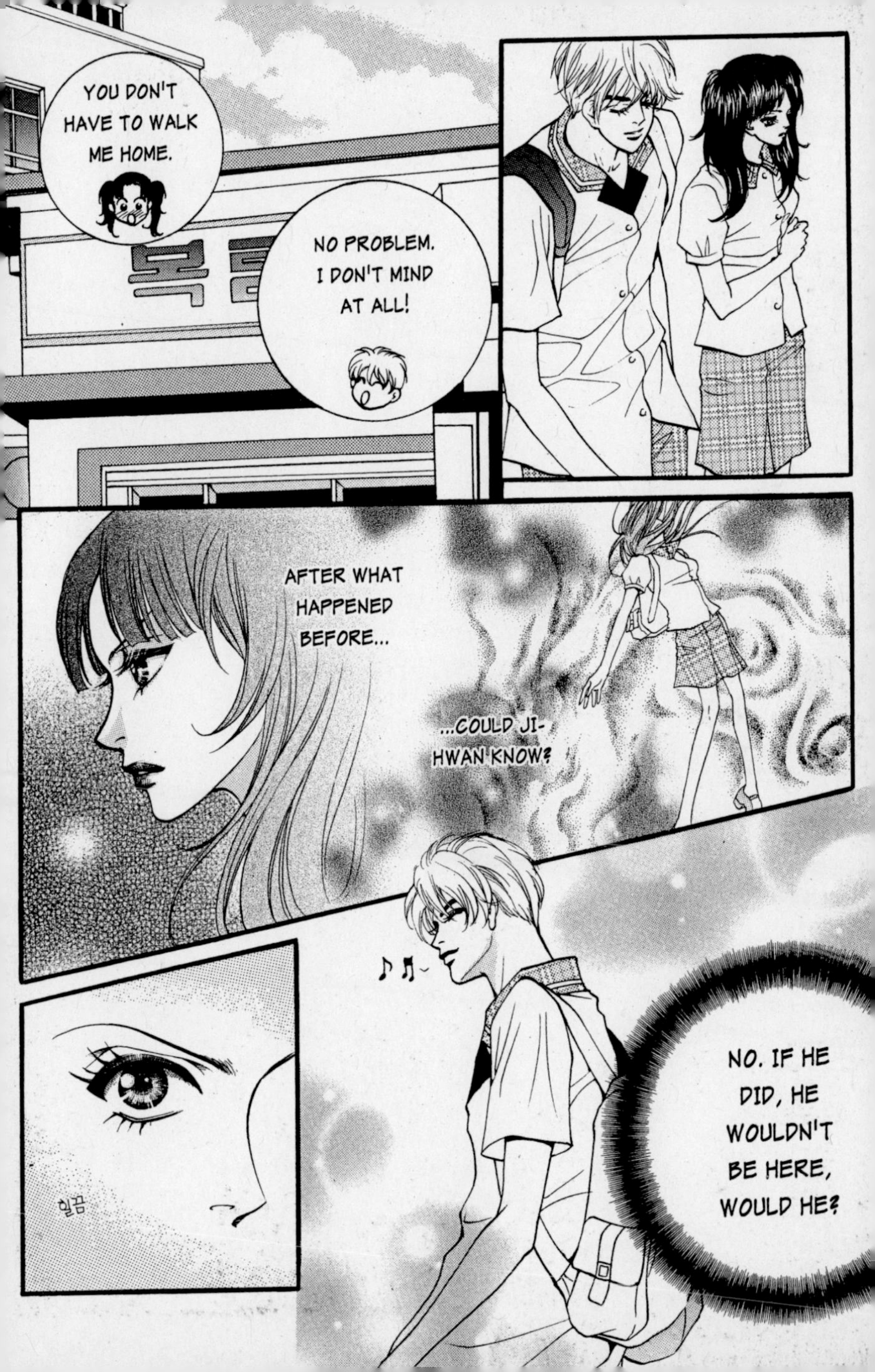
YOU DON'T HAVE TO WALK ME HOME.
NO PROBLEM. I DON'T MIND AT ALL!
AFTER WHAT HAPPENED BEFORE...
...COULD JI-HWAN KNOW?
힐끔
NO. IF HE DID, HE WOULDN'T BE HERE, WOULD HE?

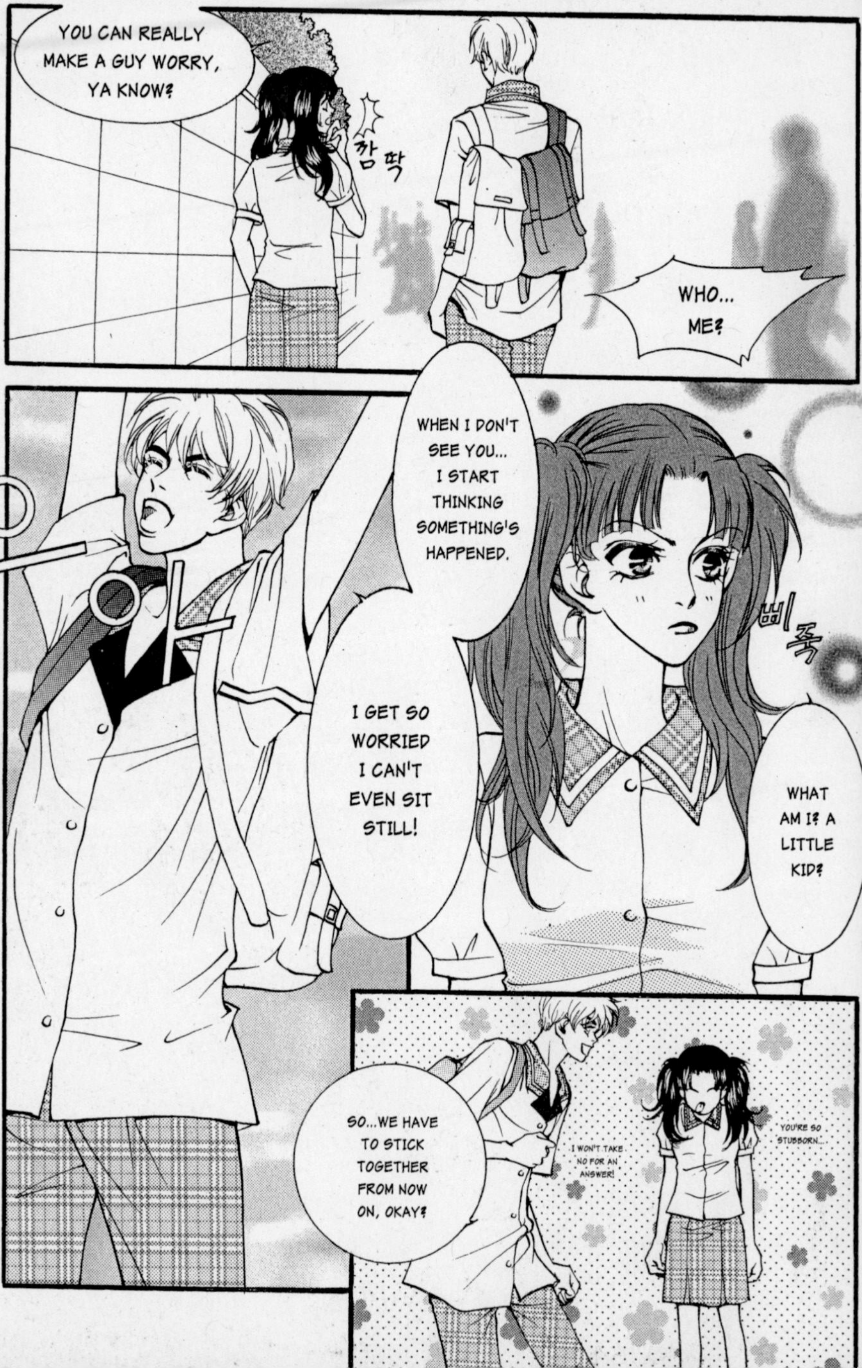
YOU CAN REALLY MAKE A GUY WORRY, YA KNOW?
깜짝
WHO... ME?
WHEN I DON'T SEE YOU... I START THINKING SOMETHING'S HAPPENED.
I GET SO WORRIED I CAN'T EVEN SIT STILL!
삐죽
WHAT AM I? A LITTLE KID?
SO...WE HAVE TO STICK TOGETHER FROM NOW ON, OKAY?
I WON'T TAKE NO FOR AN ANSWER!
YOU'RE SO STUBBORN...

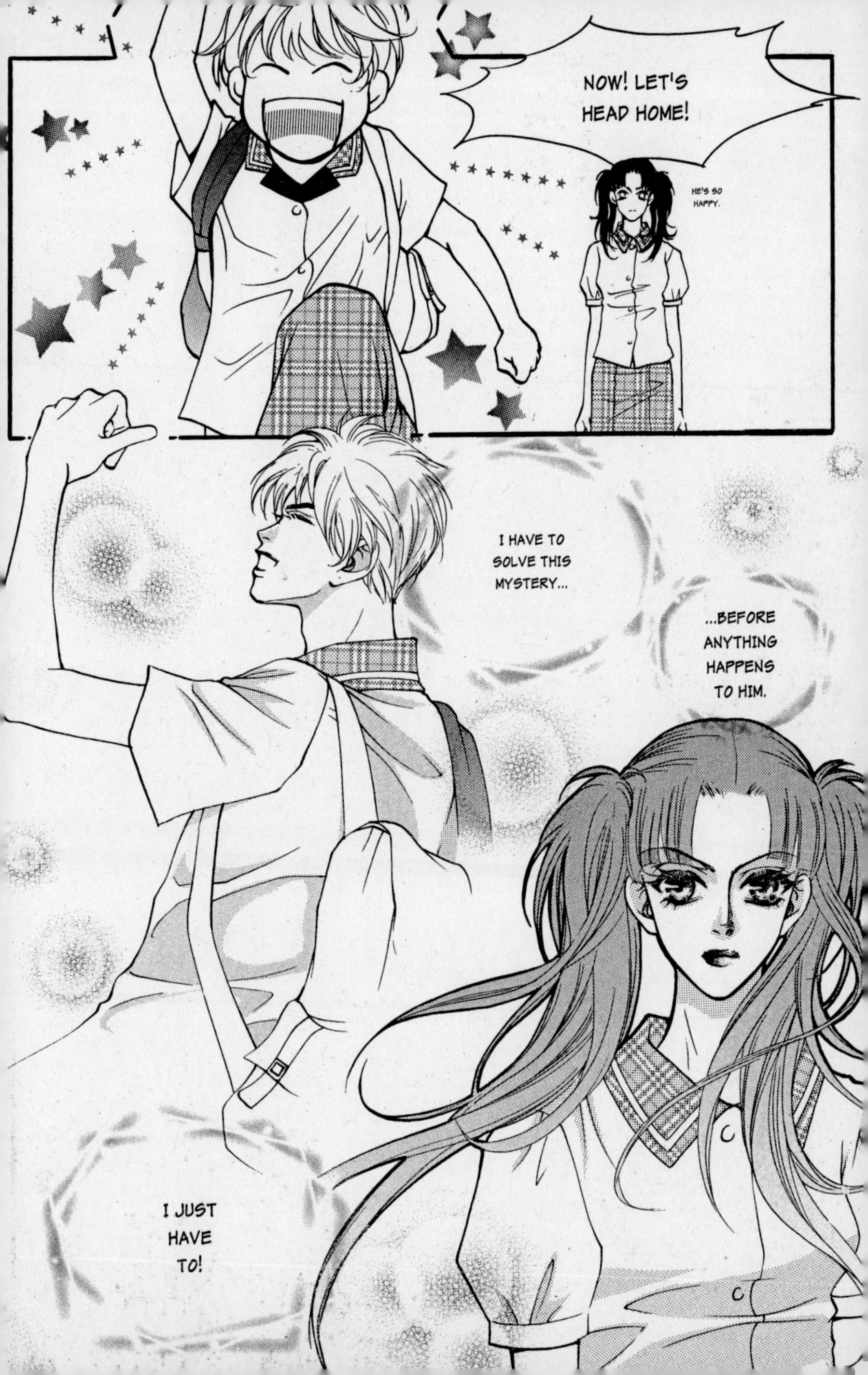
NOW! LET'S HEAD HOME!
HE'S SO HAPPY.
I HAVE TO SOLVE THIS MYSTERY...
...BEFORE ANYTHING HAPPENS TO HIM.
I JUST HAVE TO!

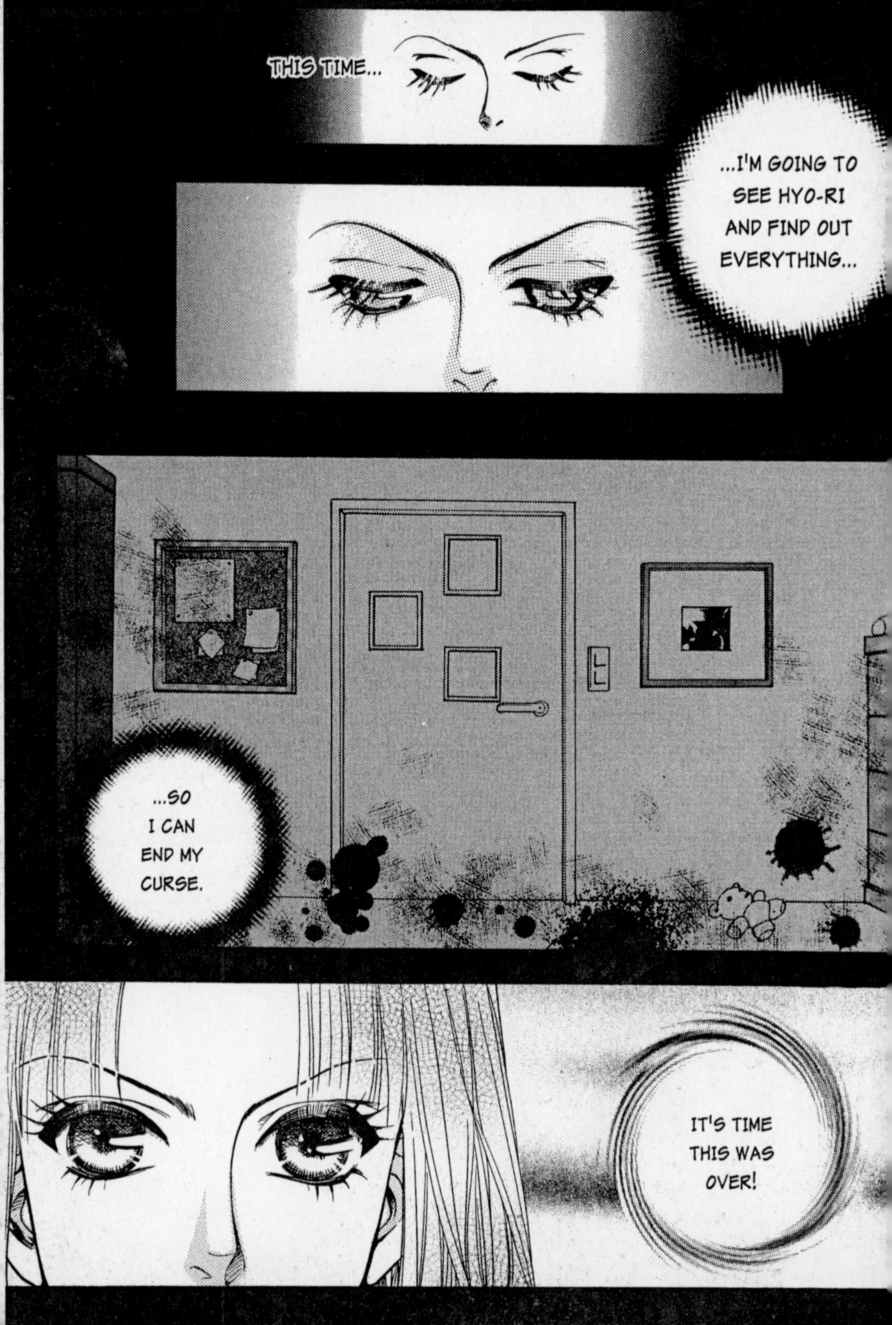
THIS TIME...
...I'M GOING TO SEE HYO-RI AND FIND OUT EVERYTHING...
...SO I CAN END MY CURSE.
IT'S TIME THIS WAS OVER!

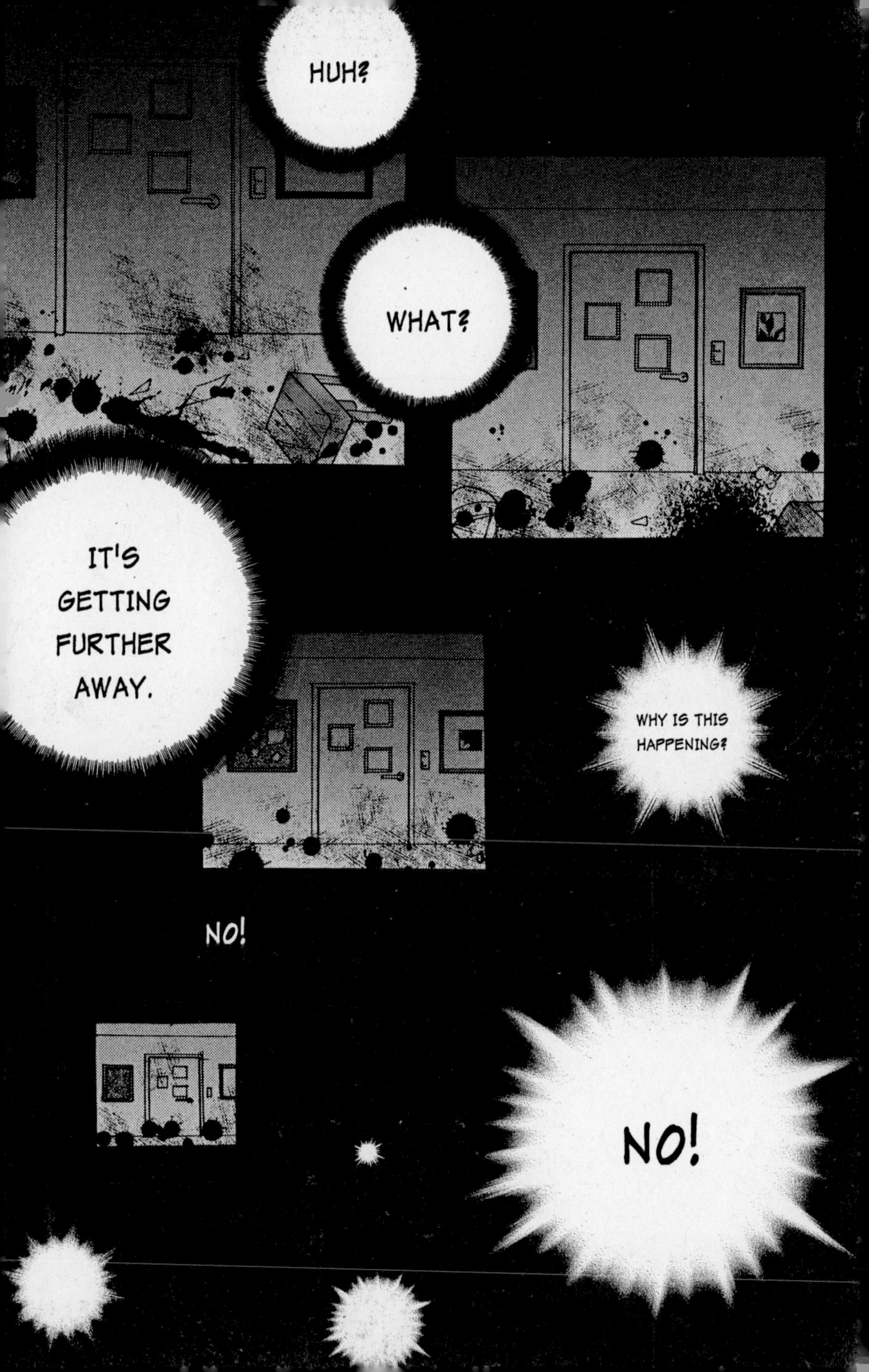
HUH?
WHAT?
IT'S GETTING FURTHER AWAY.
WHY IS THIS HAPPENING?
NO!
NO!

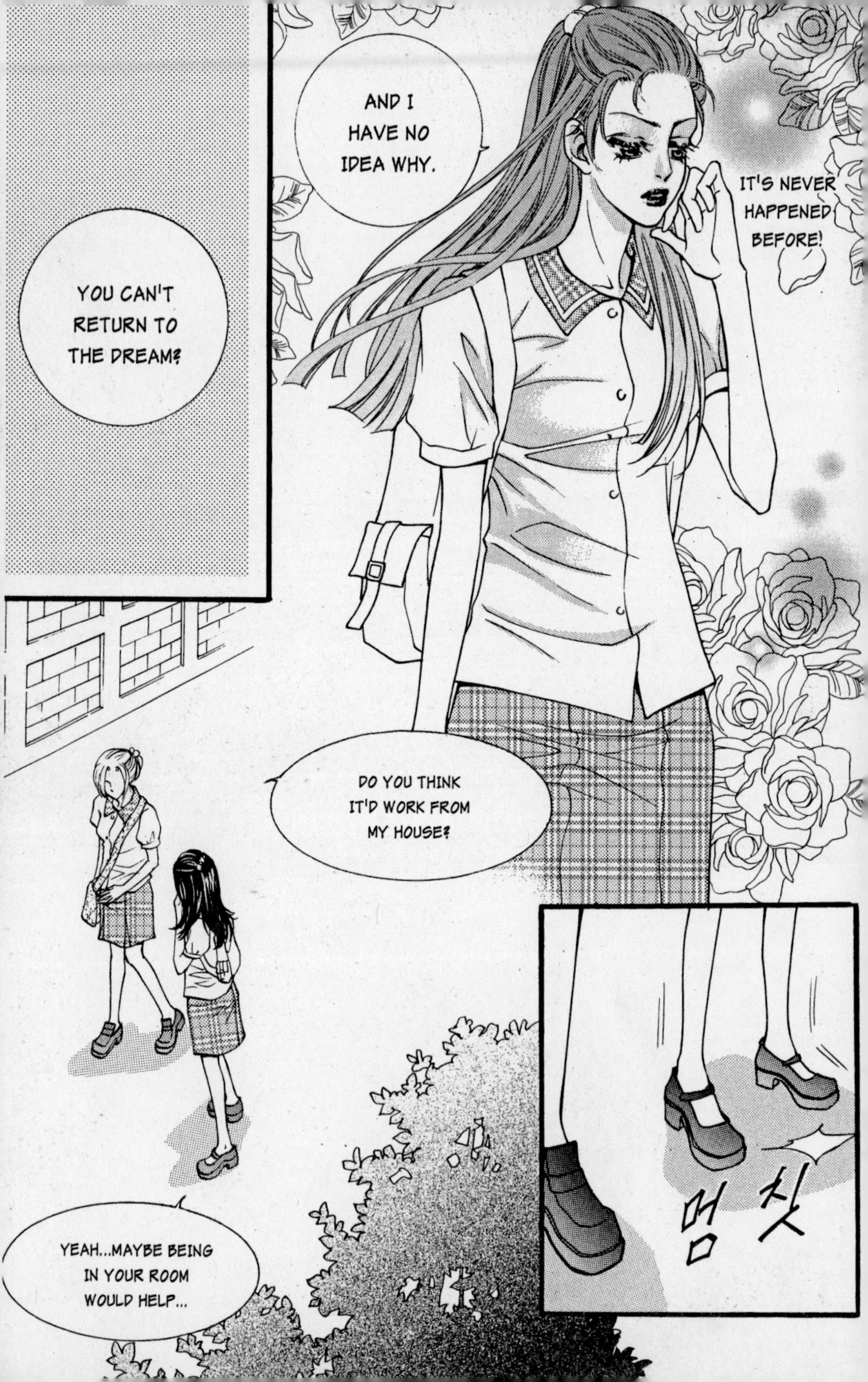
YOU CAN'T RETURN TO THE DREAM?
AND I HAVE NO IDEA WHY.
IT'S NEVER HAPPENED BEFORE!
DO YOU THINK IT'D WORK FROM MY HOUSE?
YEAH...MAYBE BEING IN YOUR ROOM WOULD HELP...
멈칫

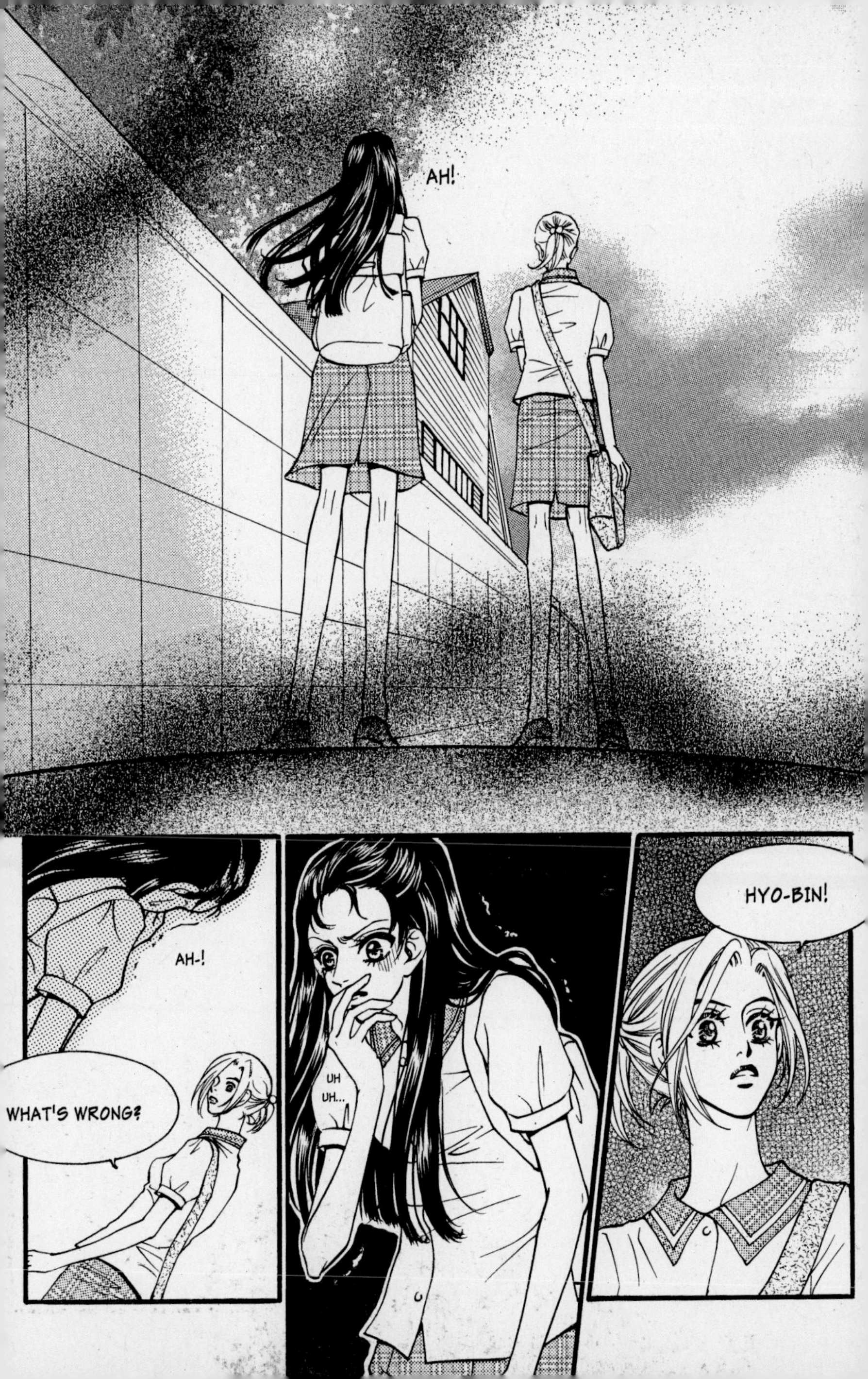
AH!
AH-!
WHAT'S WRONG?
UH UH...
HYO-BIN!

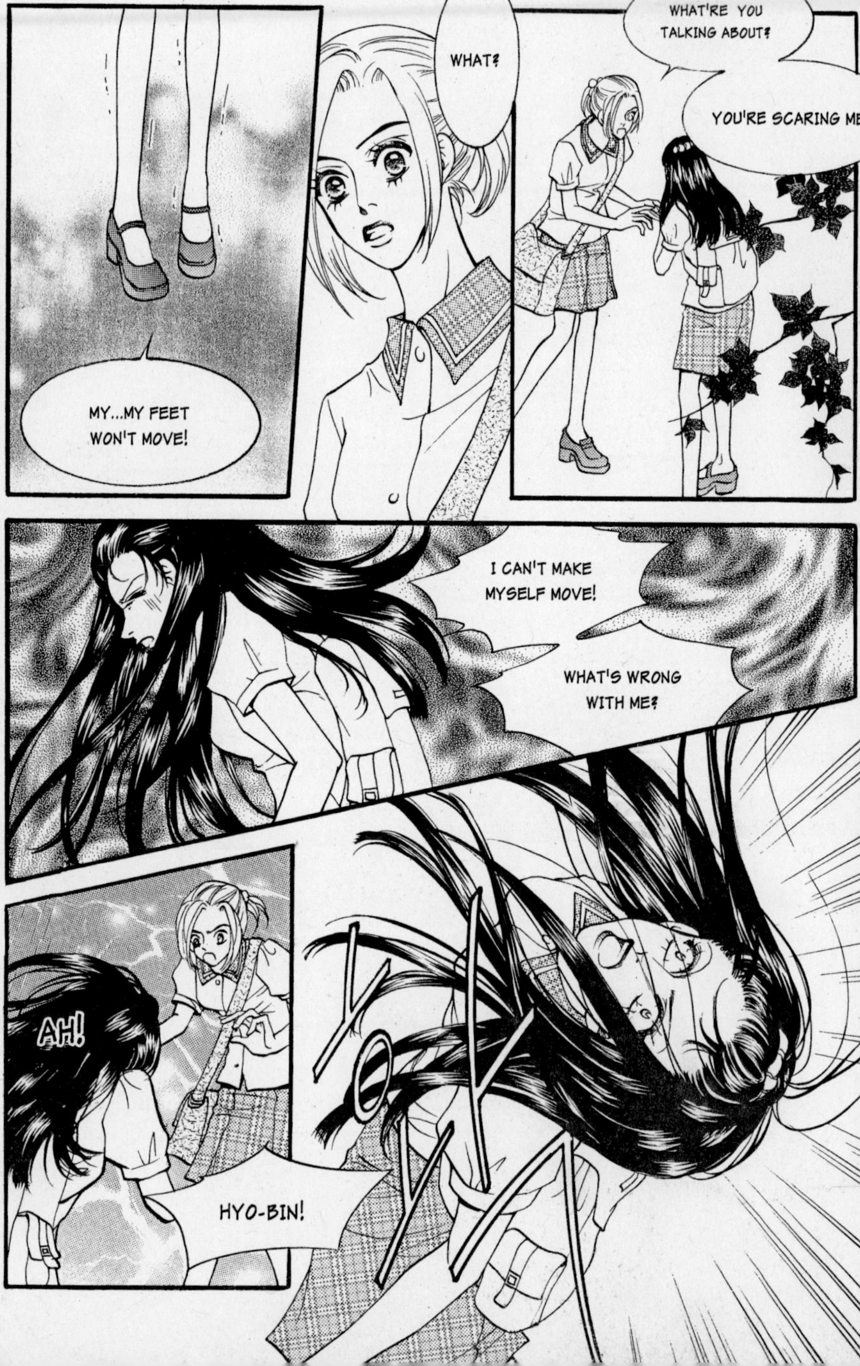
MY...MY FEET WON'T MOVE!
WHAT?
WHAT'RE YOU TALKING ABOUT?
YOU'RE SCARING ME!
I CAN'T MAKE MYSELF MOVE!
WHAT'S WRONG WITH ME?
AH!
HYO-BIN!

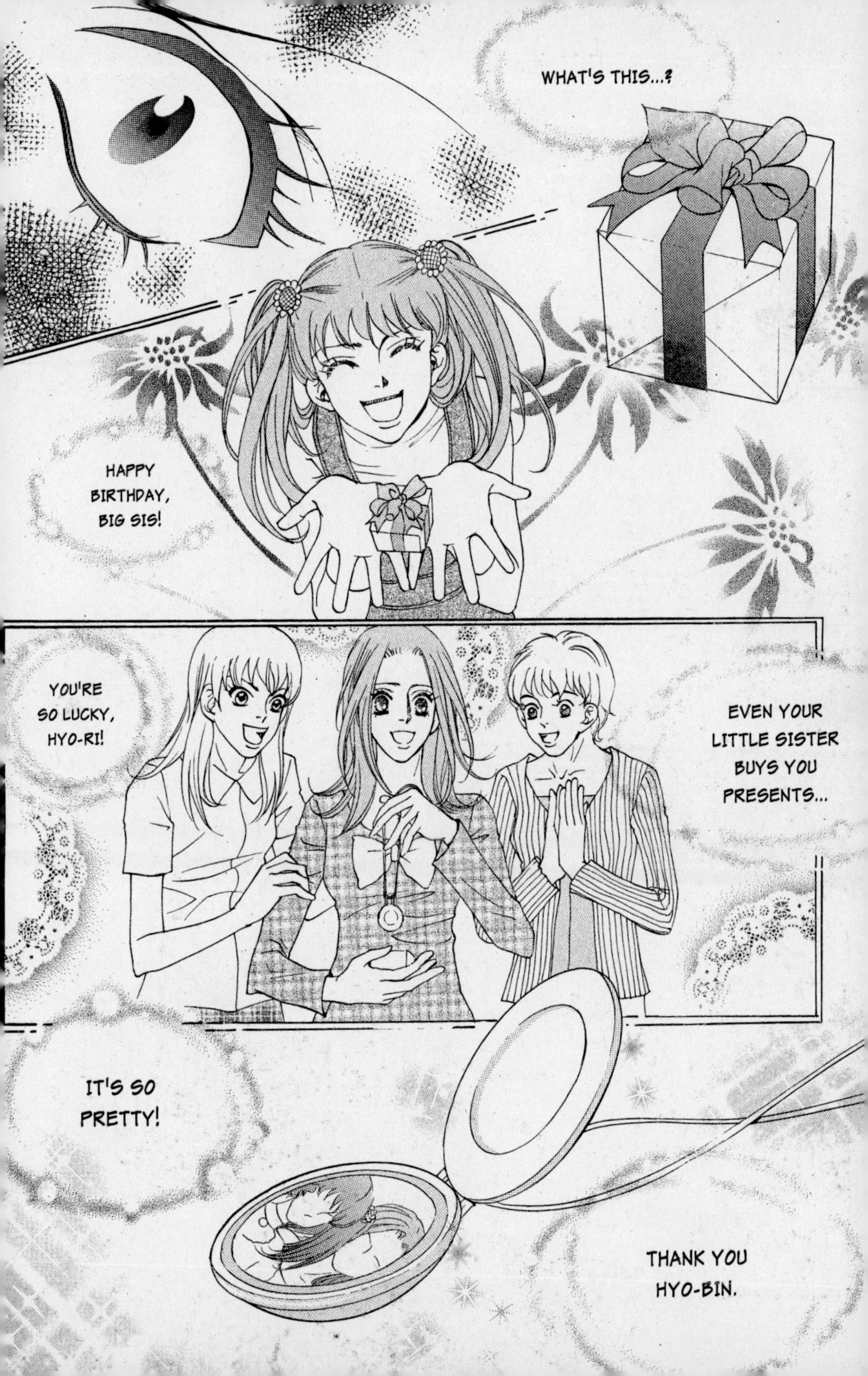
WHAT'S THIS...?
HAPPY BIRTHDAY, BIG SIS!
YOU'RE SO LUCKY, HYO-RI!
EVEN YOUR LITTLE SISTER BUYS YOU PRESENTS...
IT'S SO PRETTY!
THANK YOU HYO-BIN.

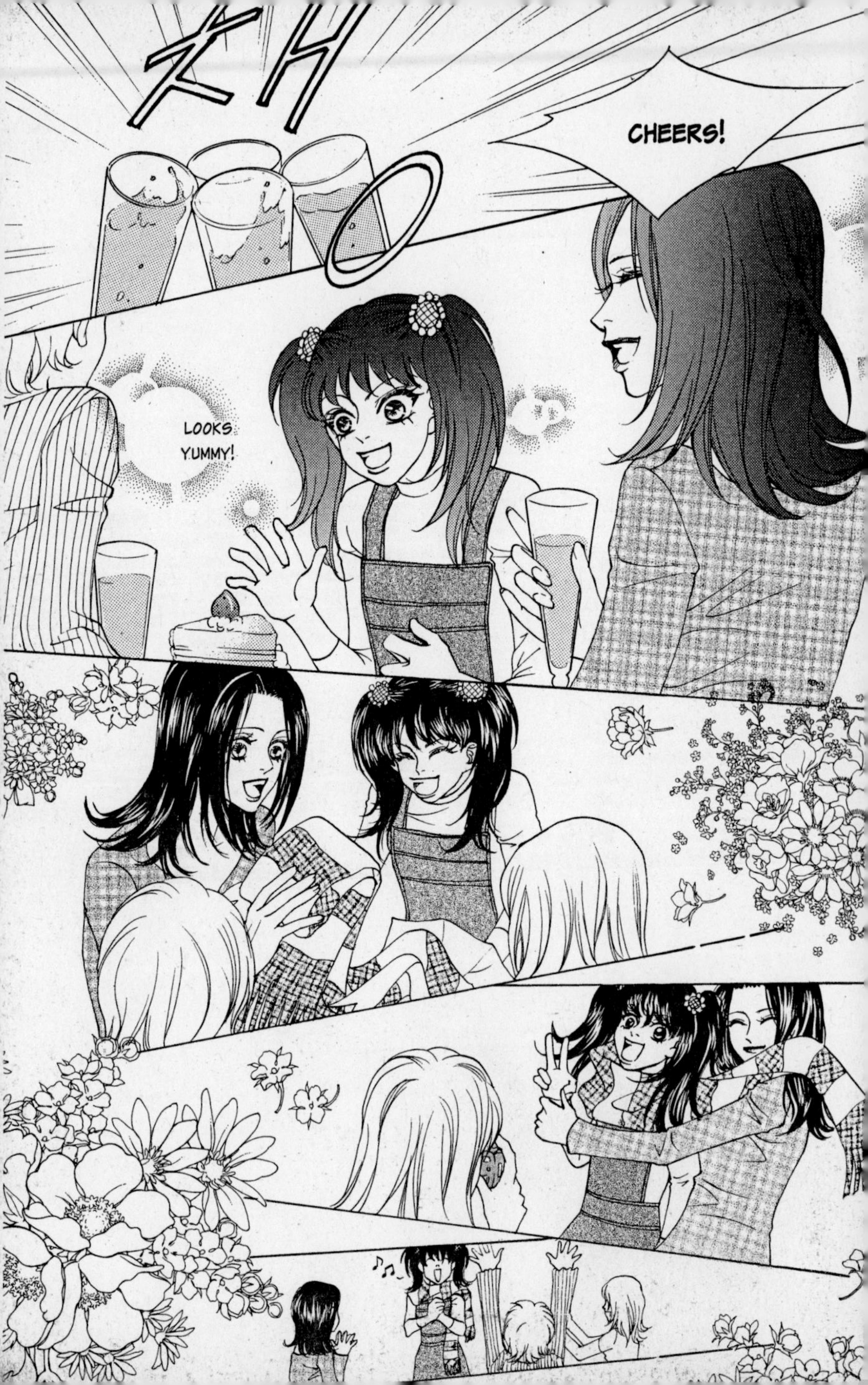
CHEERS!
LOOKS YUMMY!

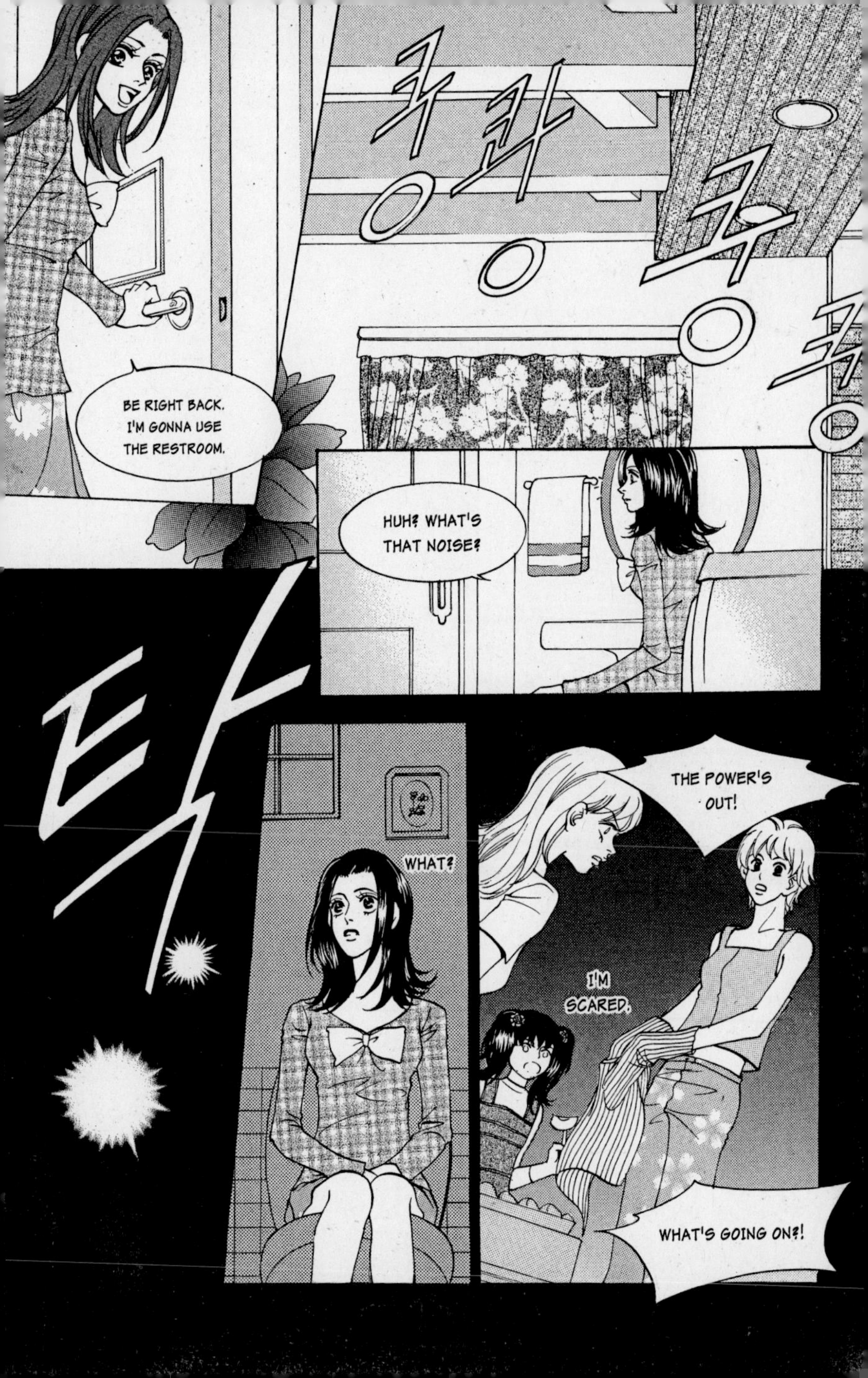
BE RIGHT BACK. I'M GONNA USE THE RESTROOM.
HUH? WHAT'S THAT NOISE?
탁
WHAT?
THE POWER'S OUT!
I'M SCARED.
WHAT'S GOING ON?!

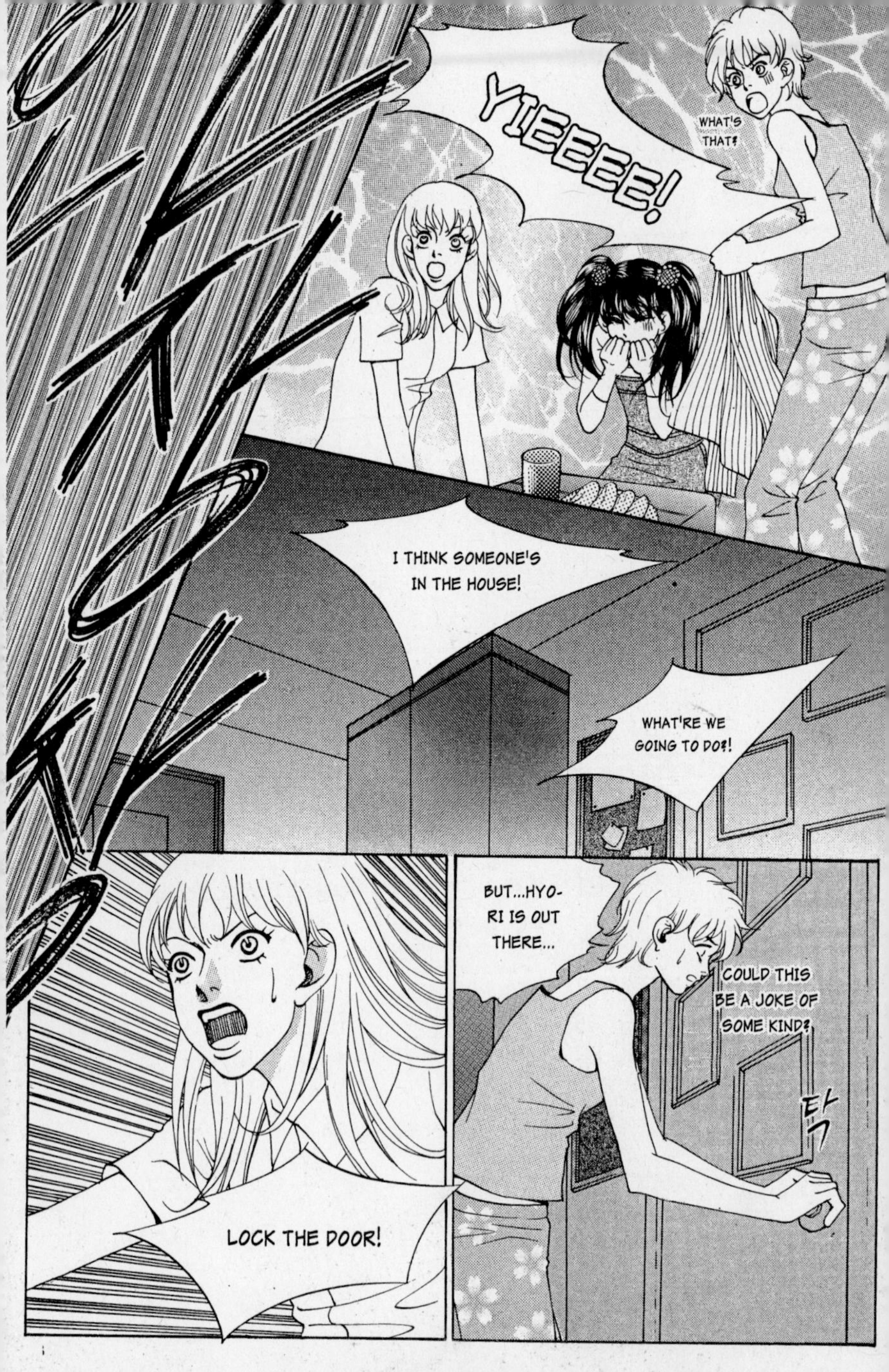
YIEEEEE!
WHAT'S THAT?
I THINK SOMEONE'S IN THE HOUSE!
WHAT'RE WE GOING TO DO?!
LOCK THE DOOR!
BUT...HYO-RI IS OUT THERE...
COULD THIS BE A JOKE OF SOME KIND?
탁

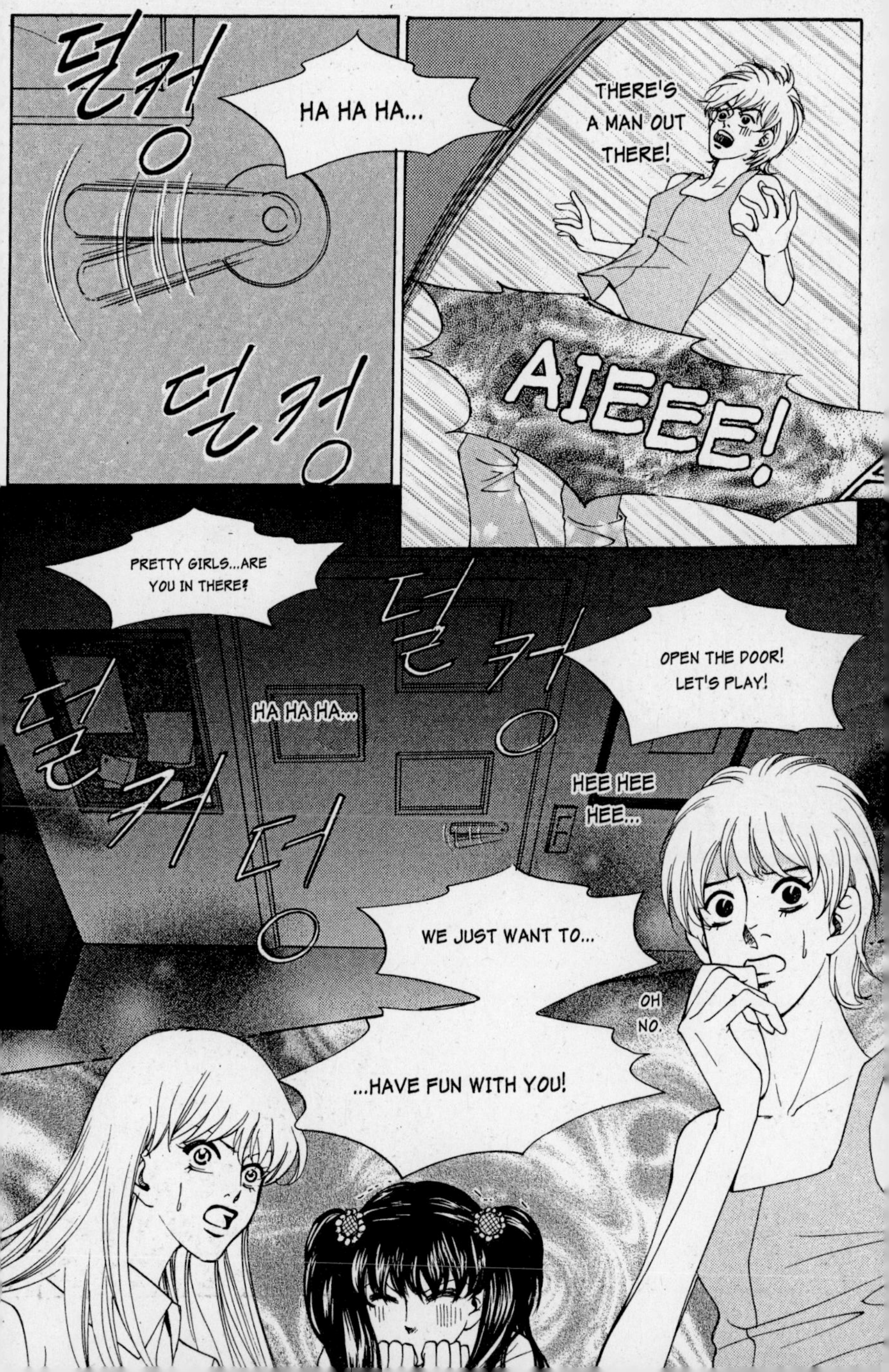
덜컹
HA HA HA...
덜컹
THERE'S A MAN OUT THERE!
AIEEE!
PRETTY GIRLS...ARE YOU IN THERE?
덜커덩
HA HA HA...
덜컹
OPEN THE DOOR! LET'S PLAY!
HEE HEE HEE...
WE JUST WANT TO...
OH NO.
...HAVE FUN WITH YOU!

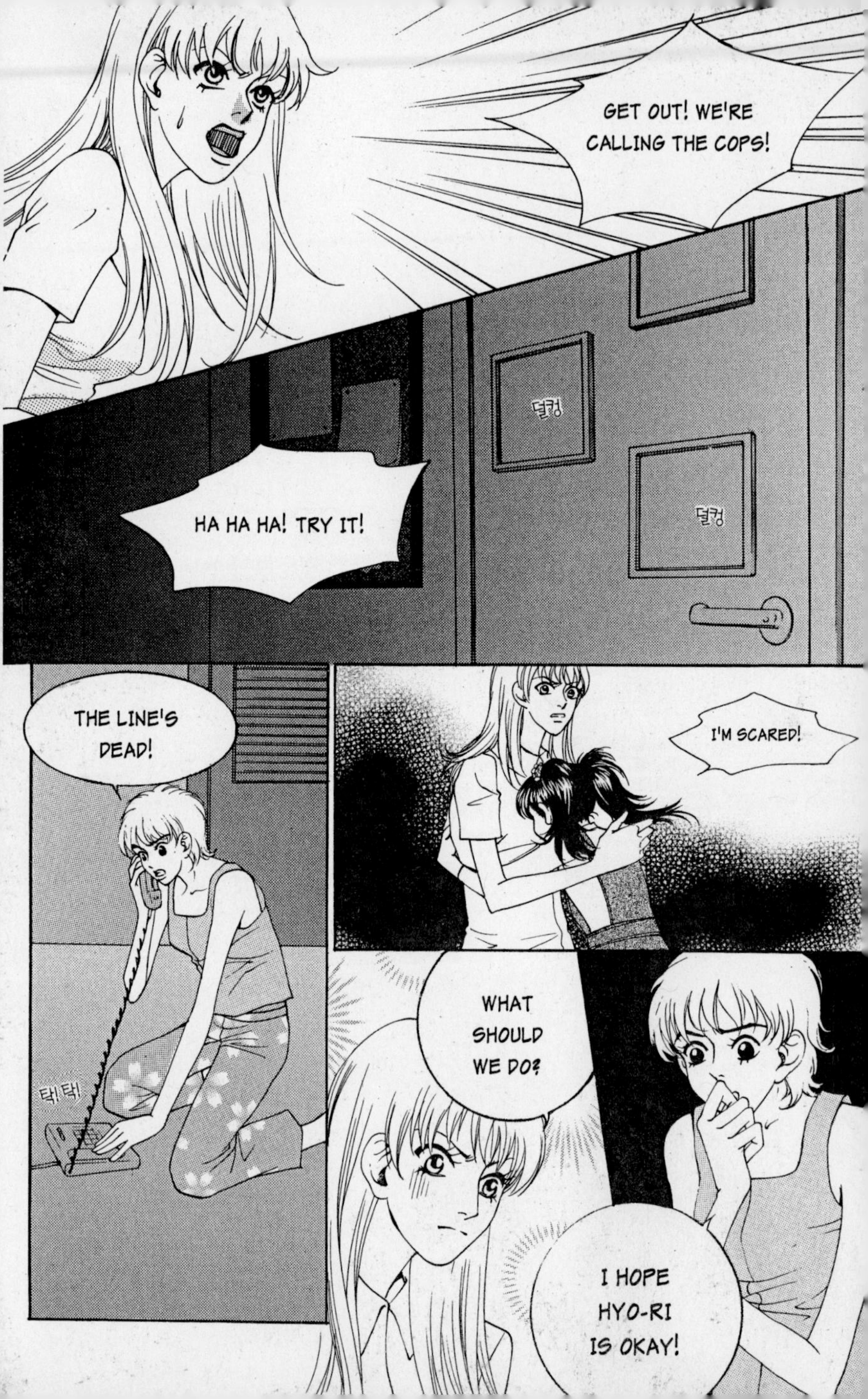
GET OUT! WE'RE CALLING THE COPS!
HA HA HA! TRY IT!
덜컹
덜컹
THE LINE'S DEAD!
탁! 탁!
I'M SCARED!
WHAT SHOULD WE DO?
I HOPE HYO-RI IS OKAY!

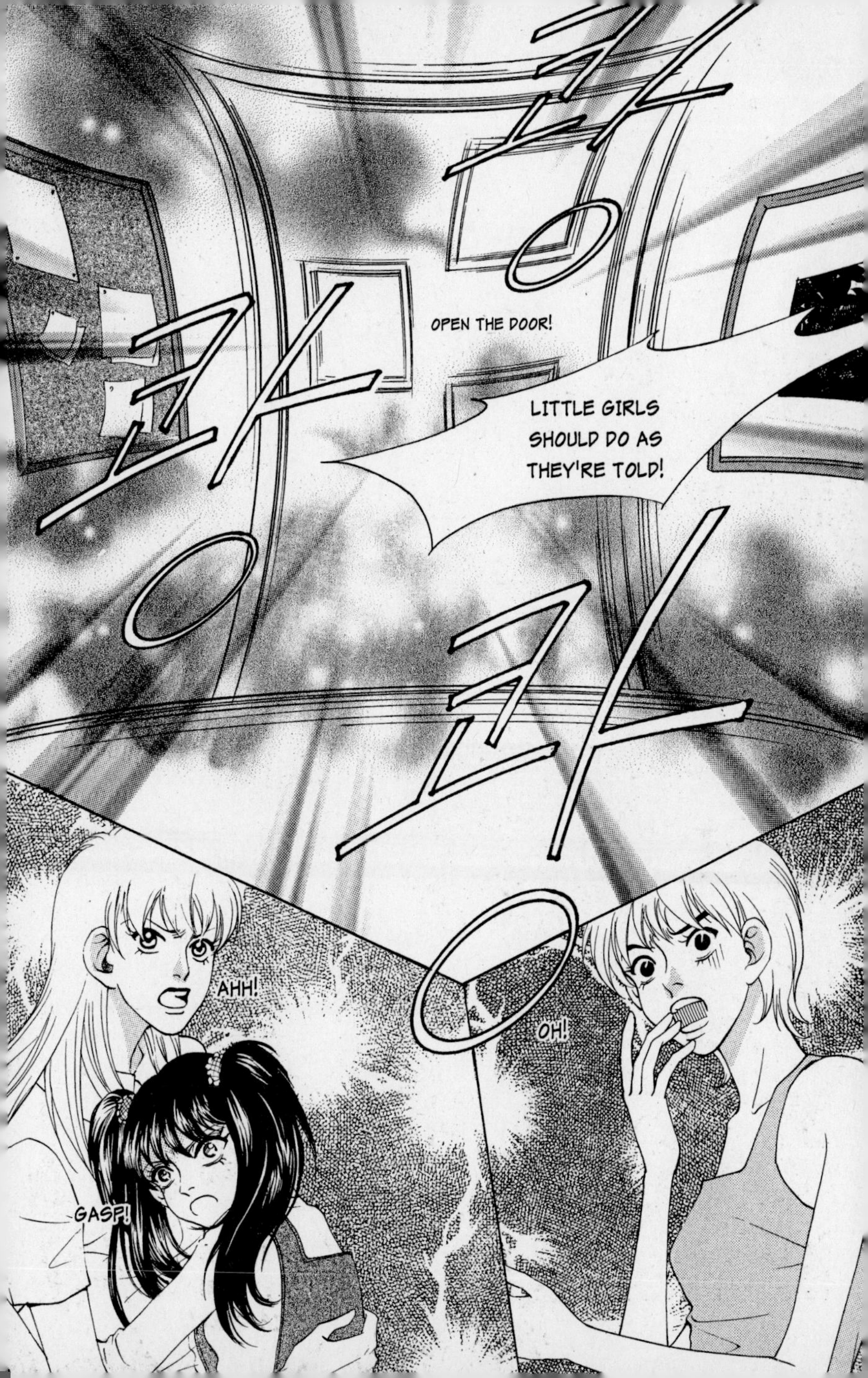
OPEN THE DOOR!
LITTLE GIRLS SHOULD DO AS THEY'RE TOLD!
AHH!
GASP!
OH!

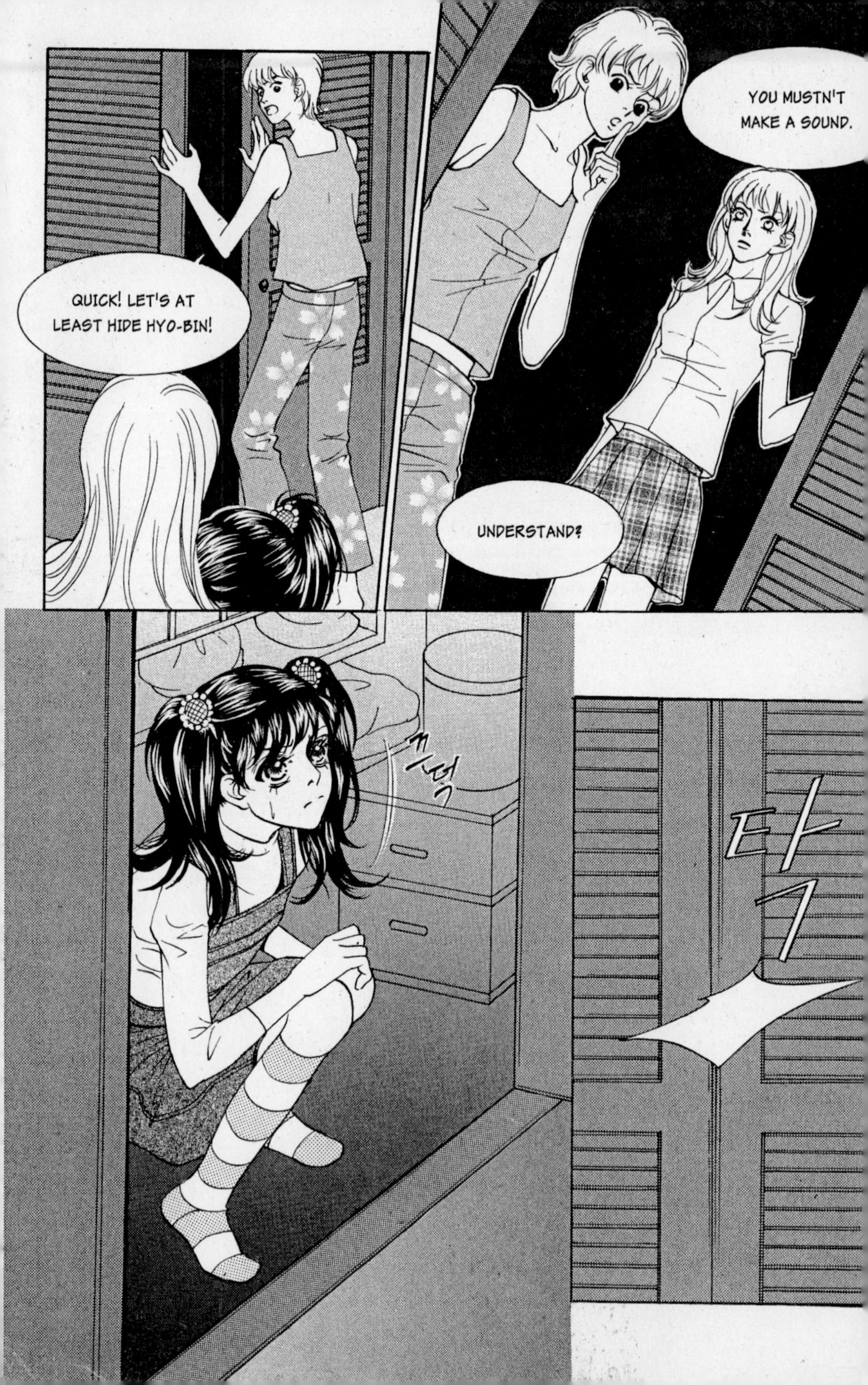
QUICK! LET'S AT LEAST HIDE HYO-BIN!
YOU MUSTN'T MAKE A SOUND.
UNDERSTAND?
끄덕
탁

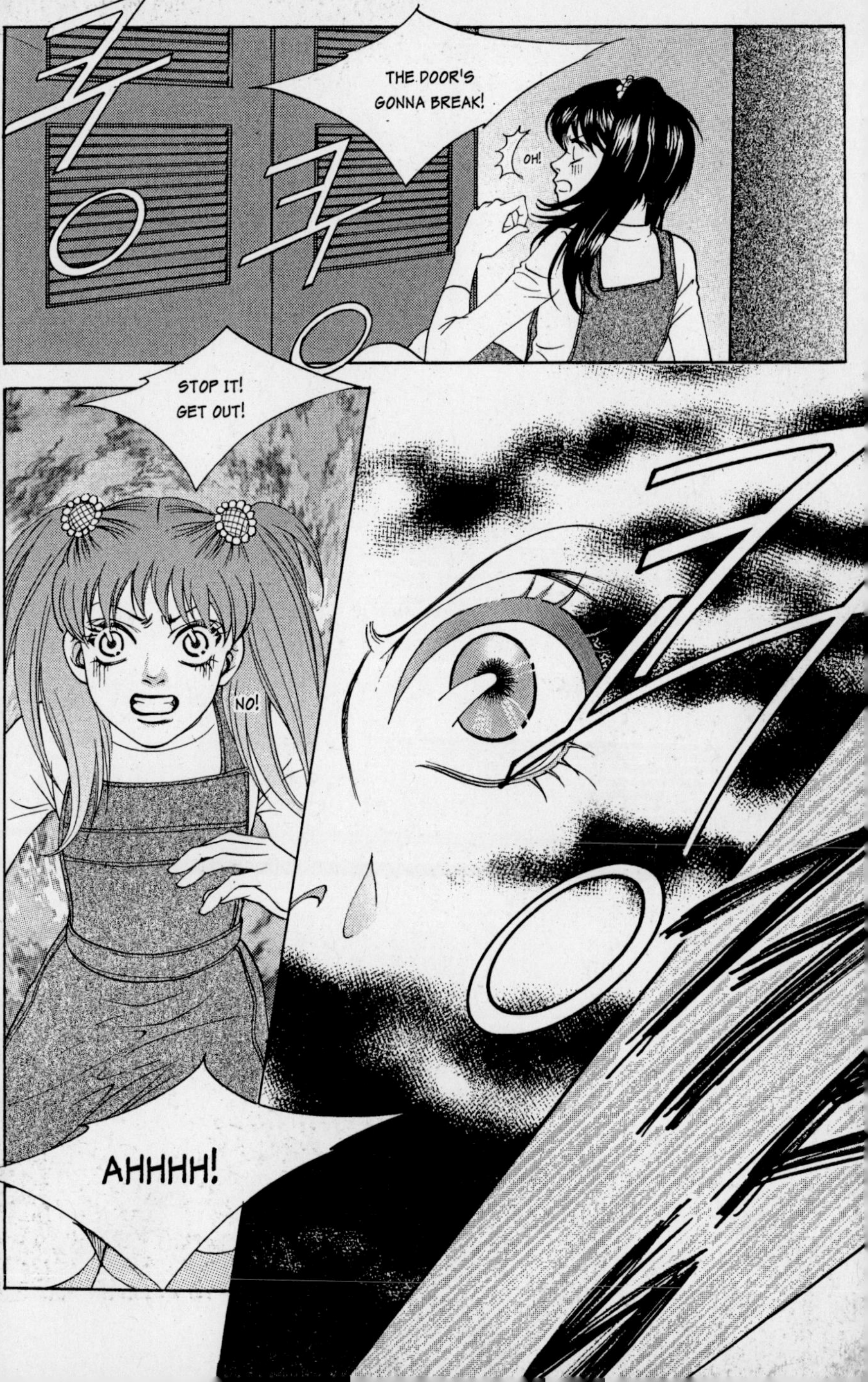
THE DOOR'S GONNA BREAK!
OH!
STOP IT! GET OUT!
NO!
AHHHH!

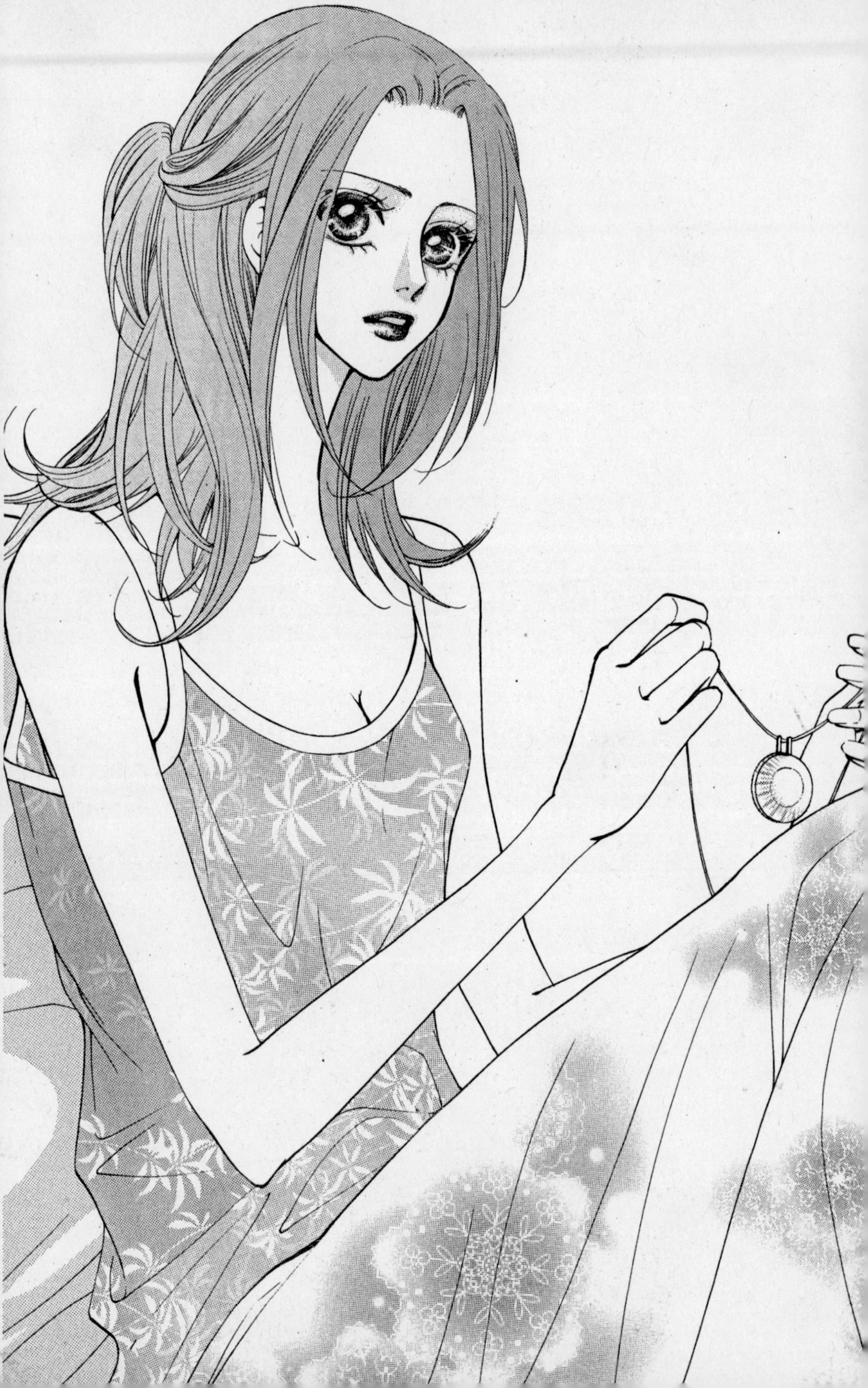

Father's Memory

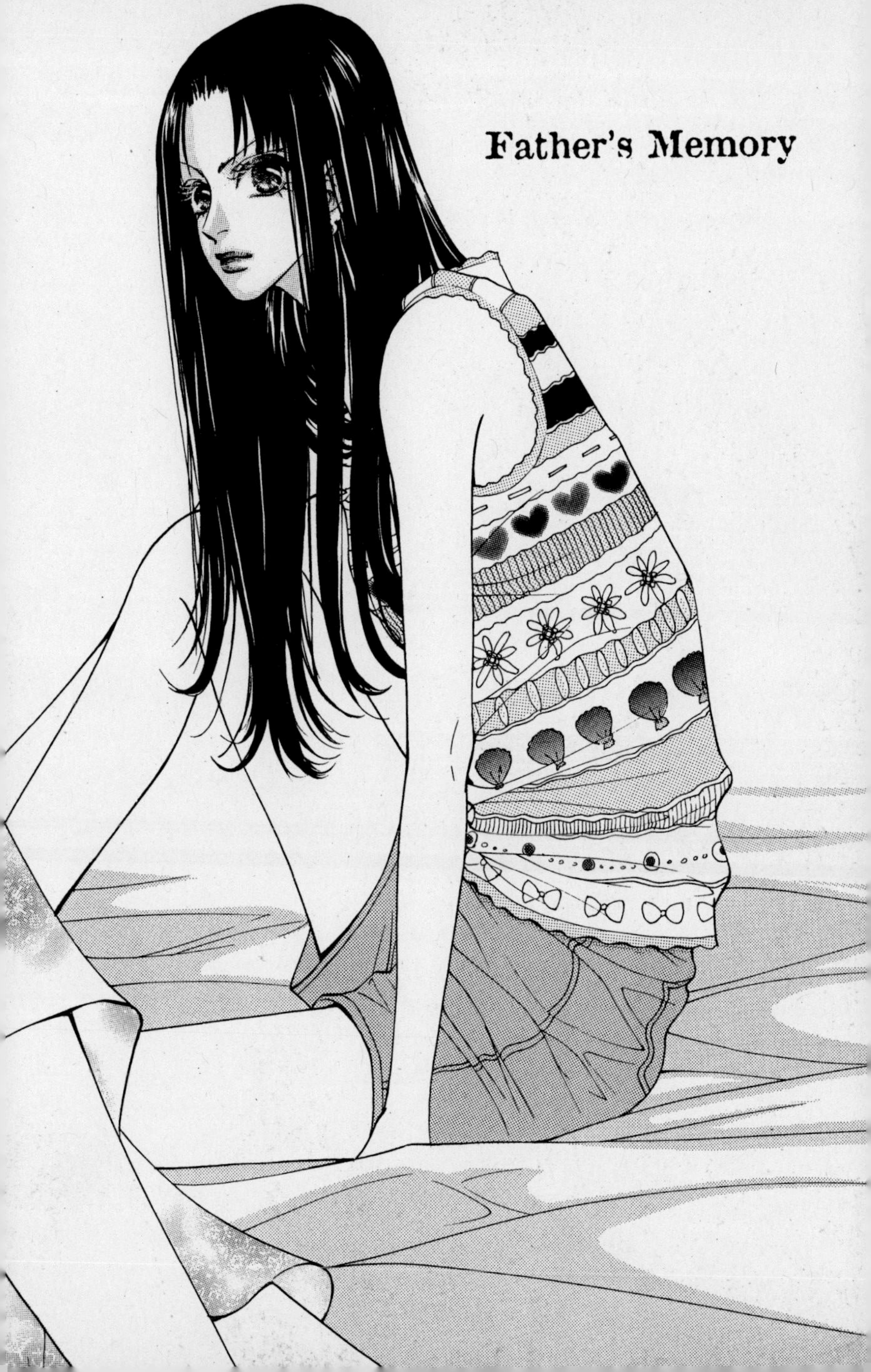

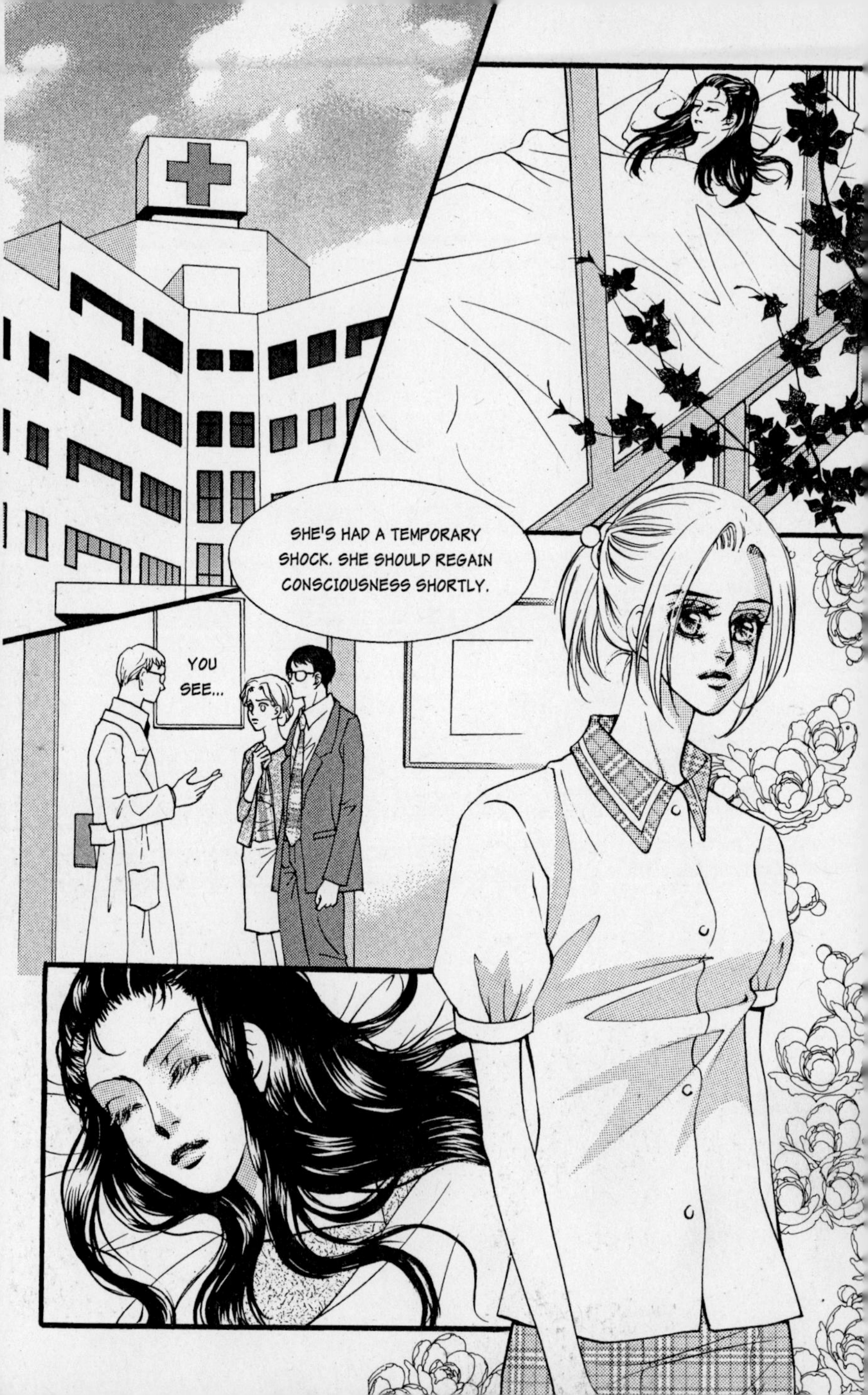
SHE'S HAD A TEMPORARY SHOCK. SHE SHOULD REGAIN CONSCIOUSNESS SHORTLY.
YOU SEE...

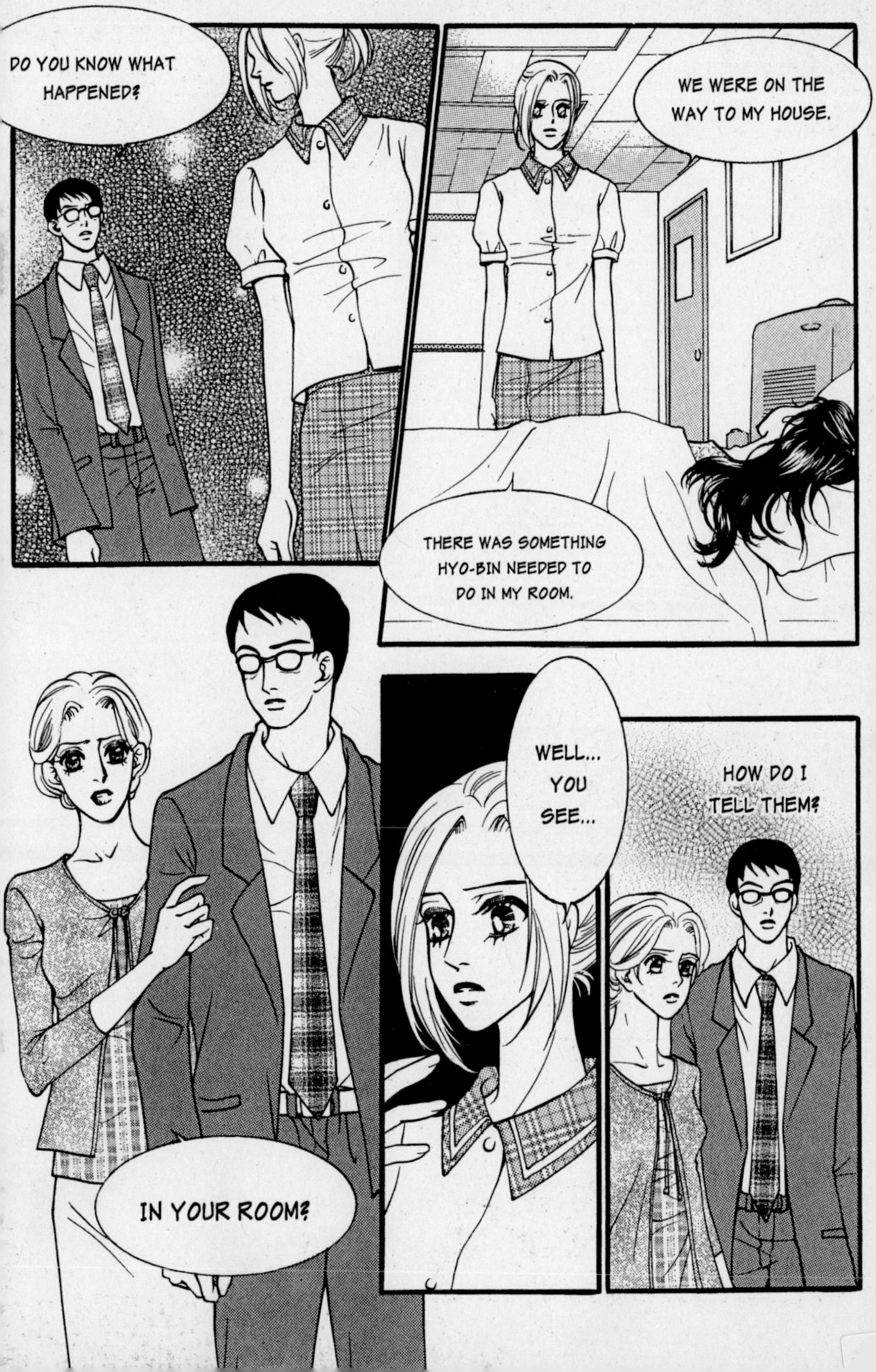
DO YOU KNOW WHAT HAPPENED?
WE WERE ON THE WAY TO MY HOUSE.
THERE WAS SOMETHING HYO-BIN NEEDED TO DO IN MY ROOM.
IN YOUR ROOM?
WELL... YOU SEE...
HOW DO I TELL THEM?

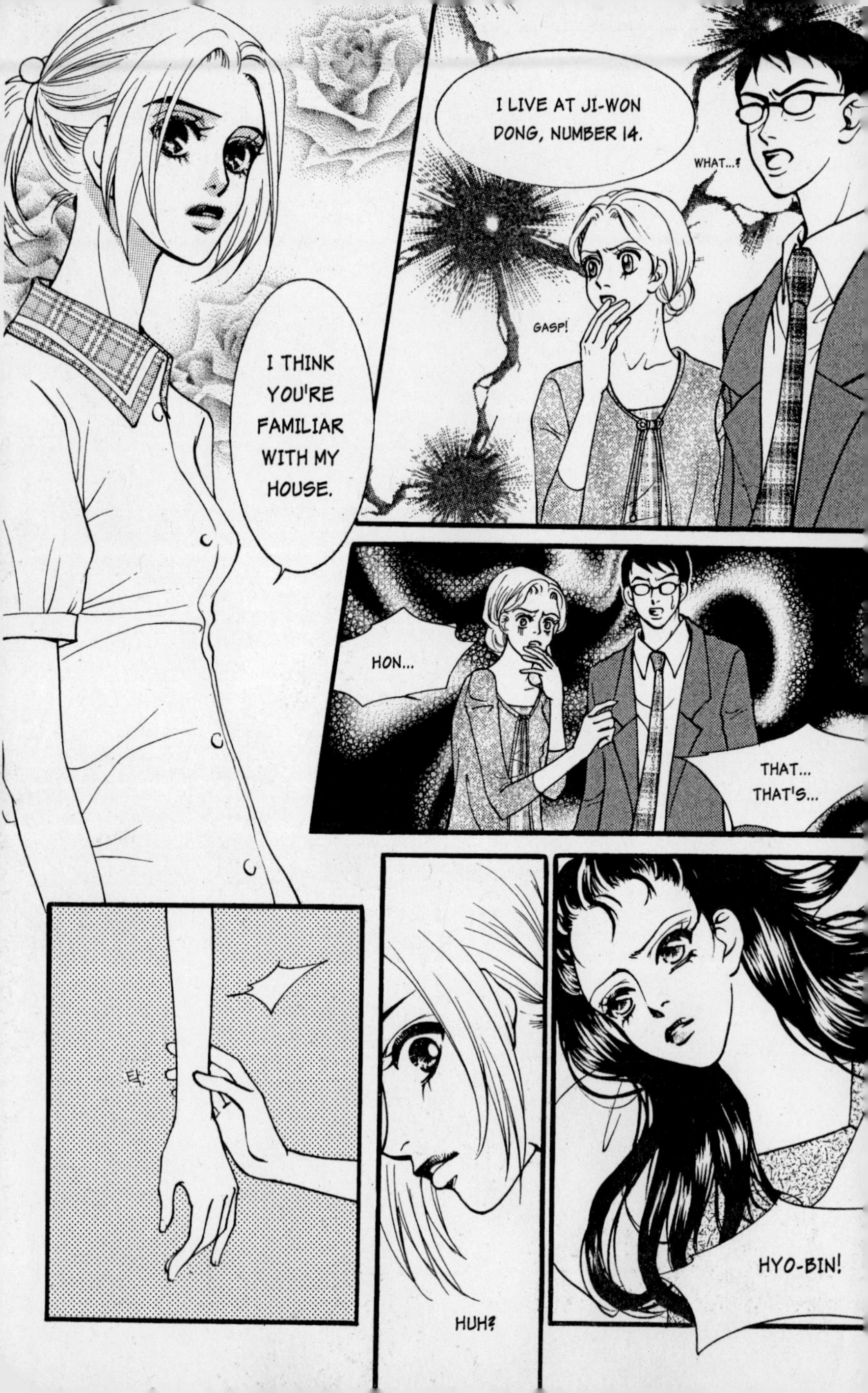
I THINK YOU'RE FAMILIAR WITH MY HOUSE.
I LIVE AT JI-WON DONG, NUMBER 14.
WHAT...?
GASP!
HON...
THAT... THAT'S...
탁
HUH?
HYO-BIN!

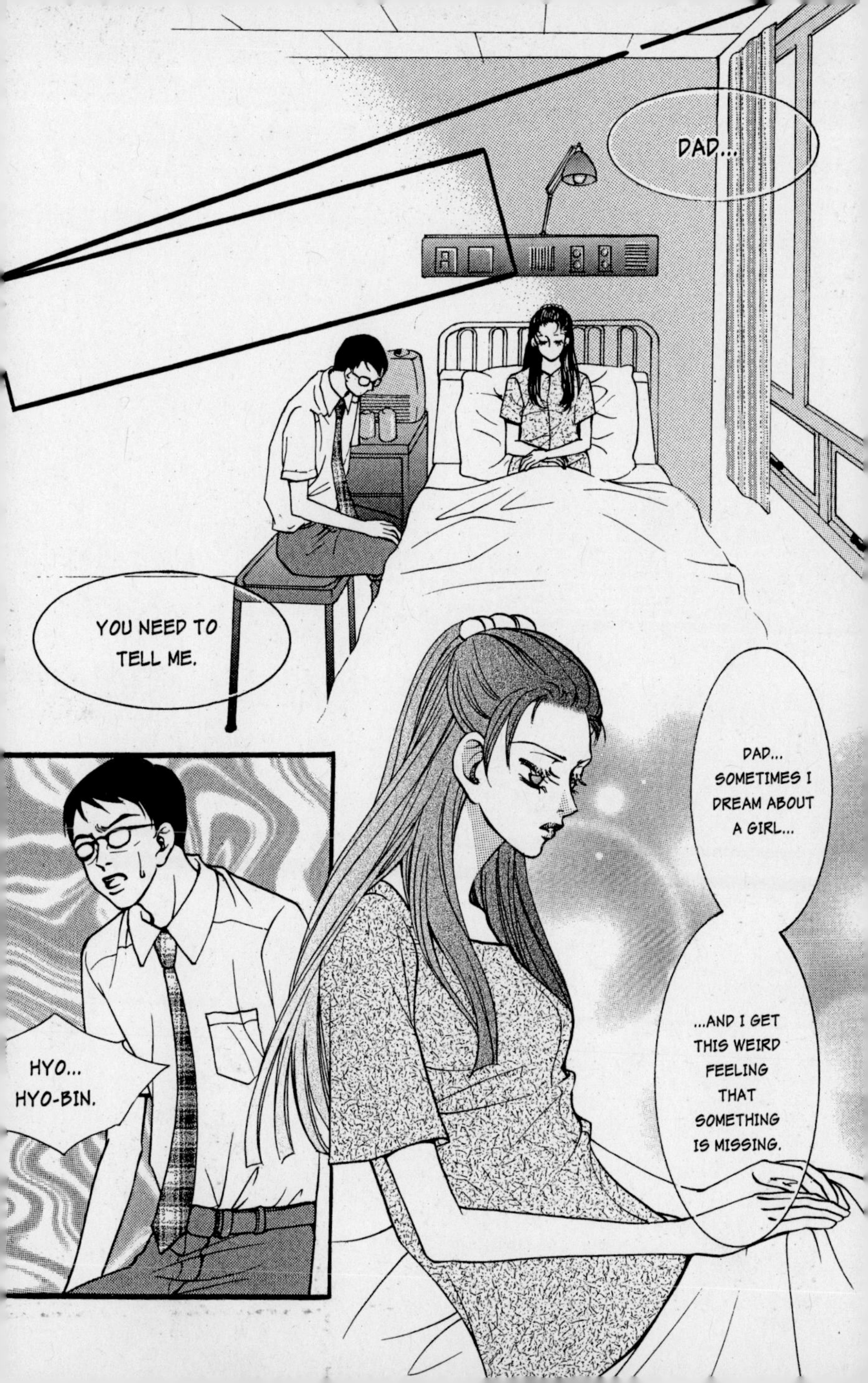
DAD...
YOU NEED TO TELL ME.
HYO... HYO-BIN.
DAD... SOMETIMES I DREAM ABOUT A GIRL...
...AND I GET THIS WEIRD FEELING THAT SOMETHING IS MISSING.

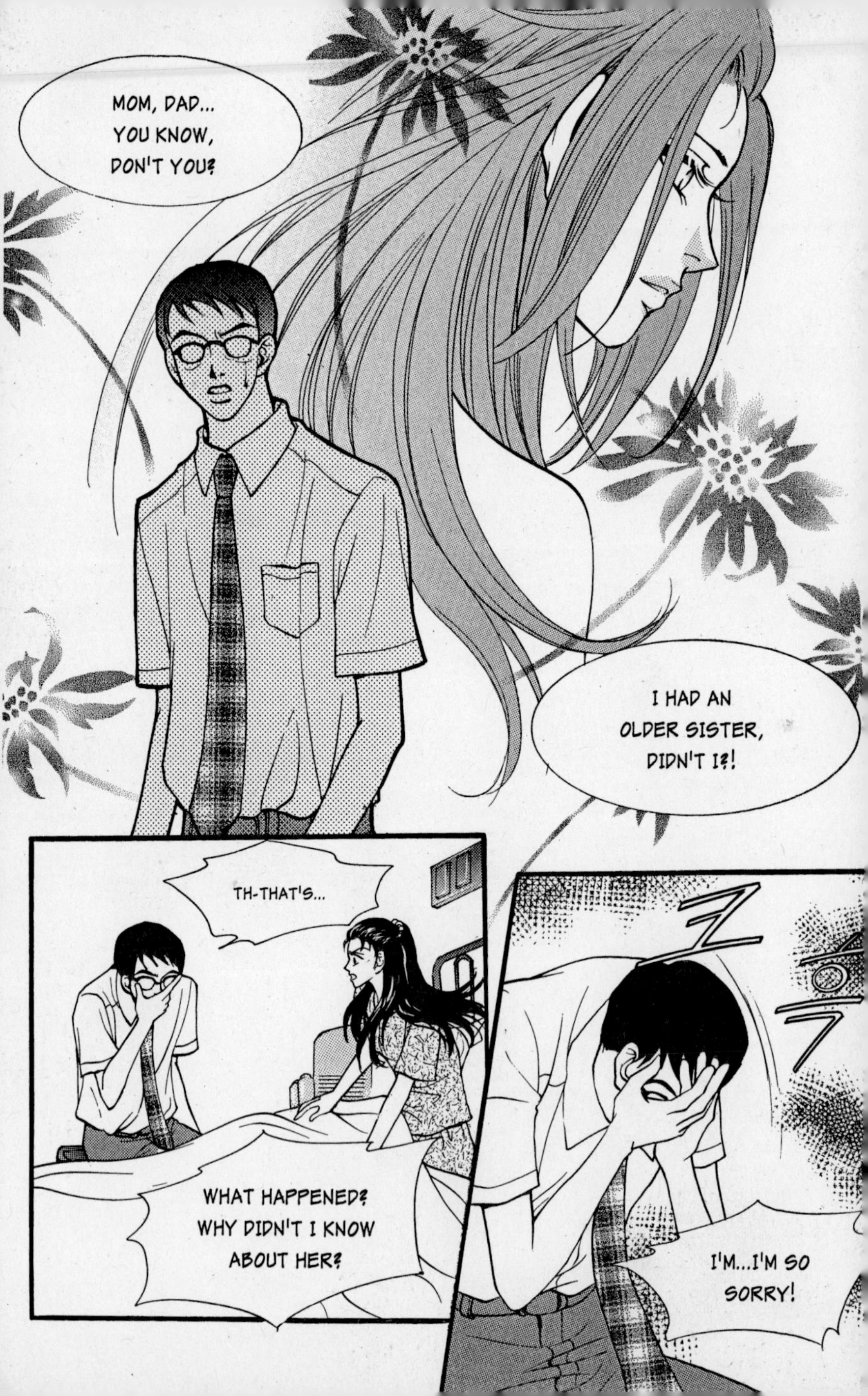
MOM, DAD... YOU KNOW, DON'T YOU?
I HAD AN OLDER SISTER, DIDN'T I?!
TH-THAT'S...
WHAT HAPPENED? WHY DIDN'T I KNOW ABOUT HER?
I'M...I'M SO SORRY!

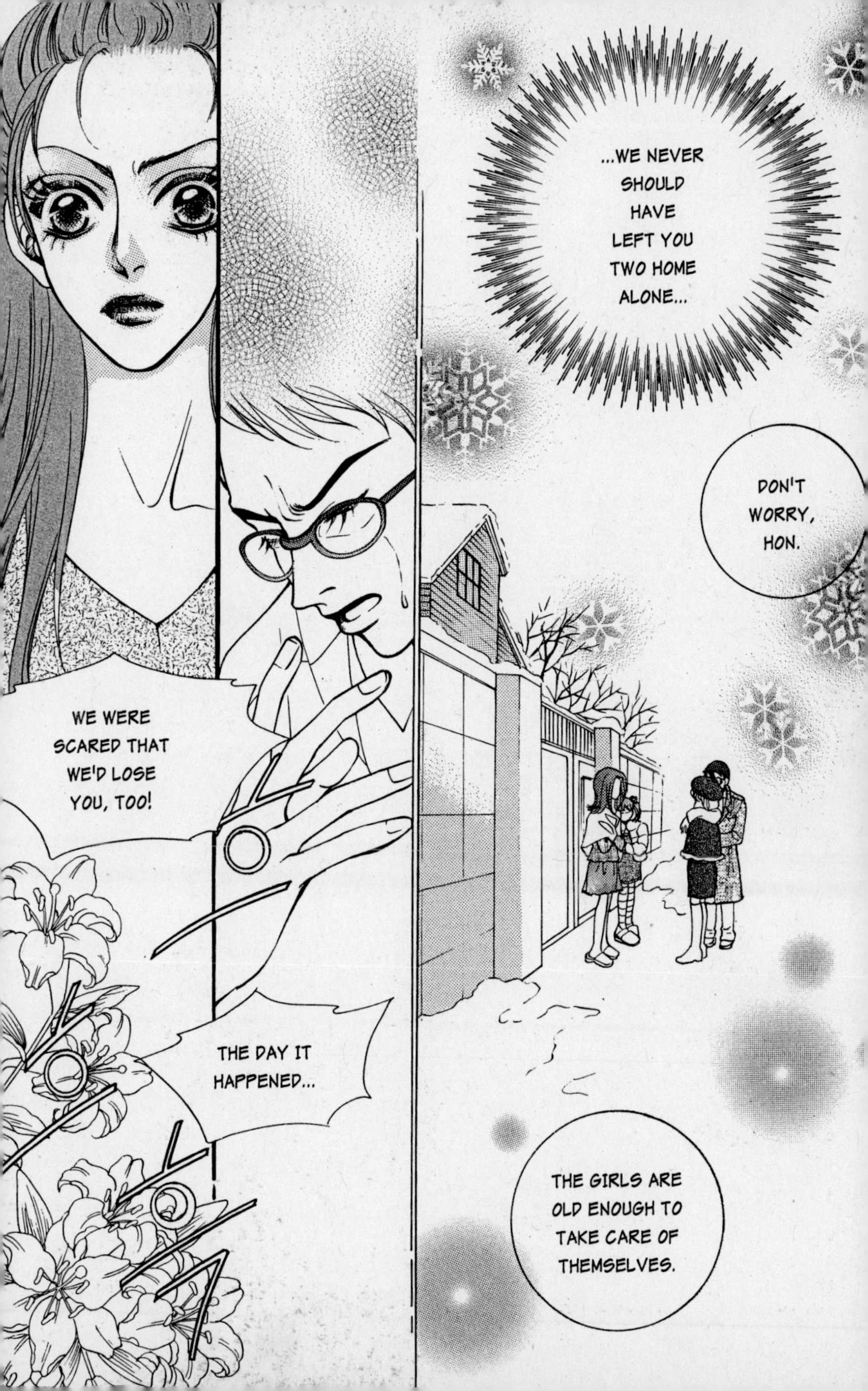
WE WERE SCARED THAT WE'D LOSE YOU, TOO!
THE DAY IT HAPPENED...
...WE NEVER SHOULD HAVE LEFT YOU TWO HOME ALONE...
DON'T WORRY, HON.
THE GIRLS ARE OLD ENOUGH TO TAKE CARE OF THEMSELVES.

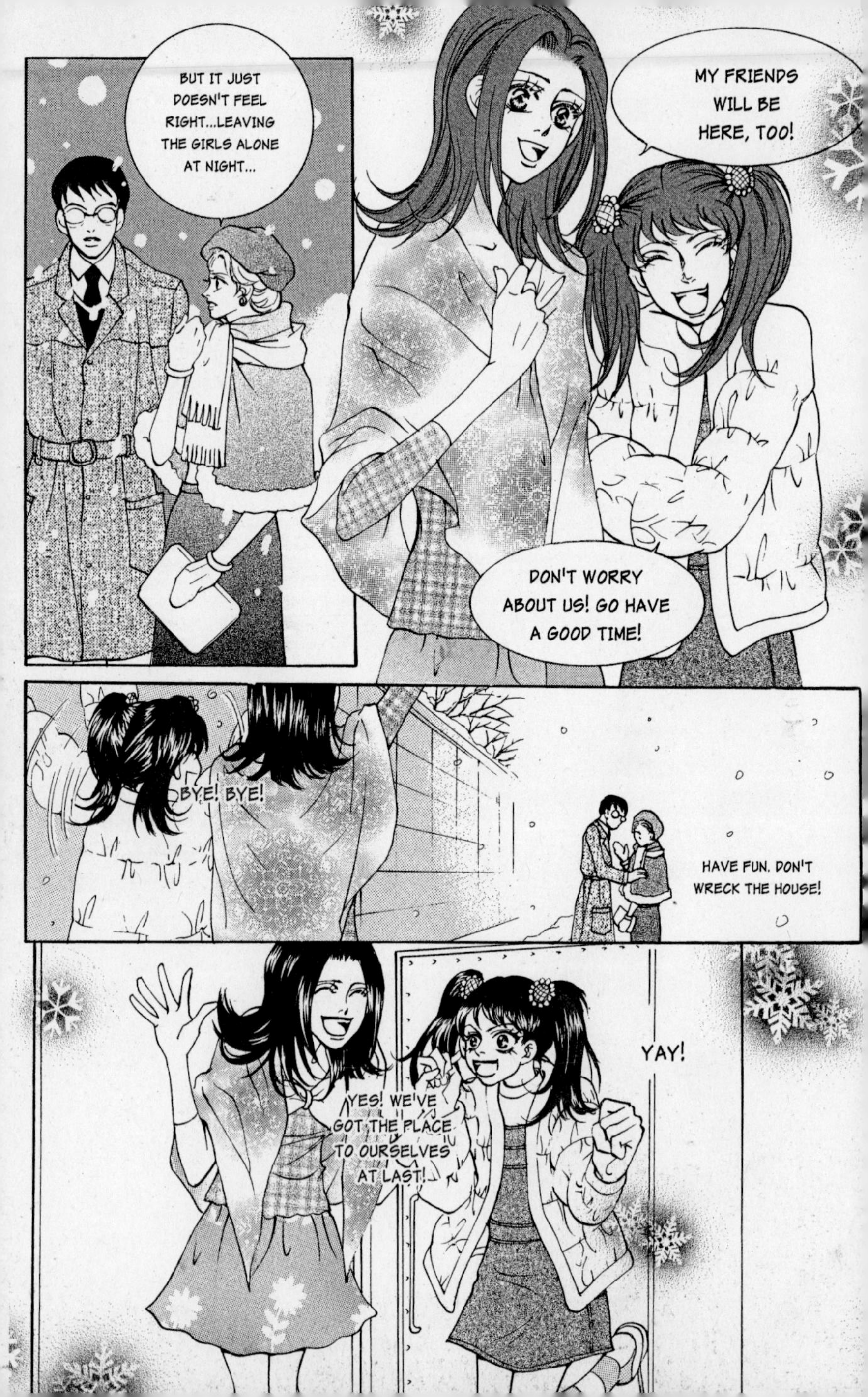
BUT IT JUST DOESN'T FEEL RIGHT...LEAVING THE GIRLS ALONE AT NIGHT...
MY FRIENDS WILL BE HERE, TOO!
DON'T WORRY ABOUT US! GO HAVE A GOOD TIME!
BYE! BYE!
HAVE FUN. DON'T WRECK THE HOUSE!
YES! WE'VE GOT THE PLACE TO OURSELVES AT LAST!
YAY!

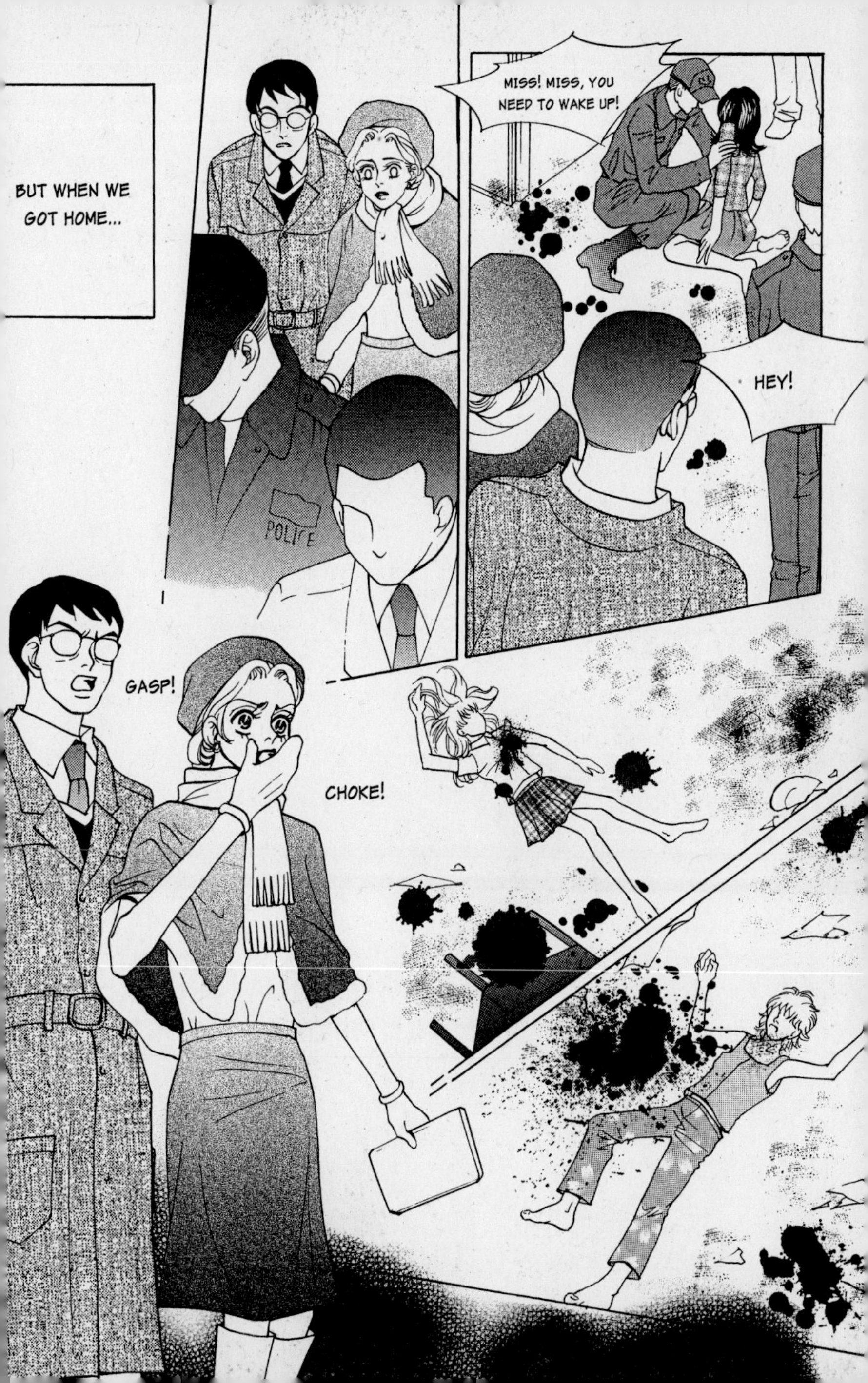
BUT WHEN WE GOT HOME...
POLICE
MISS! MISS, YOU NEED TO WAKE UP!
HEY!
GASP!
CHOKE!

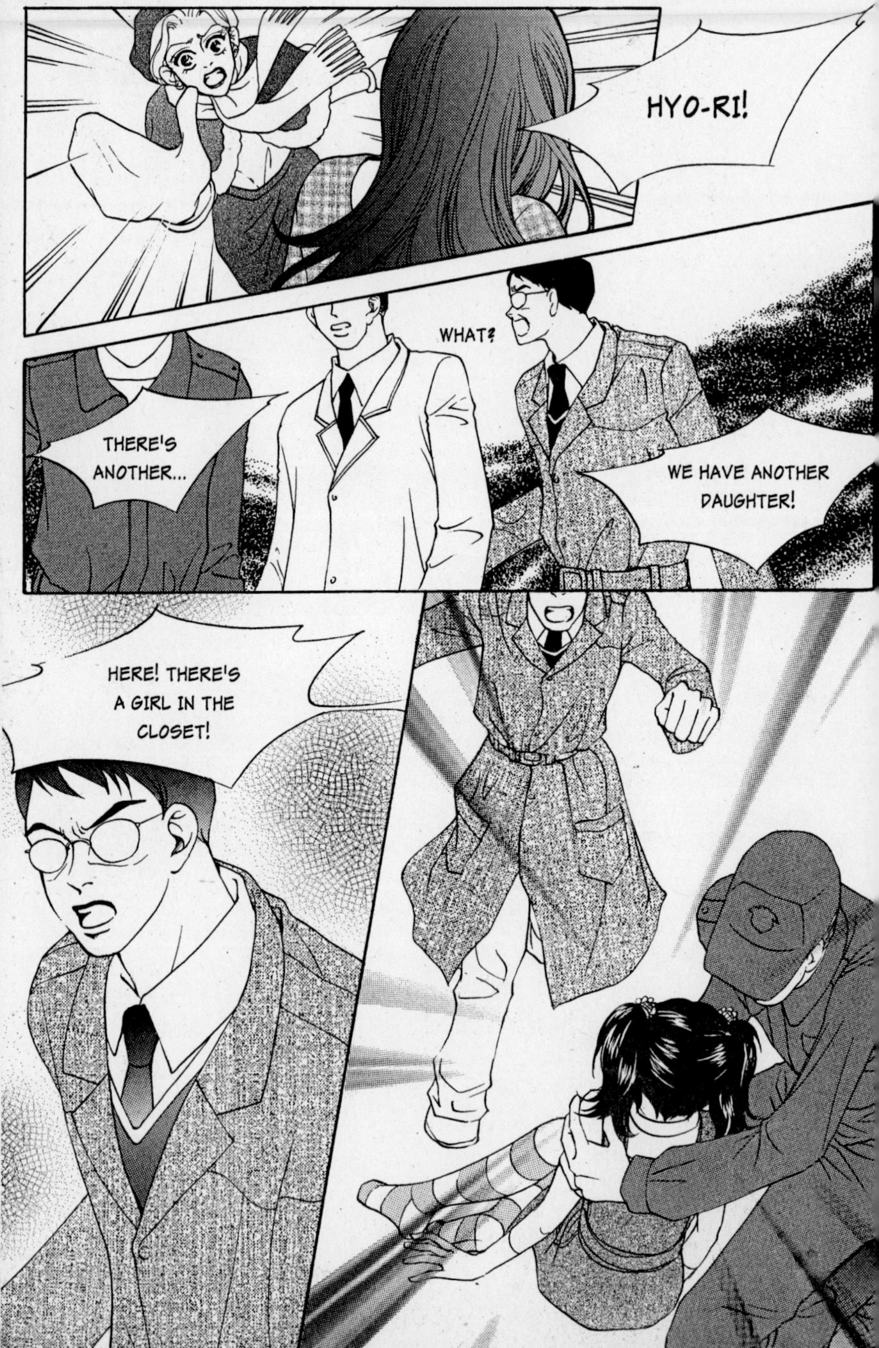
HYO-RI!
THERE'S ANOTHER...
WHAT?
WE HAVE ANOTHER DAUGHTER!
HERE! THERE'S A GIRL IN THE CLOSET!

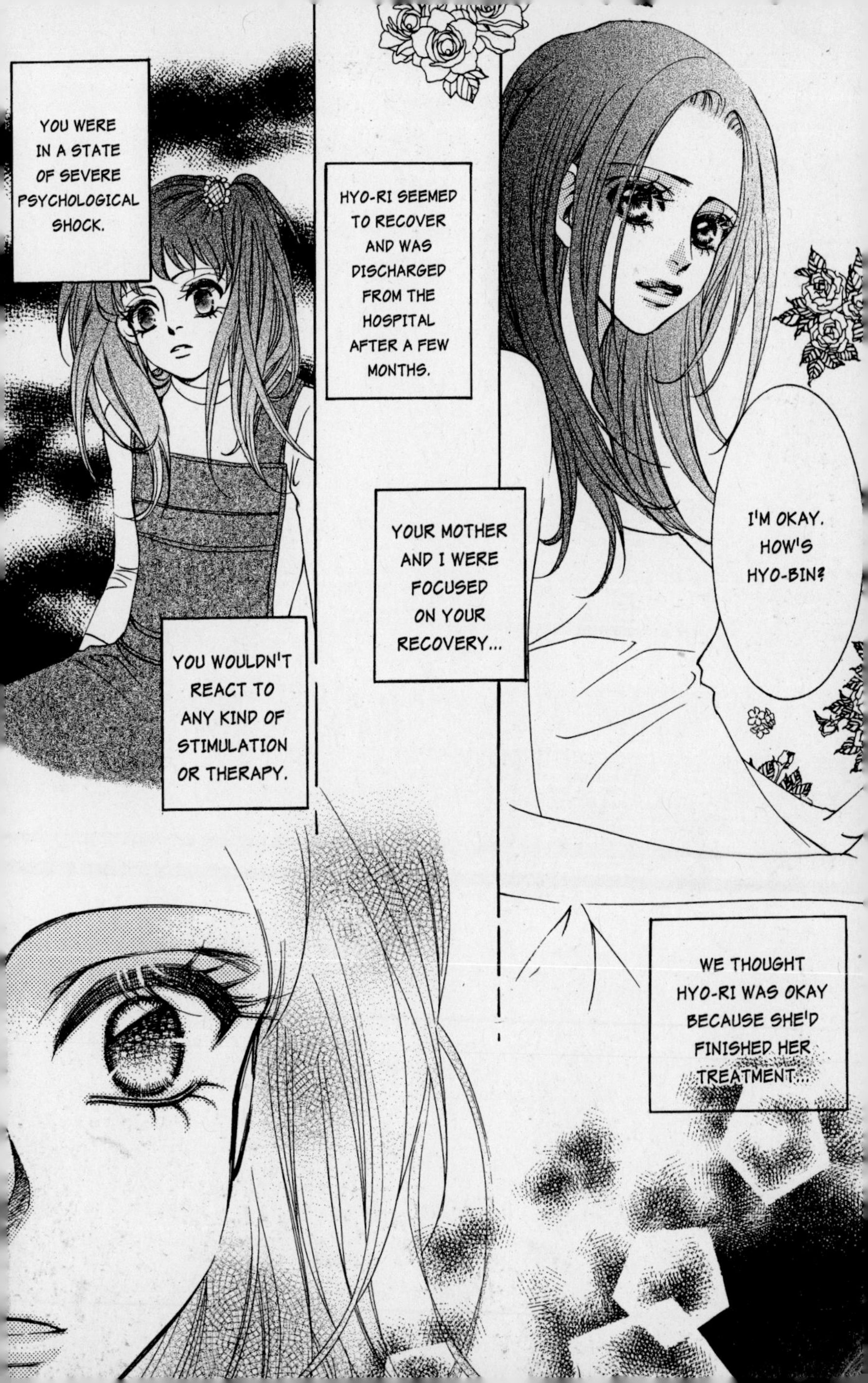
YOU WERE IN A STATE OF SEVERE PSYCHOLOGICAL SHOCK.
YOU WOULDN'T REACT TO ANY KIND OF STIMULATION OR THERAPY.
HYO-RI SEEMED TO RECOVER AND WAS DISCHARGED FROM THE HOSPITAL AFTER A FEW MONTHS.
YOUR MOTHER AND I WERE FOCUSED ON YOUR RECOVERY...
I'M OKAY. HOW'S HYO-BIN?
WE THOUGHT HYO-RI WAS OKAY BECAUSE SHE'D FINISHED HER TREATMENT...

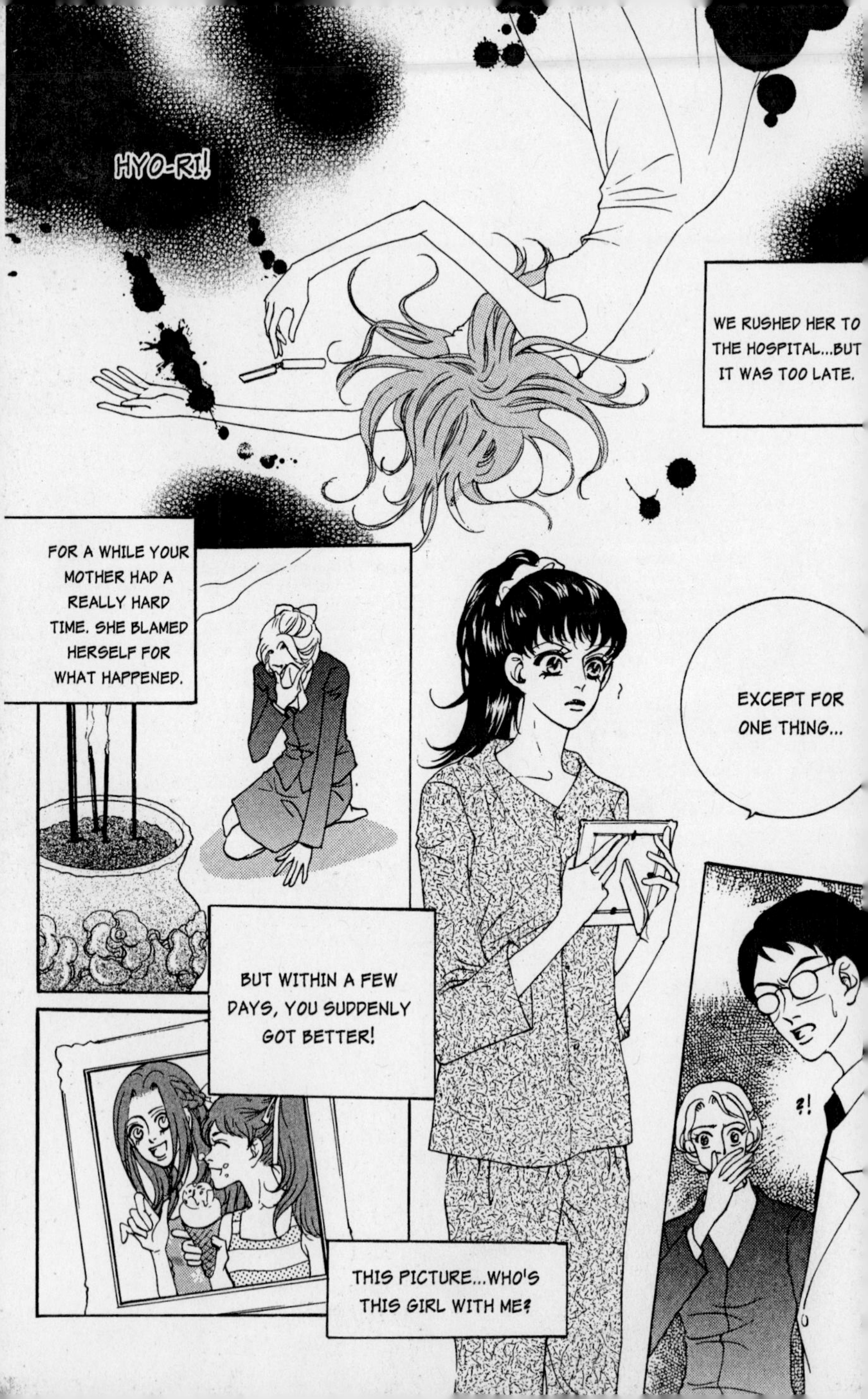
HYO-RI!
WE RUSHED HER TO THE HOSPITAL...BUT IT WAS TOO LATE.
FOR A WHILE YOUR MOTHER HAD A REALLY HARD TIME. SHE BLAMED HERSELF FOR WHAT HAPPENED.
EXCEPT FOR ONE THING...
BUT WITHIN A FEW DAYS, YOU SUDDENLY GOT BETTER!
?!
THIS PICTURE...WHO'S THIS GIRL WITH ME?

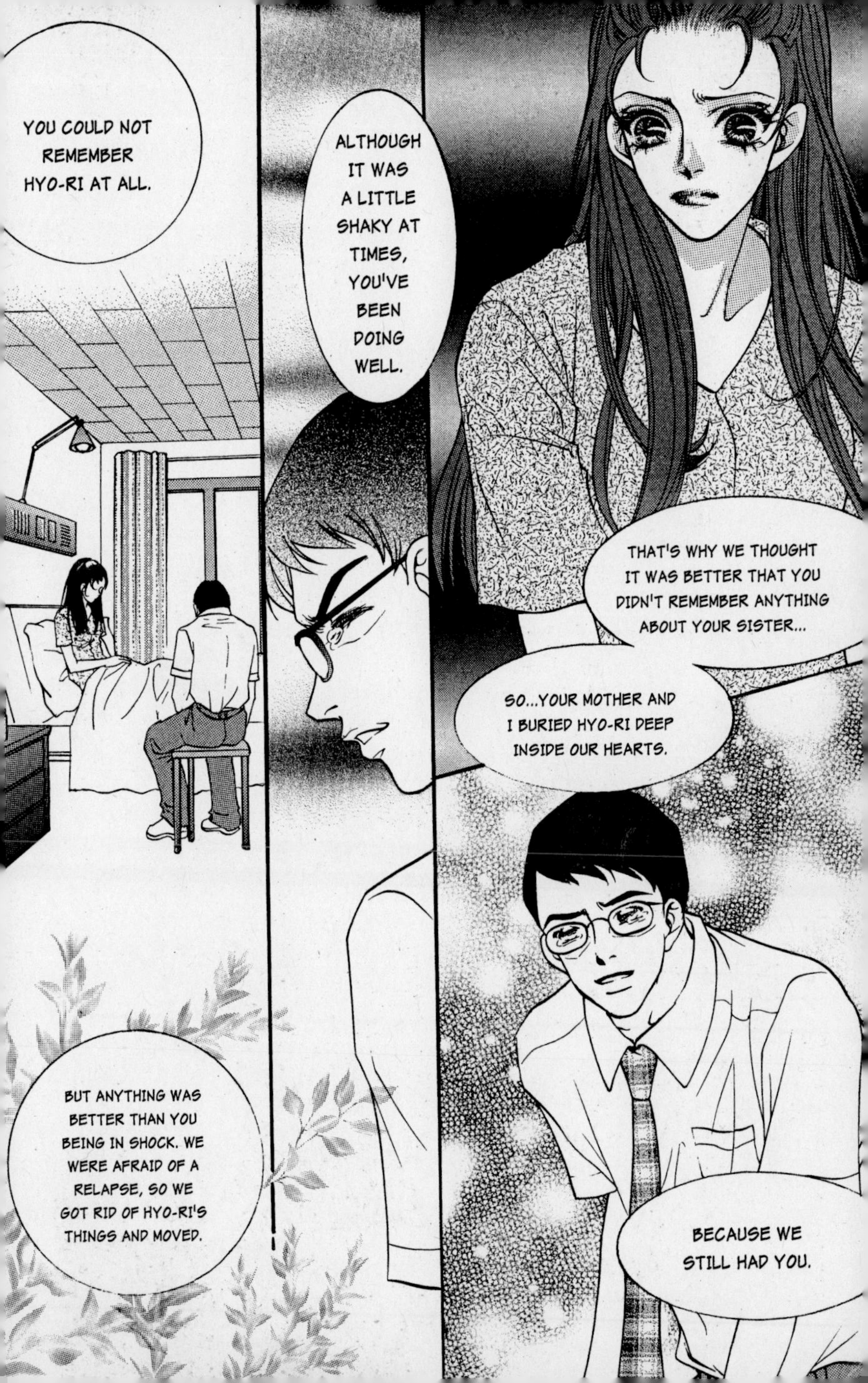

YOU COULD NOT REMEMBER HYO-RI AT ALL.
BUT ANYTHING WAS BETTER THAN YOU BEING IN SHOCK. WE WERE AFRAID OF A RELAPSE, SO WE GOT RID OF HYO-RI'S THINGS AND MOVED.
ALTHOUGH IT WAS A LITTLE SHAKY AT TIMES, YOU'VE BEEN DOING WELL.
THAT'S WHY WE THOUGHT IT WAS BETTER THAT YOU DIDN'T REMEMBER ANYTHING ABOUT YOUR SISTER...
SO...YOUR MOTHER AND I BURIED HYO-RI DEEP INSIDE OUR HEARTS.
BECAUSE WE STILL HAD YOU.

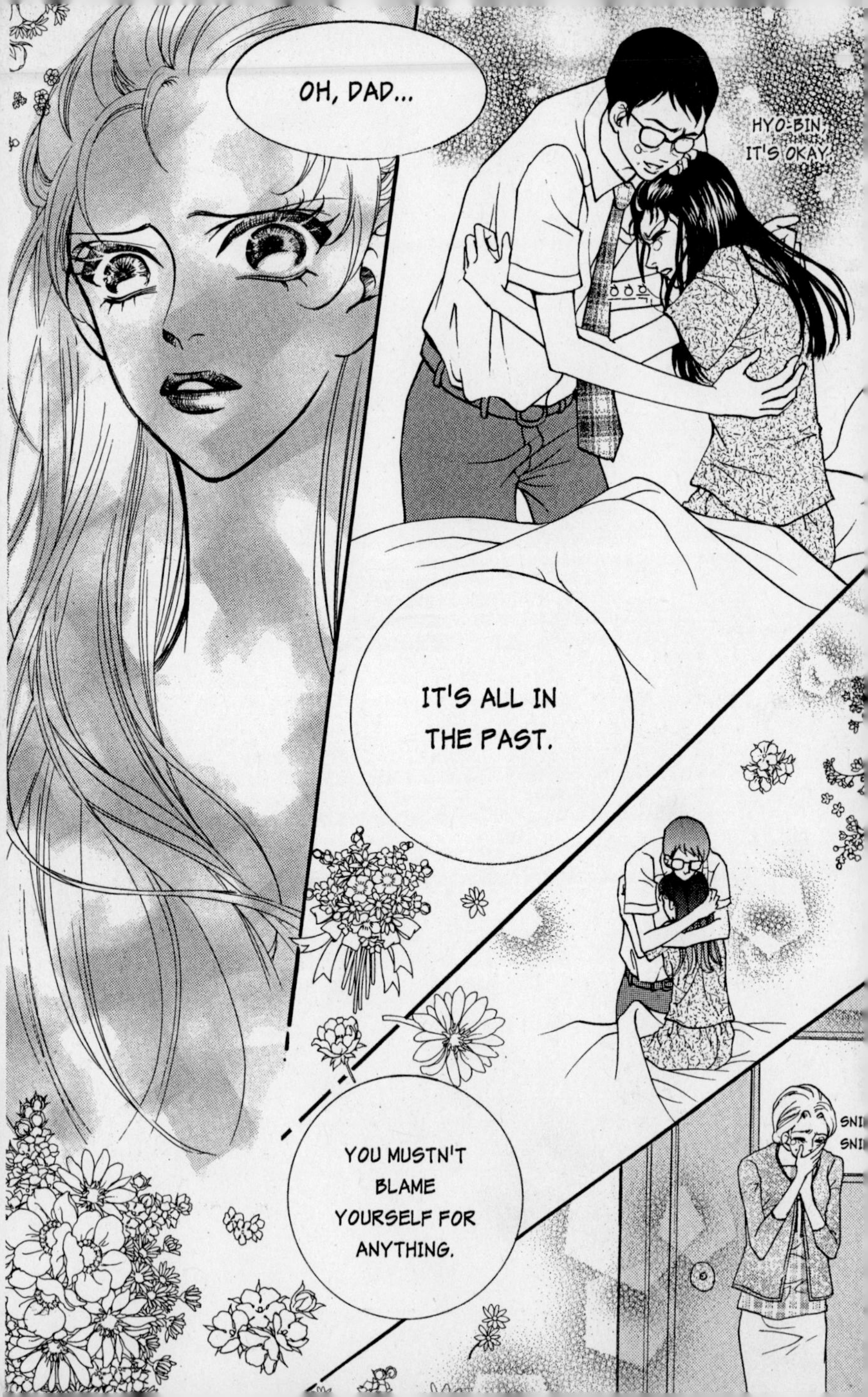
OH, DAD...
HYO-BIN, IT'S OKAY.
IT'S ALL IN THE PAST.
YOU MUSTN'T BLAME YOURSELF FOR ANYTHING.
SNI
SNI

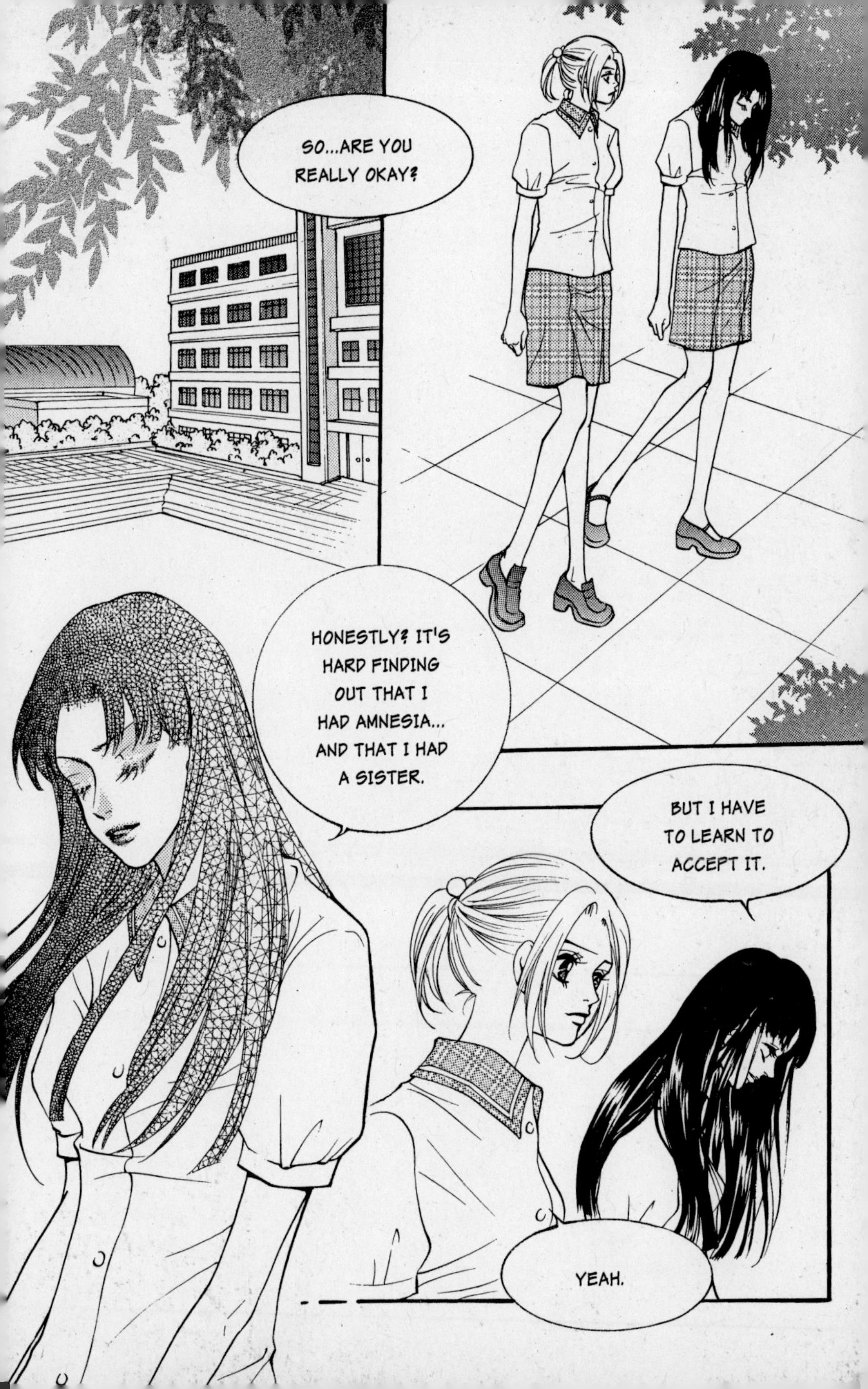
SO...ARE YOU REALLY OKAY?
HONESTLY? IT'S HARD FINDING OUT THAT I HAD AMNESIA... AND THAT I HAD A SISTER.
BUT I HAVE TO LEARN TO ACCEPT IT.
YEAH.

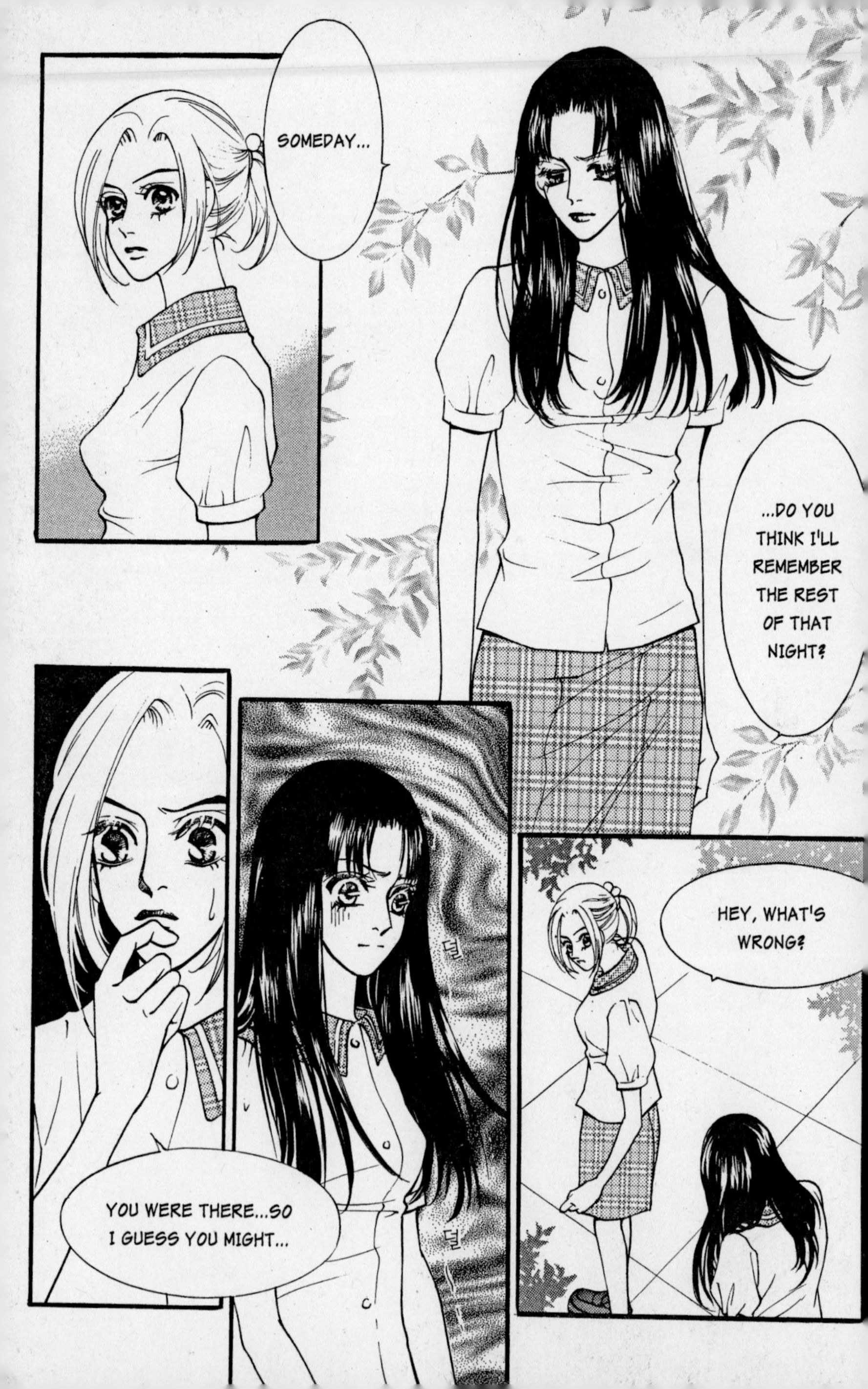
SOMEDAY...
...DO YOU THINK I'LL REMEMBER THE REST OF THAT NIGHT?
YOU WERE THERE...SO I GUESS YOU MIGHT...
덜
덜
HEY, WHAT'S WRONG?

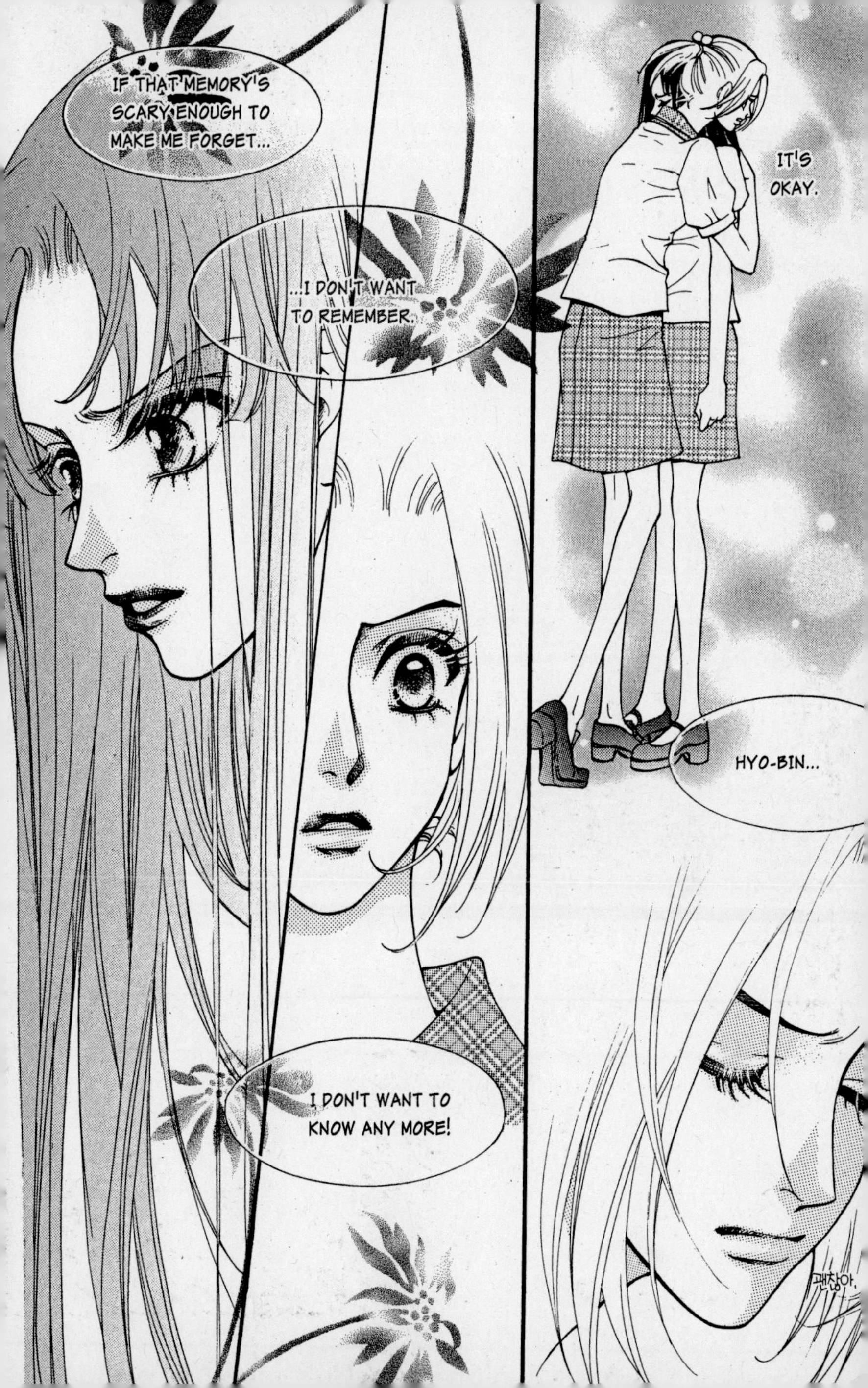
IF THAT MEMORY'S SCARY ENOUGH TO MAKE ME FORGET...
...I DON'T WANT TO REMEMBER.
I DON'T WANT TO KNOW ANY MORE!
IT'S OKAY.
HYO-BIN...
괜찮아.

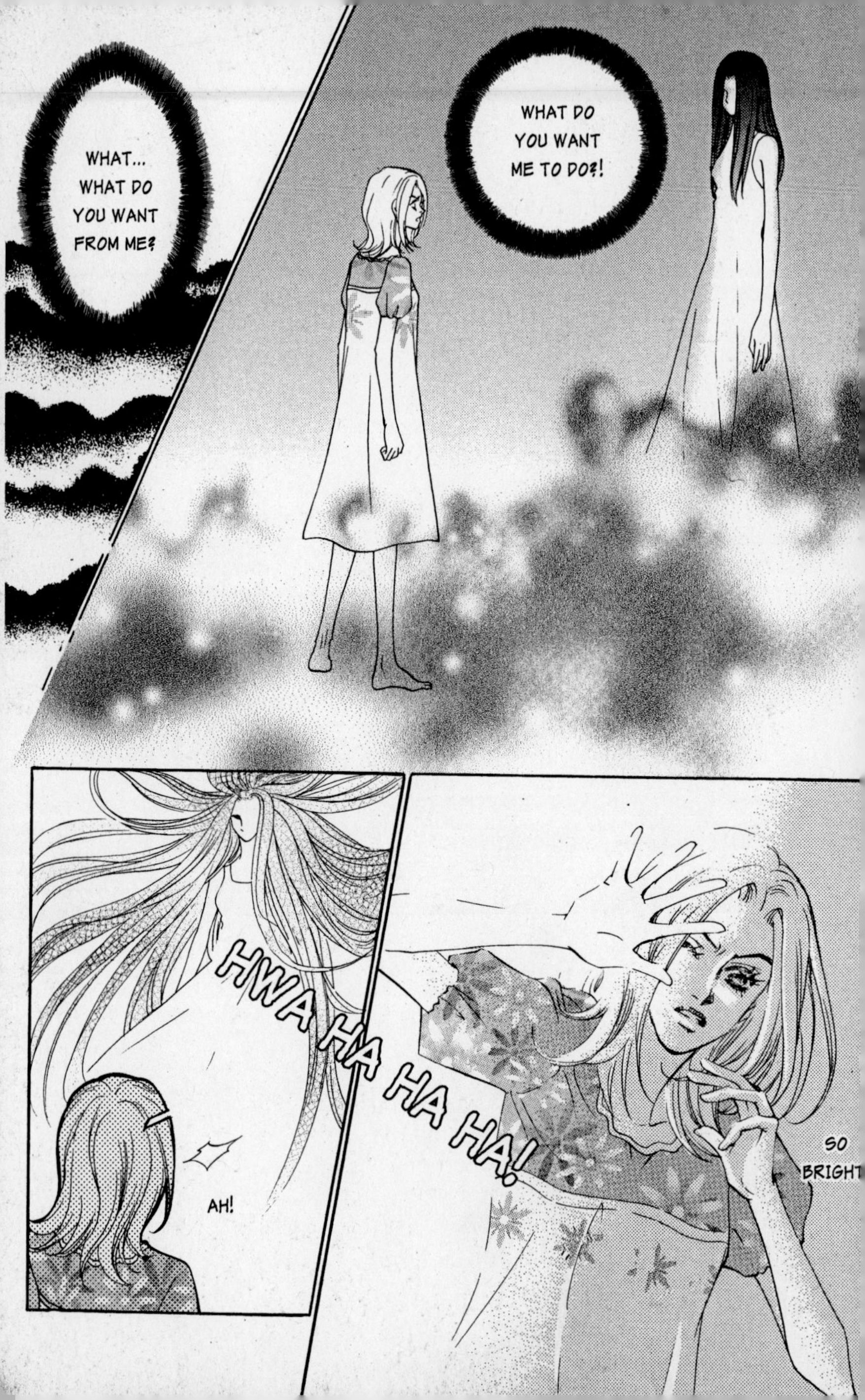
WHAT... WHAT DO YOU WANT FROM ME?
WHAT DO YOU WANT ME TO DO?!
AH!
HWA HA HA HA!
SO BRIGHT

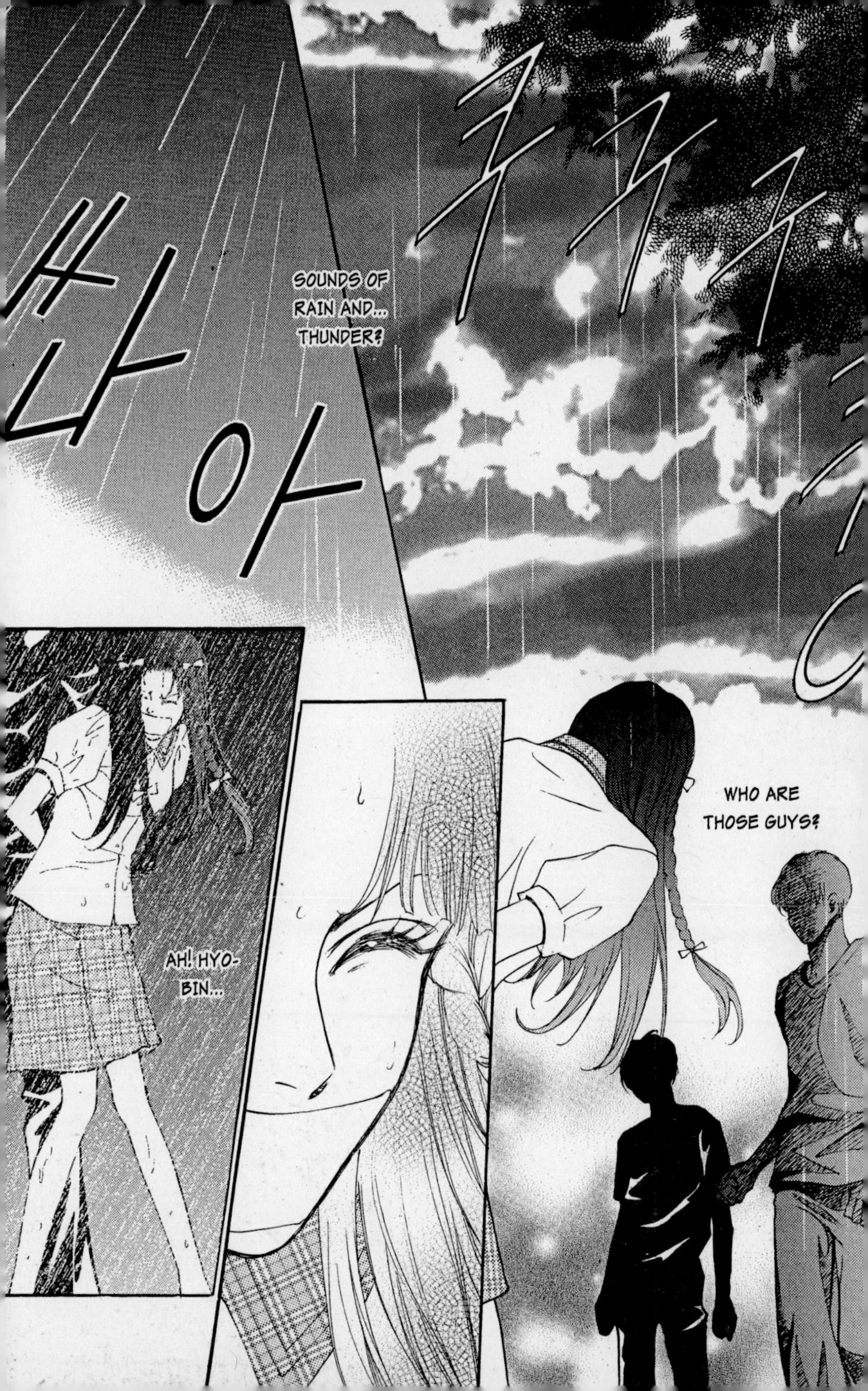
SOUNDS OF RAIN AND... THUNDER?
AH! HYO-BIN...
WHO ARE THOSE GUYS?

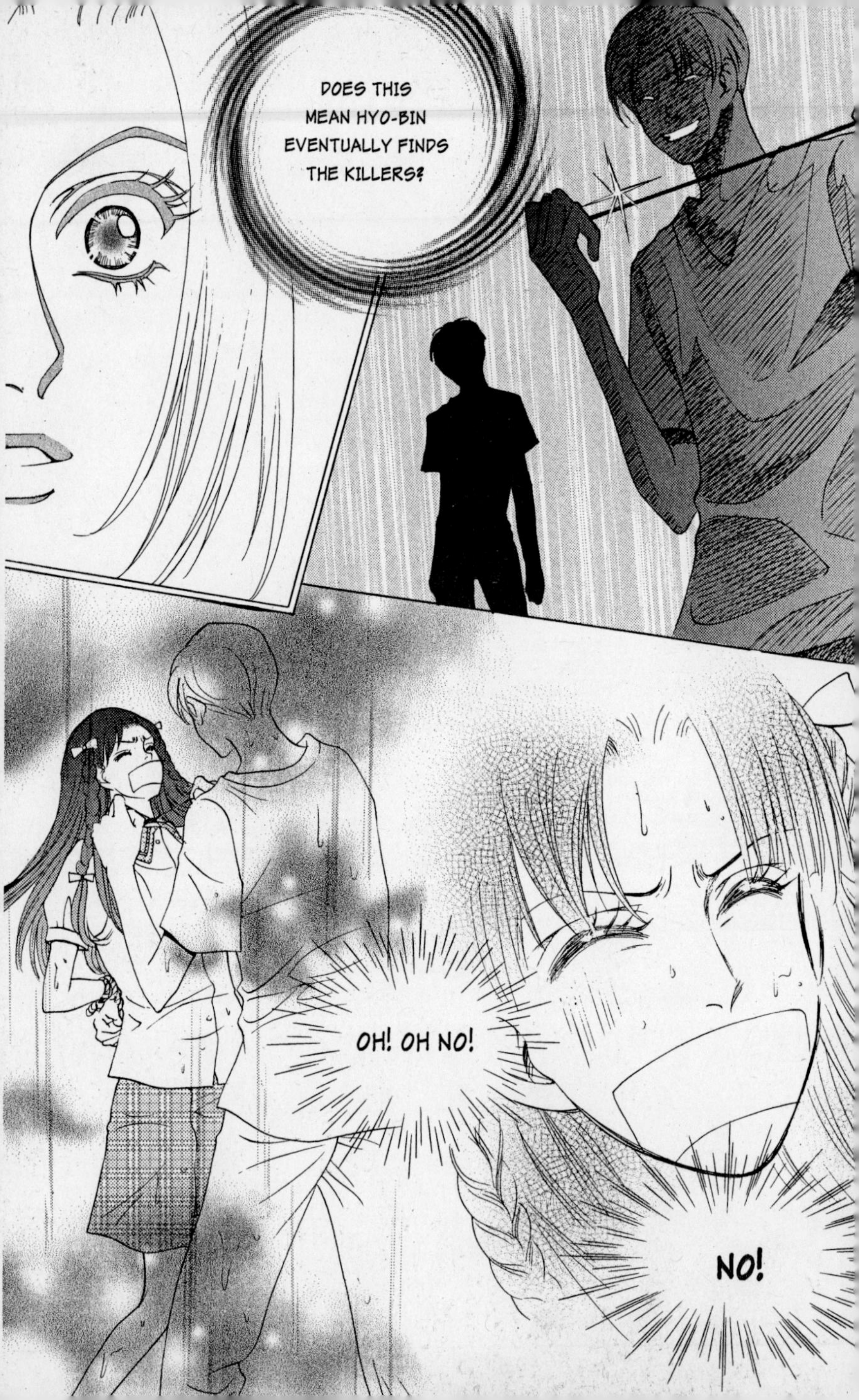
DOES THIS MEAN HYO-BIN EVENTUALLY FINDS THE KILLERS?
OH! OH NO!
NO!

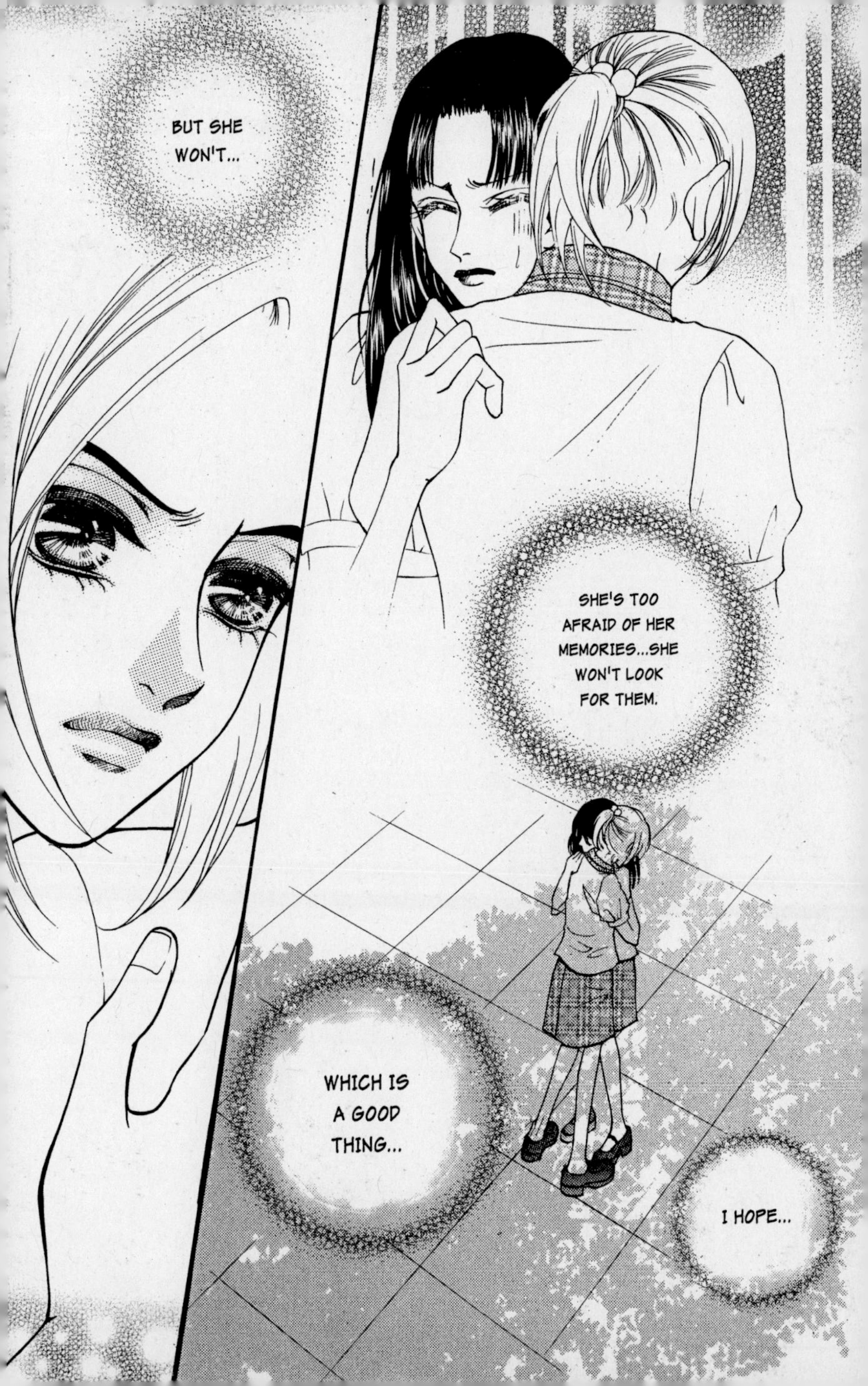
BUT SHE WON'T...
SHE'S TOO AFRAID OF HER MEMORIES...SHE WON'T LOOK FOR THEM.
WHICH IS A GOOD THING...
I HOPE...

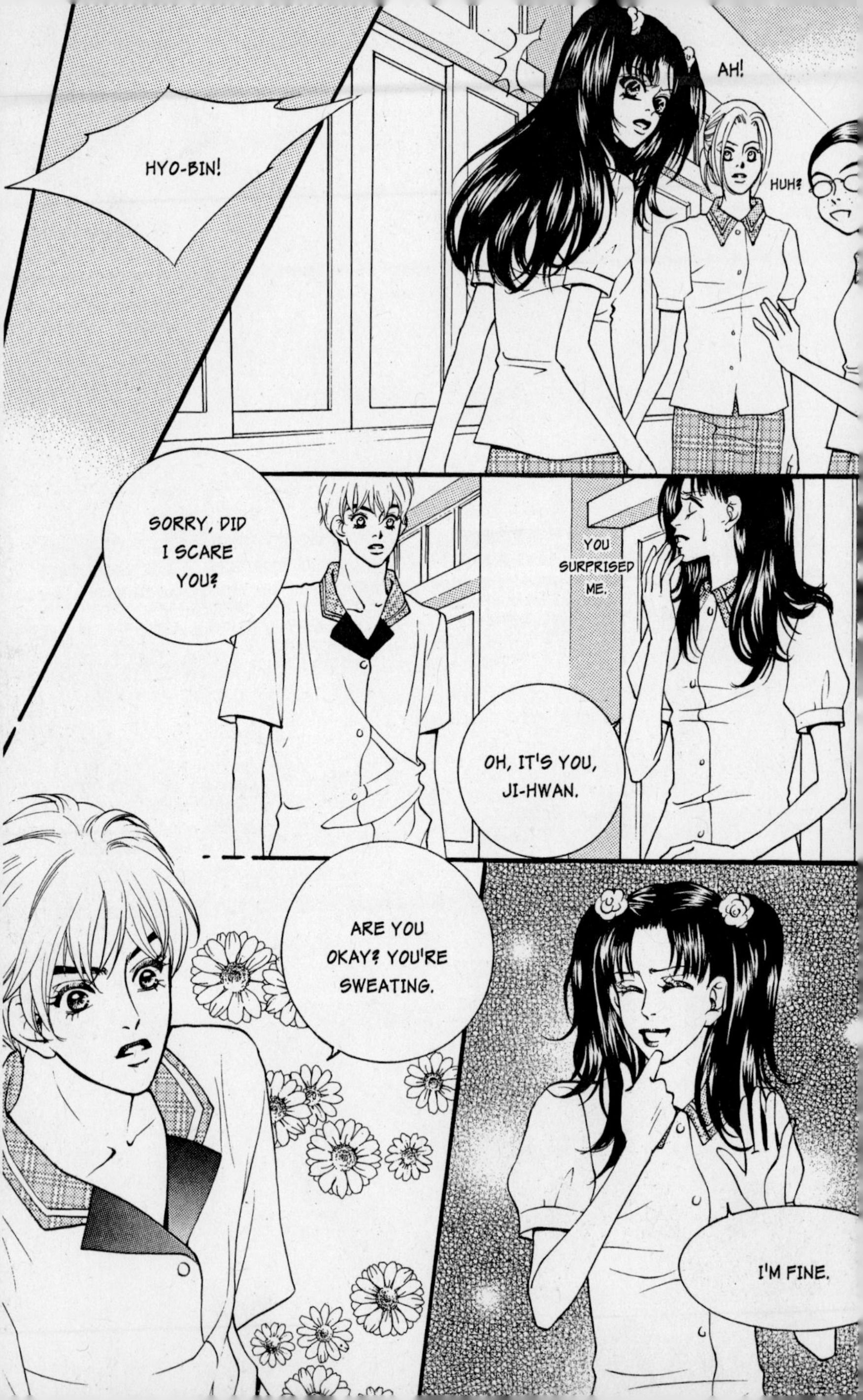
HYO-BIN!
AH!
HUH?
SORRY, DID I SCARE YOU?
YOU SURPRISED ME.
OH, IT'S YOU, JI-HWAN.
ARE YOU OKAY? YOU'RE SWEATING.
I'M FINE.

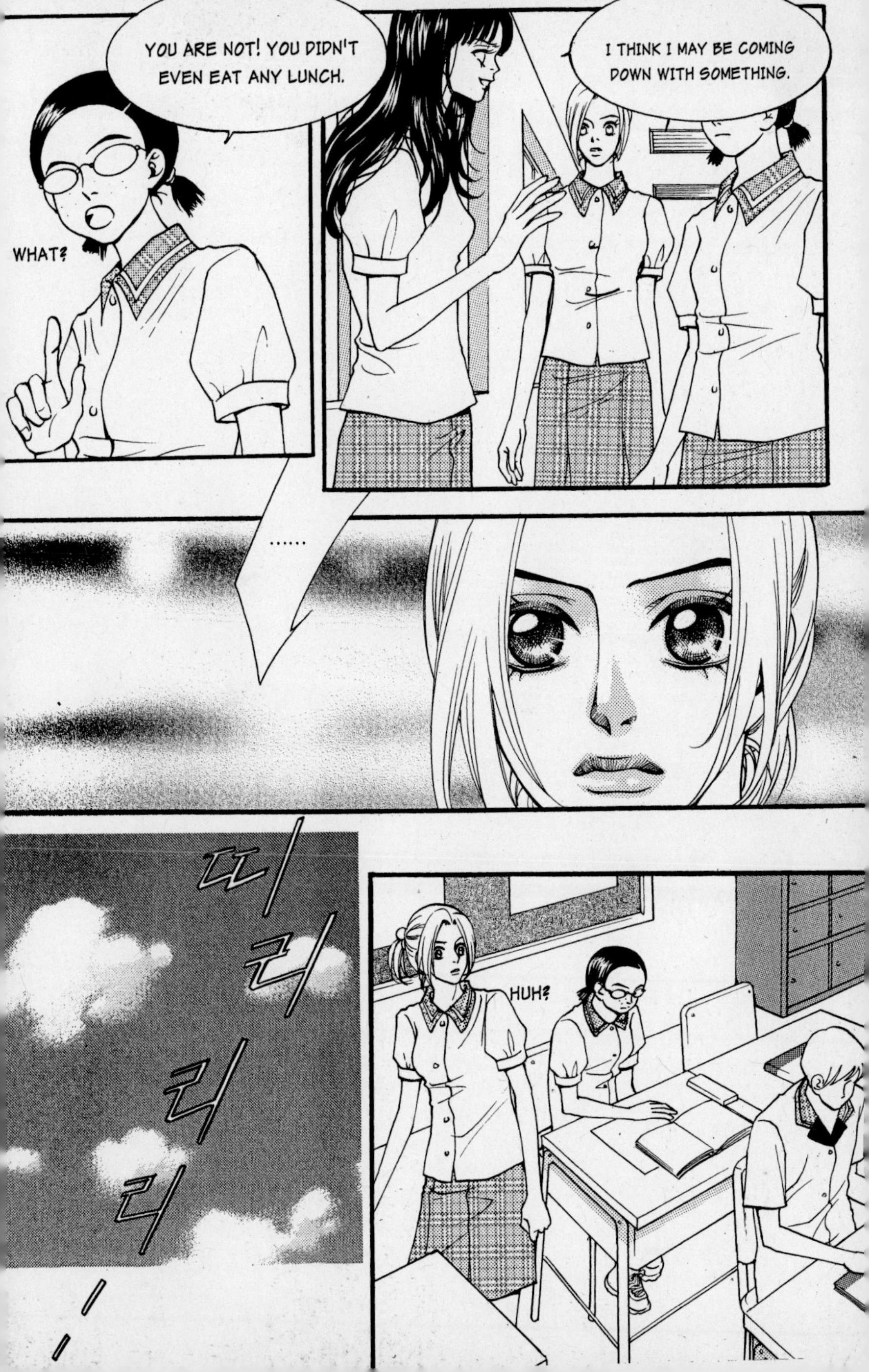
YOU ARE NOT! YOU DIDN'T EVEN EAT ANY LUNCH.
WHAT?
I THINK I MAY BE COMING DOWN WITH SOMETHING.
......
떠
러
러
러
HUH?

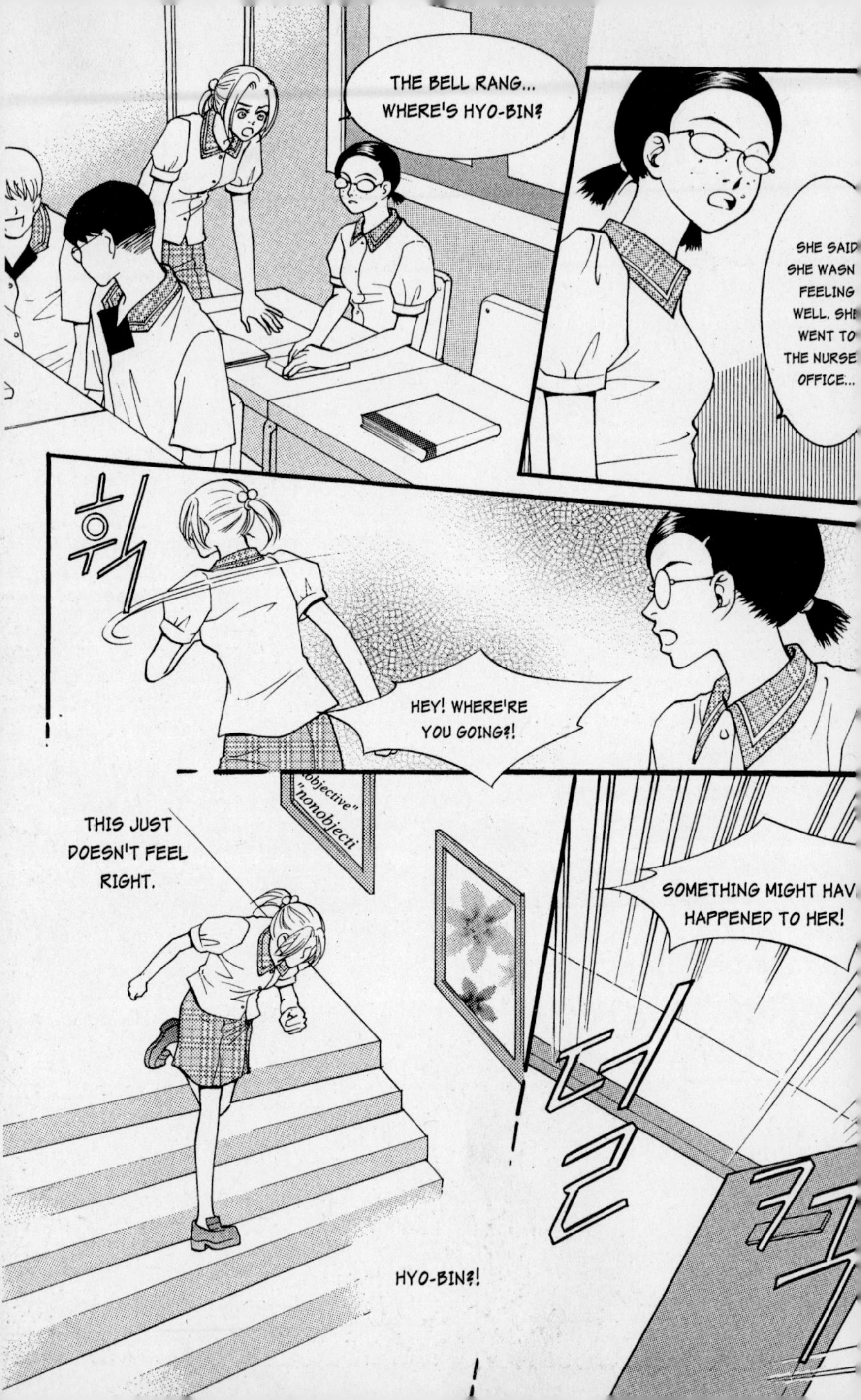
THE BELL RANG... WHERE'S HYO-BIN?
SHE SAID SHE WASN FEELING WELL. SHE WENT TO THE NURSE OFFICE...
휙
HEY! WHERE'RE YOU GOING?!
THIS JUST DOESN'T FEEL RIGHT.
"objective" "nonobjecti
SOMETHING MIGHT HAV HAPPENED TO HER!
HYO-BIN?!

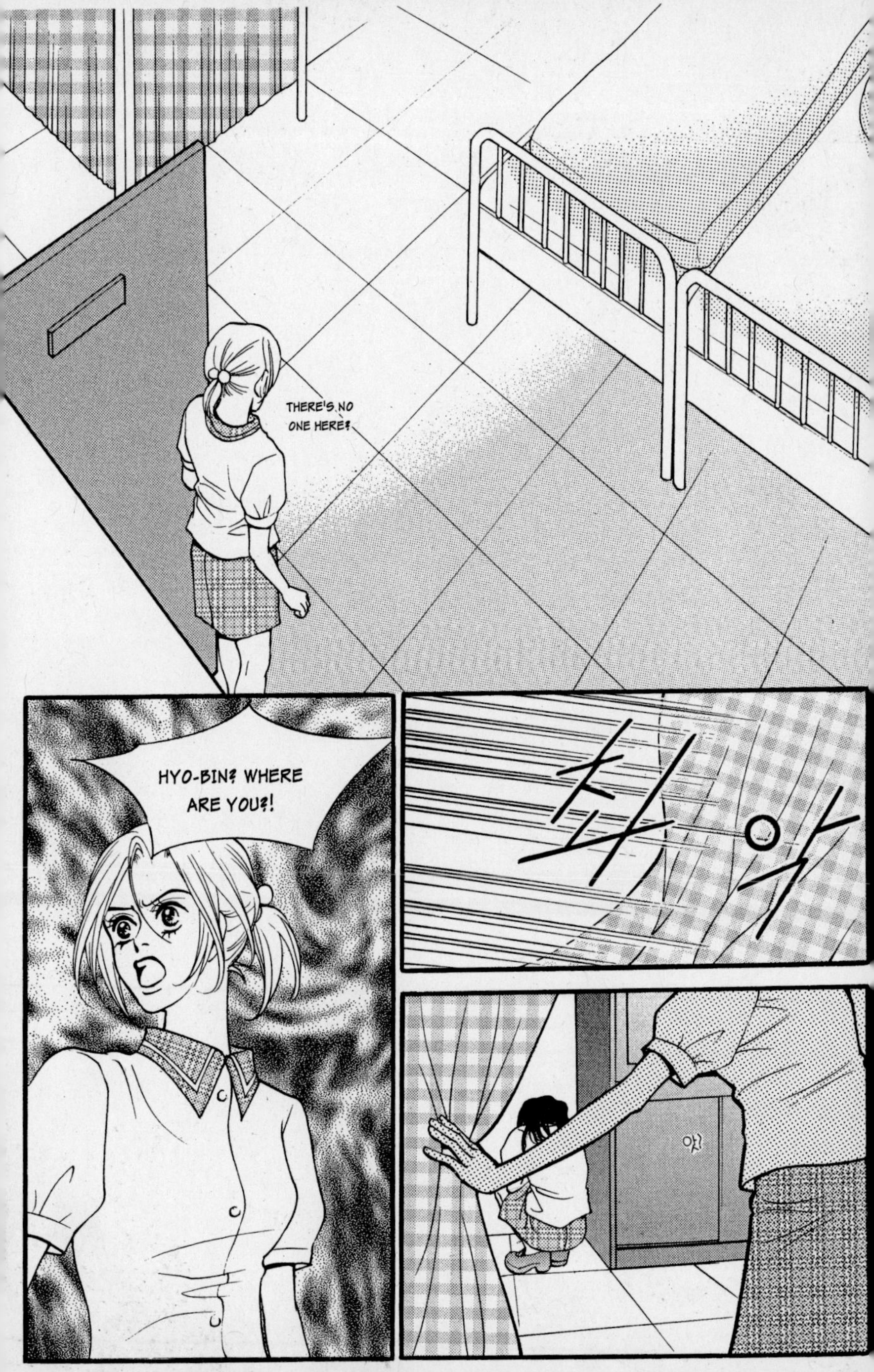
THERE'S NO ONE HERE?
HYO-BIN? WHERE ARE YOU?!
촤악

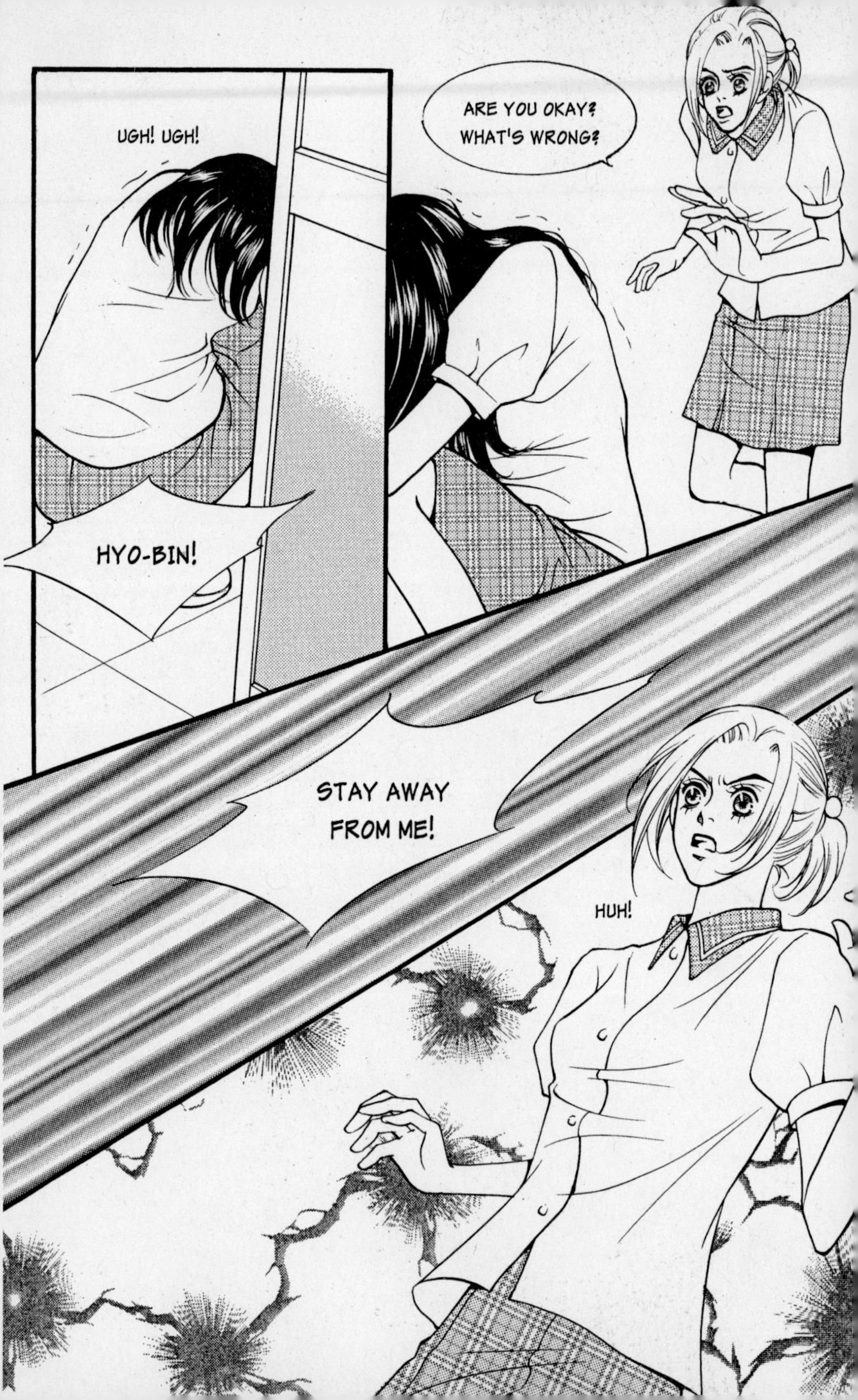
UGH! UGH!
ARE YOU OKAY? WHAT'S WRONG?
HYO-BIN!
STAY AWAY FROM ME!
HUH!

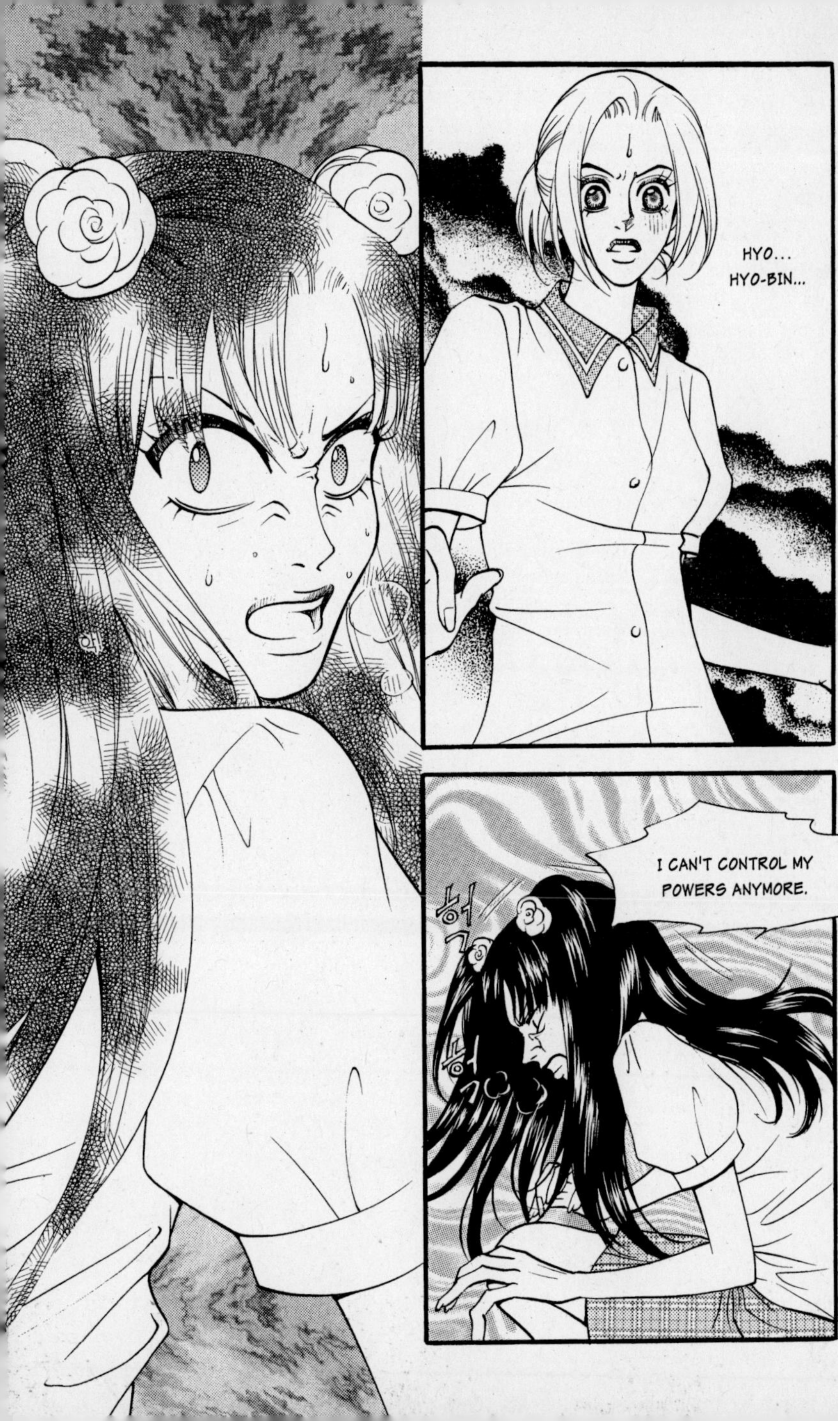
HYO...
HYO-BIN...
I CAN'T CONTROL MY POWERS ANYMORE.

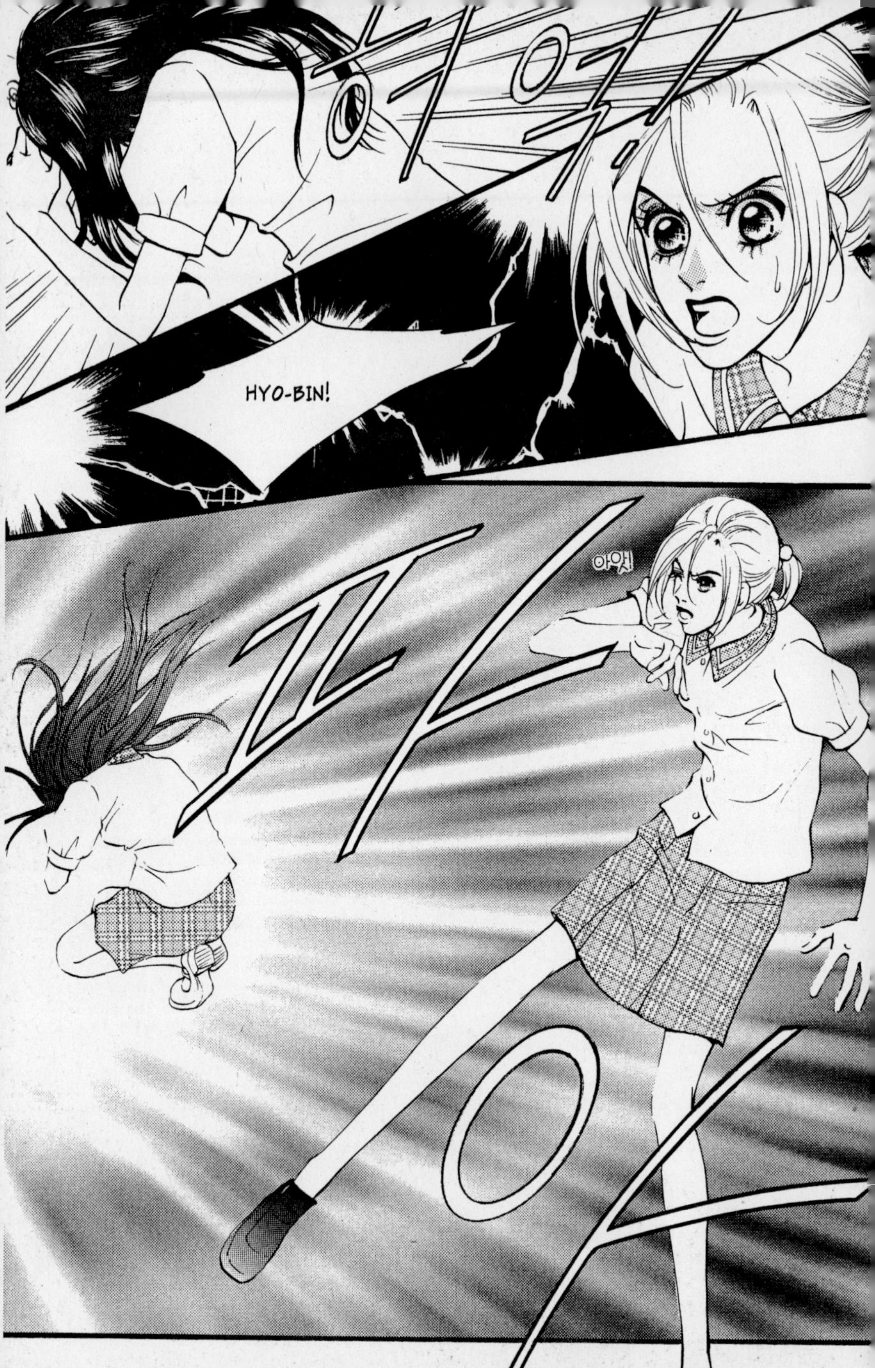
HYO-BIN!
야앗!

Feelings That Crossed Paths

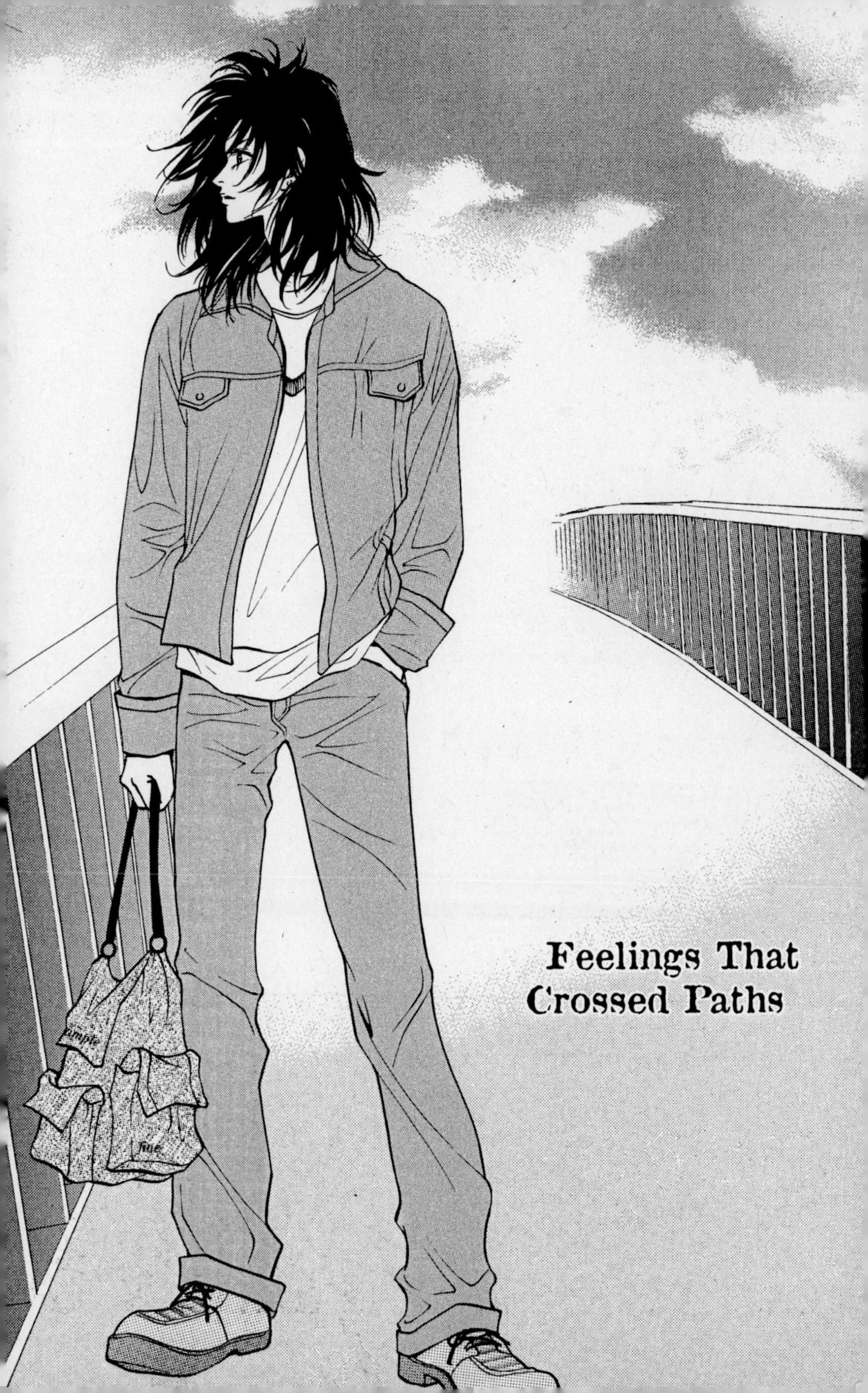

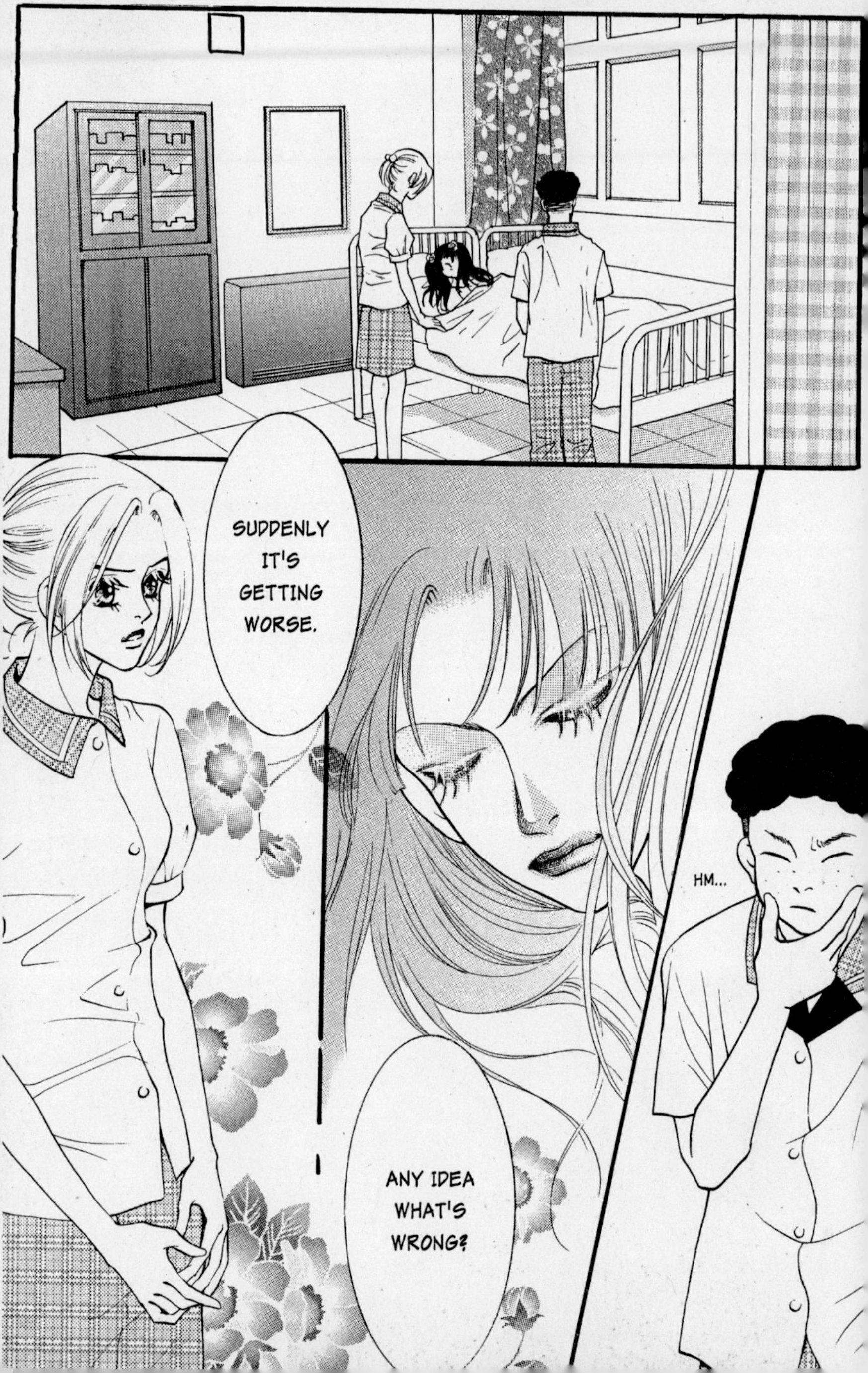
SUDDENLY IT'S GETTING WORSE.
ANY IDEA WHAT'S WRONG?
HM...

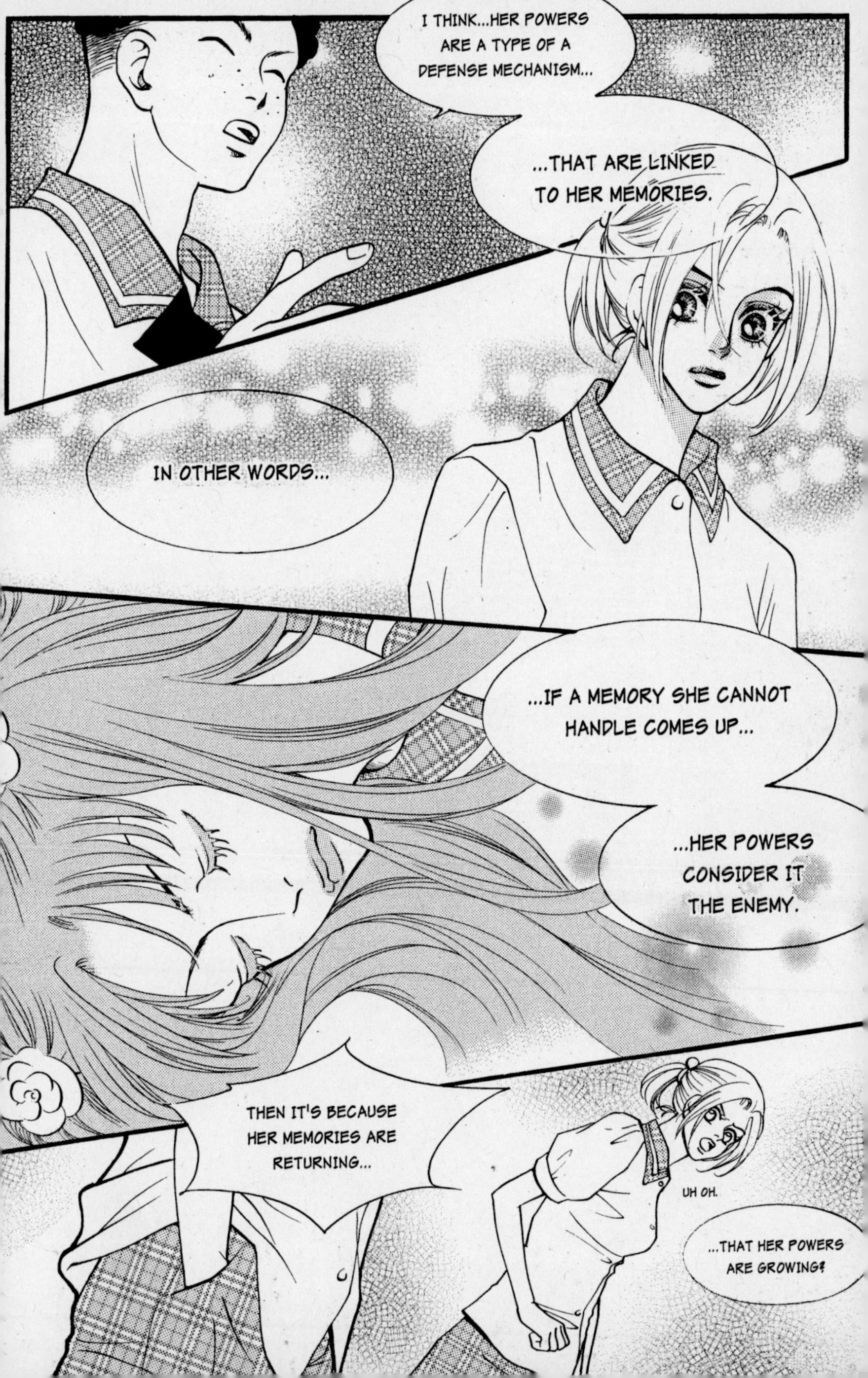
I THINK...HER POWERS ARE A TYPE OF A DEFENSE MECHANISM...
...THAT ARE LINKED TO HER MEMORIES.
IN OTHER WORDS...
...IF A MEMORY SHE CANNOT HANDLE COMES UP...
...HER POWERS CONSIDER IT THE ENEMY.
THEN IT'S BECAUSE HER MEMORIES ARE RETURNING...
UH OH.
...THAT HER POWERS ARE GROWING?

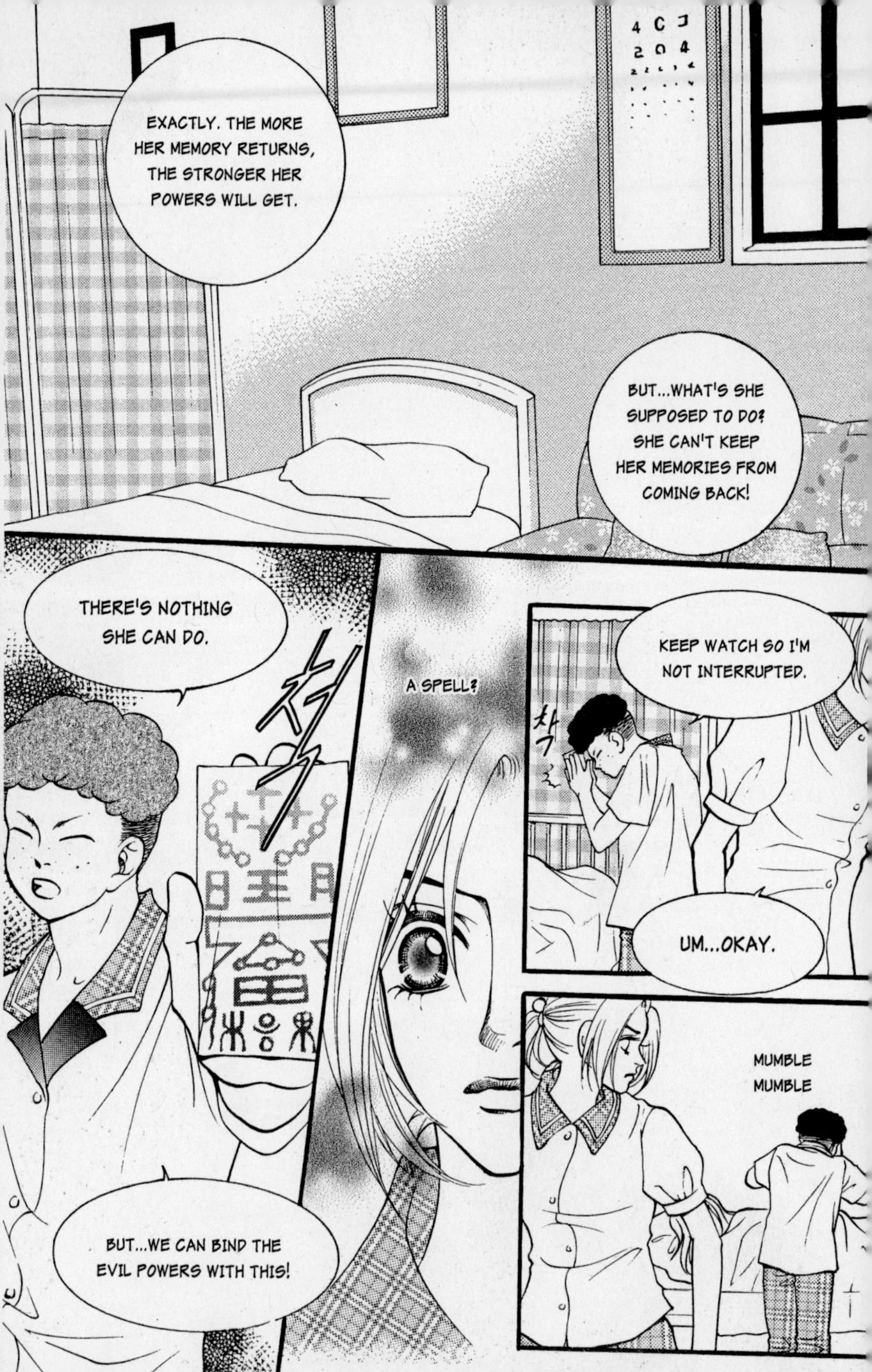
EXACTLY. THE MORE HER MEMORY RETURNS, THE STRONGER HER POWERS WILL GET.
BUT...WHAT'S SHE SUPPOSED TO DO? SHE CAN'T KEEP HER MEMORIES FROM COMING BACK!
THERE'S NOTHING SHE CAN DO.
BUT...WE CAN BIND THE EVIL POWERS WITH THIS!
A SPELL?
KEEP WATCH SO I'M NOT INTERRUPTED.
착
UM...OKAY.
MUMBLE
MUMBLE

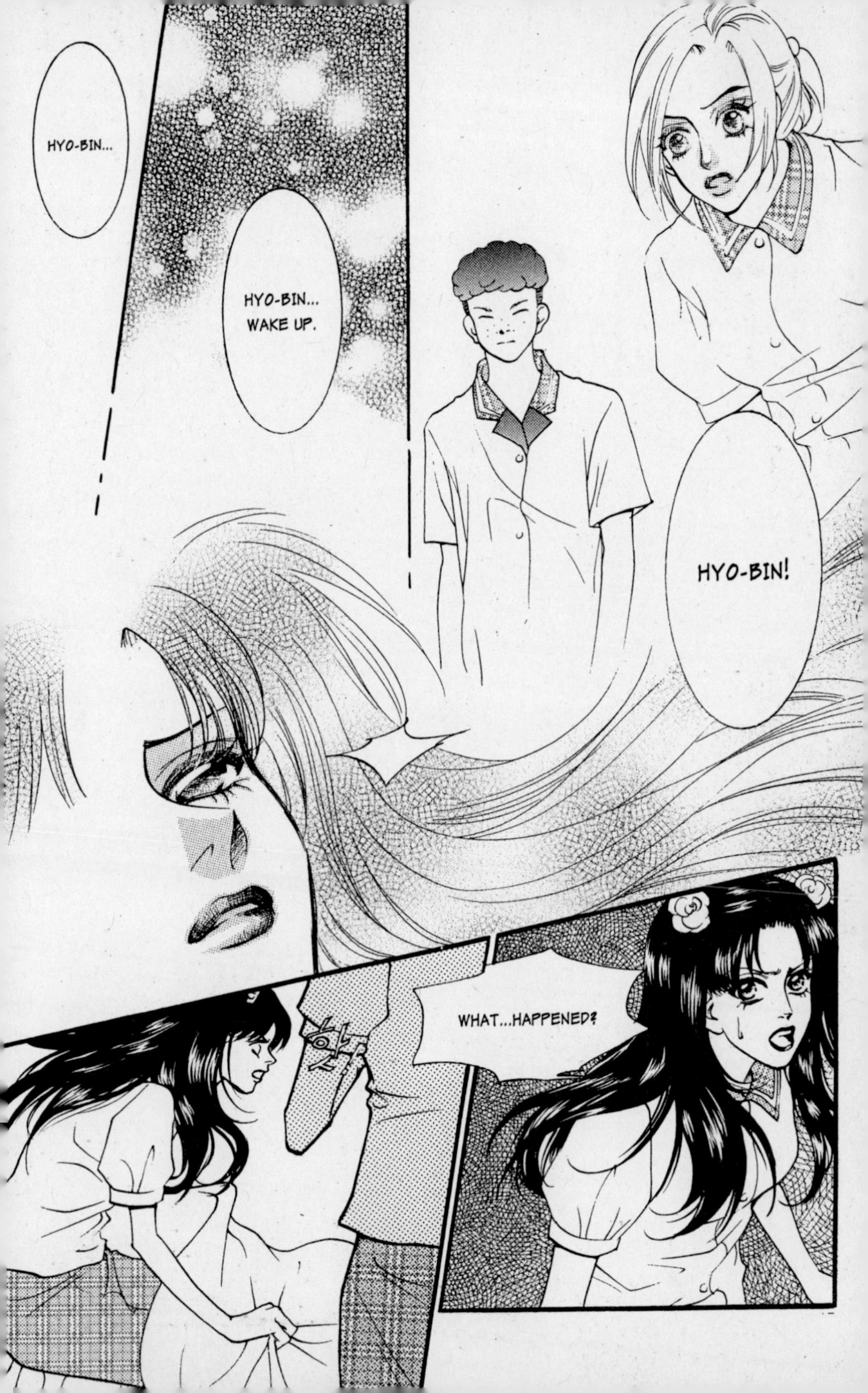
HYO-BIN...
HYO-BIN... WAKE UP.
HYO-BIN!
WHAT...HAPPENED?

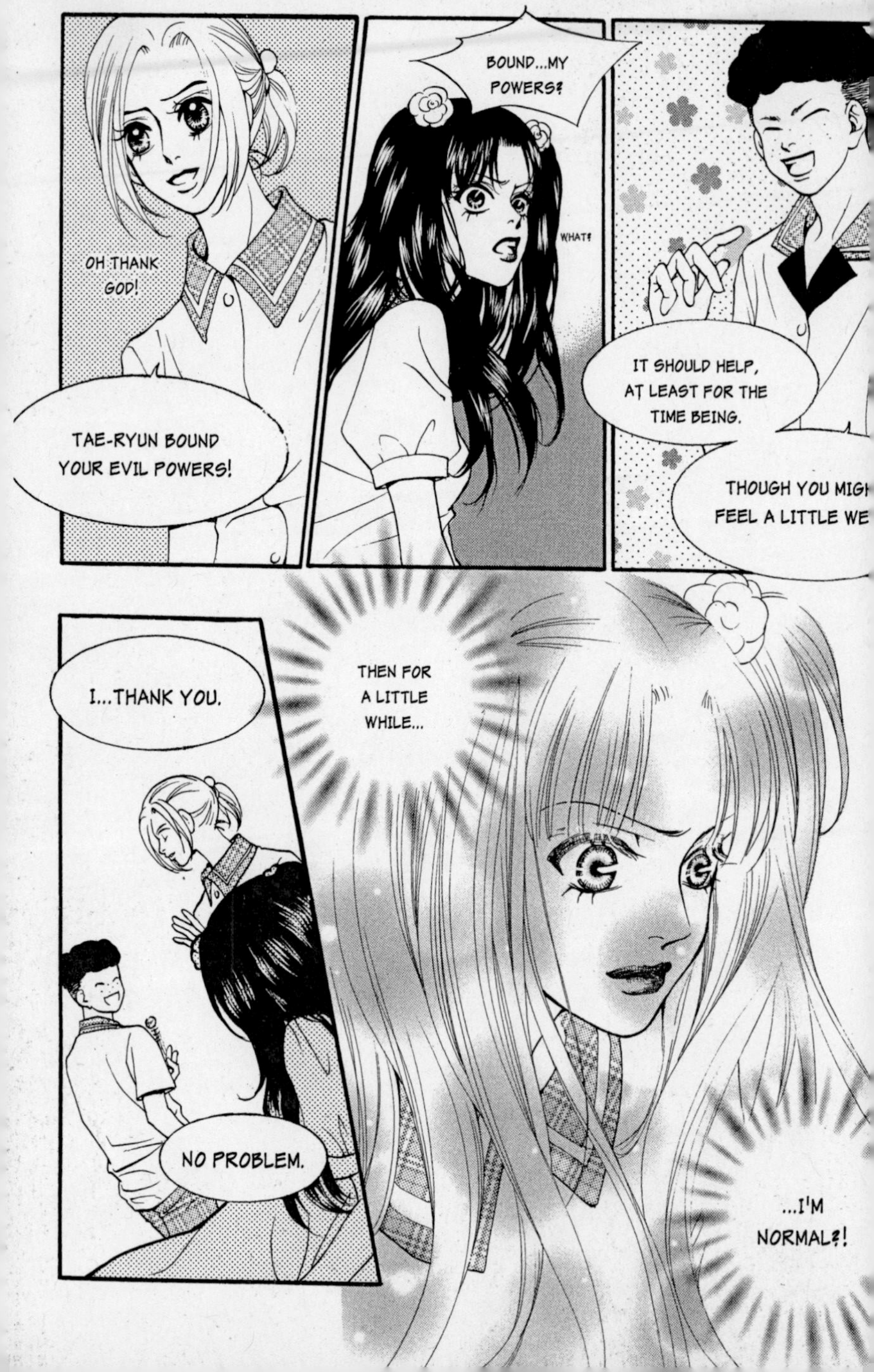
OH THANK GOD!
TAE-RYUN BOUND YOUR EVIL POWERS!
BOUND...MY POWERS?
WHAT?
IT SHOULD HELP, AT LEAST FOR THE TIME BEING.
THOUGH YOU MIGI FEEL A LITTLE WE
I...THANK YOU.
NO PROBLEM.
THEN FOR A LITTLE WHILE...
...I'M NORMAL?!

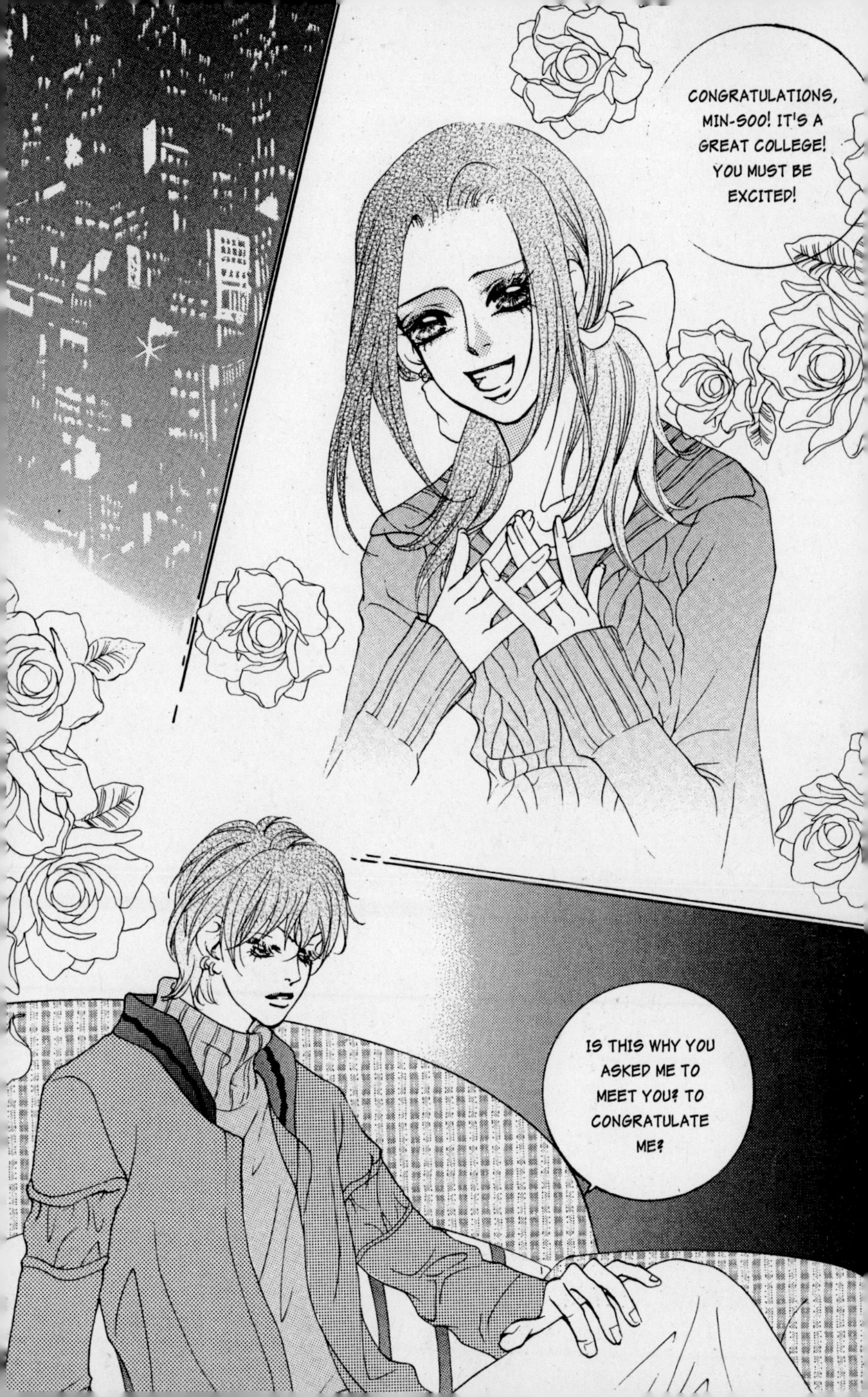
CONGRATULATIONS, MIN-SOO! IT'S A GREAT COLLEGE! YOU MUST BE EXCITED!
IS THIS WHY YOU ASKED ME TO MEET YOU? TO CONGRATULATE ME?

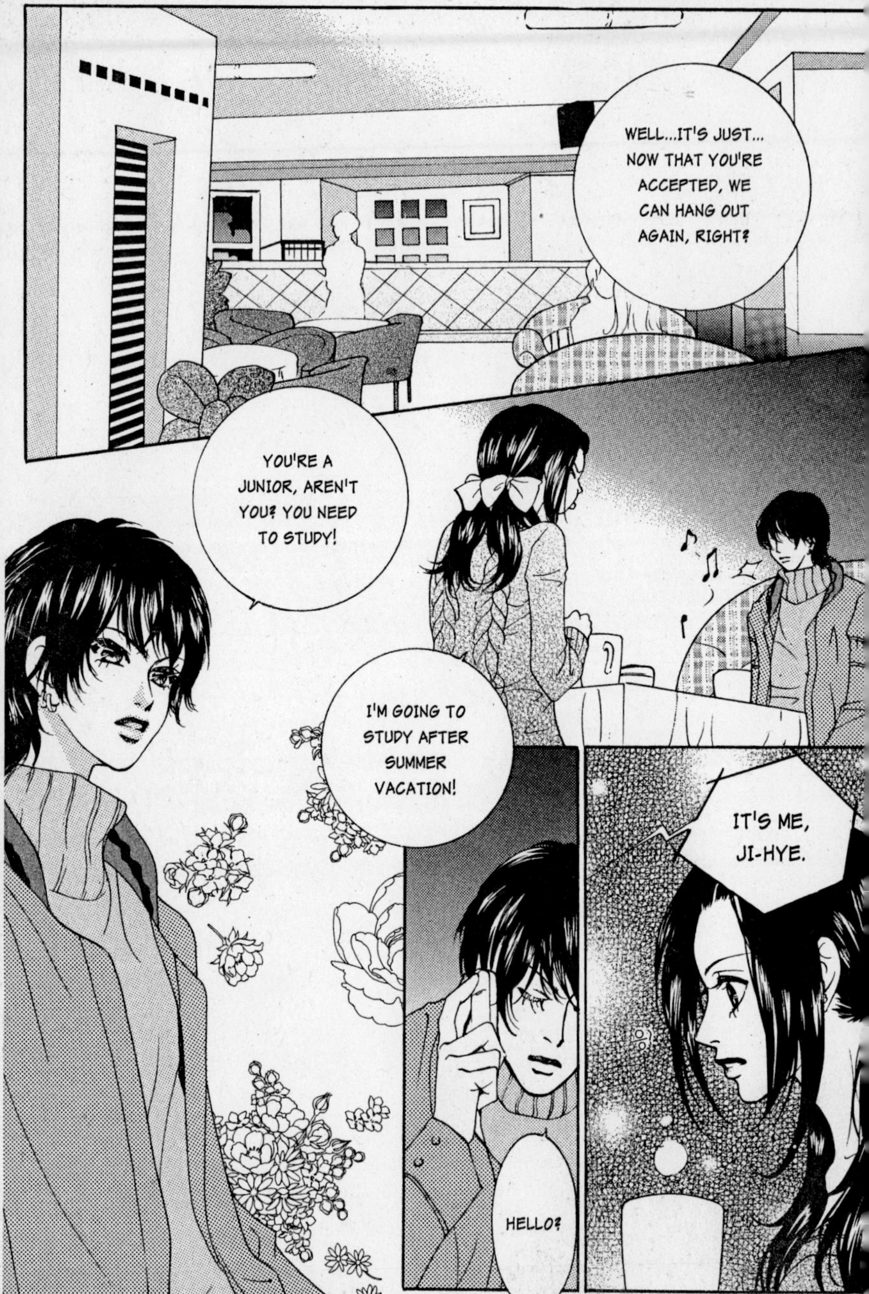
WELL...IT'S JUST... NOW THAT YOU'RE ACCEPTED, WE CAN HANG OUT AGAIN, RIGHT?
YOU'RE A JUNIOR, AREN'T YOU? YOU NEED TO STUDY!
I'M GOING TO STUDY AFTER SUMMER VACATION!
IT'S ME, JI-HYE.
HELLO?

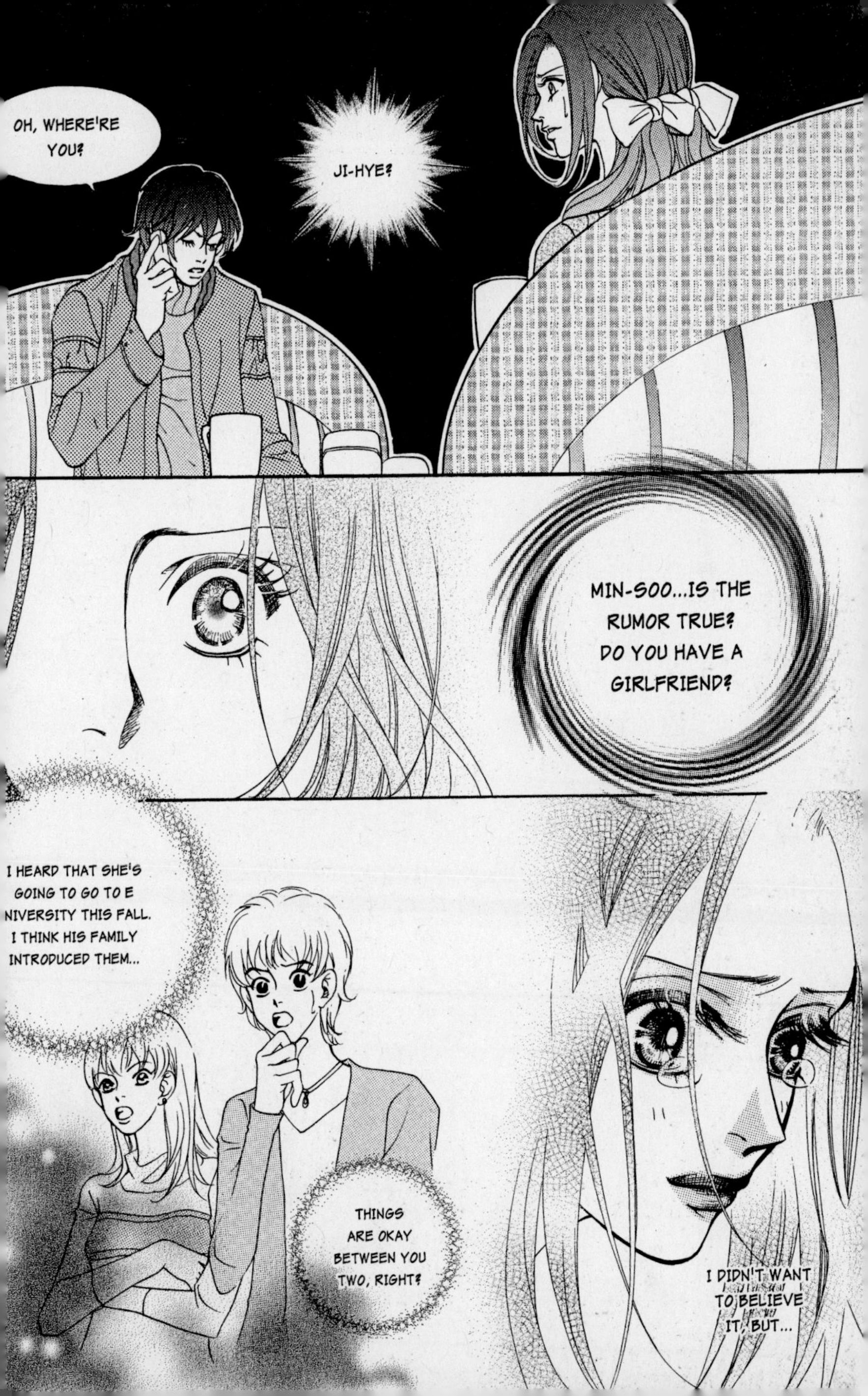

OH, WHERE'RE YOU?
JI-HYE?
MIN-SOO...IS THE RUMOR TRUE? DO YOU HAVE A GIRLFRIEND?
I HEARD THAT SHE'S GOING TO GO TO E NIVERSITY THIS FALL. I THINK HIS FAMILY INTRODUCED THEM...
THINGS ARE OKAY BETWEEN YOU TWO, RIGHT?
I DIDN'T WANT TO BELIEVE IT, BUT...

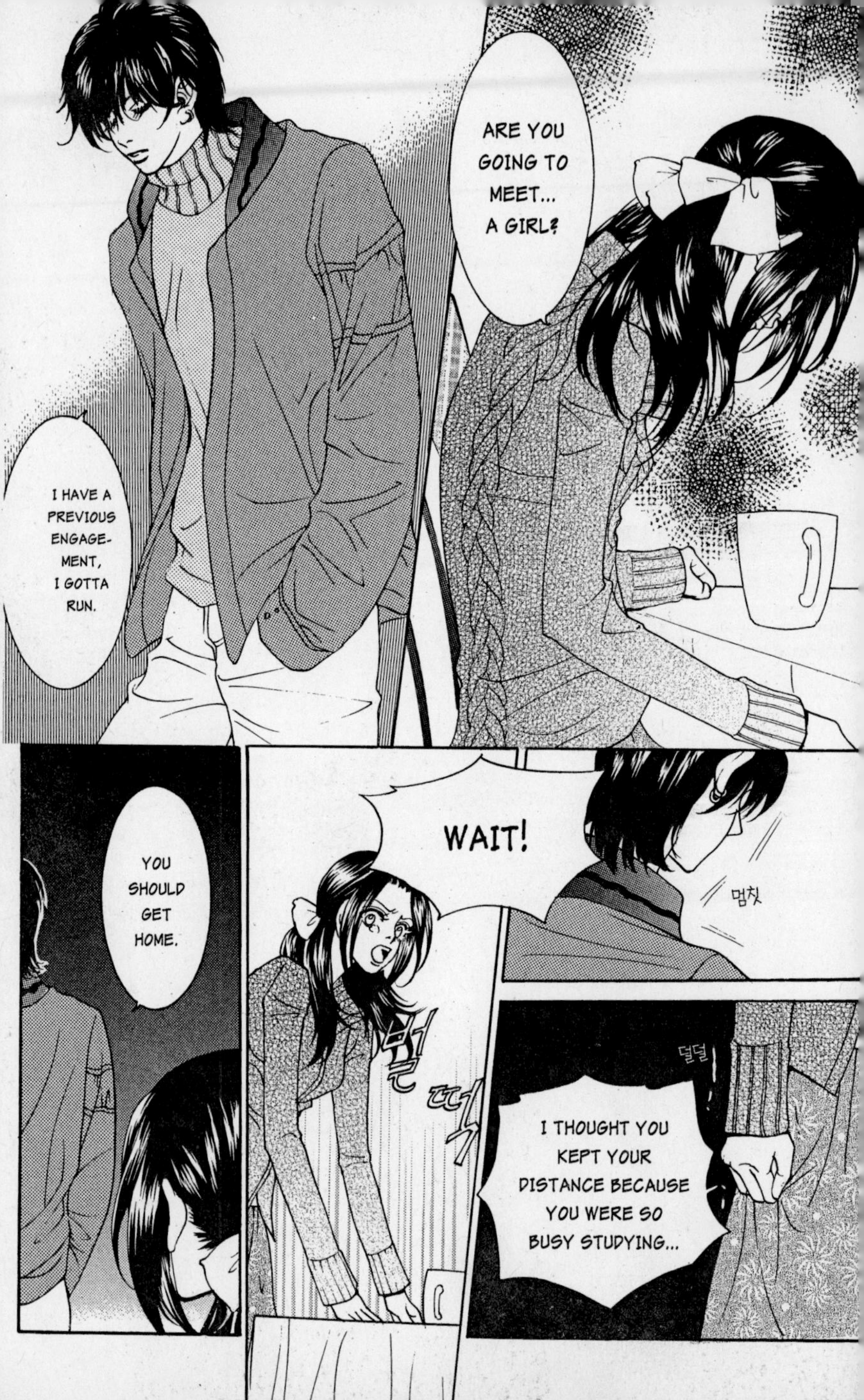
I HAVE A PREVIOUS ENGAGE-MENT, I GOTTA RUN.
ARE YOU GOING TO MEET... A GIRL?
YOU SHOULD GET HOME.
WAIT!
멈칫
벌떡
덜덜
I THOUGHT YOU KEPT YOUR DISTANCE BECAUSE YOU WERE SO BUSY STUDYING...

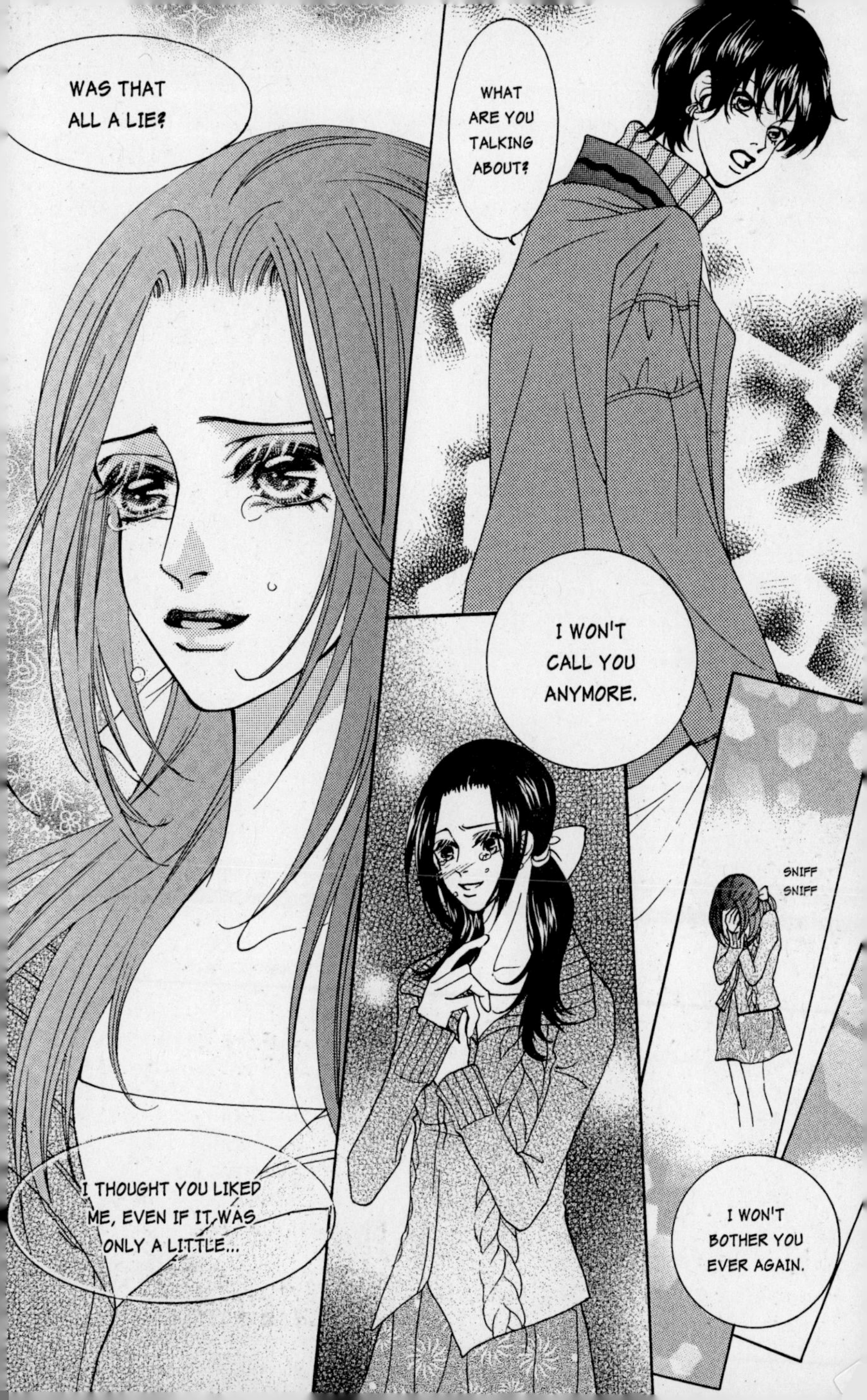

WAS THAT ALL A LIE?
I THOUGHT YOU LIKED ME, EVEN IF IT WAS ONLY A LITTLE...
WHAT ARE YOU TALKING ABOUT?
I WON'T CALL YOU ANYMORE.
SNIFF SNIFF
I WON'T BOTHER YOU EVER AGAIN.

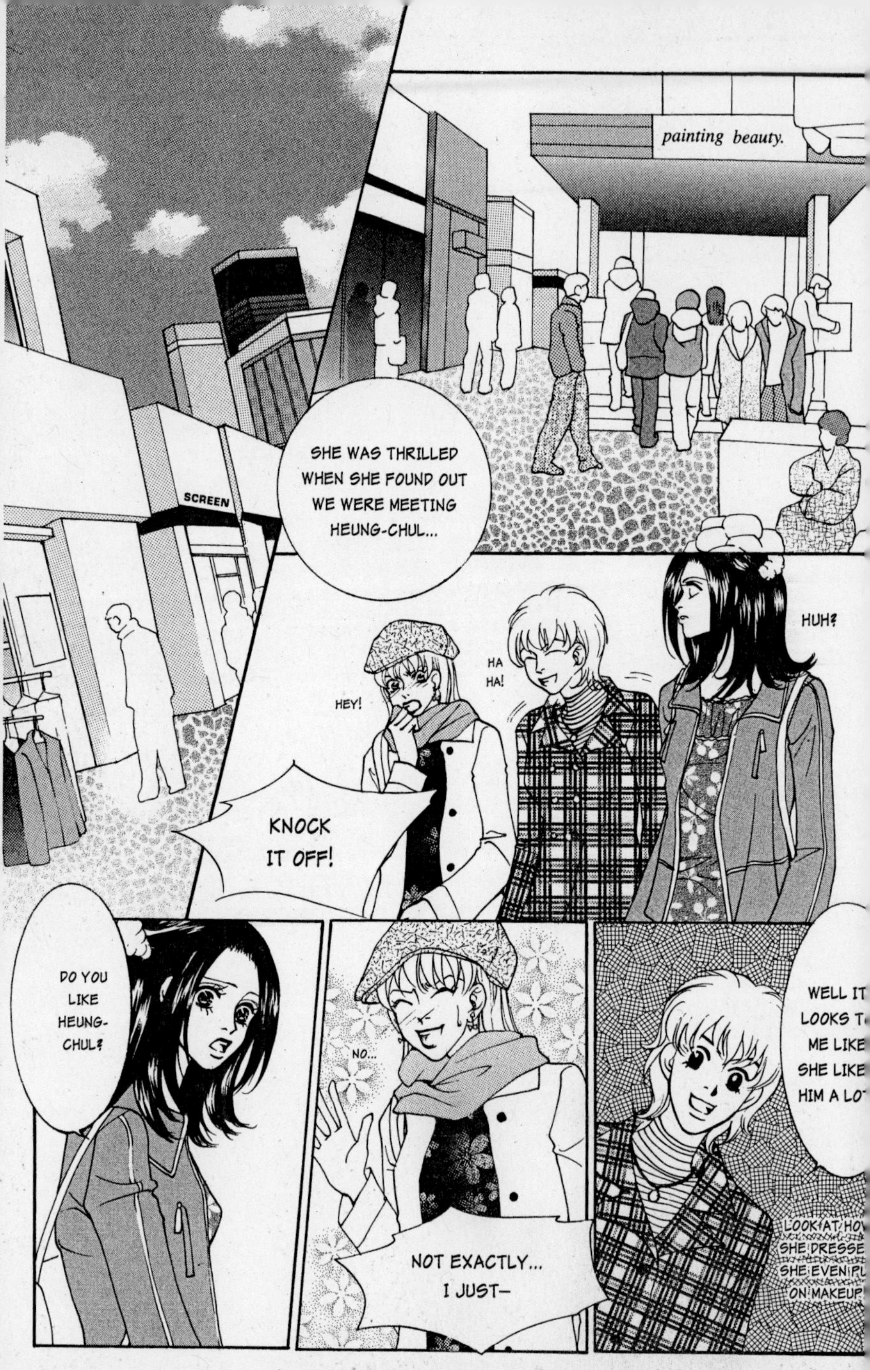
SCREEN
painting beauty.
SHE WAS THRILLED WHEN SHE FOUND OUT WE WERE MEETING HEUNG-CHUL...
HEY!
HA HA!
HUH?
KNOCK IT OFF!
DO YOU LIKE HEUNG-CHUL?
NO...
NOT EXACTLY... I JUST-
WELL IT LOOKS T ME LIKE SHE LIKE HIM A LO
LOOK AT HO SHE DRESSE SHE EVEN P ON MAKEUP

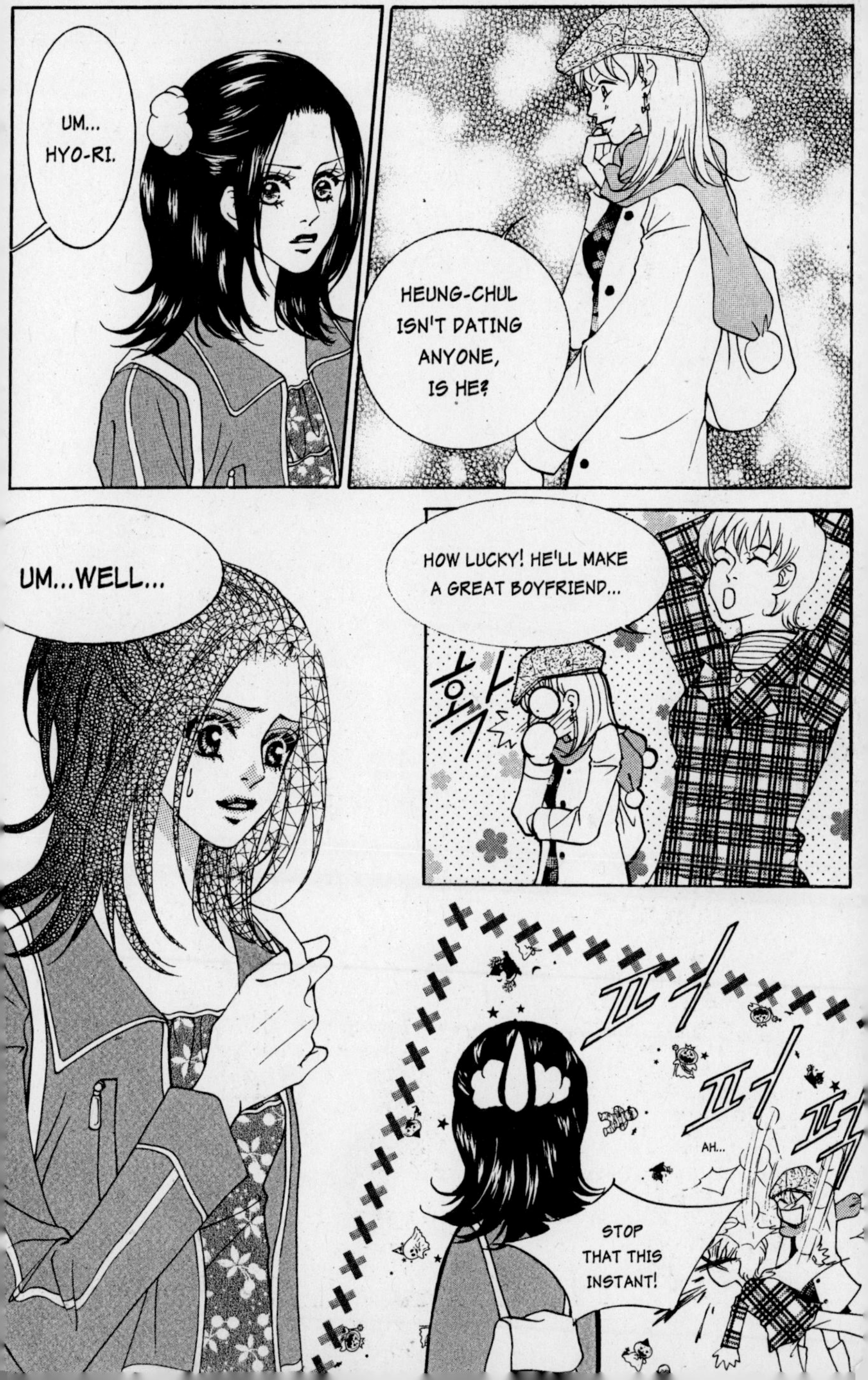
UM... HYO-RI.
HEUNG-CHUL ISN'T DATING ANYONE, IS HE?
UM...WELL...
HOW LUCKY! HE'LL MAKE A GREAT BOYFRIEND...
AH...
STOP THAT THIS INSTANT!

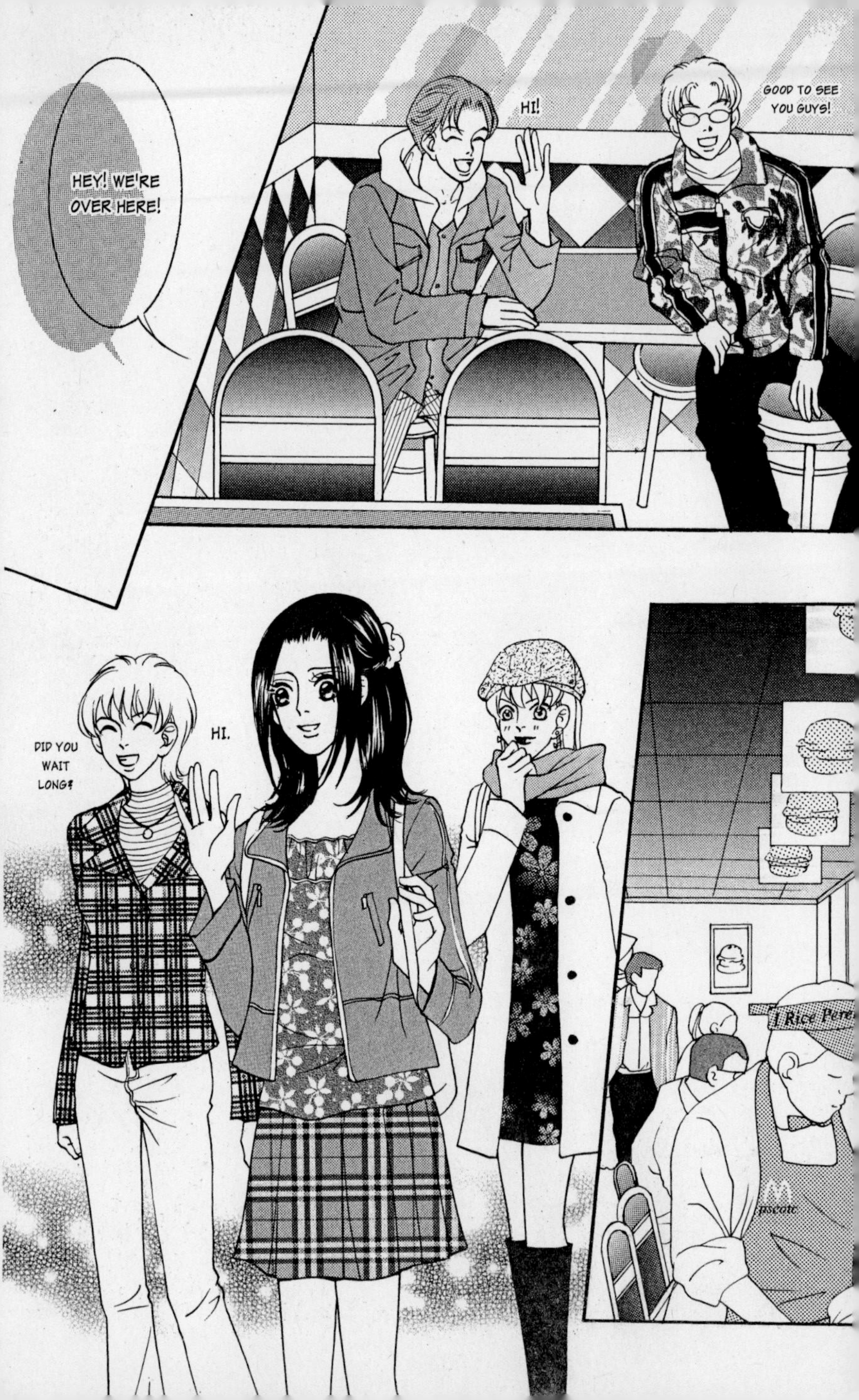
HEY! WE'RE OVER HERE!
HI!
GOOD TO SEE YOU GUYS!
DID YOU WAIT LONG?
HI.

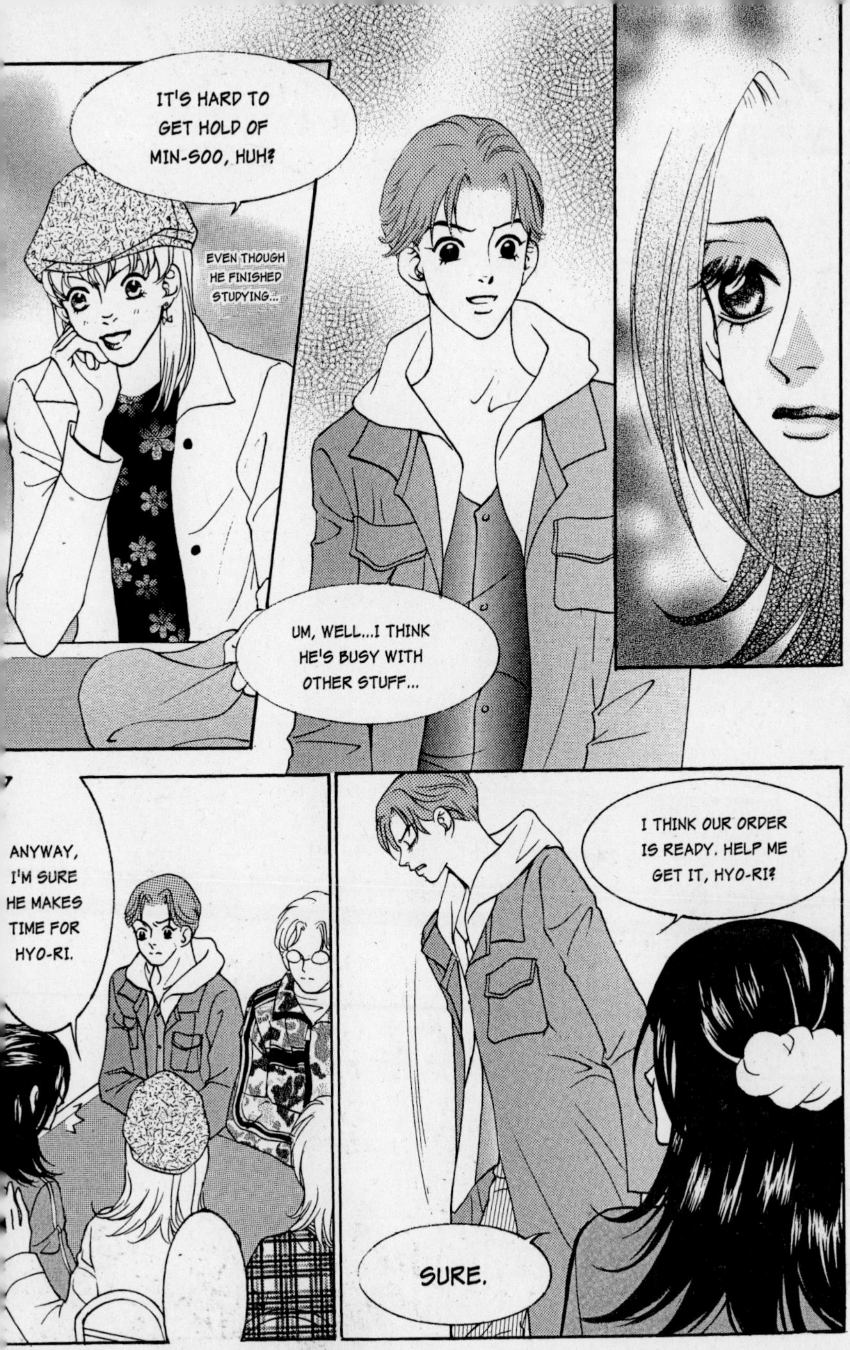
IT'S HARD TO GET HOLD OF MIN-SOO, HUH?
EVEN THOUGH HE FINISHED STUDYING...
UM, WELL...I THINK HE'S BUSY WITH OTHER STUFF...
ANYWAY, I'M SURE HE MAKES TIME FOR HYO-RI.
I THINK OUR ORDER IS READY. HELP ME GET IT, HYO-RI?
SURE.

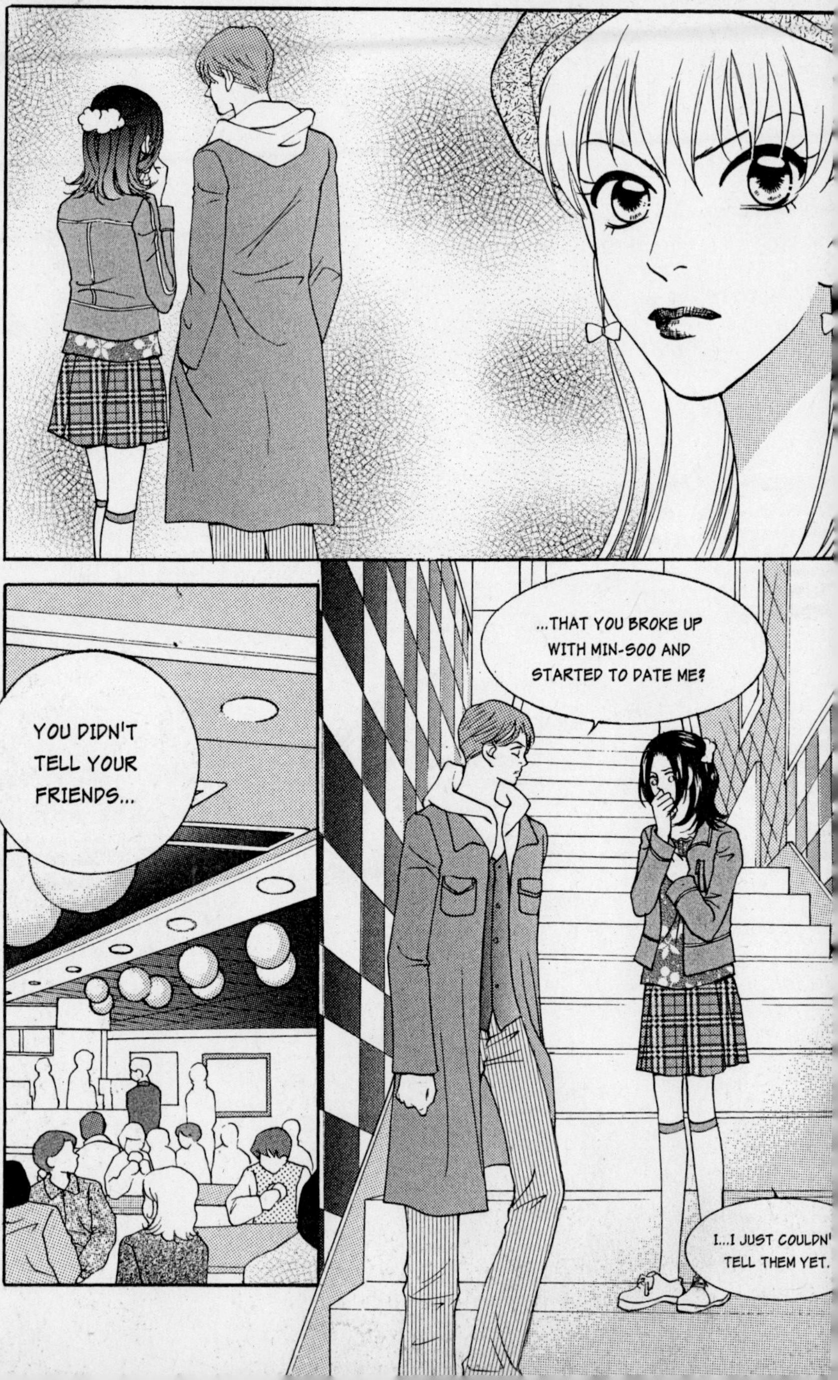
YOU DIDN'T TELL YOUR FRIENDS...
...THAT YOU BROKE UP WITH MIN-SOO AND STARTED TO DATE ME?
I...I JUST COULDN' TELL THEM YET.

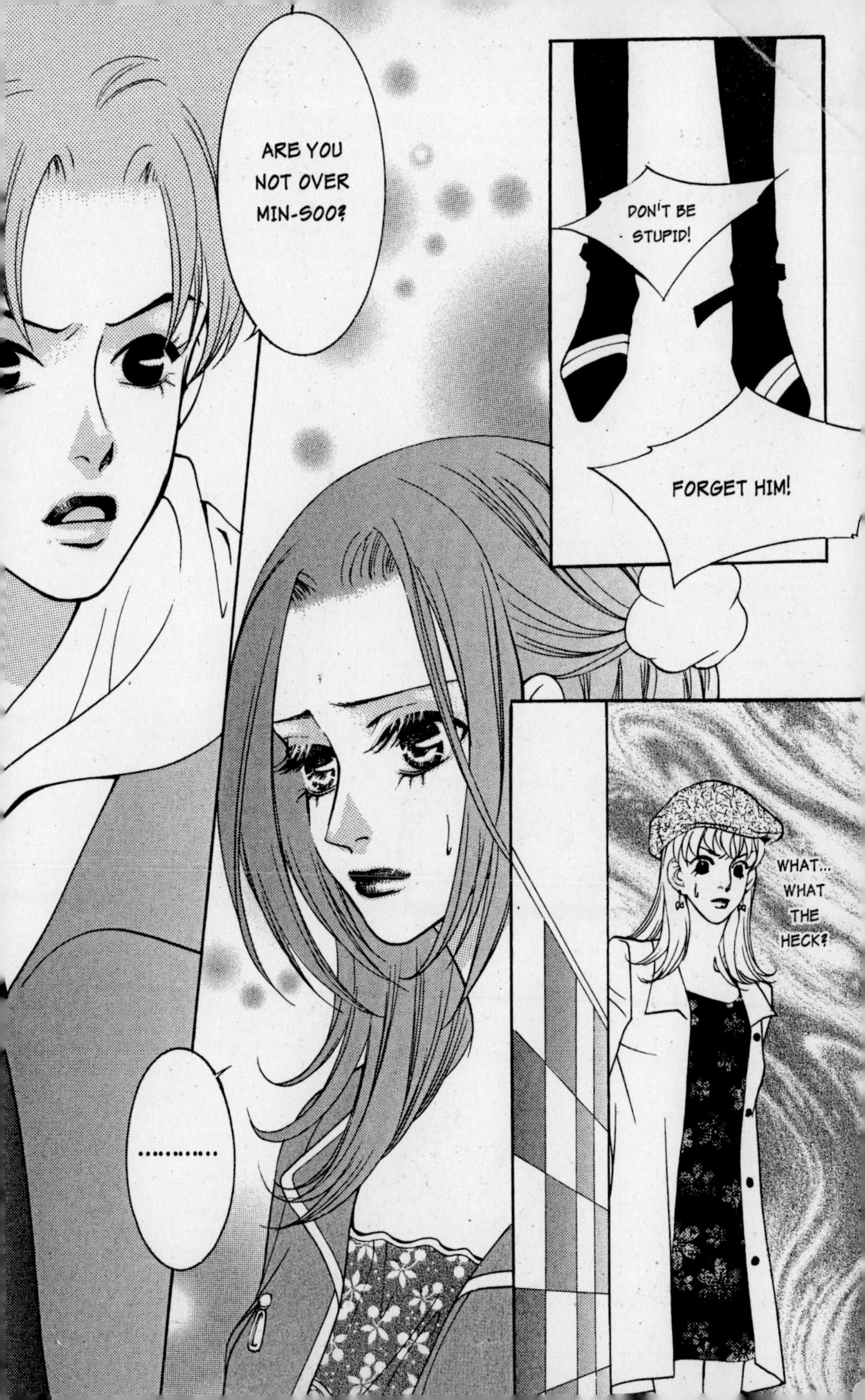
ARE YOU NOT OVER MIN-SOO?
....
DON'T BE STUPID!
FORGET HIM!
WHAT... WHAT THE HECK?

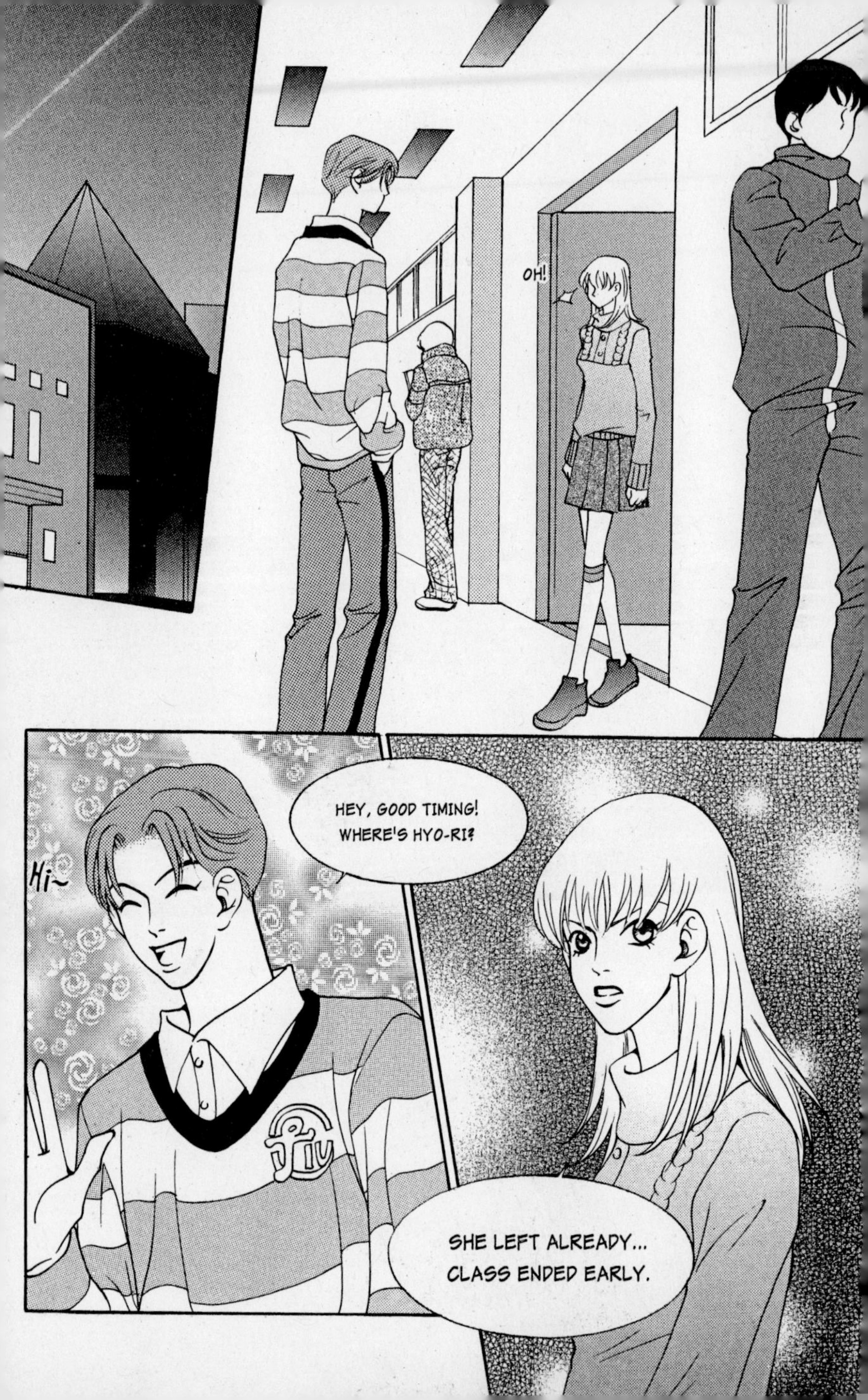
OH!
Hi~
HEY, GOOD TIMING! WHERE'S HYO-RI?
SHE LEFT ALREADY... CLASS ENDED EARLY.

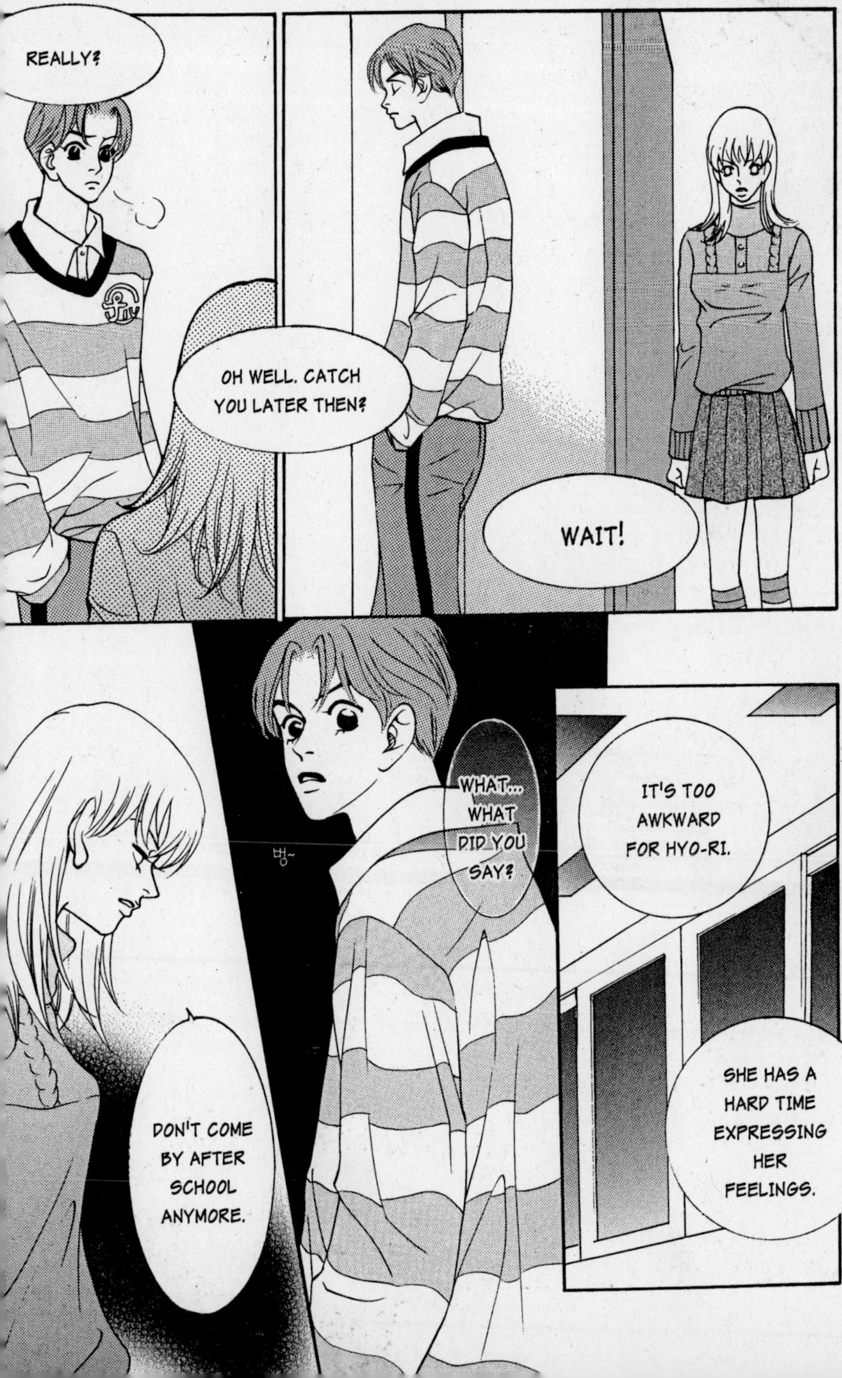
REALLY?
OH WELL. CATCH YOU LATER THEN?
WAIT!
DON'T COME BY AFTER SCHOOL ANYMORE.
WHAT... WHAT DID YOU SAY?
벙~
IT'S TOO AWKWARD FOR HYO-RI.
SHE HAS A HARD TIME EXPRESSING HER FEELINGS.

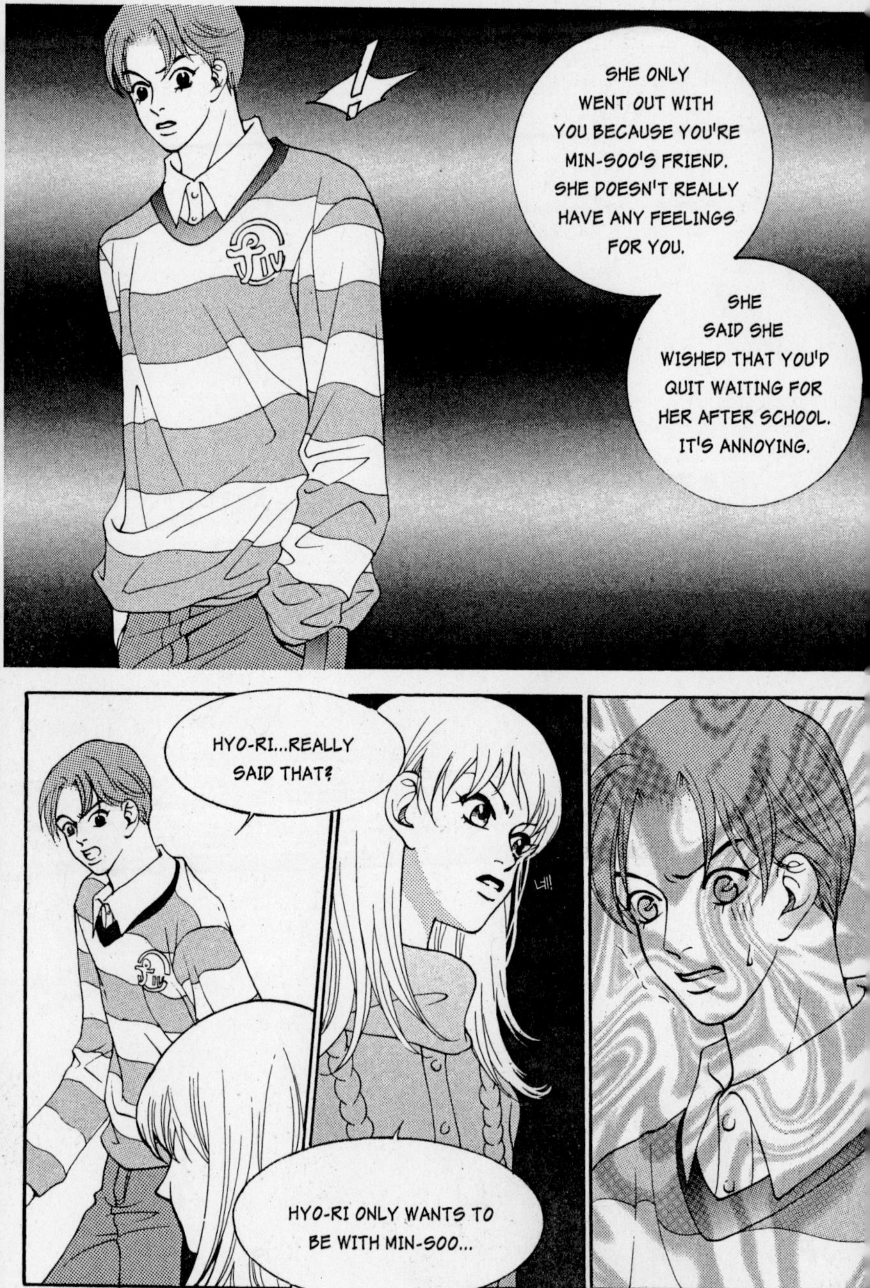
!
SHE ONLY WENT OUT WITH YOU BECAUSE YOU'RE MIN-SOO'S FRIEND. SHE DOESN'T REALLY HAVE ANY FEELINGS FOR YOU.
SHE SAID SHE WISHED THAT YOU'D QUIT WAITING FOR HER AFTER SCHOOL. IT'S ANNOYING.
HYO-RI...REALLY SAID THAT?
HYO-RI ONLY WANTS TO BE WITH MIN-SOO...

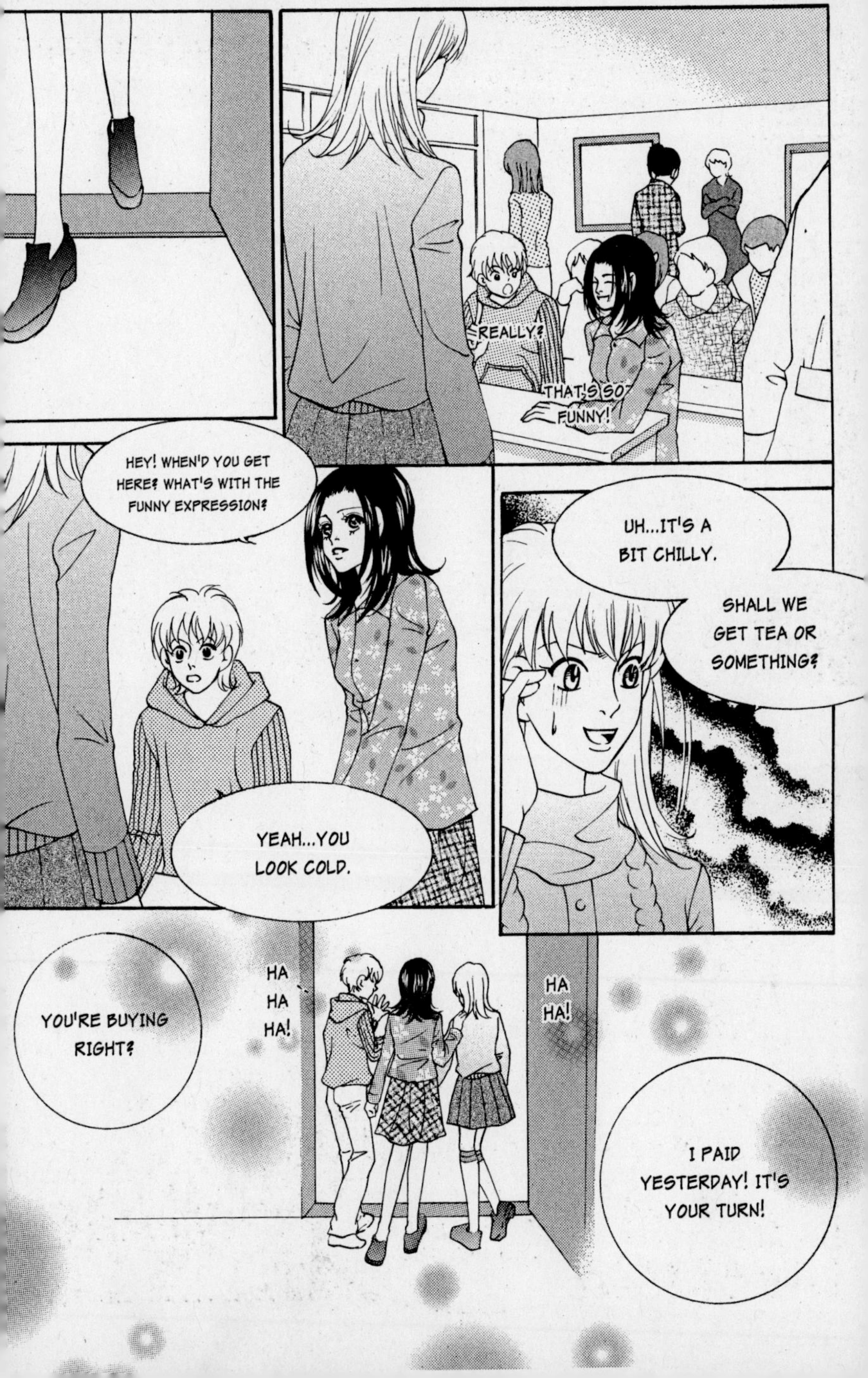

REALLY?
THAT'S SO FUNNY!
HEY! WHEN'D YOU GET HERE? WHAT'S WITH THE FUNNY EXPRESSION?
YEAH...YOU LOOK COLD.
UH...IT'S A BIT CHILLY.
SHALL WE GET TEA OR SOMETHING?
YOU'RE BUYING RIGHT?
HA HA HA!
HA HA!
I PAID YESTERDAY! IT'S YOUR TURN!

Visitor

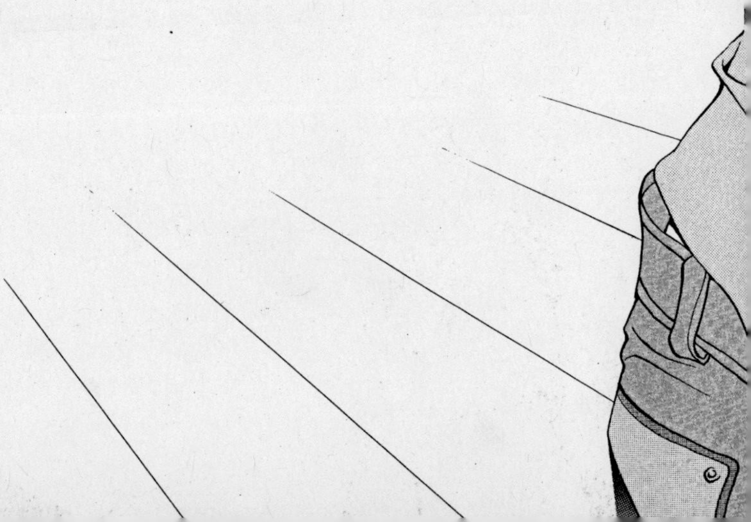

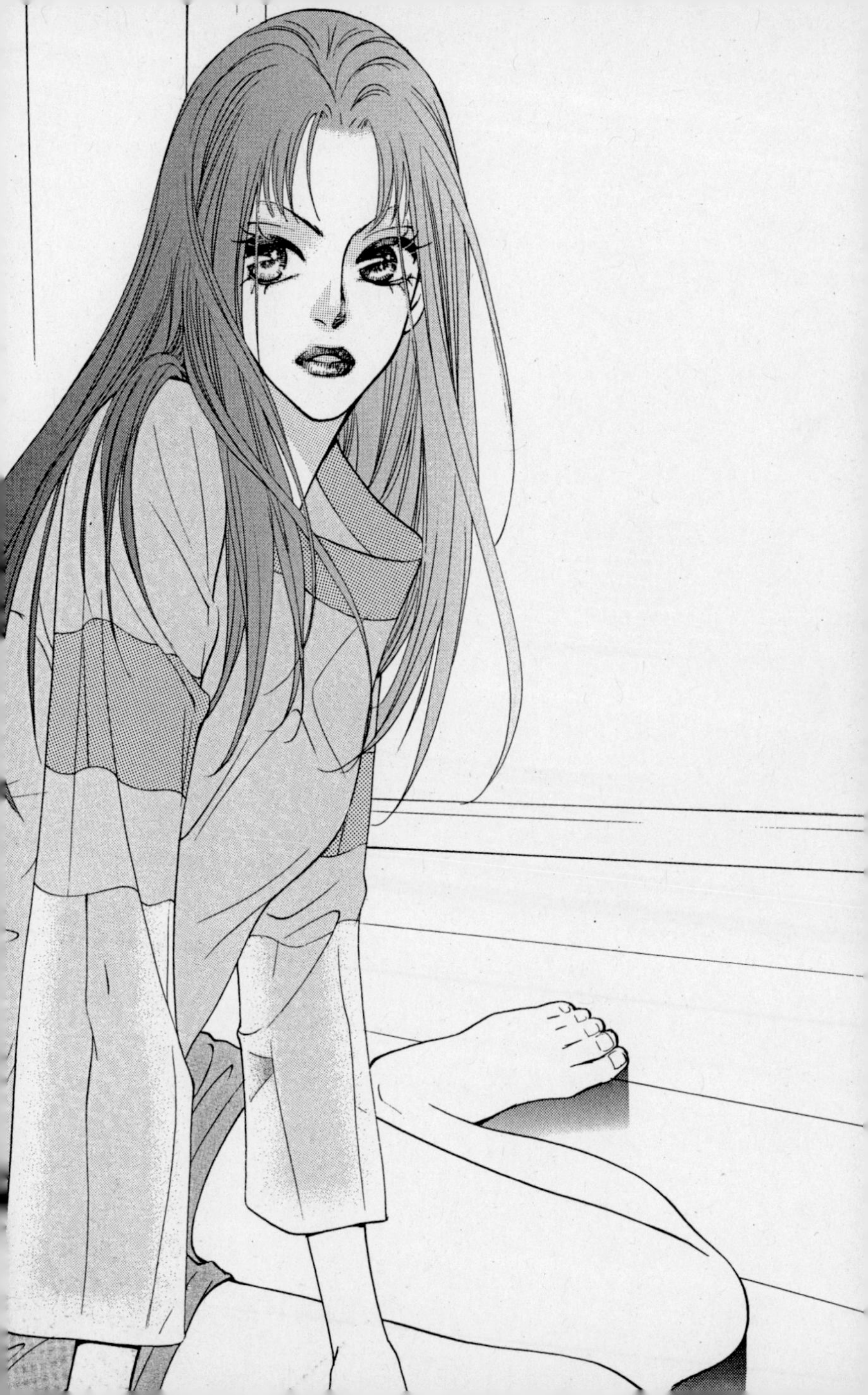

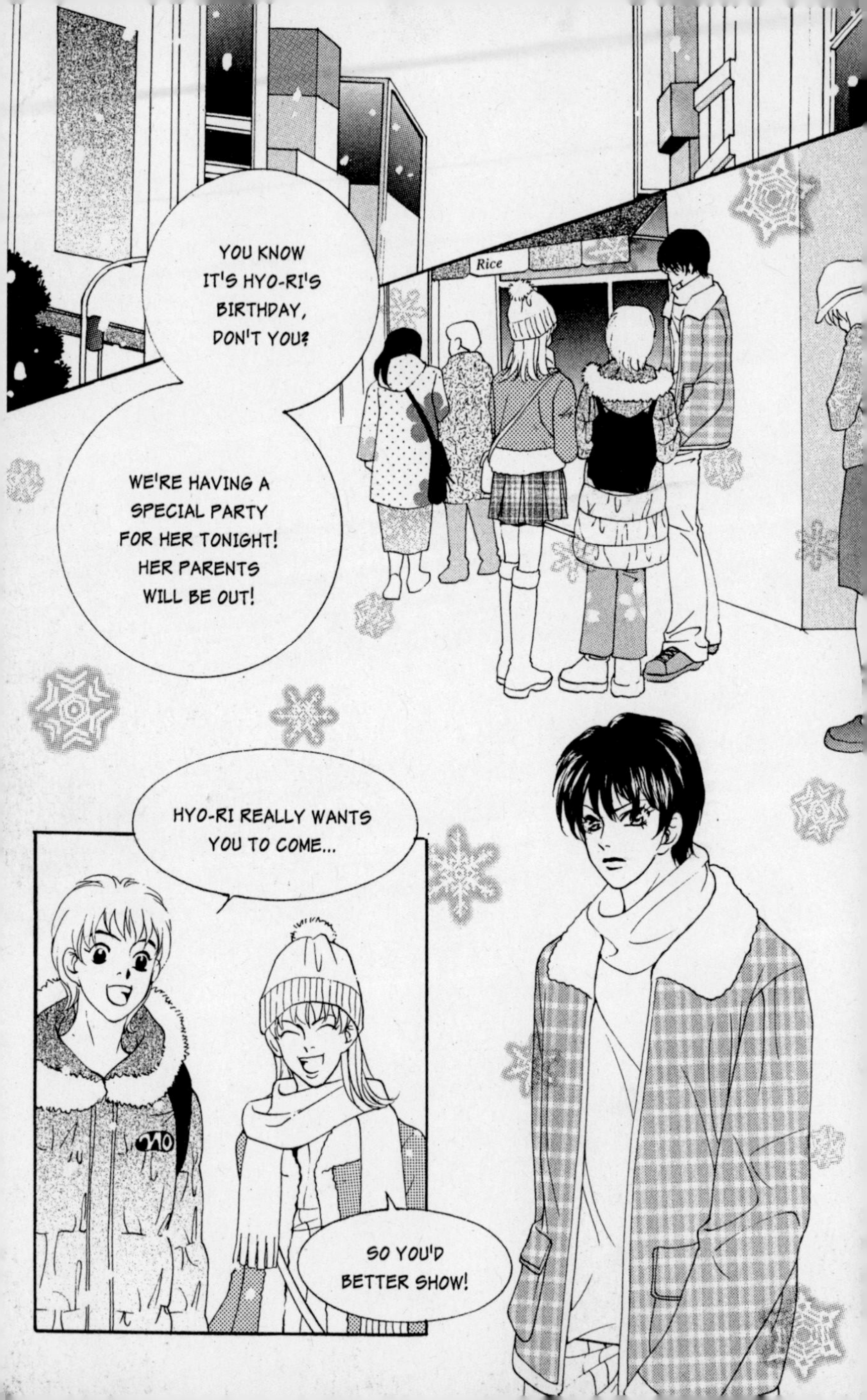
Rice
YOU KNOW IT'S HYO-RI'S BIRTHDAY, DON'T YOU?
WE'RE HAVING A SPECIAL PARTY FOR HER TONIGHT! HER PARENTS WILL BE OUT!
HYO-RI REALLY WANTS YOU TO COME...
SO YOU'D BETTER SHOW!

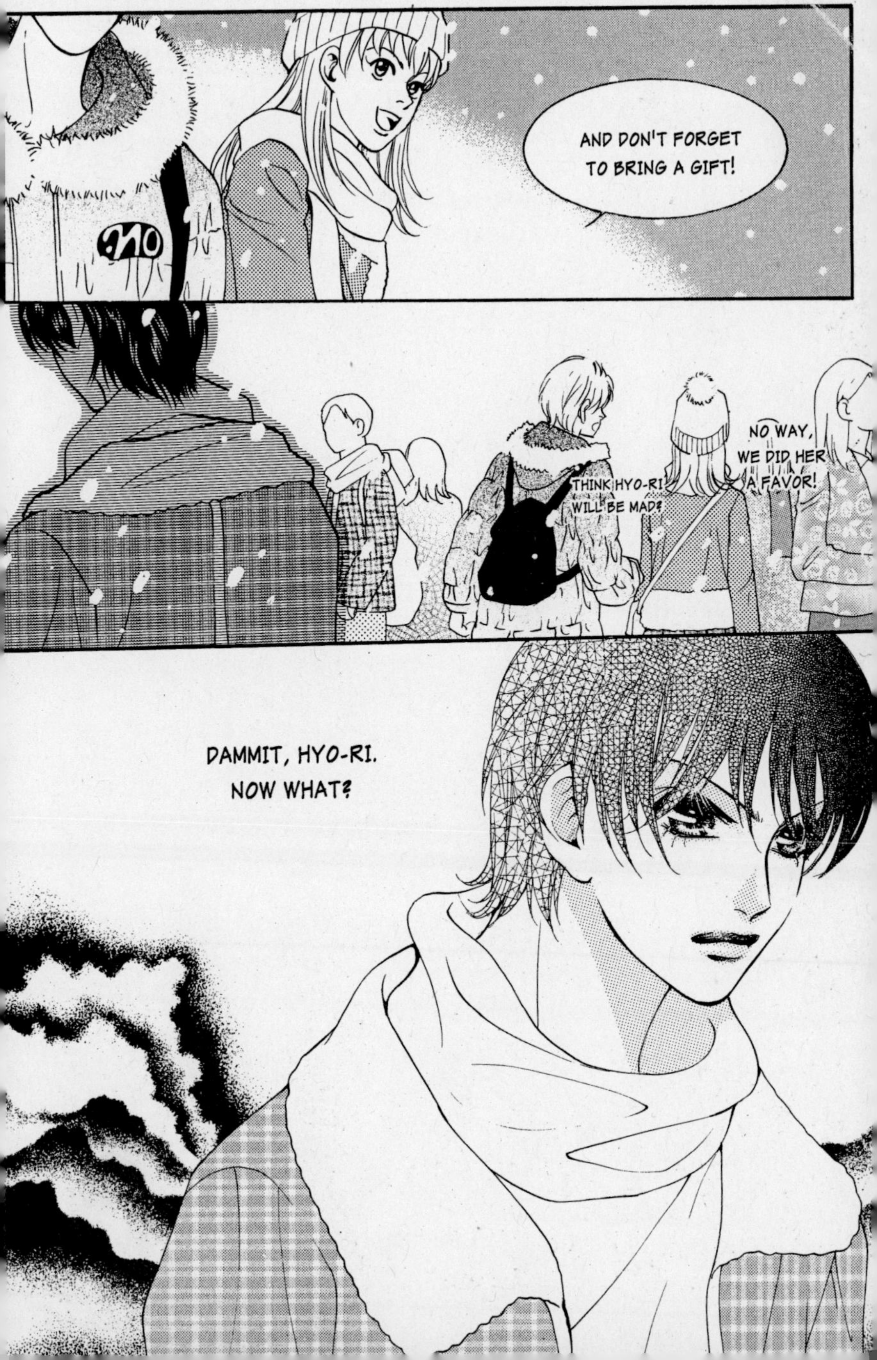
AND DON'T FORGET TO BRING A GIFT!
THINK HYO-RI WILL BE MAD?
NO WAY, WE DID HER A FAVOR!
DAMMIT, HYO-RI. NOW WHAT?

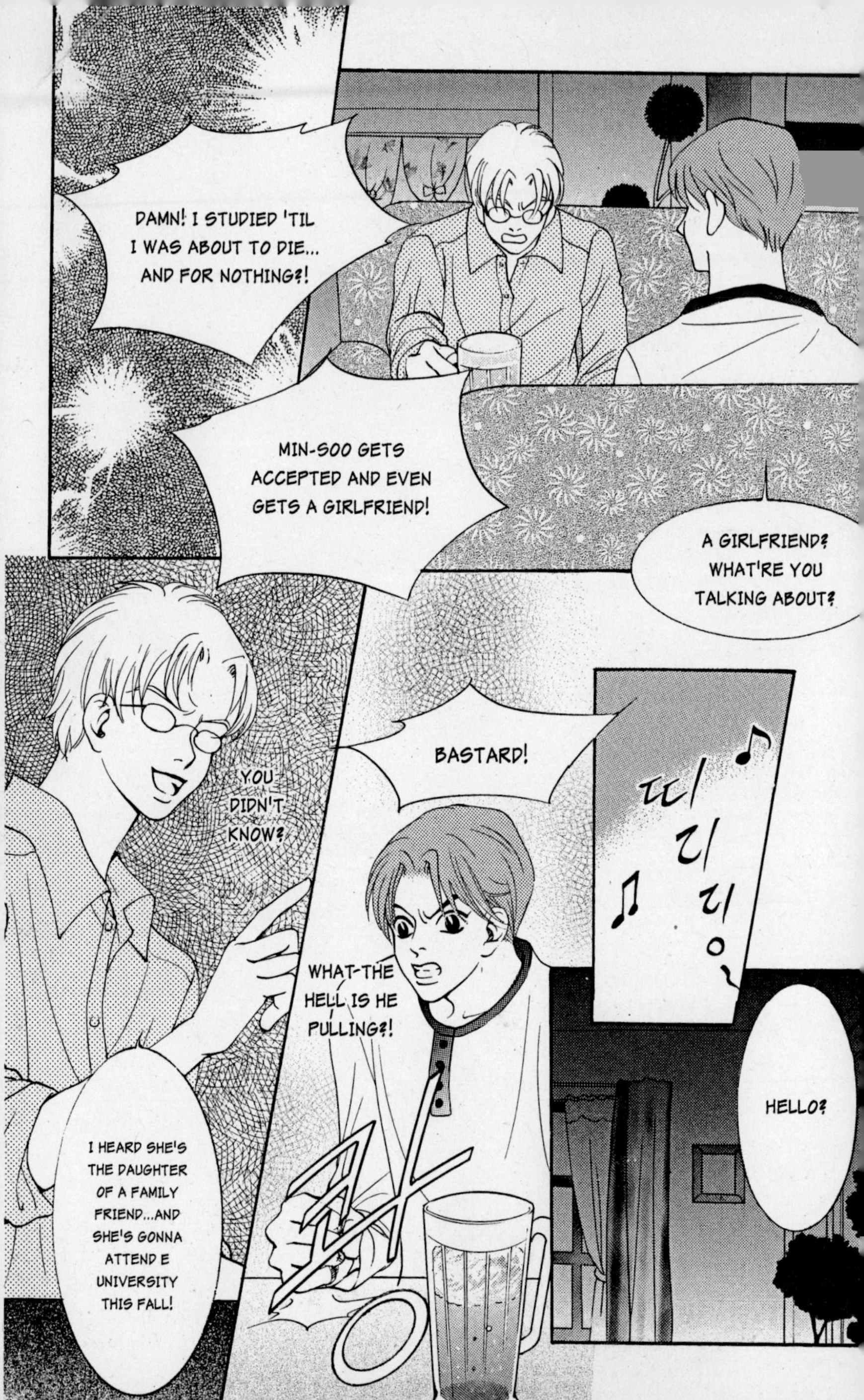
DAMN! I STUDIED 'TIL I WAS ABOUT TO DIE... AND FOR NOTHING?!
MIN-SOO GETS ACCEPTED AND EVEN GETS A GIRLFRIEND!
A GIRLFRIEND? WHAT'RE YOU TALKING ABOUT?
YOU DIDN'T KNOW?
I HEARD SHE'S THE DAUGHTER OF A FAMILY FRIEND...AND SHE'S GONNA ATTEND E UNIVERSITY THIS FALL!
BASTARD!
WHAT THE HELL IS HE PULLING?!
띠리리ㅇ~
HELLO?

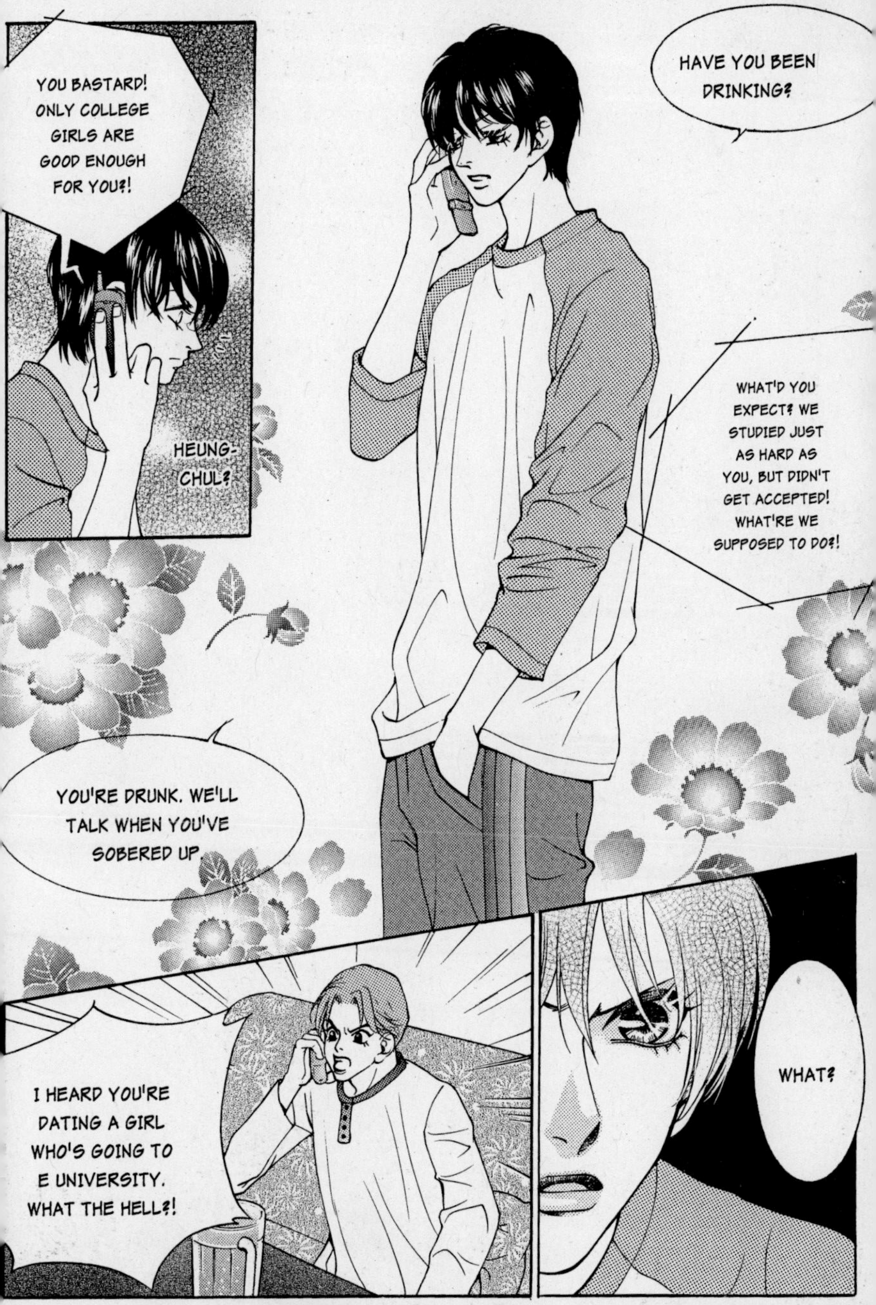
YOU BASTARD! ONLY COLLEGE GIRLS ARE GOOD ENOUGH FOR YOU?!
HEUNG-CHUL?
HAVE YOU BEEN DRINKING?
WHAT'D YOU EXPECT? WE STUDIED JUST AS HARD AS YOU, BUT DIDN'T GET ACCEPTED! WHAT'RE WE SUPPOSED TO DO?!
YOU'RE DRUNK. WE'LL TALK WHEN YOU'VE SOBERED UP.
I HEARD YOU'RE DATING A GIRL WHO'S GOING TO E UNIVERSITY. WHAT THE HELL?!
WHAT?

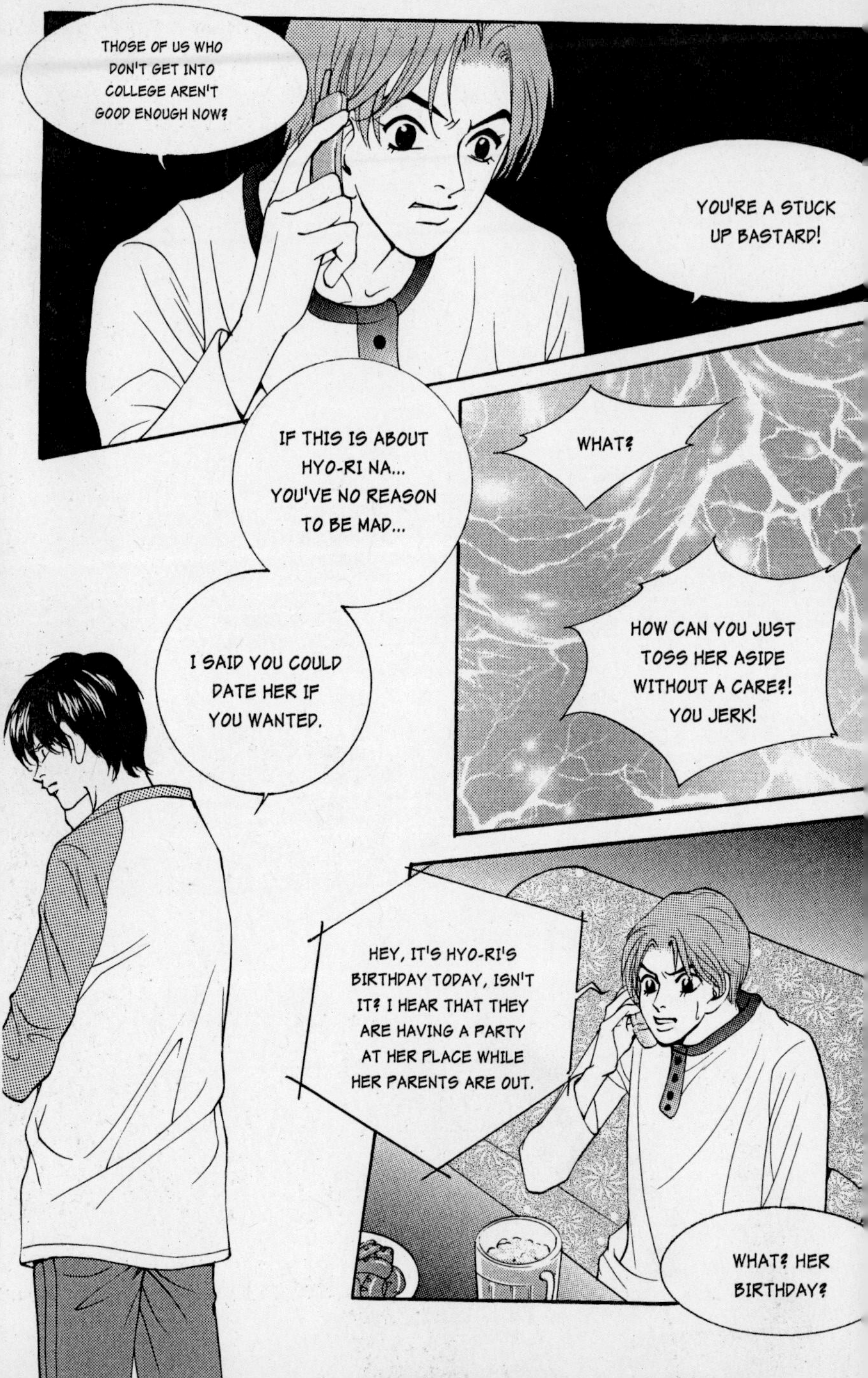
THOSE OF US WHO DON'T GET INTO COLLEGE AREN'T GOOD ENOUGH NOW?
YOU'RE A STUCK UP BASTARD!
IF THIS IS ABOUT HYO-RI NA... YOU'VE NO REASON TO BE MAD...
I SAID YOU COULD DATE HER IF YOU WANTED.
WHAT?
HOW CAN YOU JUST TOSS HER ASIDE WITHOUT A CARE?! YOU JERK!
HEY, IT'S HYO-RI'S BIRTHDAY TODAY, ISN'T IT? I HEAR THAT THEY ARE HAVING A PARTY AT HER PLACE WHILE HER PARENTS ARE OUT.
WHAT? HER BIRTHDAY?

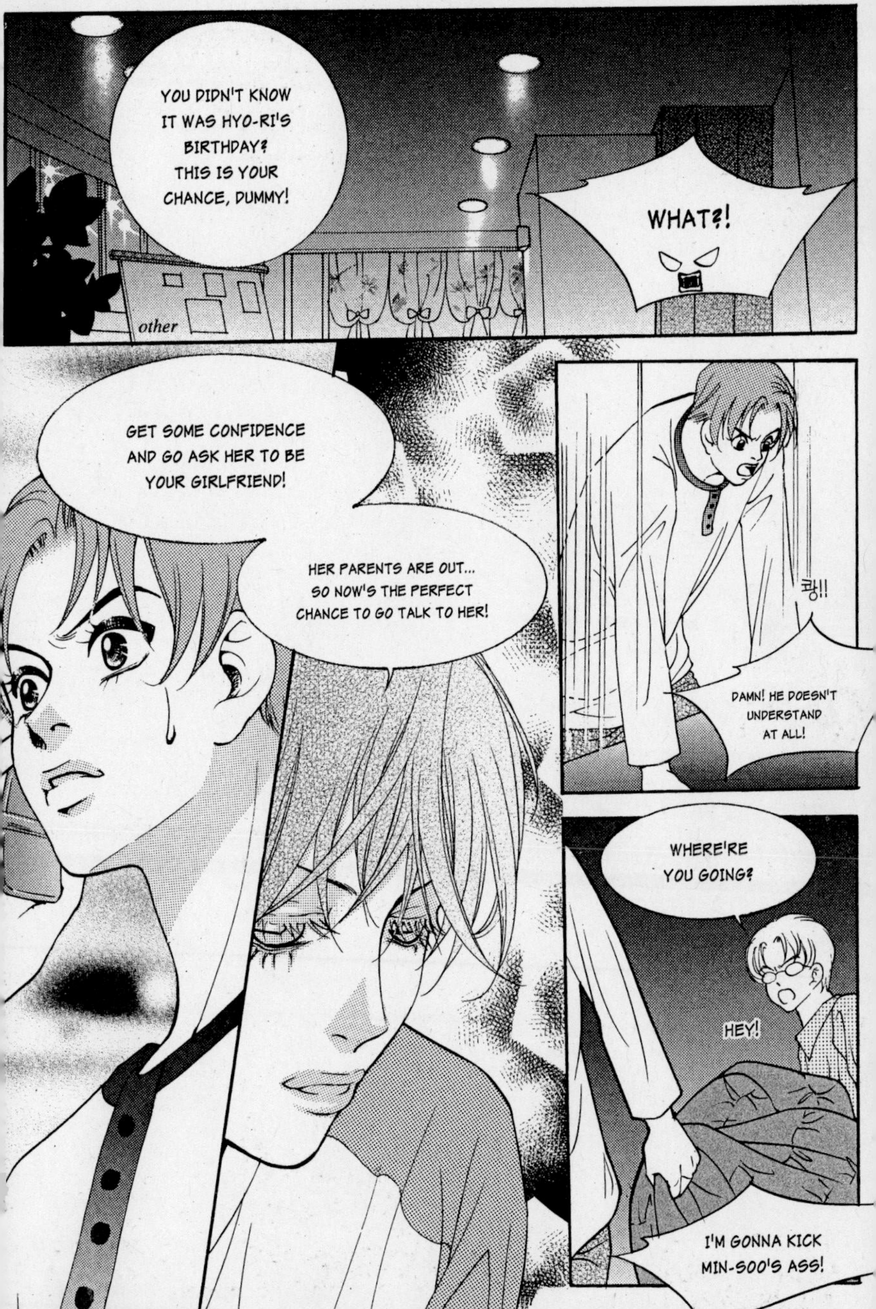
YOU DIDN'T KNOW IT WAS HYO-RI'S BIRTHDAY? THIS IS YOUR CHANCE, DUMMY!
other
WHAT?!
GET SOME CONFIDENCE AND GO ASK HER TO BE YOUR GIRLFRIEND!
HER PARENTS ARE OUT... SO NOW'S THE PERFECT CHANCE TO GO TALK TO HER!
쾅!!
DAMN! HE DOESN'T UNDERSTAND AT ALL!
WHERE'RE YOU GOING?
HEY!
I'M GONNA KICK MIN-SOO'S ASS!

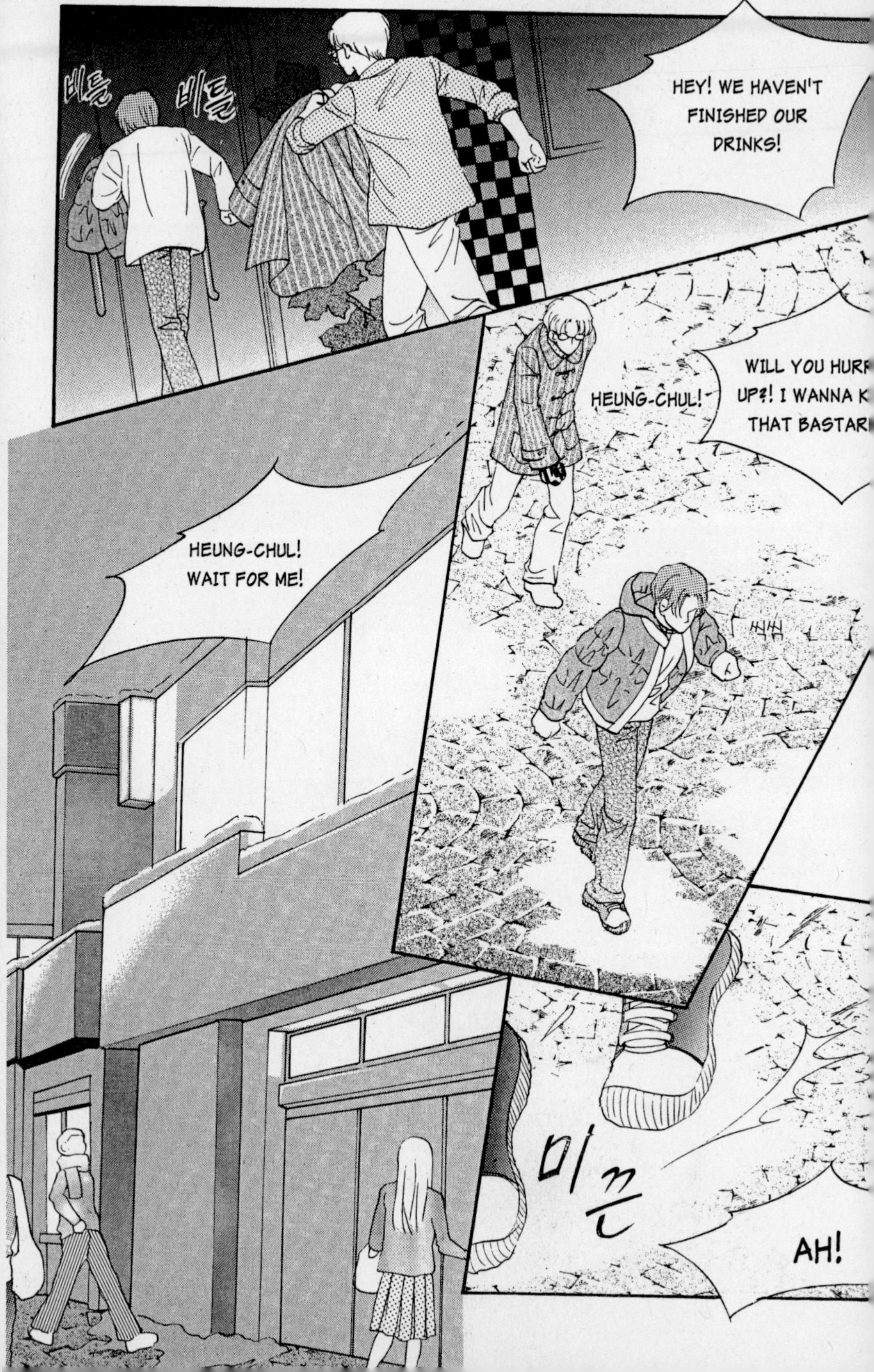
비틀 비틀
HEY! WE HAVEN'T FINISHED OUR DRINKS!
HEUNG-CHUL! WAIT FOR ME!
HEUNG-CHUL!
WILL YOU HURR UP?! I WANNA K THAT BASTAR
씩씩
미끈
AH!

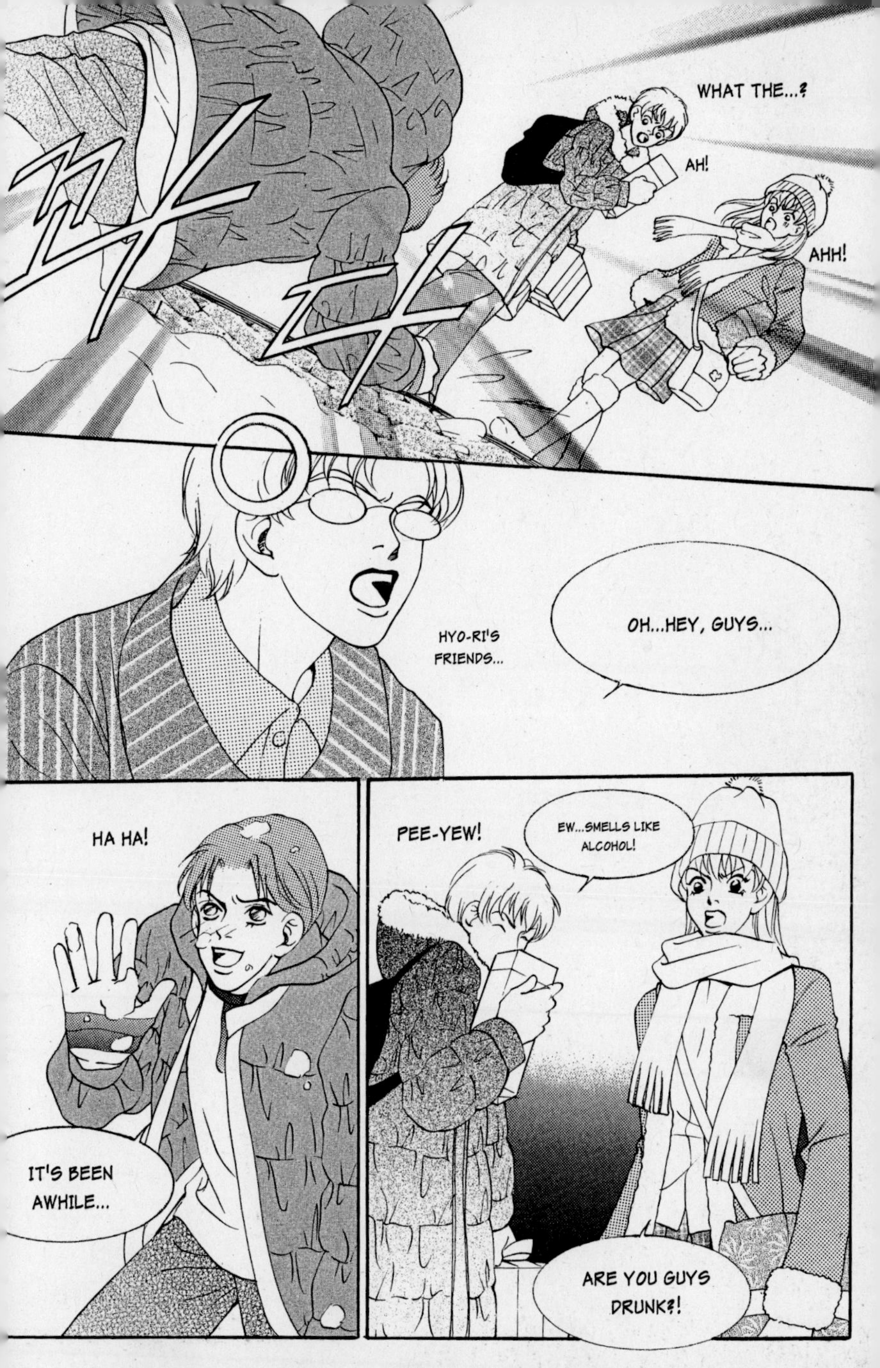
WHAT THE...?
AH!
AHH!
HYO-RI'S FRIENDS...
OH...HEY, GUYS...
HA HA!
IT'S BEEN AWHILE...
PEE-YEW!
EW...SMELLS LIKE ALCOHOL!
ARE YOU GUYS DRUNK?!

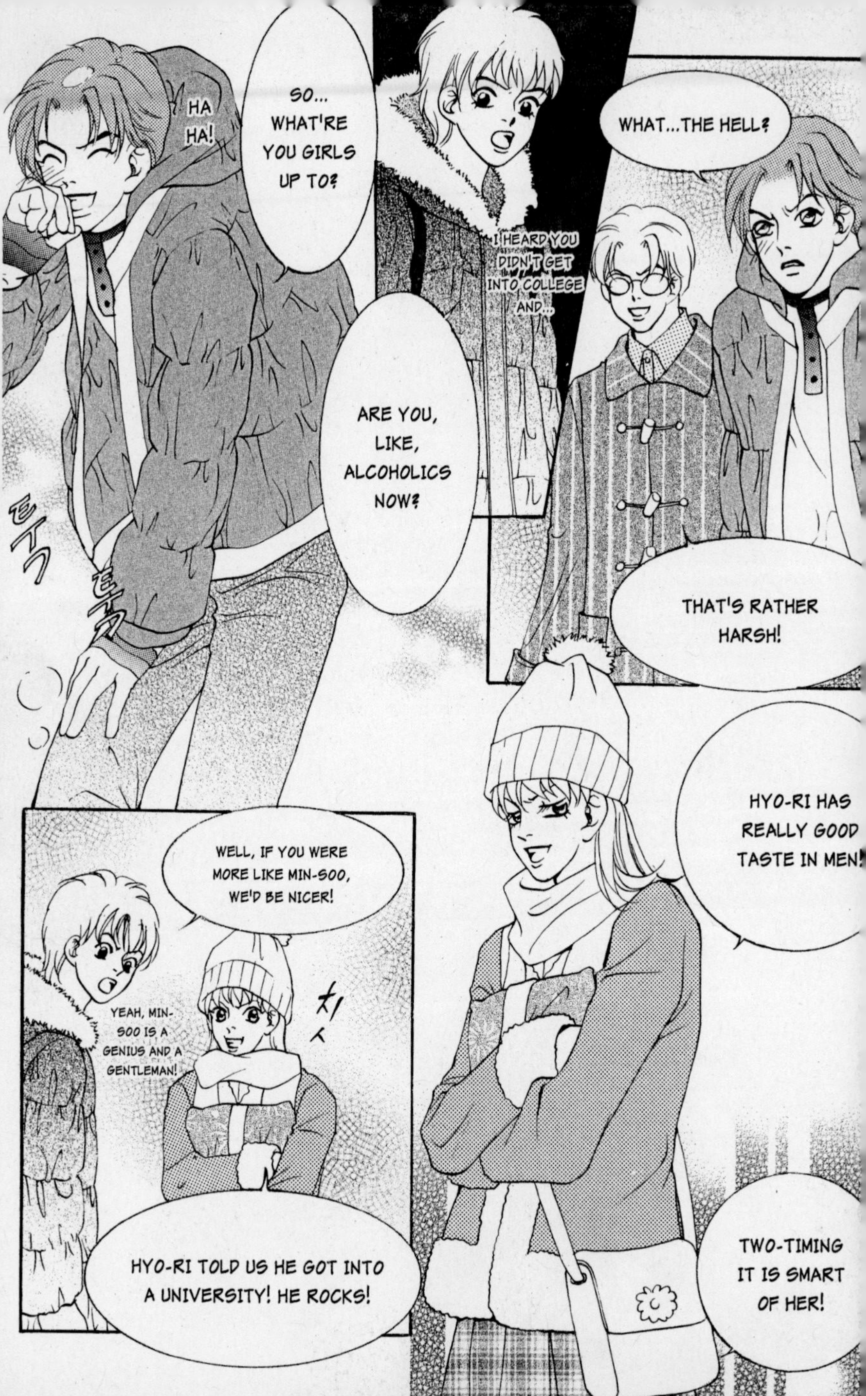
HA HA!
SO... WHAT'RE YOU GIRLS UP TO?
I HEARD YOU DIDN'T GET INTO COLLEGE AND...
ARE YOU, LIKE, ALCOHOLICS NOW?
WHAT...THE HELL?
THAT'S RATHER HARSH!
WELL, IF YOU WERE MORE LIKE MIN-SOO, WE'D BE NICER!
YEAH, MIN-SOO IS A GENIUS AND A GENTLEMAN!
HYO-RI TOLD US HE GOT INTO A UNIVERSITY! HE ROCKS!
HYO-RI HAS REALLY GOOD TASTE IN MEN!
TWO-TIMING IT IS SMART OF HER!

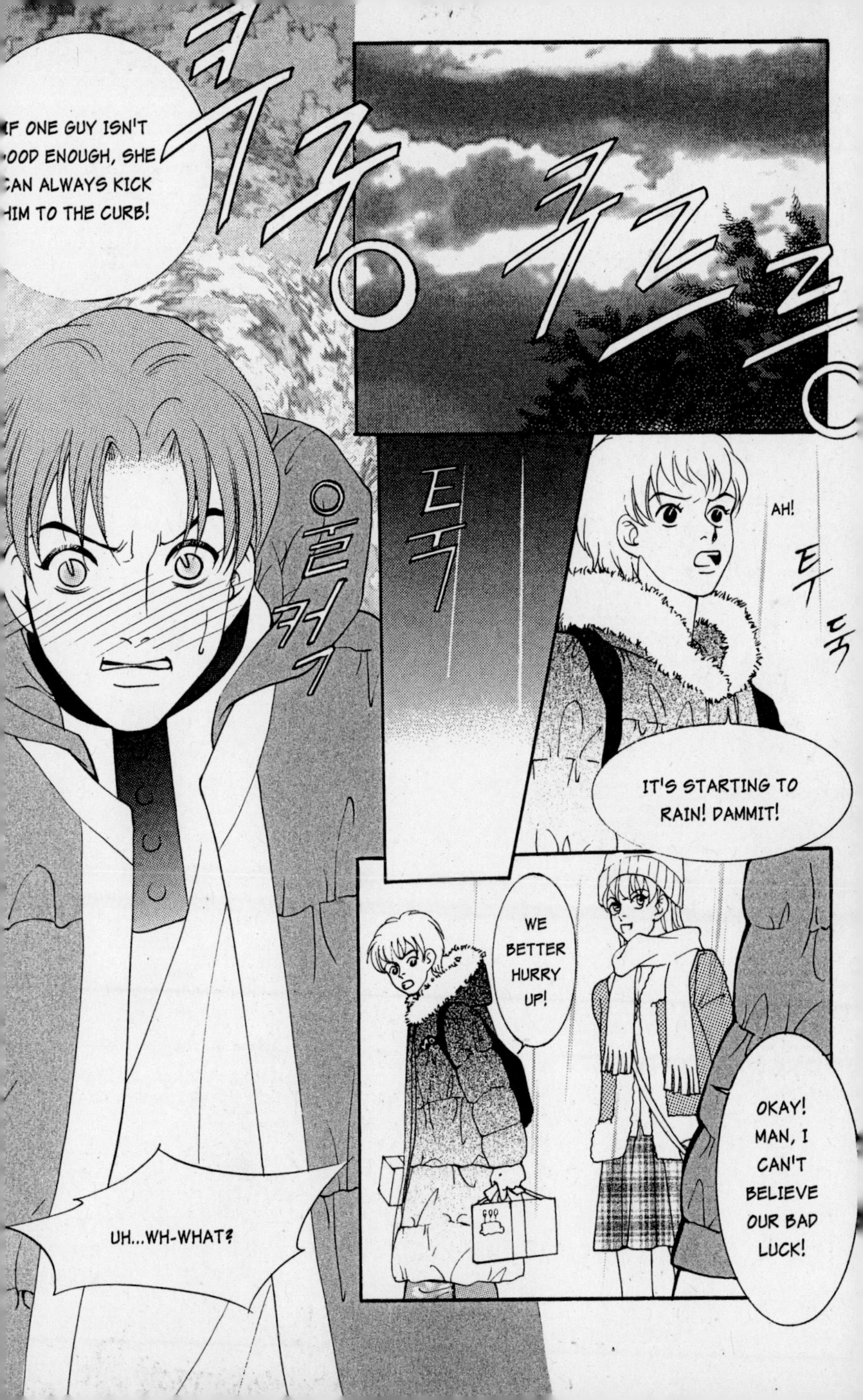
IF ONE GUY ISN'T GOOD ENOUGH, SHE CAN ALWAYS KICK HIM TO THE CURB!
UH...WH-WHAT?
AH!
IT'S STARTING TO RAIN! DAMMIT!
WE BETTER HURRY UP!
OKAY! MAN, I CAN'T BELIEVE OUR BAD LUCK!

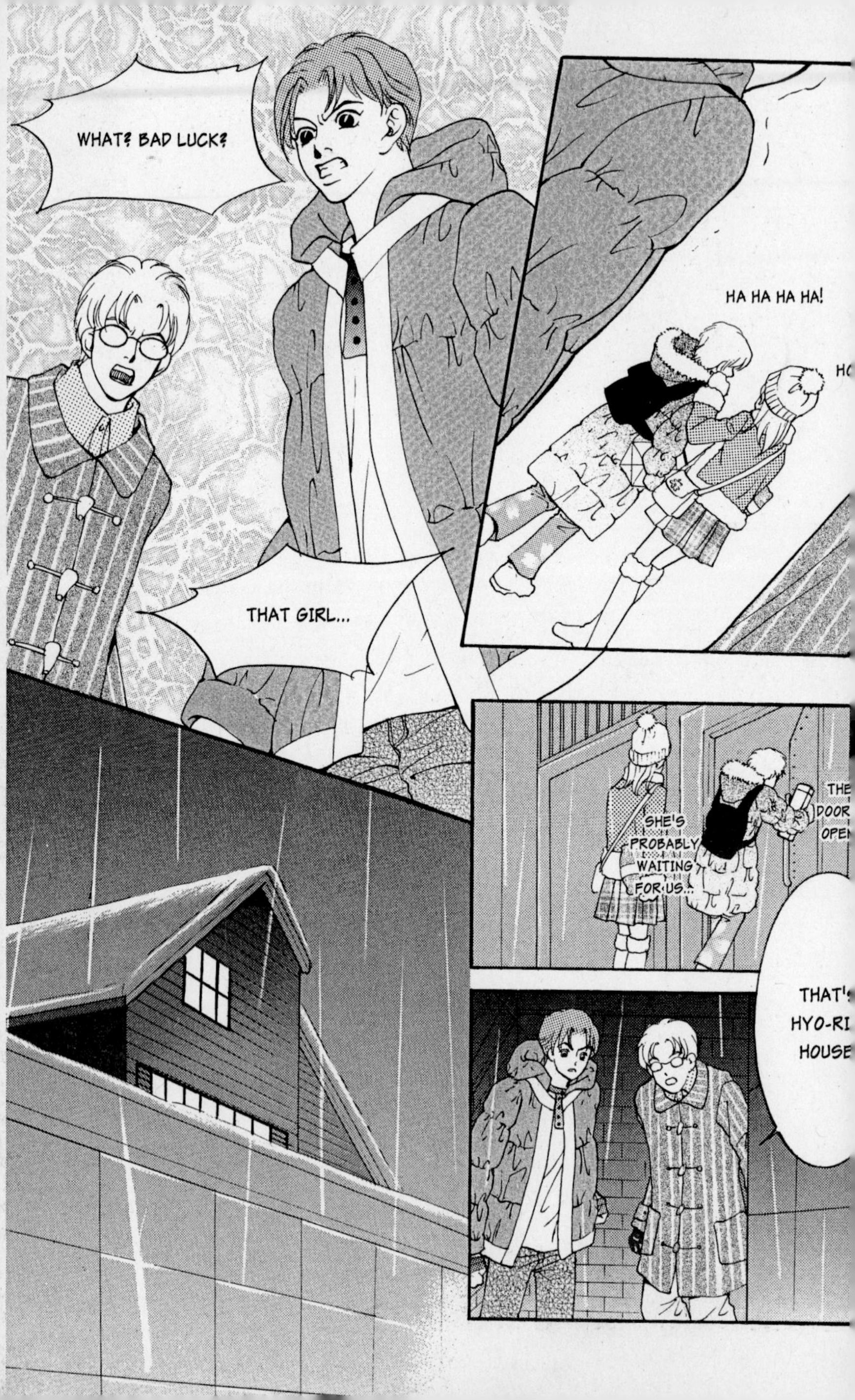

WHAT? BAD LUCK?
THAT GIRL...
HA HA HA HA!
HO
SHE'S PROBABLY WAITING FOR US...
THE DOOR OPE
THAT'S HYO-RI HOUSE

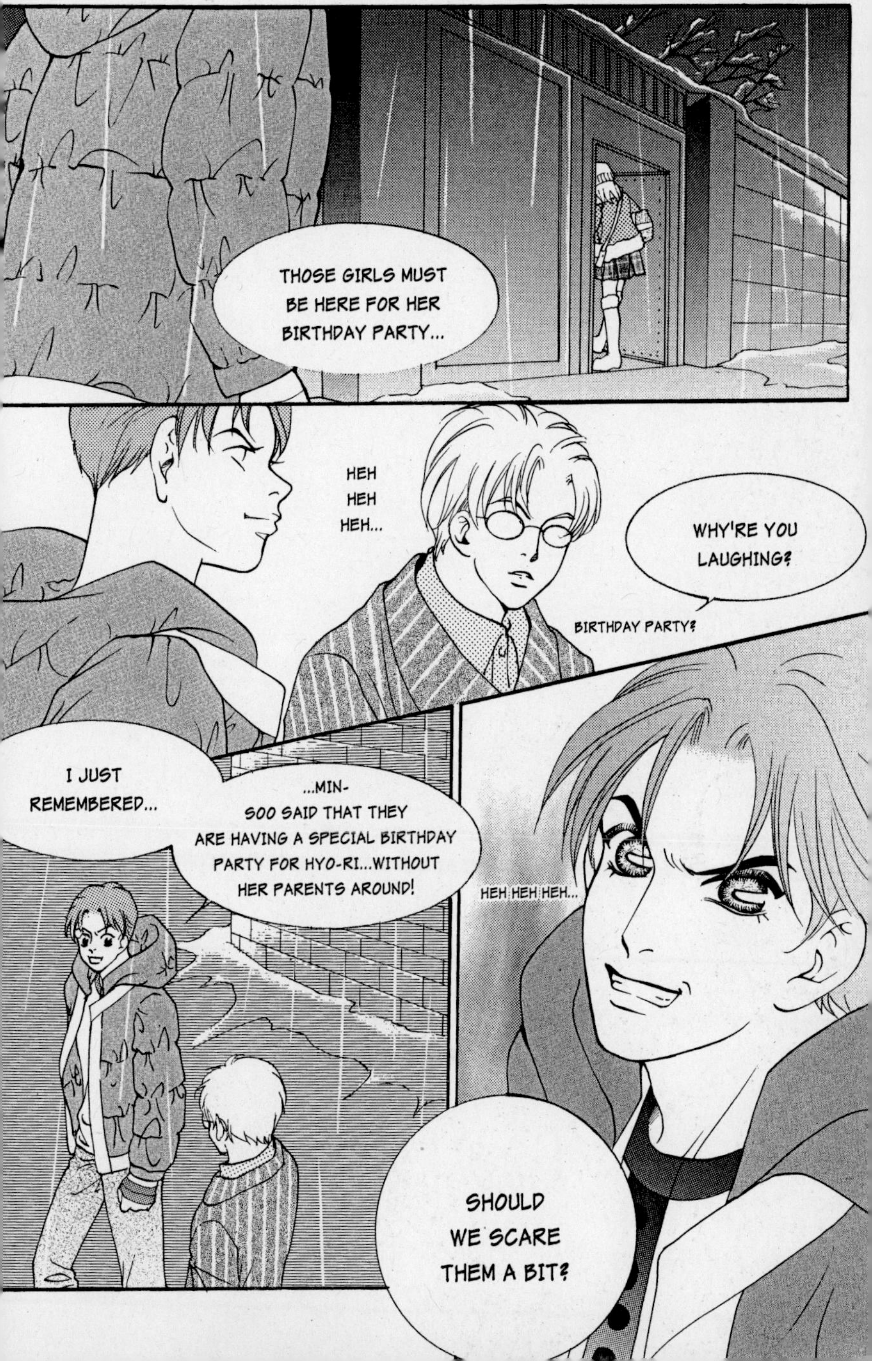
THOSE GIRLS MUST BE HERE FOR HER BIRTHDAY PARTY...
HEH HEH HEH...
WHY'RE YOU LAUGHING?
BIRTHDAY PARTY?
I JUST REMEMBERED...
...MIN-SOO SAID THAT THEY ARE HAVING A SPECIAL BIRTHDAY PARTY FOR HYO-RI...WITHOUT HER PARENTS AROUND!
HEH HEH HEH...
SHOULD WE SCARE THEM A BIT?

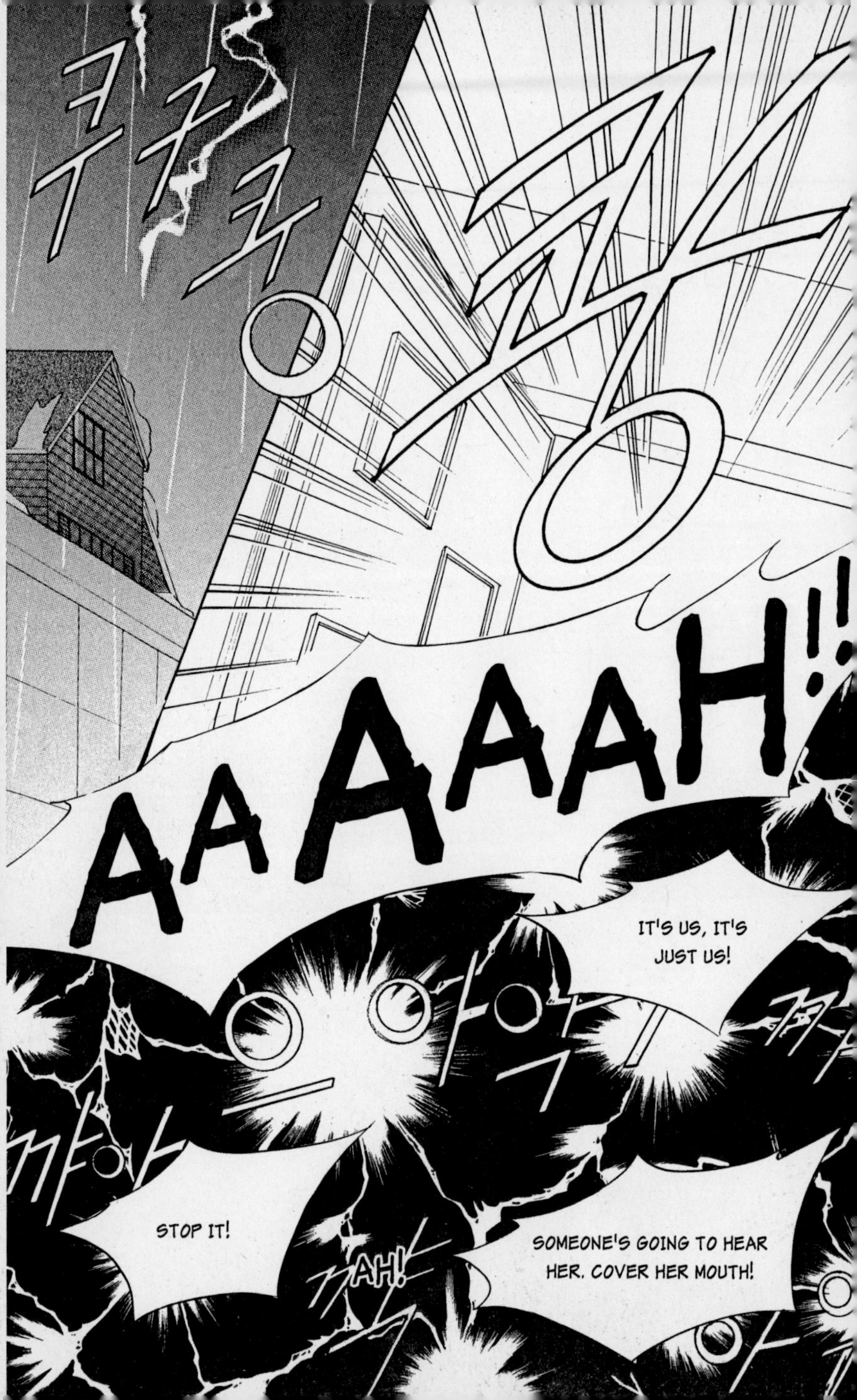
AAAAAH!!
IT'S US, IT'S JUST US!
STOP IT!
AH!
SOMEONE'S GOING TO HEAR HER. COVER HER MOUTH!

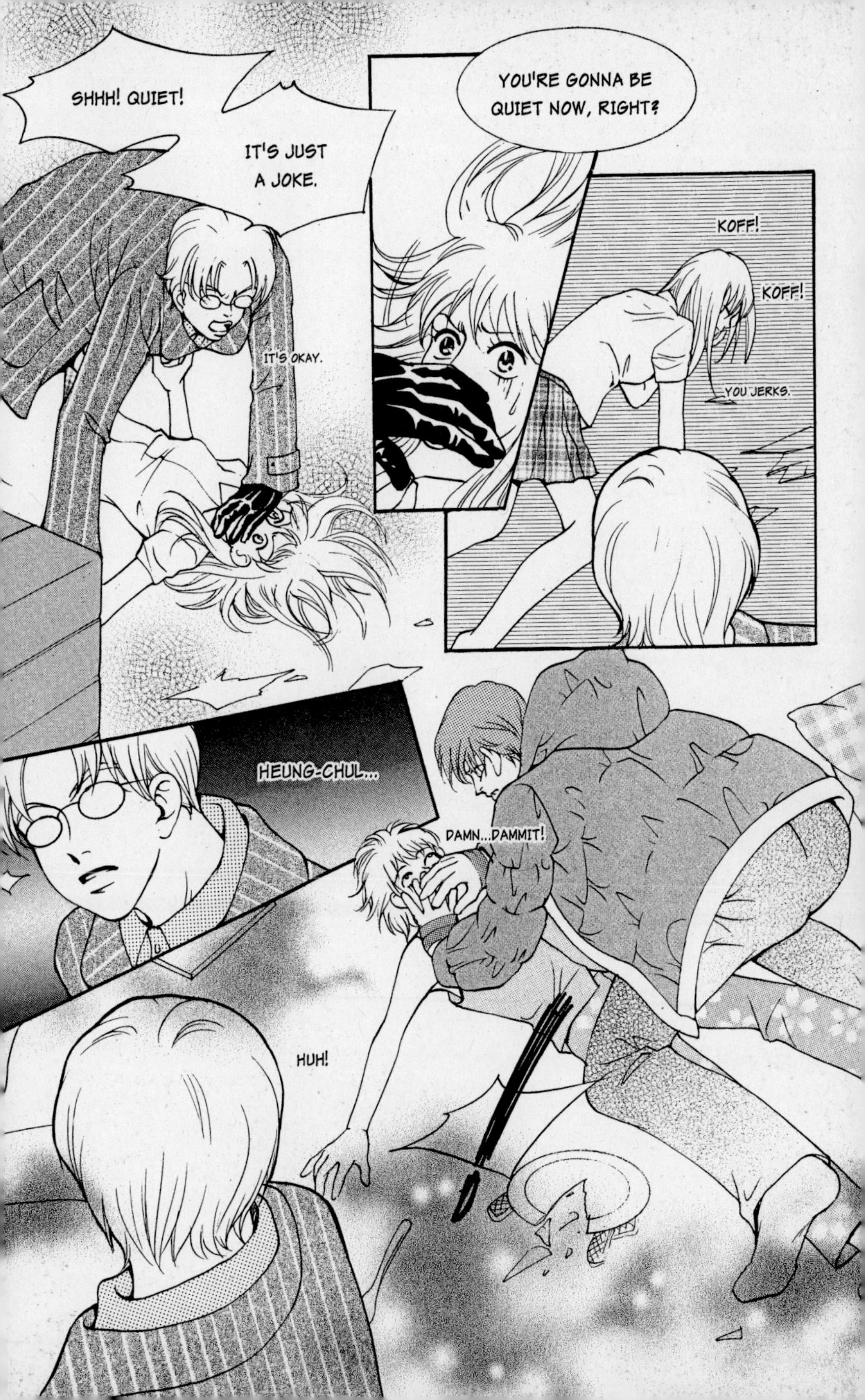
SHHH! QUIET!
IT'S JUST A JOKE.
IT'S OKAY.
YOU'RE GONNA BE QUIET NOW, RIGHT?
KOFF!
KOFF!
YOU JERKS.
HEUNG-CHUL...
DAMN...DAMMIT!
HUH!

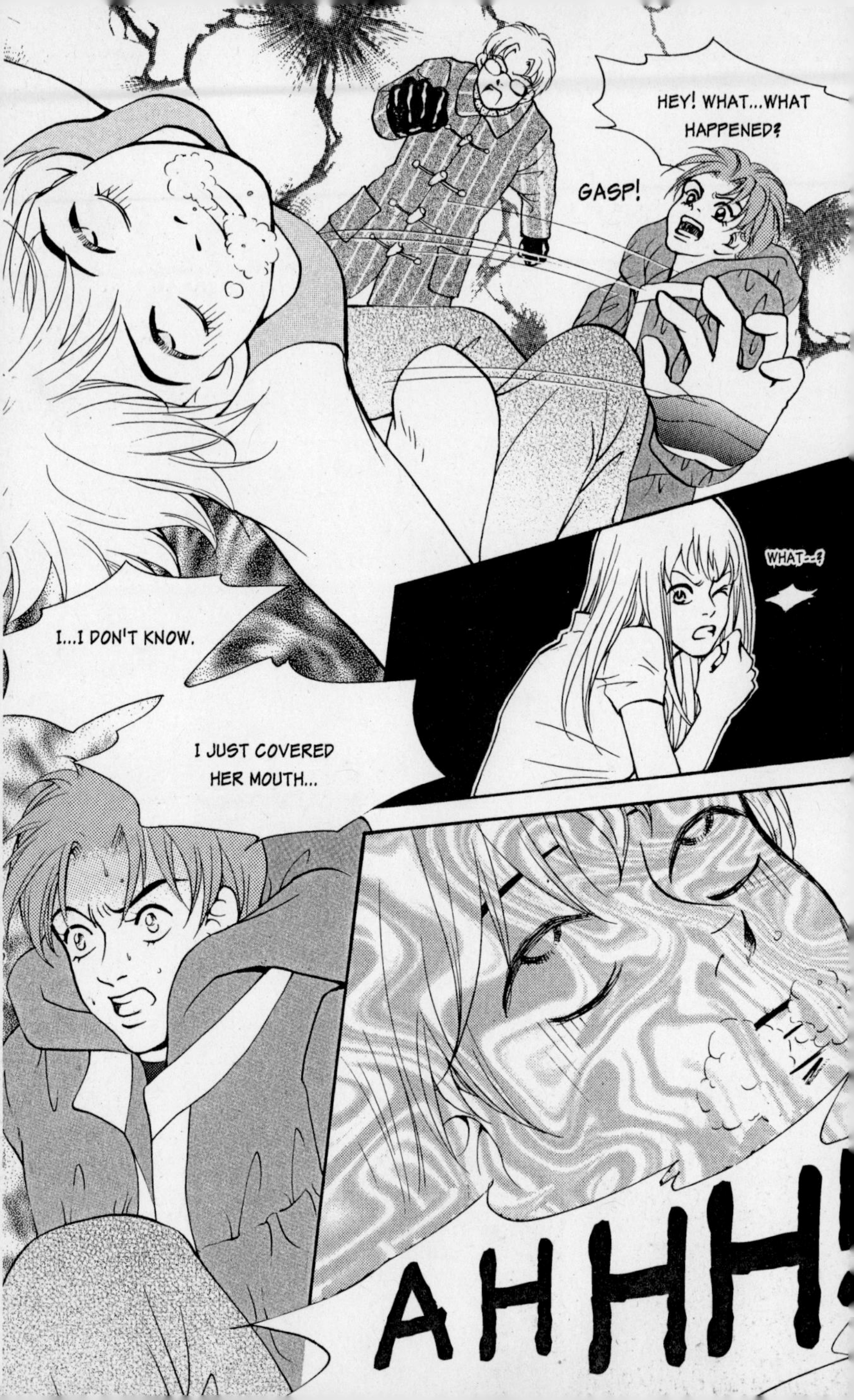

GASP!
HEY! WHAT...WHAT HAPPENED?
I...I DON'T KNOW.
I JUST COVERED HER MOUTH...
WHAT--!
AHHH!

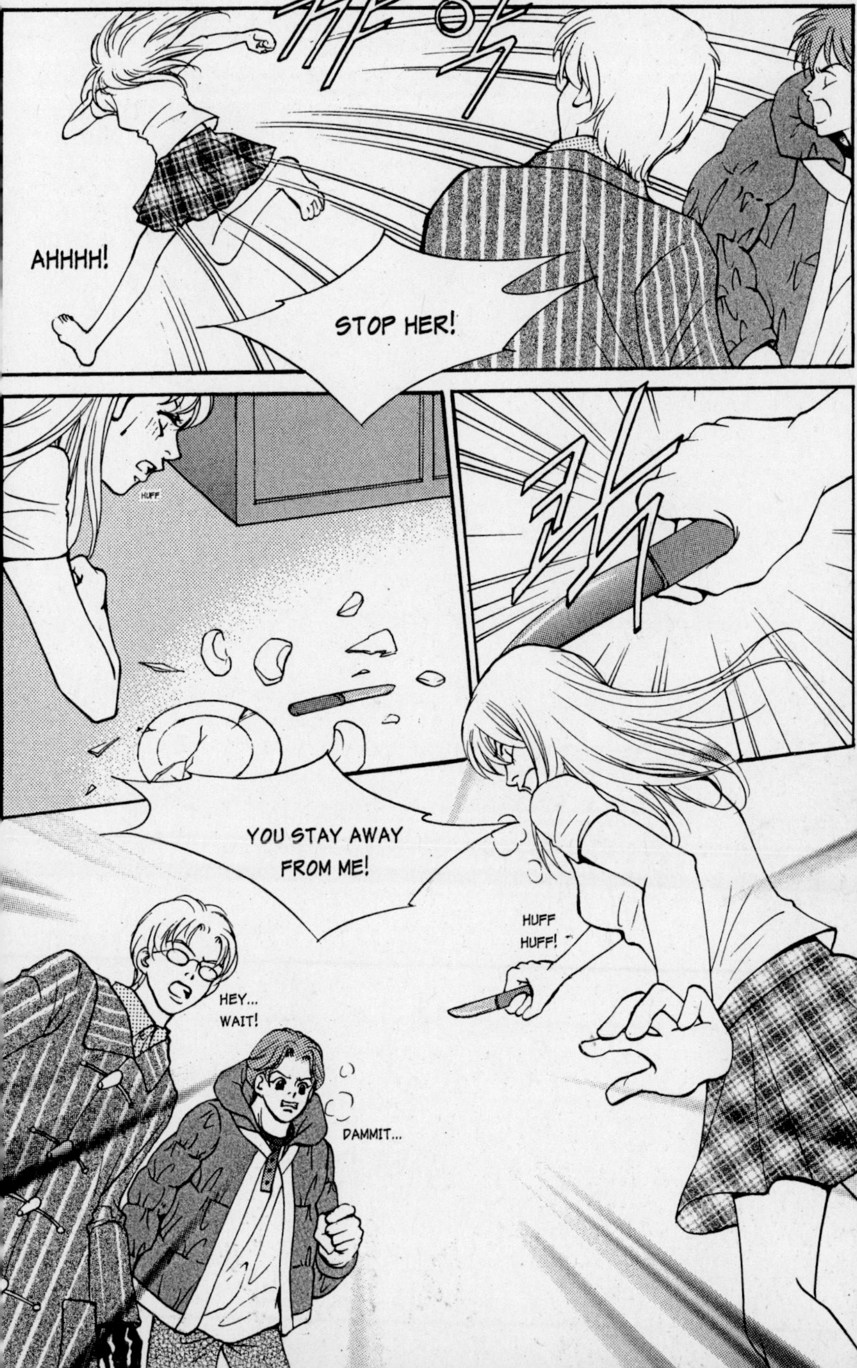
AHHHH!
STOP HER!
HUFF
콱
YOU STAY AWAY FROM ME!
HUFF HUFF!
HEY... WAIT!
DAMMIT...

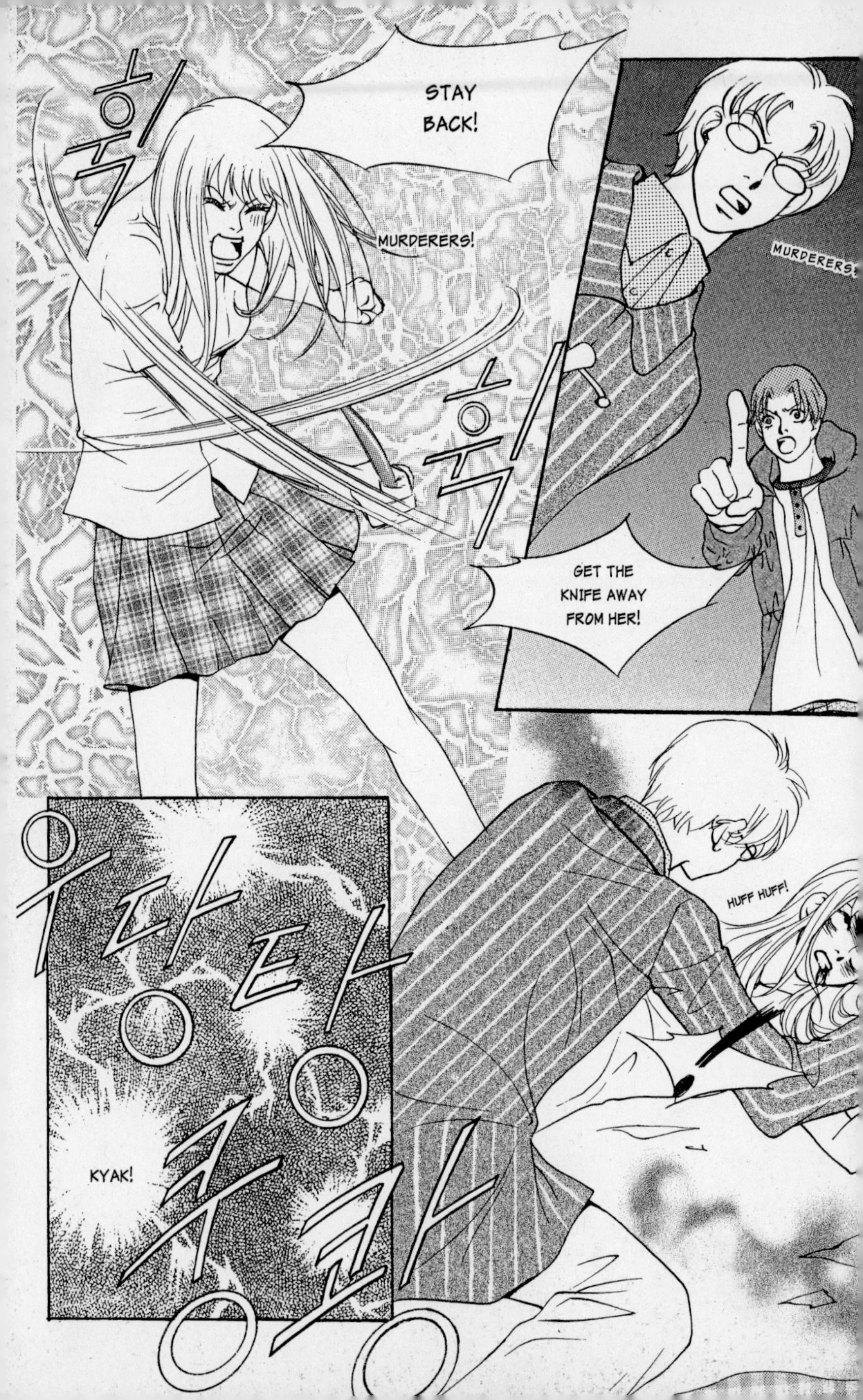
STAY BACK!
MURDERERS!
MURDERERS!
GET THE KNIFE AWAY FROM HER!
KYAK!
HUFF HUFF!

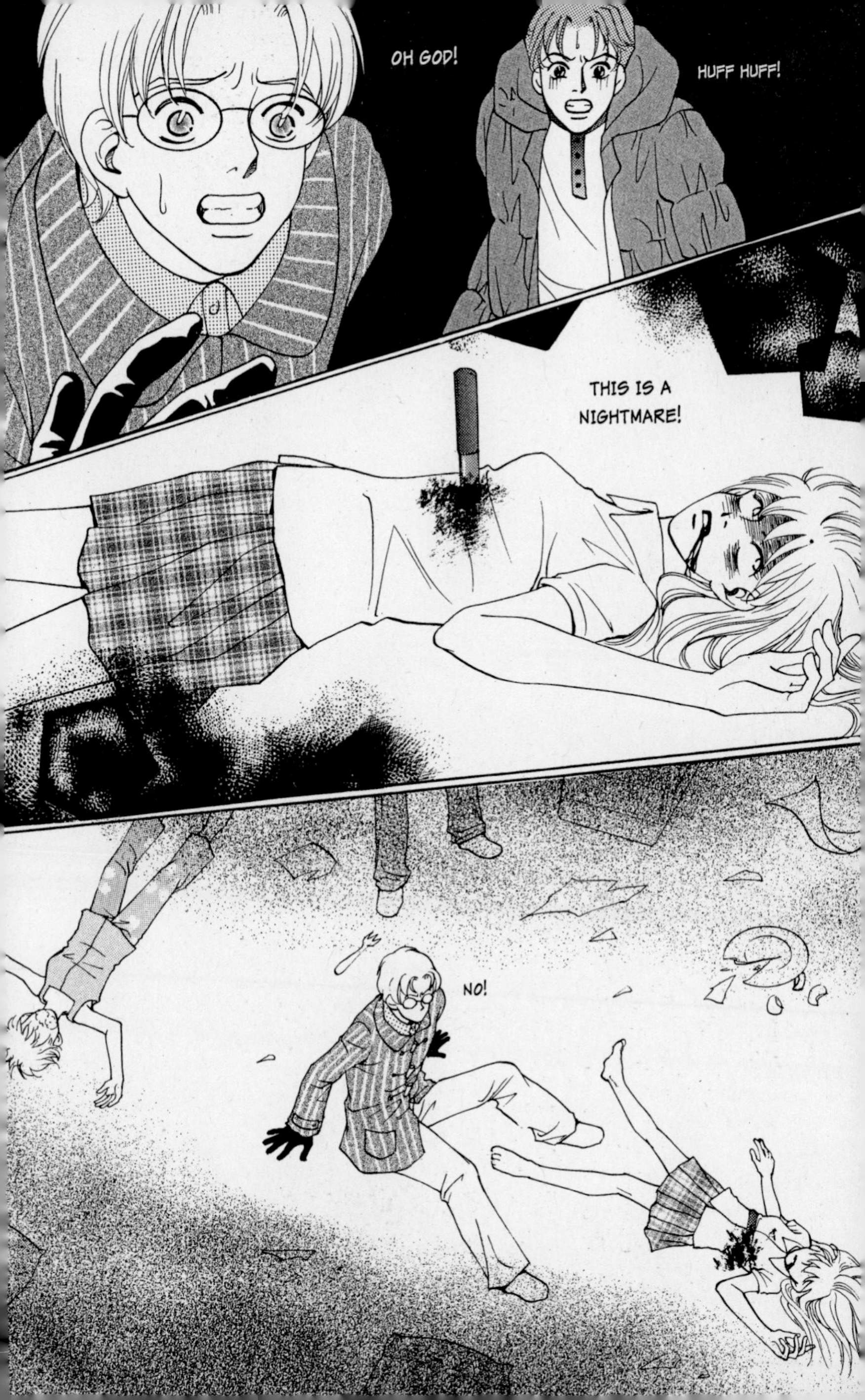
OH GOD!
HUFF HUFF!
THIS IS A NIGHTMARE!
NO!

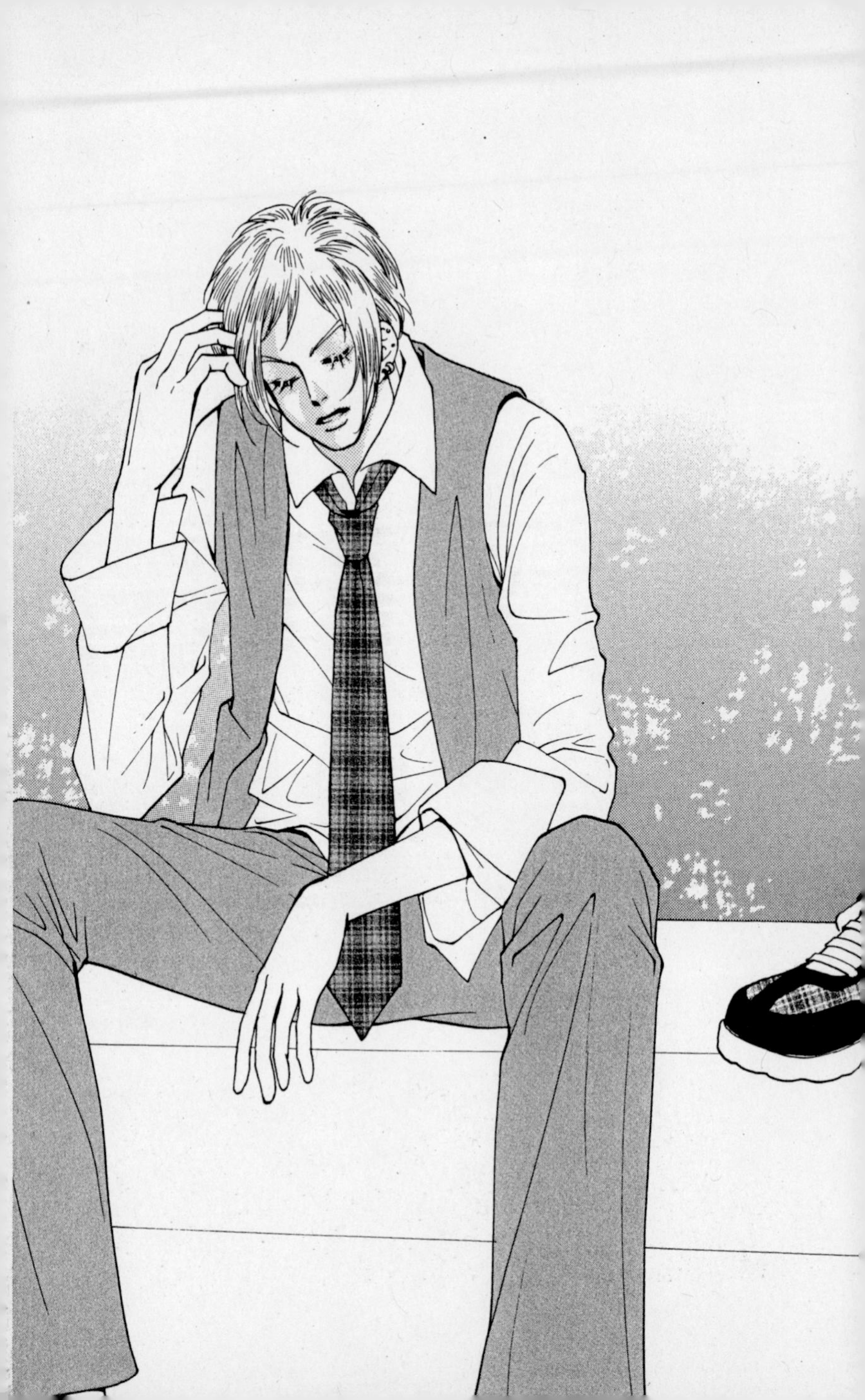

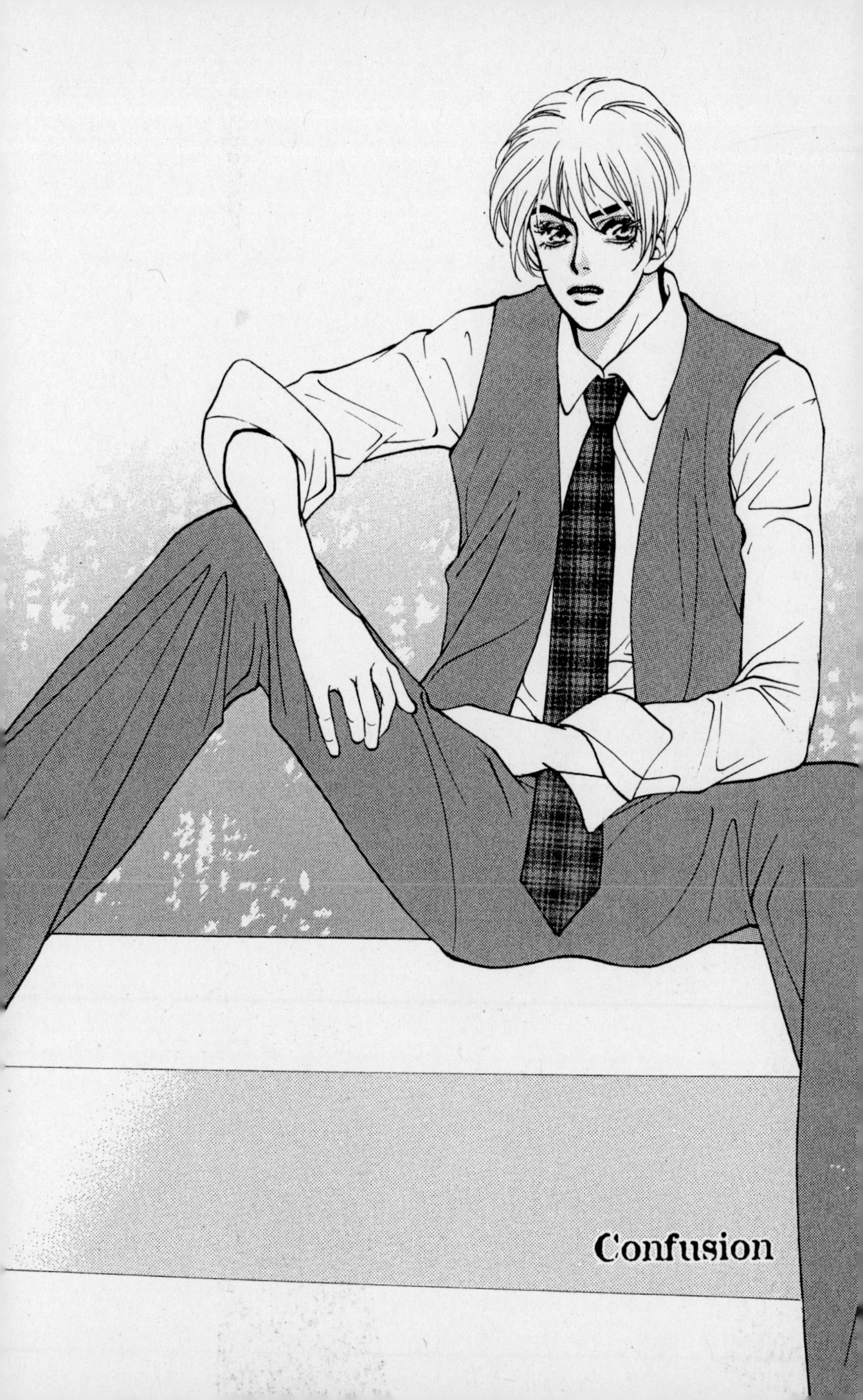
Confusion

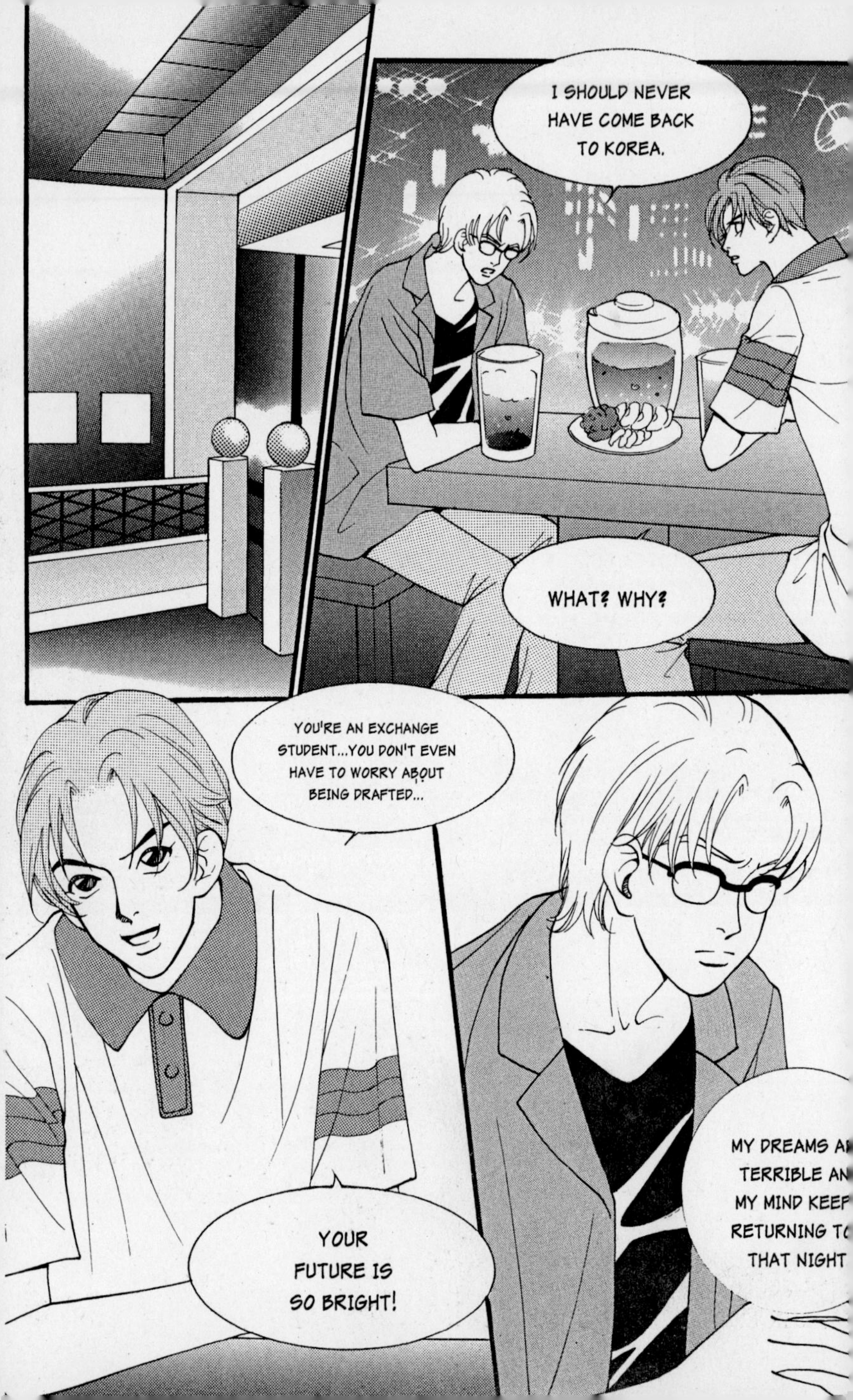
I SHOULD NEVER HAVE COME BACK TO KOREA.
WHAT? WHY?
YOU'RE AN EXCHANGE STUDENT...YOU DON'T EVEN HAVE TO WORRY ABOUT BEING DRAFTED...
YOUR FUTURE IS SO BRIGHT!

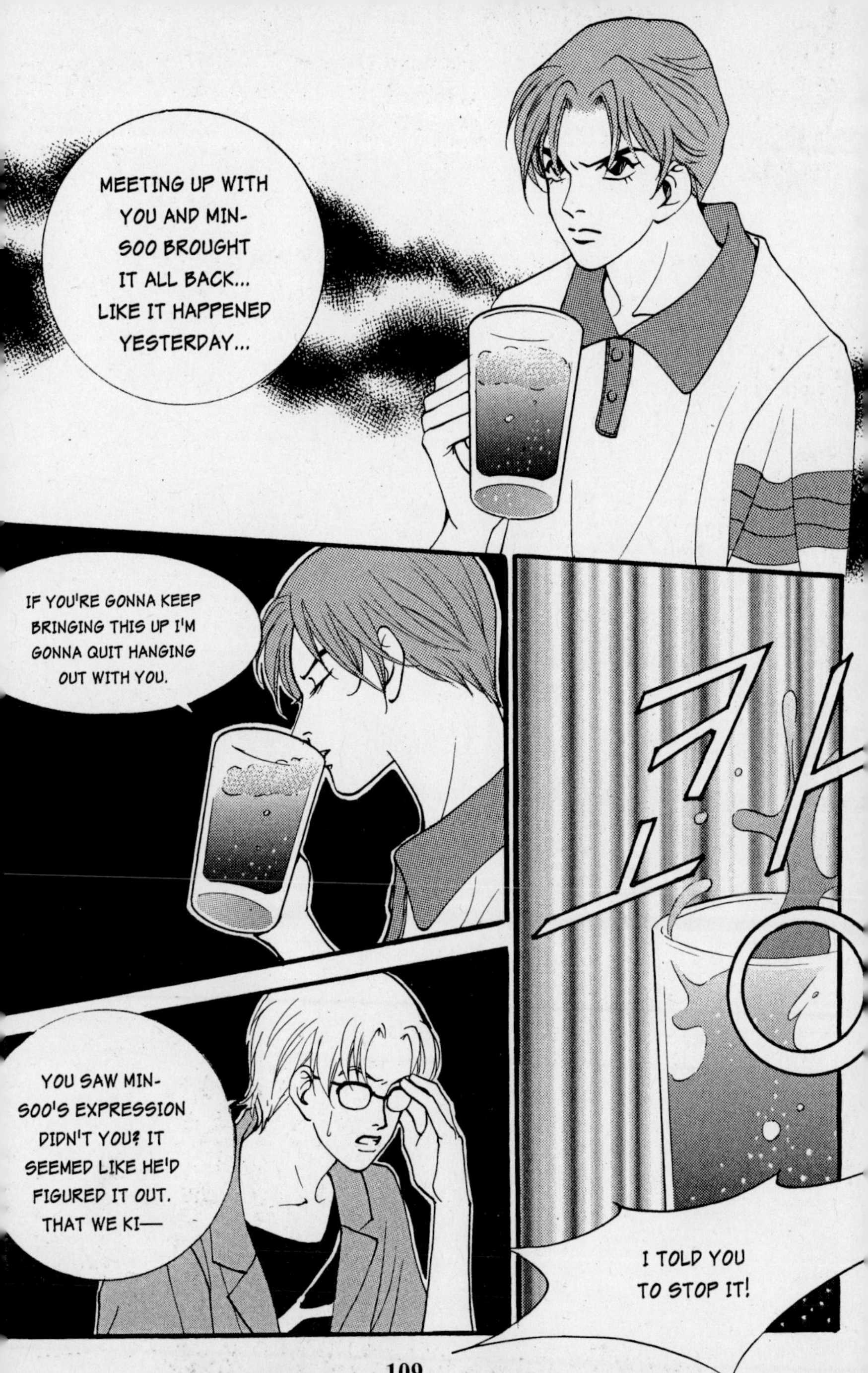
MEETING UP WITH YOU AND MIN-SOO BROUGHT IT ALL BACK... LIKE IT HAPPENED YESTERDAY...
IF YOU'RE GONNA KEEP BRINGING THIS UP I'M GONNA QUIT HANGING OUT WITH YOU.
YOU SAW MIN-SOO'S EXPRESSION DIDN'T YOU? IT SEEMED LIKE HE'D FIGURED IT OUT. THAT WE KI—
I TOLD YOU TO STOP IT!

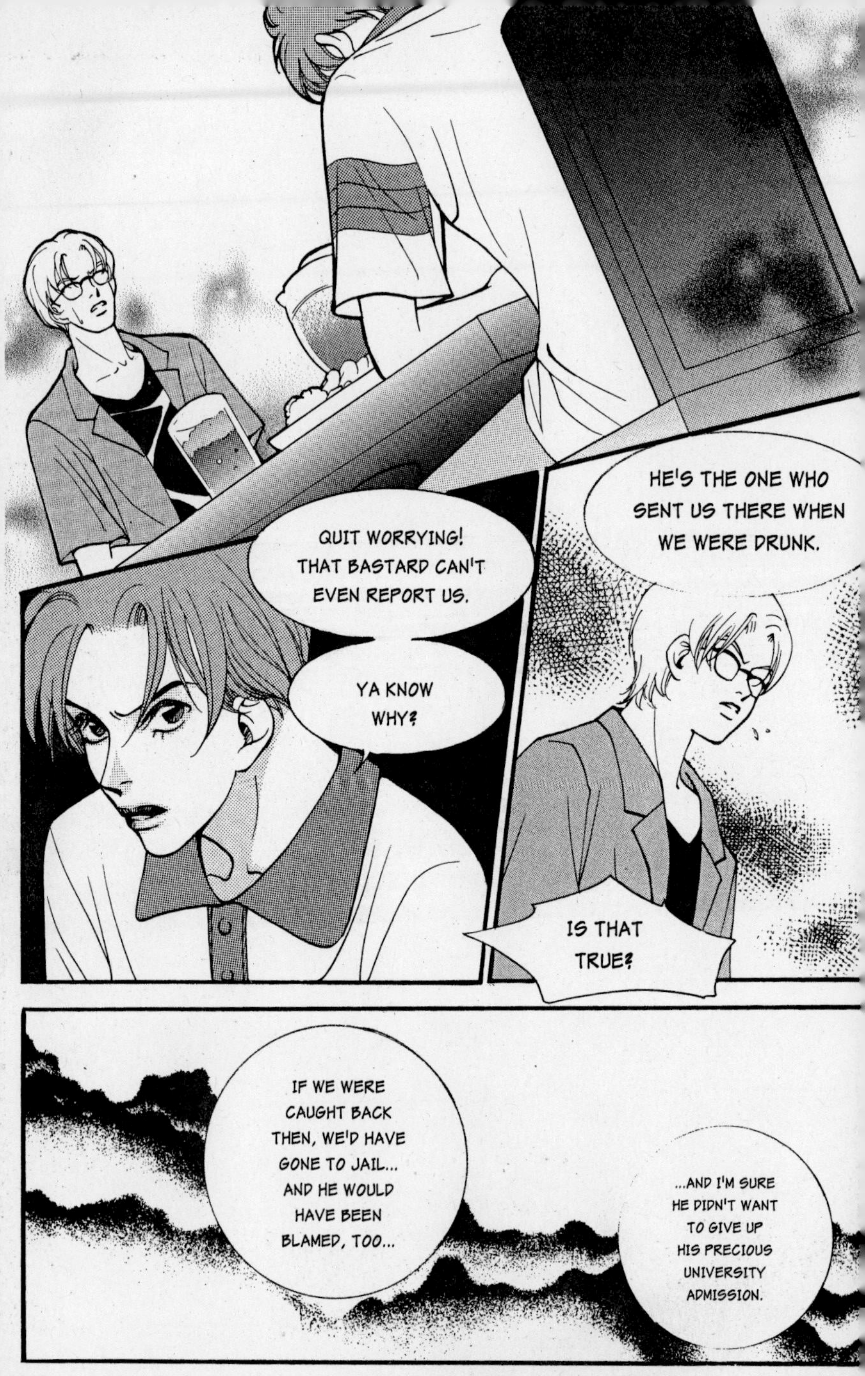
QUIT WORRYING! THAT BASTARD CAN'T EVEN REPORT US.
YA KNOW WHY?
HE'S THE ONE WHO SENT US THERE WHEN WE WERE DRUNK.
IS THAT TRUE?
IF WE WERE CAUGHT BACK THEN, WE'D HAVE GONE TO JAIL... AND HE WOULD HAVE BEEN BLAMED, TOO...
...AND I'M SURE HE DIDN'T WANT TO GIVE UP HIS PRECIOUS UNIVERSITY ADMISSION.

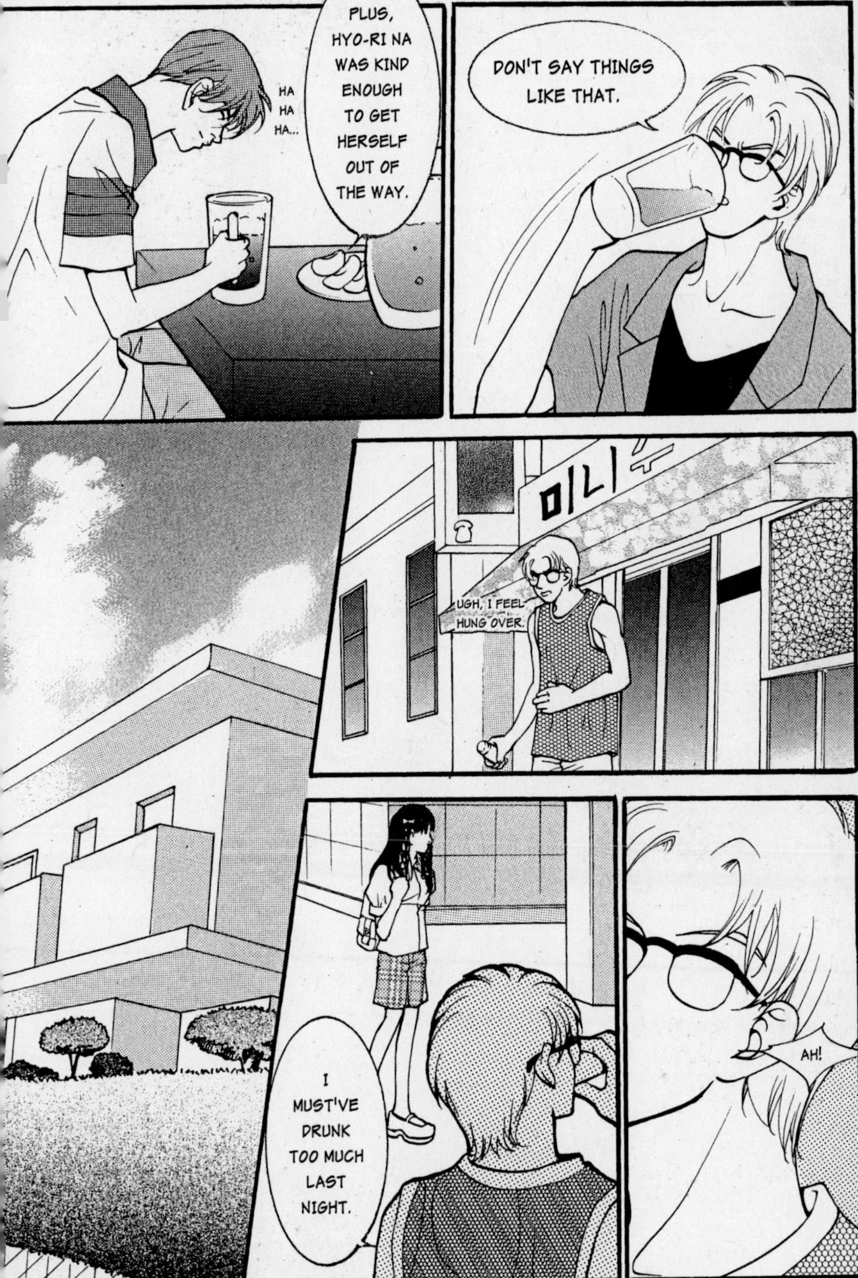
HA HA HA...
PLUS, HYO-RI NA WAS KIND ENOUGH TO GET HERSELF OUT OF THE WAY.
DON'T SAY THINGS LIKE THAT.
미니수
UGH, I FEEL HUNG OVER.
I MUST'VE DRUNK TOO MUCH LAST NIGHT.
AH!

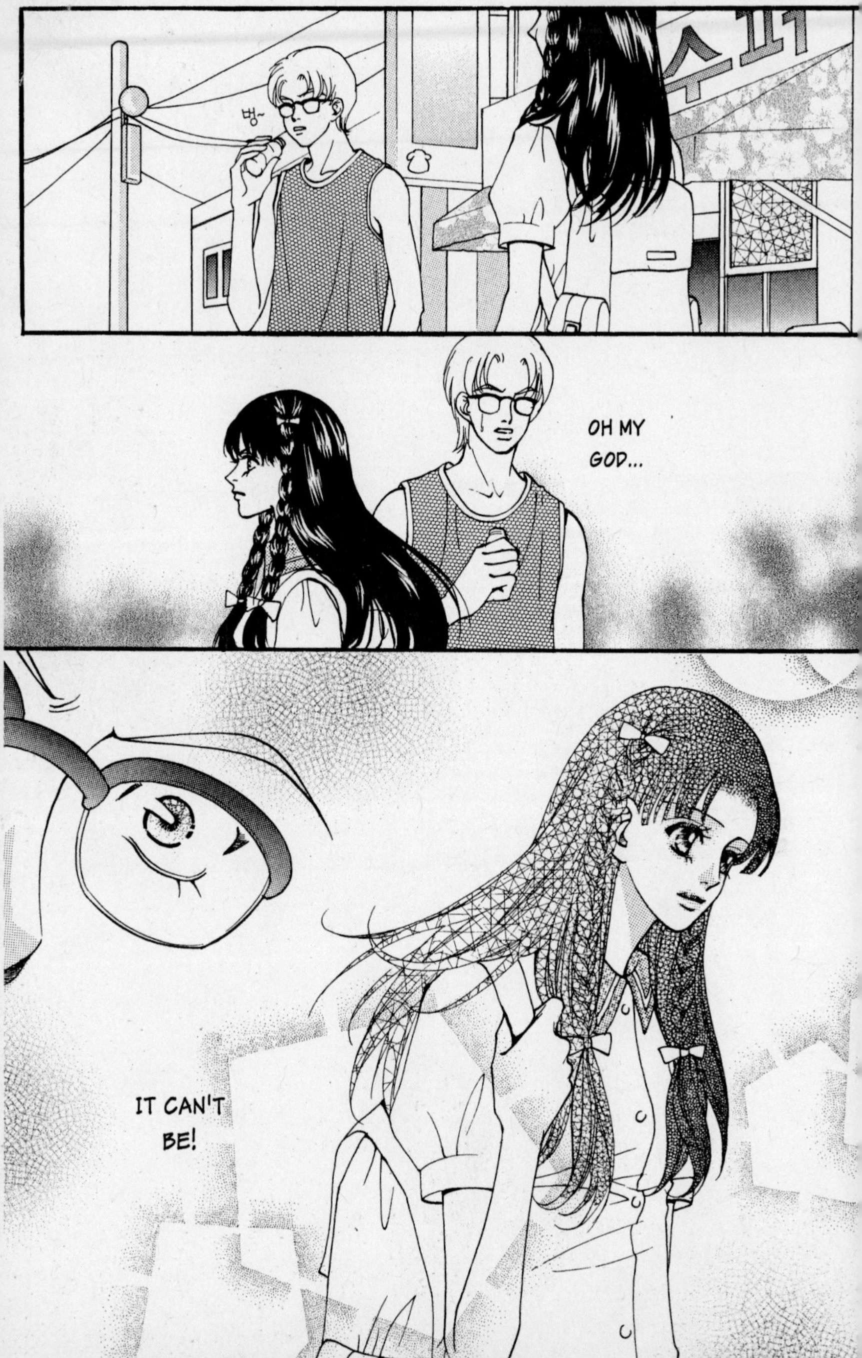
벙~
OH MY GOD...
IT CAN'T BE!

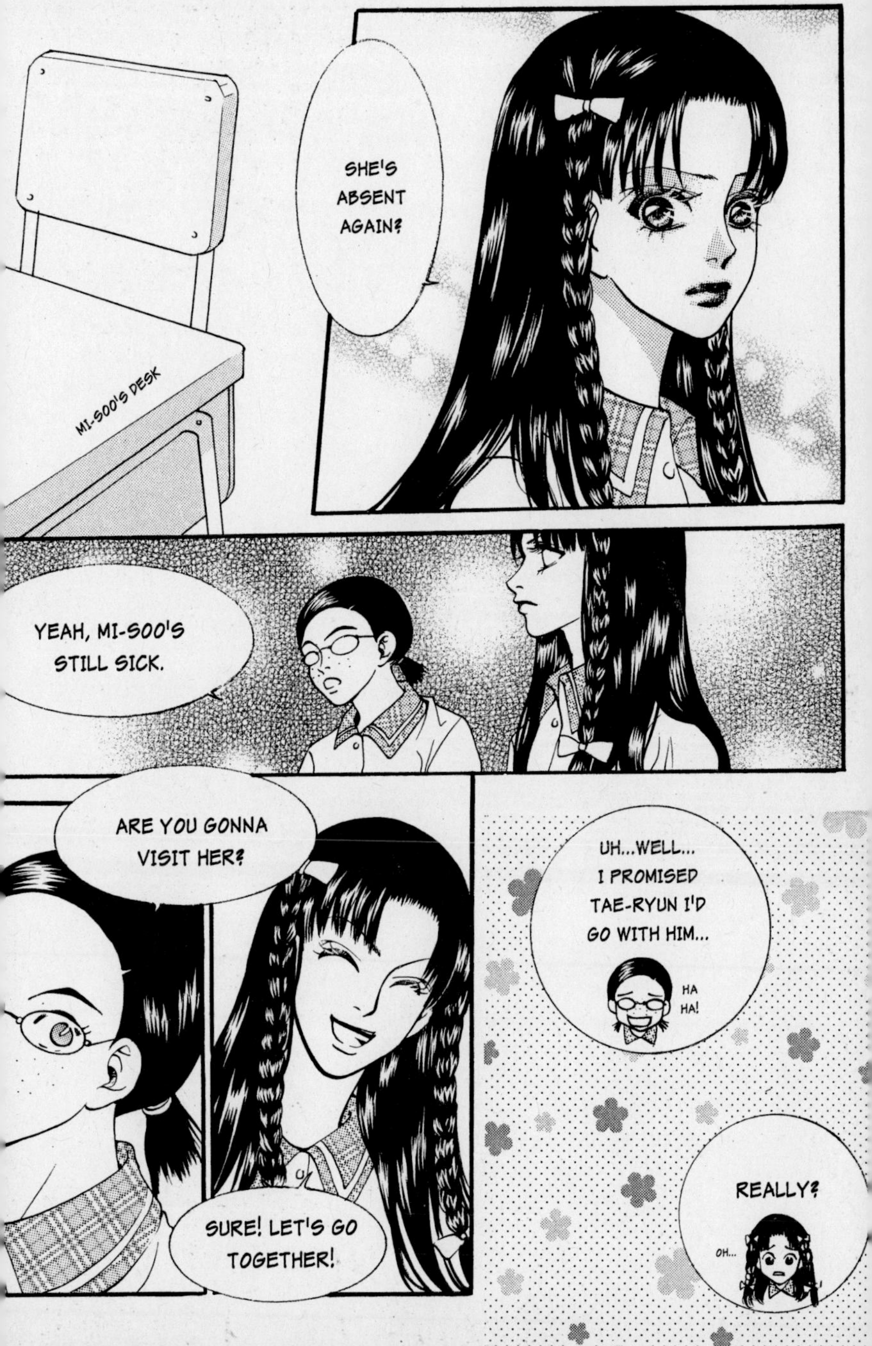
MI-SOO'S DESK
SHE'S ABSENT AGAIN?
YEAH, MI-SOO'S STILL SICK.
ARE YOU GONNA VISIT HER?
SURE! LET'S GO TOGETHER!
UH...WELL... I PROMISED TAE-RYUN I'D GO WITH HIM...
HA HA!
REALLY?
OH...

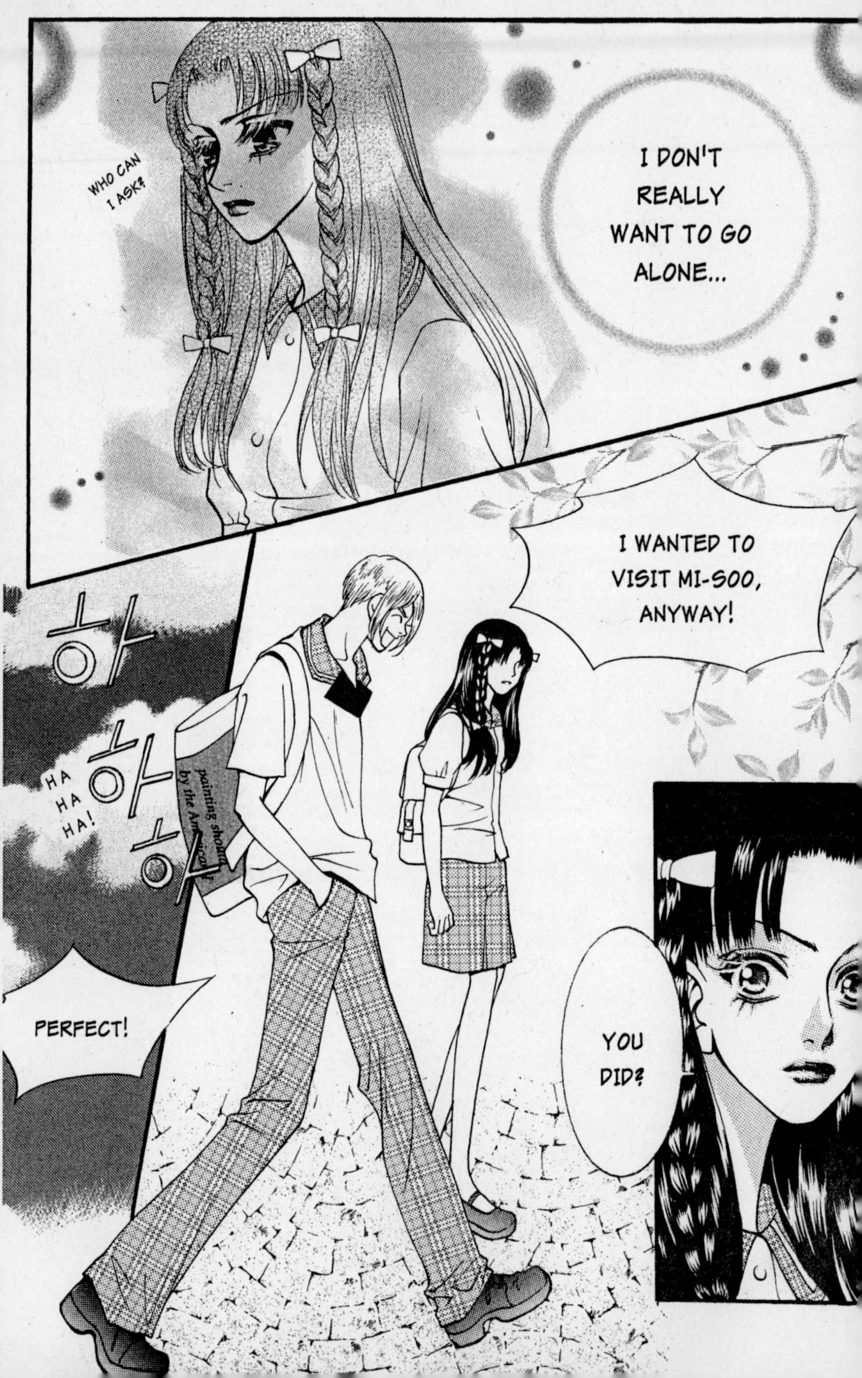
WHO CAN I ASK?
I DON'T REALLY WANT TO GO ALONE...
I WANTED TO VISIT MI-SOO, ANYWAY!
YOU DID?
하하하
HA HA HA!
PERFECT!

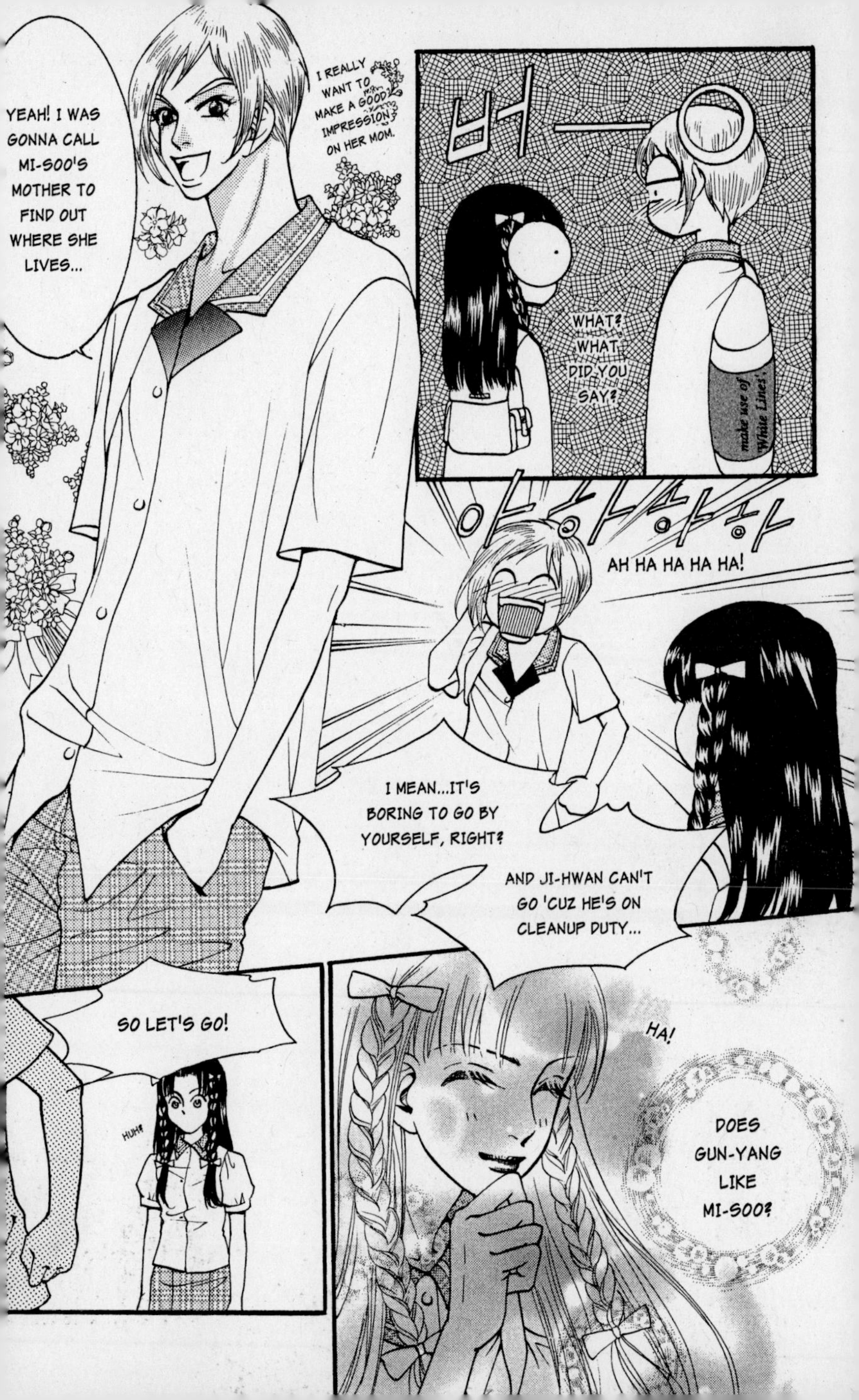
YEAH! I WAS GONNA CALL MI-SOO'S MOTHER TO FIND OUT WHERE SHE LIVES...
I REALLY WANT TO MAKE A GOOD IMPRESSION ON HER MOM.
WHAT? WHAT DID YOU SAY?
make use of 'White Lines'
AH HA HA HA HA!
I MEAN...IT'S BORING TO GO BY YOURSELF, RIGHT?
AND JI-HWAN CAN'T GO 'CUZ HE'S ON CLEANUP DUTY...
SO LET'S GO!
HUH?
HA!
DOES GUN-YANG LIKE MI-SOO?

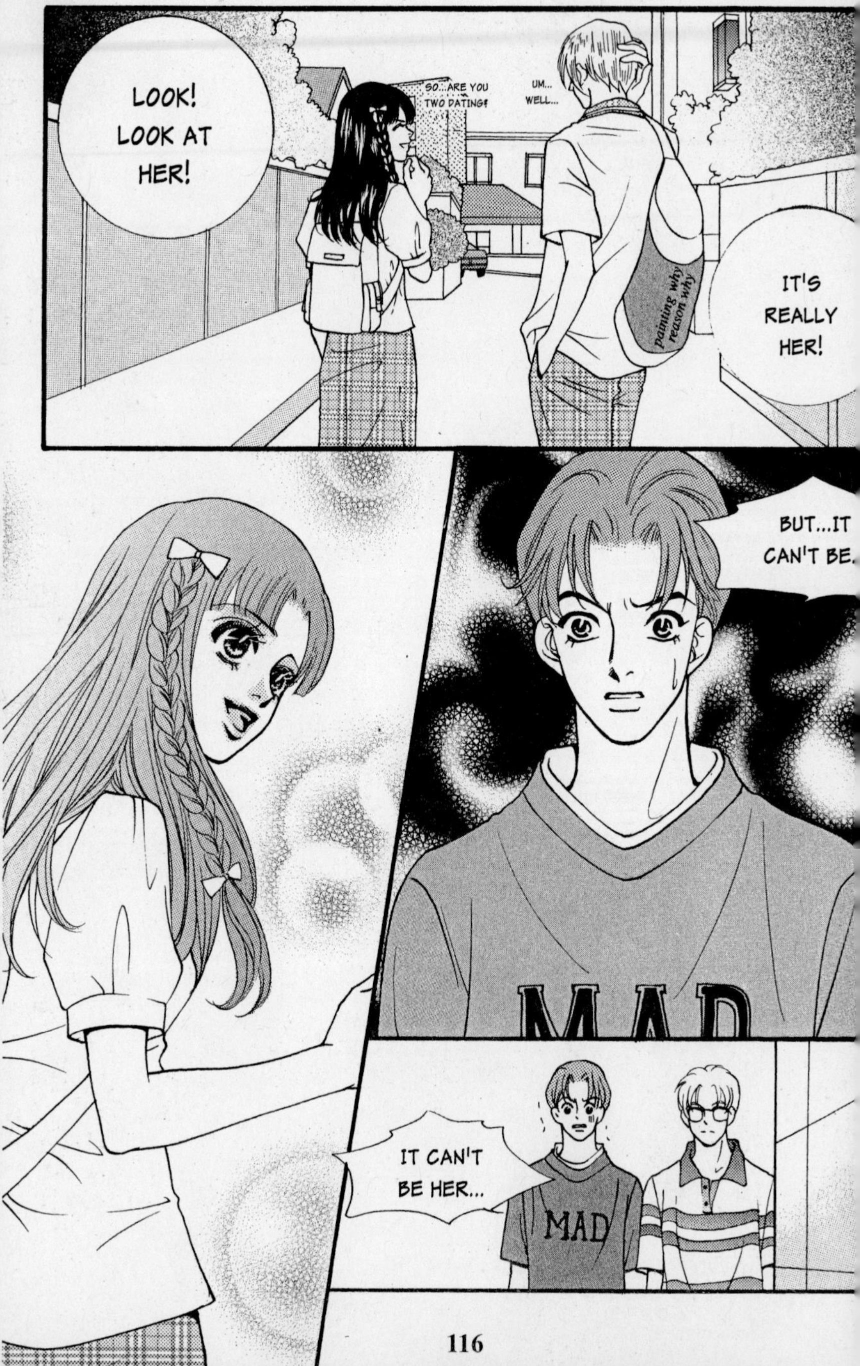
LOOK! LOOK AT HER!
SO...ARE YOU TWO DATING?
UM... WELL...
painting why reason why
IT'S REALLY HER!
BUT...IT CAN'T BE.
MAD
IT CAN'T BE HER...
MAD

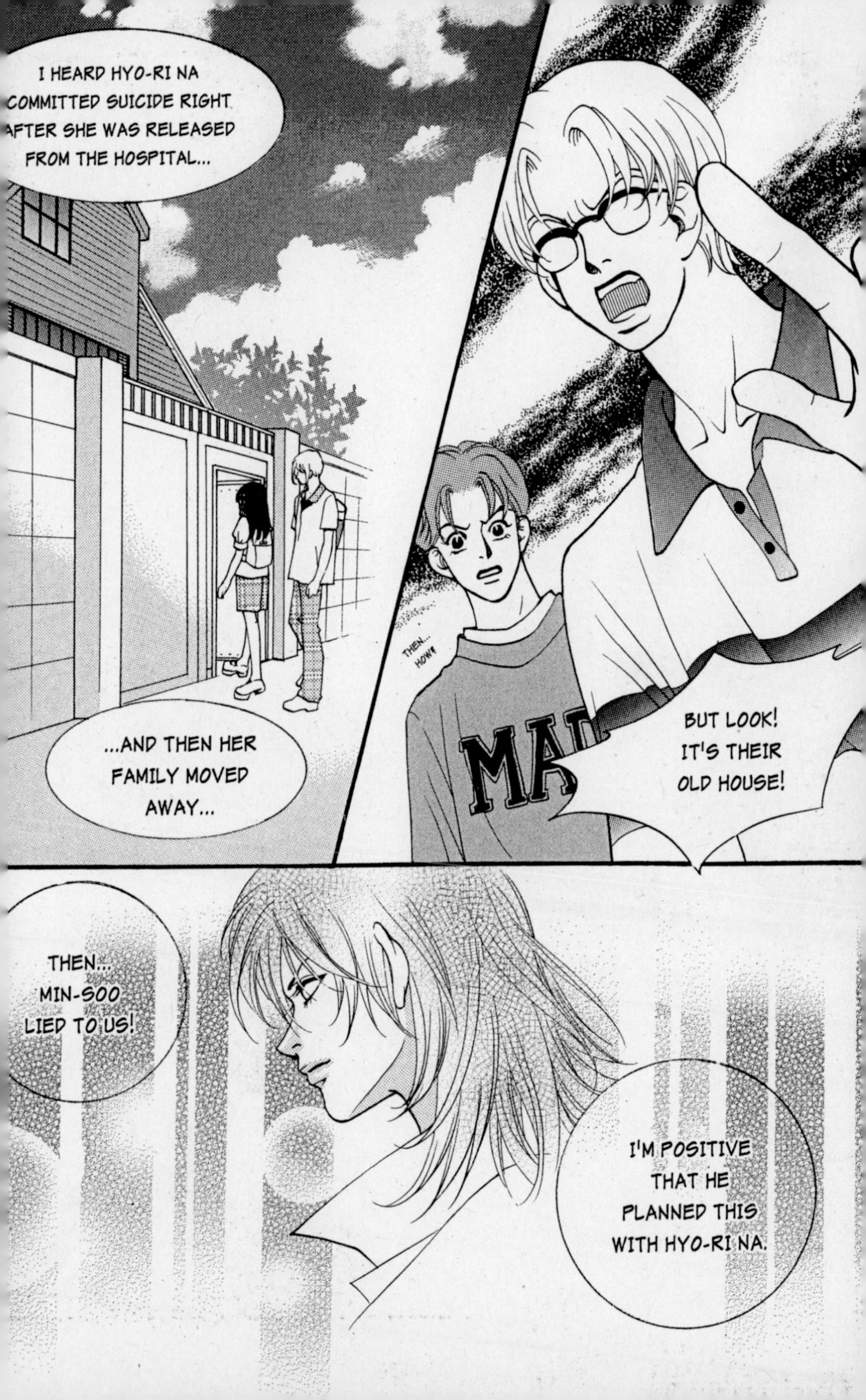
I HEARD HYO-RI NA COMMITTED SUICIDE RIGHT AFTER SHE WAS RELEASED FROM THE HOSPITAL...
...AND THEN HER FAMILY MOVED AWAY...
THEN... HOW?
BUT LOOK! IT'S THEIR OLD HOUSE!
THEN... MIN-SOO LIED TO US!
I'M POSITIVE THAT HE PLANNED THIS WITH HYO-RI NA.

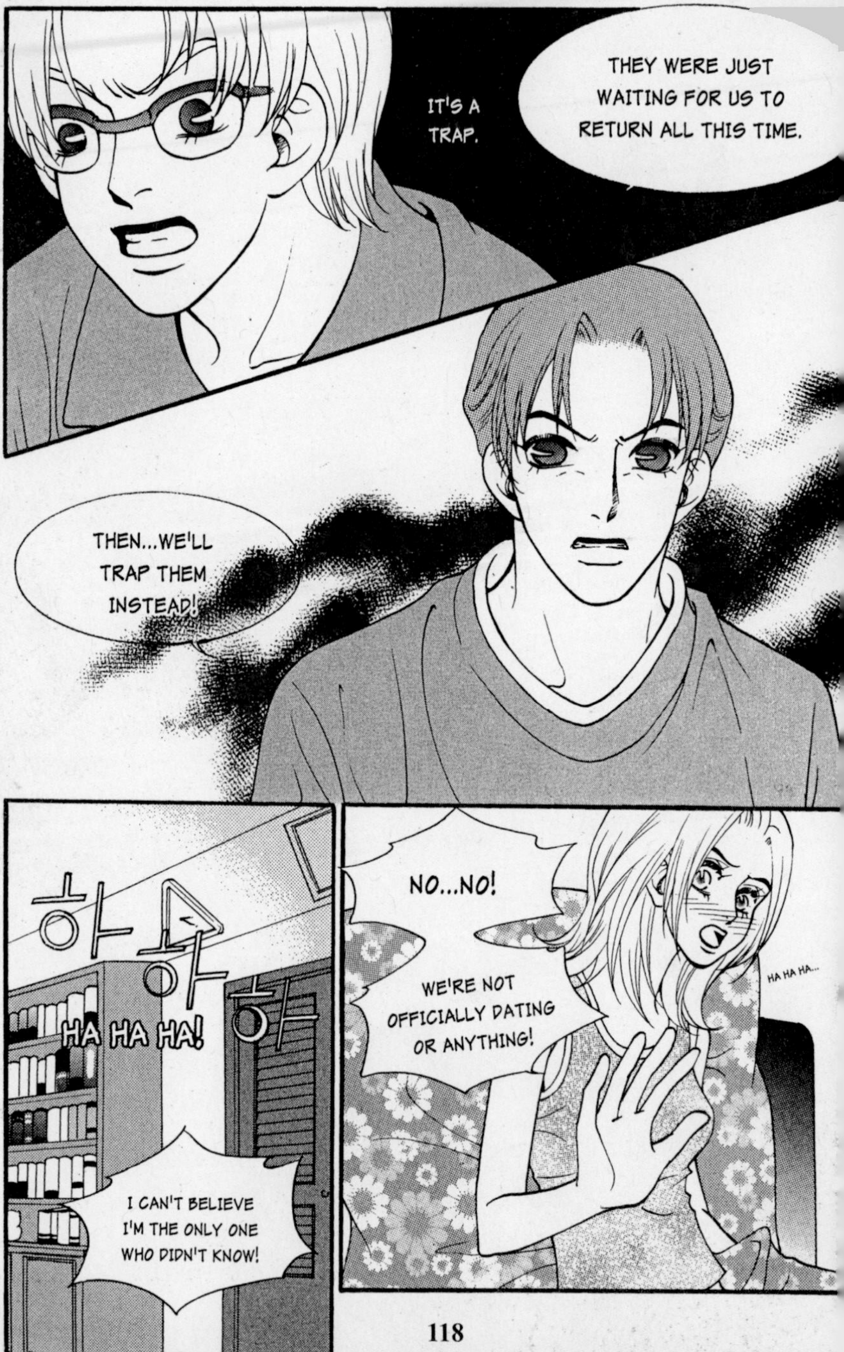
IT'S A TRAP.
THEY WERE JUST WAITING FOR US TO RETURN ALL THIS TIME.
THEN...WE'LL TRAP THEM INSTEAD!
하하하
HA HA HA!
I CAN'T BELIEVE I'M THE ONLY ONE WHO DIDN'T KNOW!
NO...NO!
WE'RE NOT OFFICIALLY DATING OR ANYTHING!
HA HA HA...

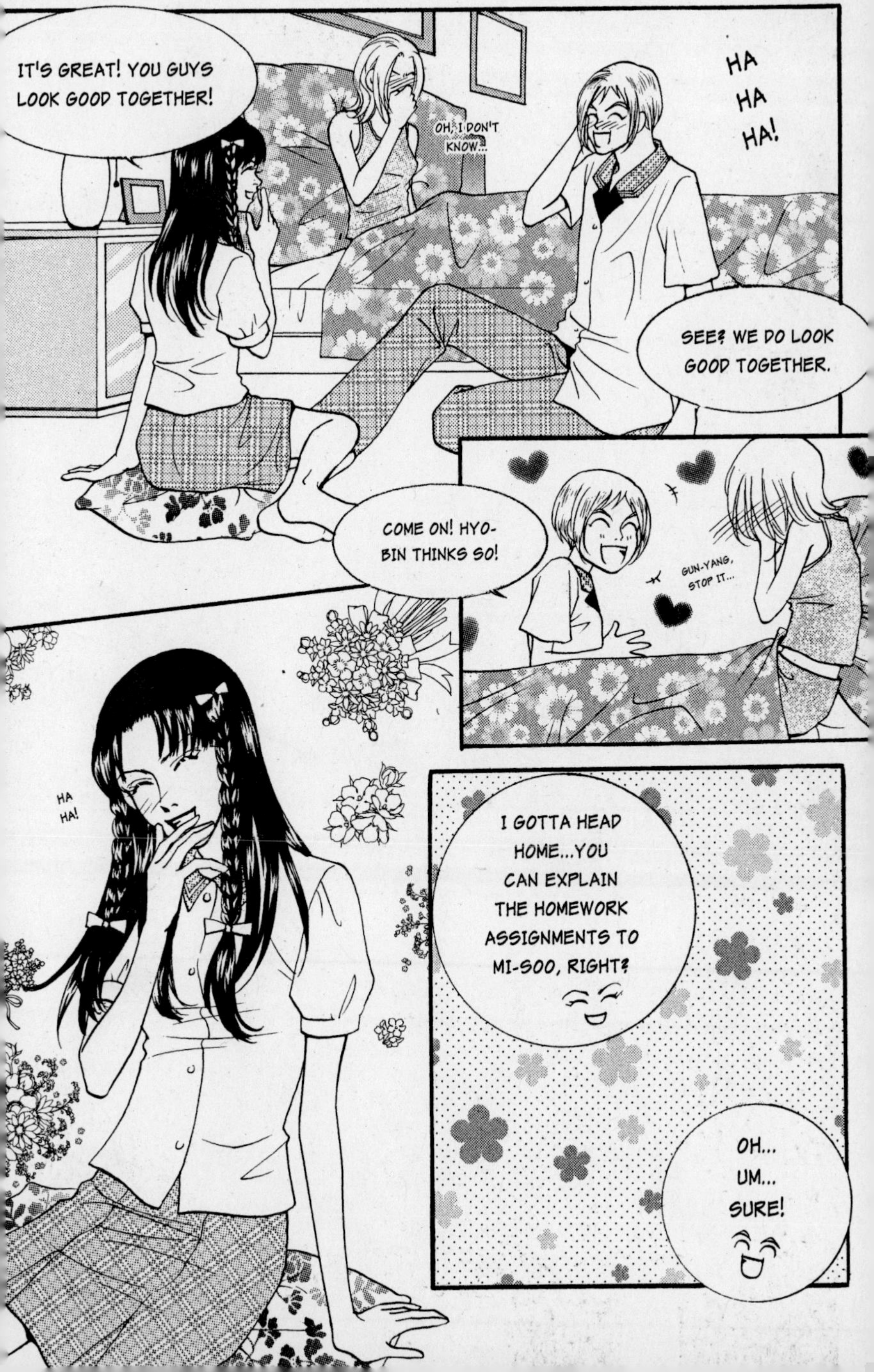
IT'S GREAT! YOU GUYS LOOK GOOD TOGETHER!
OH, I DON'T KNOW...
HA HA HA!
SEE? WE DO LOOK GOOD TOGETHER.
COME ON! HYO-BIN THINKS SO!
GUN-YANG, STOP IT...
HA HA!
I GOTTA HEAD HOME...YOU CAN EXPLAIN THE HOMEWORK ASSIGNMENTS TO MI-SOO, RIGHT?
OH... UM... SURE!

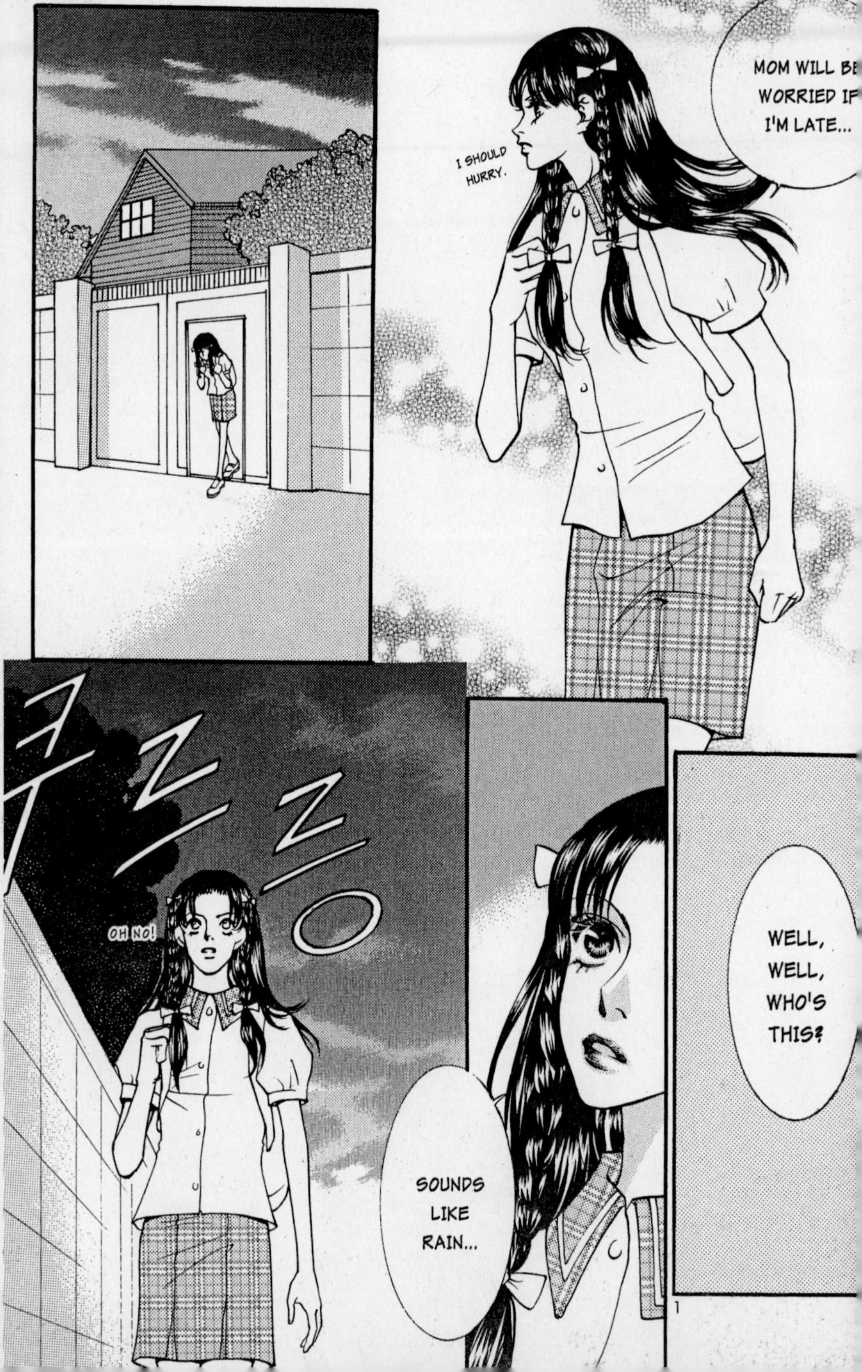
I SHOULD HURRY.
MOM WILL BE WORRIED IF I'M LATE...
OH NO!
SOUNDS LIKE RAIN...
WELL, WELL, WHO'S THIS?

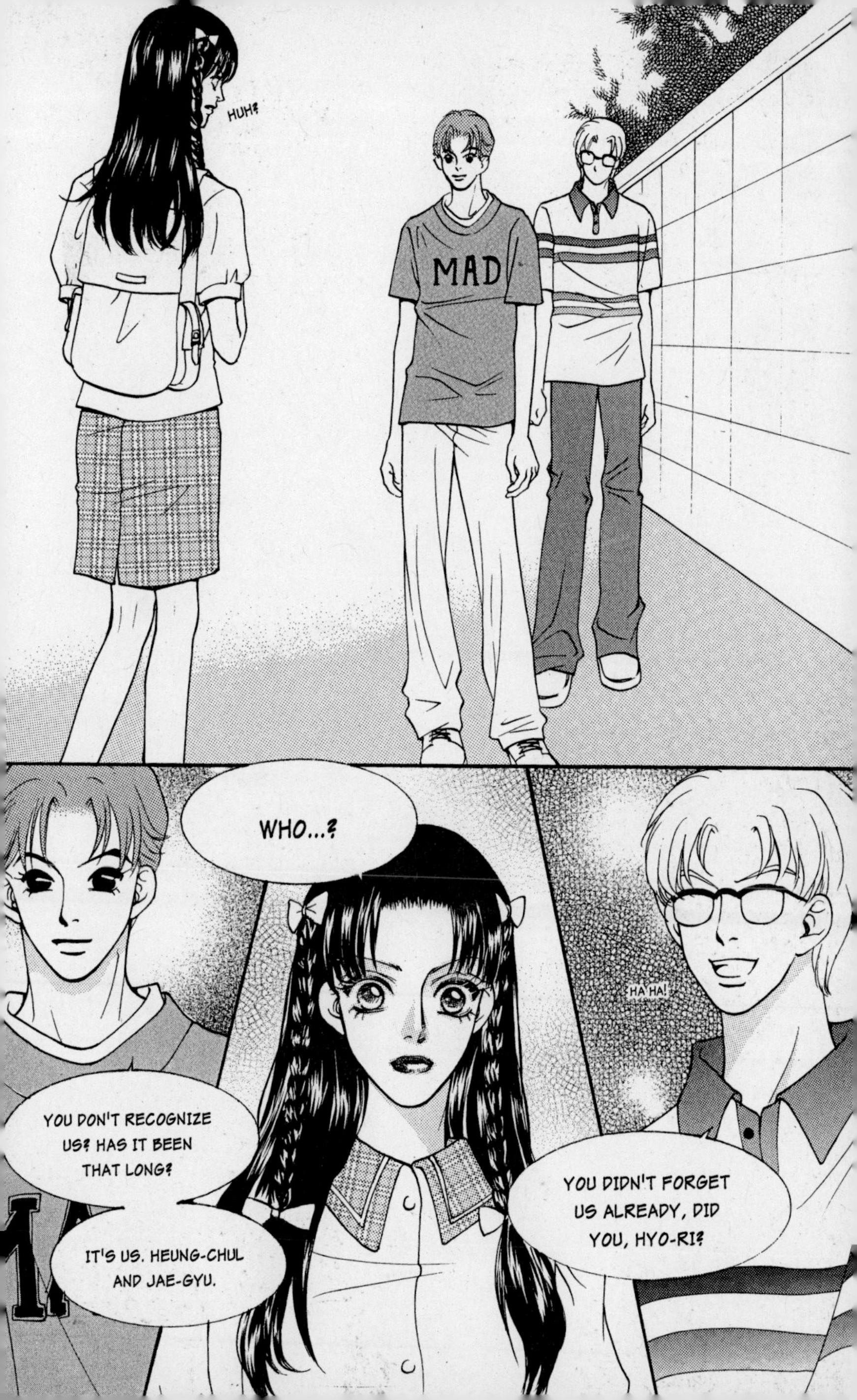
HUH?
WHO...?
YOU DON'T RECOGNIZE US? HAS IT BEEN THAT LONG?
IT'S US. HEUNG-CHUL AND JAE-GYU.
HA HA!
YOU DIDN'T FORGET US ALREADY, DID YOU, HYO-RI?

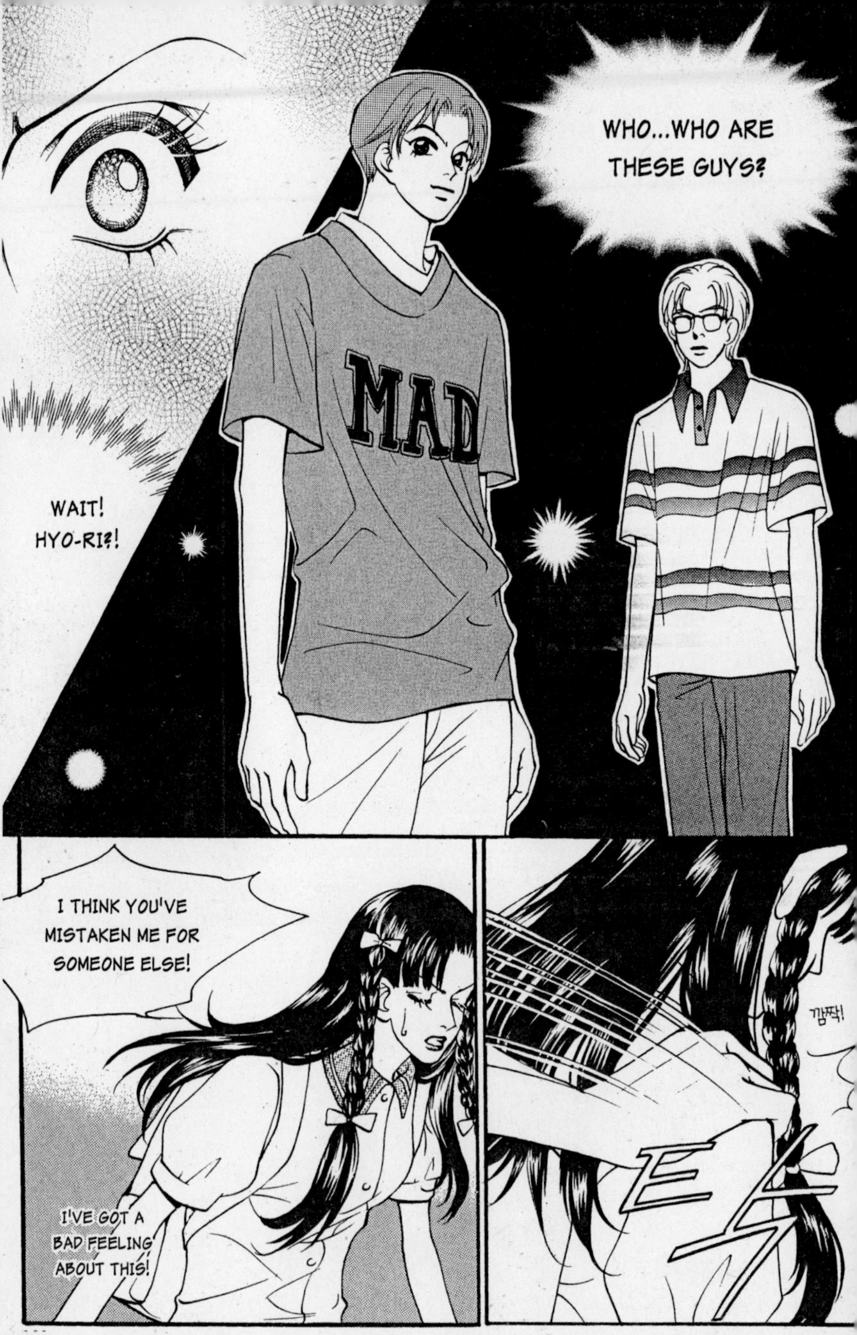
WHO...WHO ARE THESE GUYS?
WAIT! HYO-RI?!
I THINK YOU'VE MISTAKEN ME FOR SOMEONE ELSE!
I'VE GOT A BAD FEELING ABOUT THIS!
깜짝!

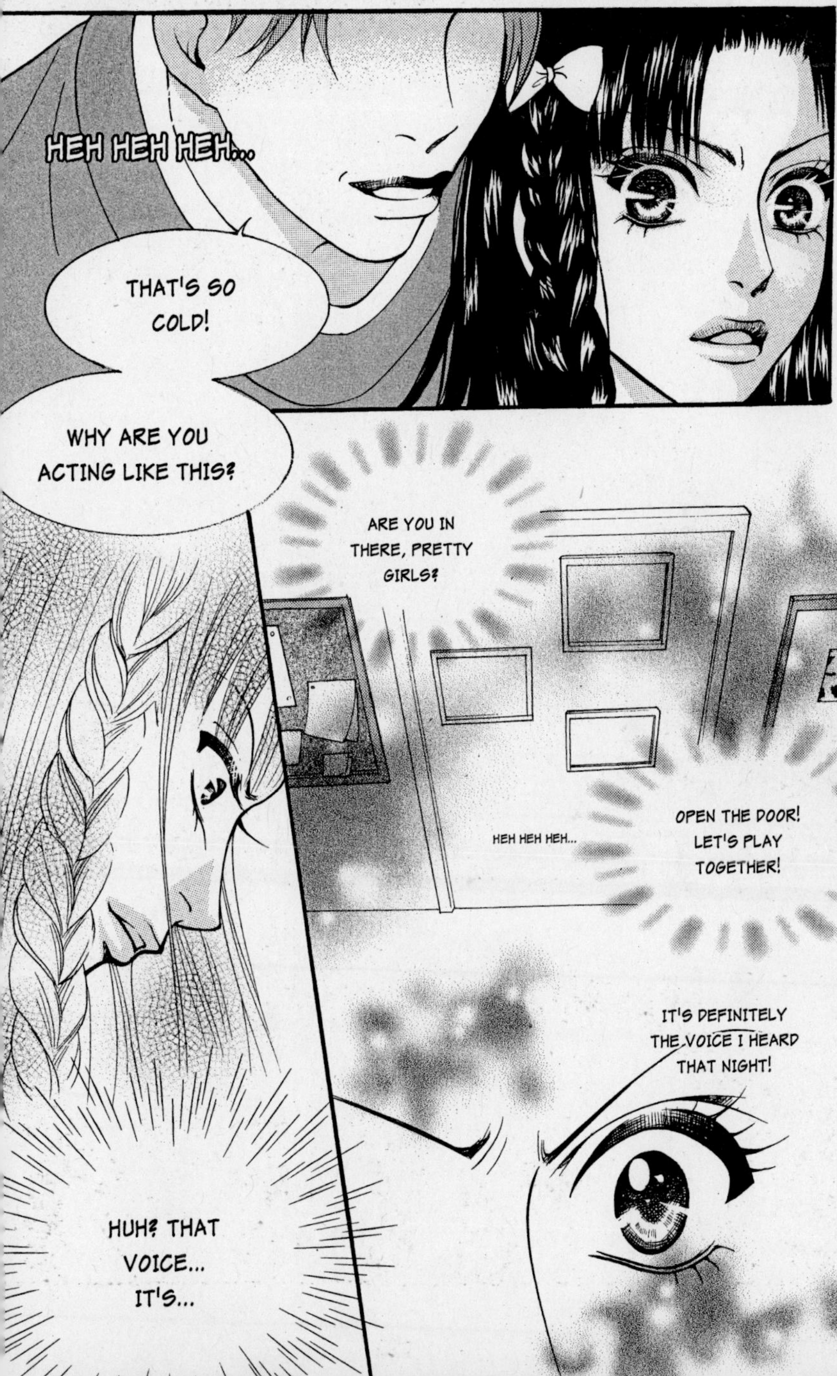
HEH HEH HEH...
THAT'S SO COLD!
WHY ARE YOU ACTING LIKE THIS?
HUH? THAT VOICE... IT'S...
ARE YOU IN THERE, PRETTY GIRLS?
HEH HEH HEH...
OPEN THE DOOR! LET'S PLAY TOGETHER!
IT'S DEFINITELY THE VOICE I HEARD THAT NIGHT!

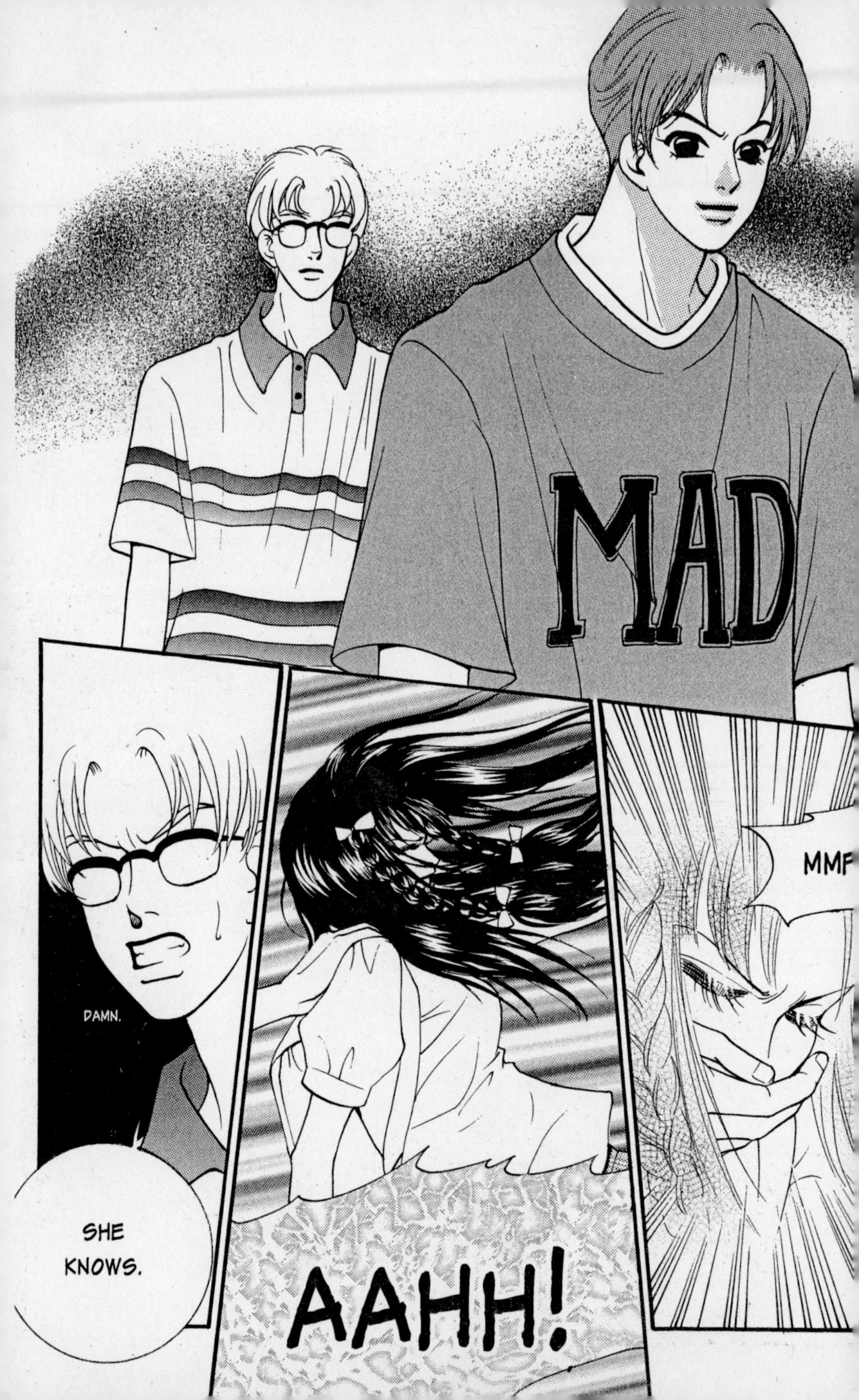
MAD
DAMN.
SHE KNOWS.
AAHH!
MMF

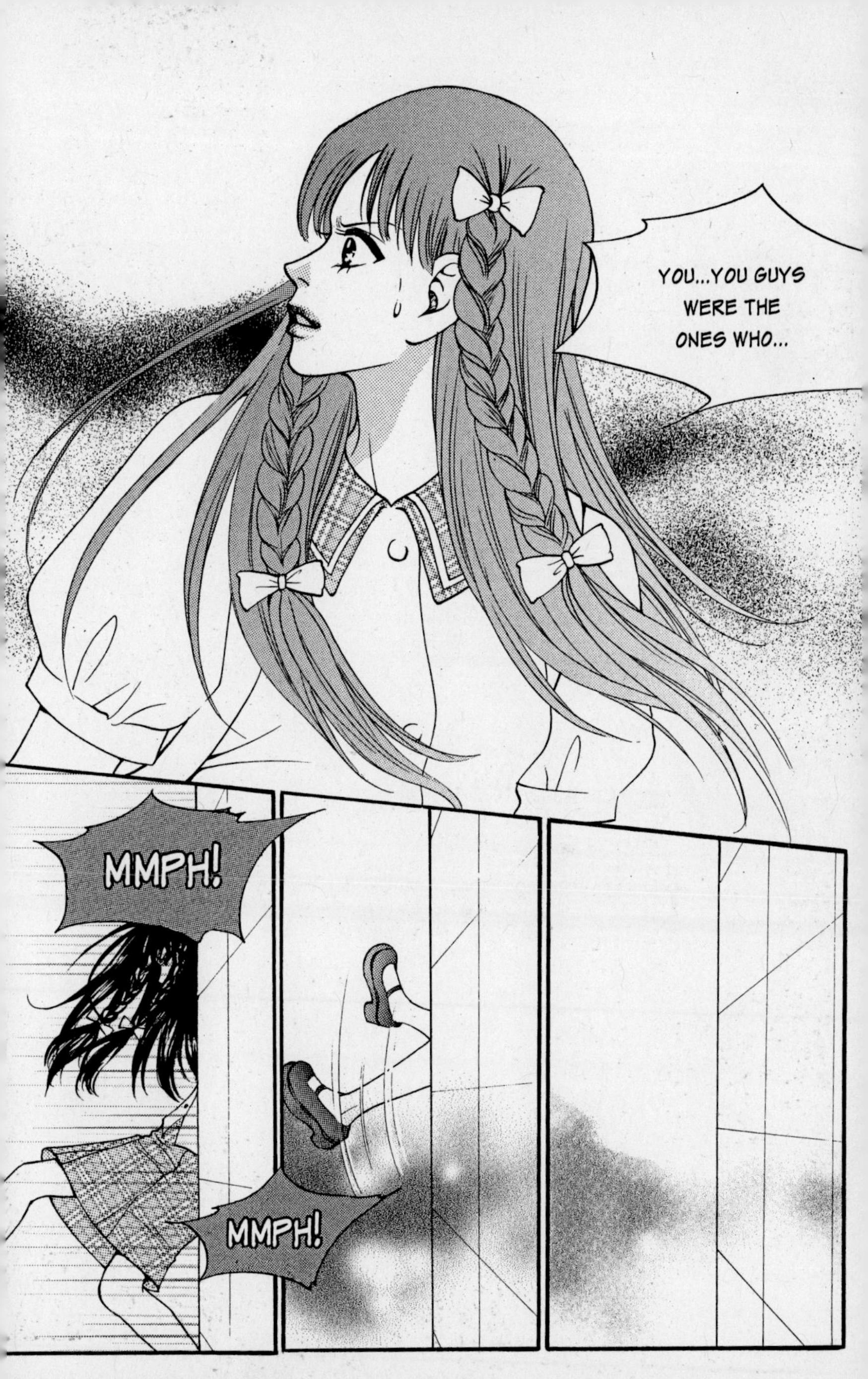
YOU...YOU GUYS WERE THE ONES WHO...
MMPH!
MMPH!

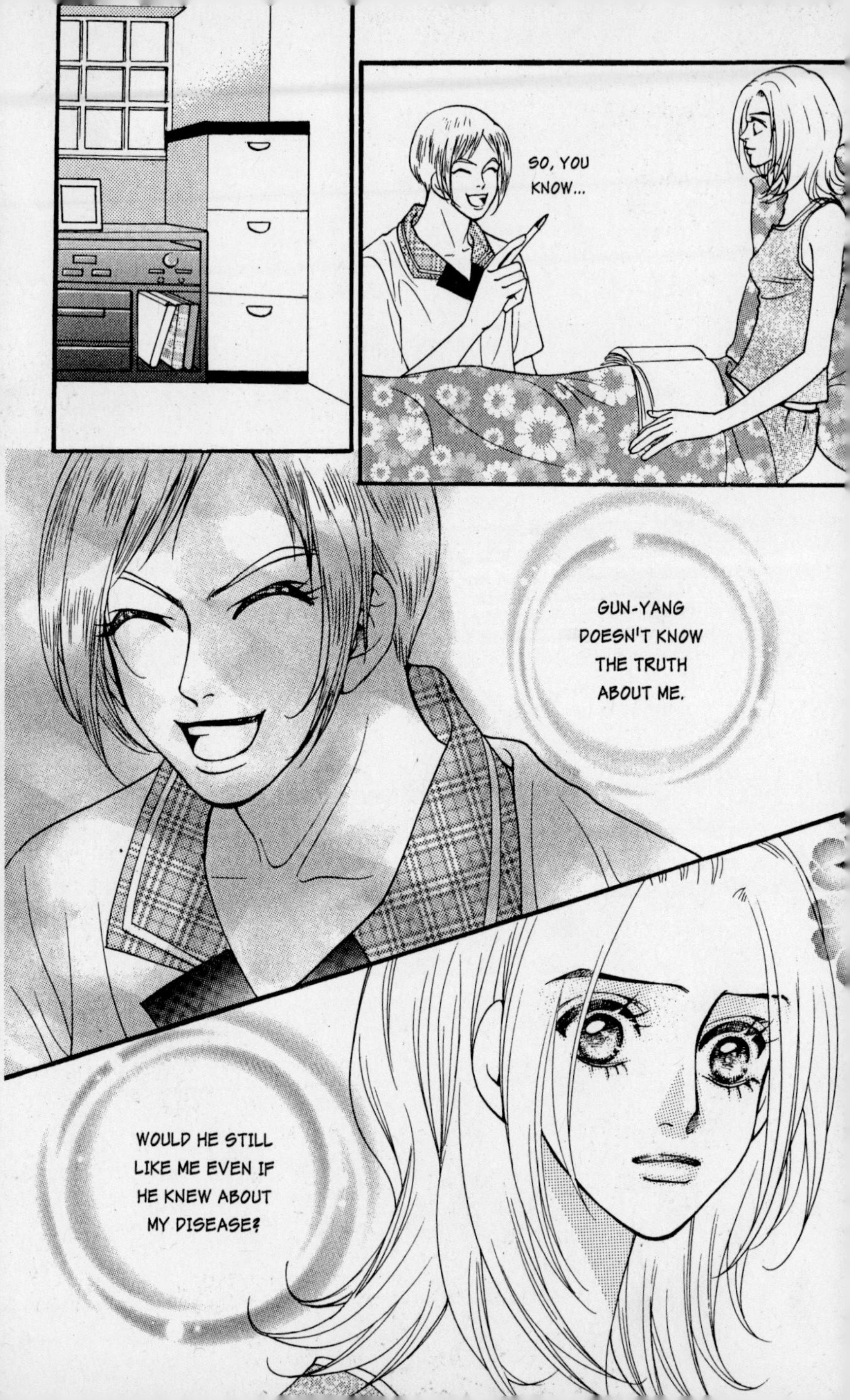
SO, YOU KNOW...
GUN-YANG DOESN'T KNOW THE TRUTH ABOUT ME.
WOULD HE STILL LIKE ME EVEN IF HE KNEW ABOUT MY DISEASE?

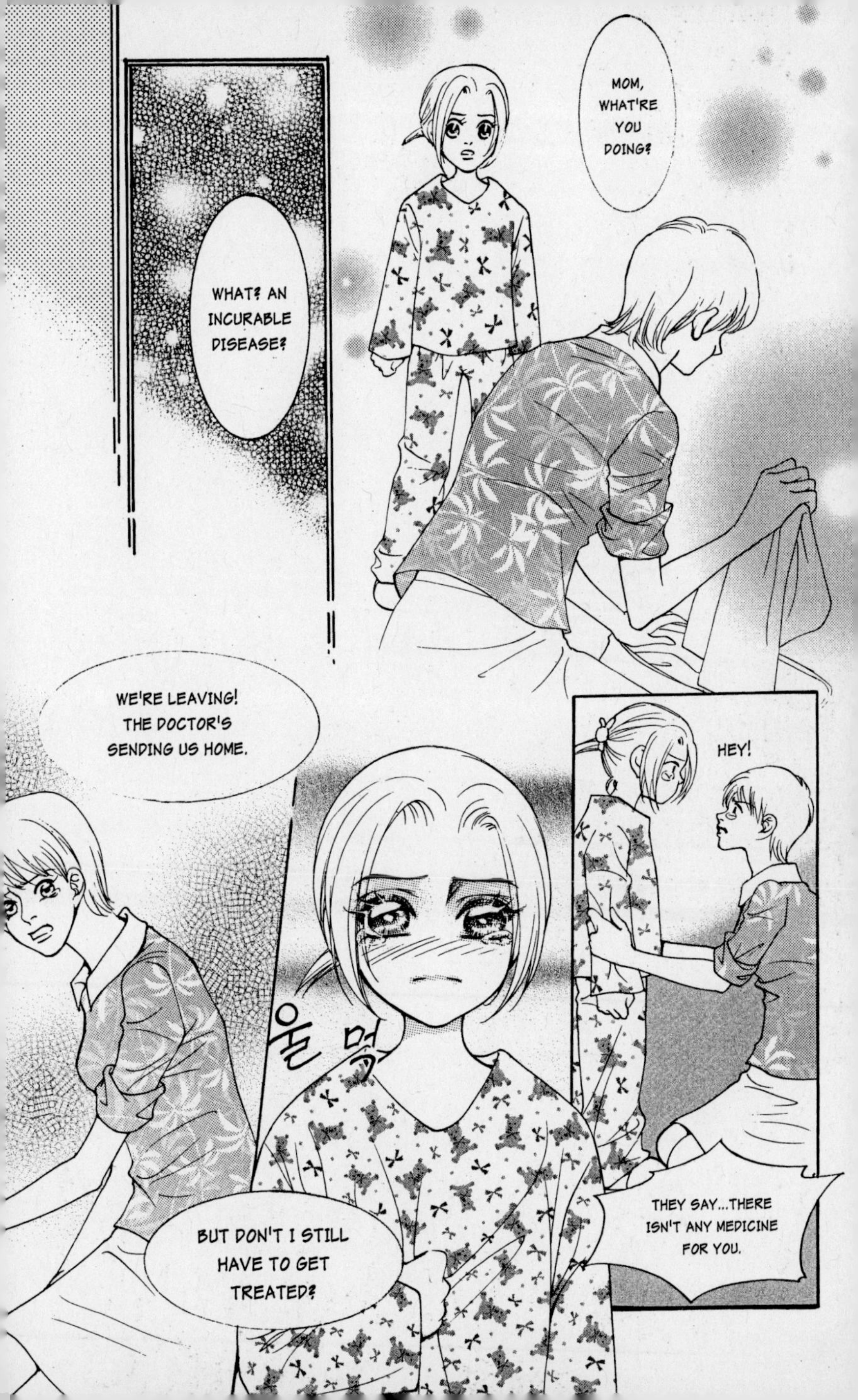
WHAT? AN INCURABLE DISEASE?
MOM, WHAT'RE YOU DOING?
WE'RE LEAVING! THE DOCTOR'S SENDING US HOME.
BUT DON'T I STILL HAVE TO GET TREATED?
울
HEY!
THEY SAY...THERE ISN'T ANY MEDICINE FOR YOU.

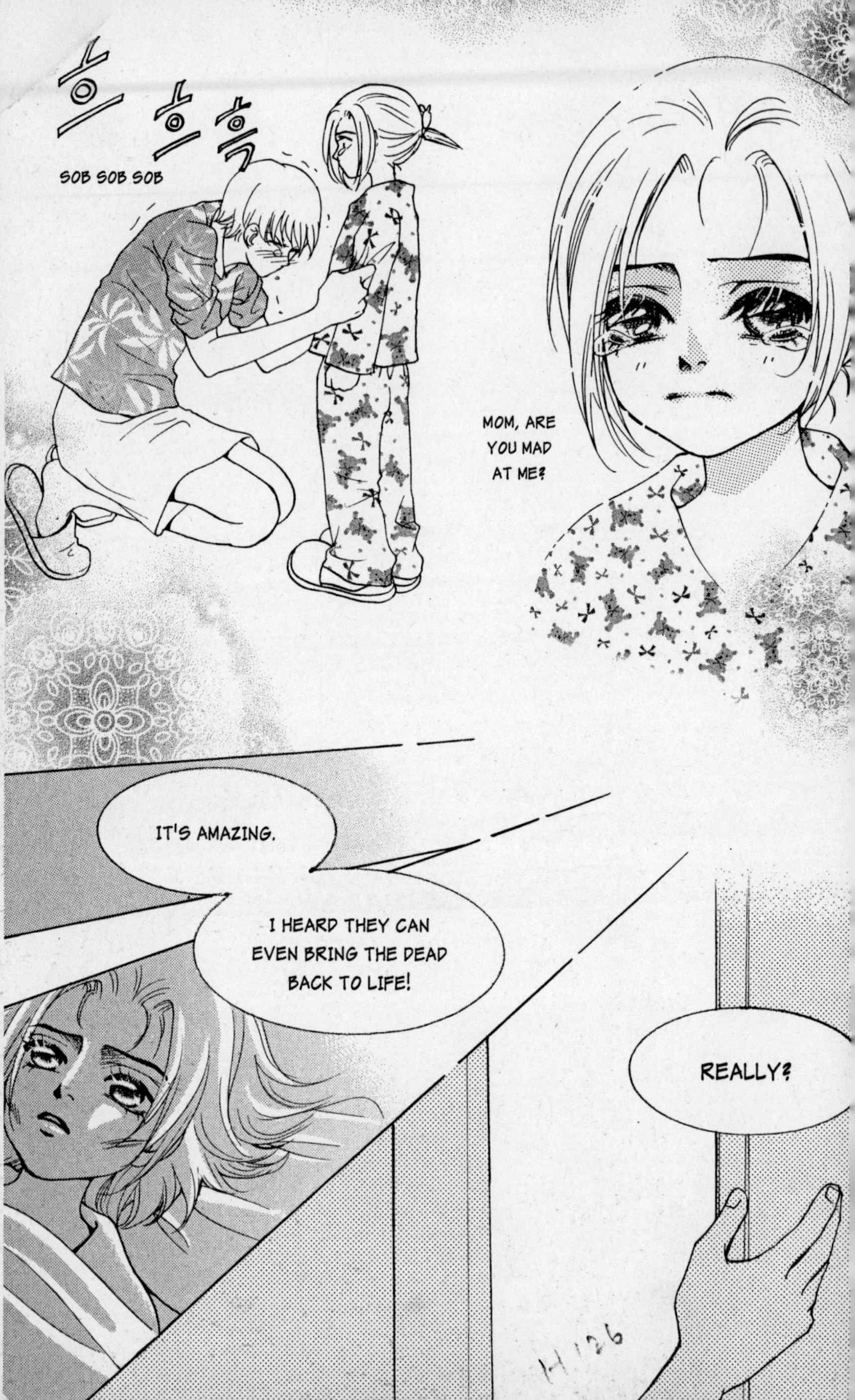
흐 흐흑
SOB SOB SOB
MOM, ARE YOU MAD AT ME?
IT'S AMAZING.
I HEARD THEY CAN EVEN BRING THE DEAD BACK TO LIFE!
REALLY?

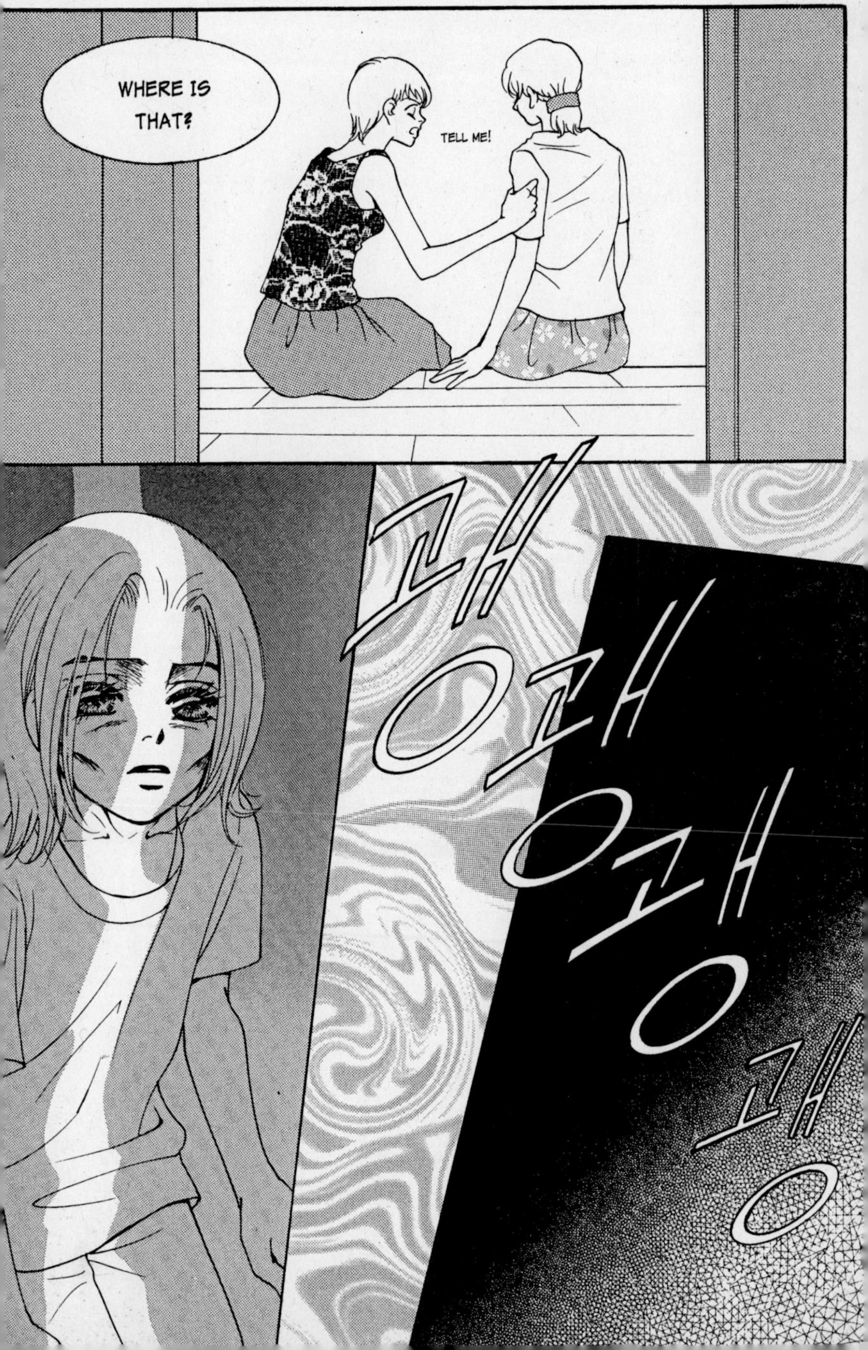
WHERE IS THAT?
TELL ME!

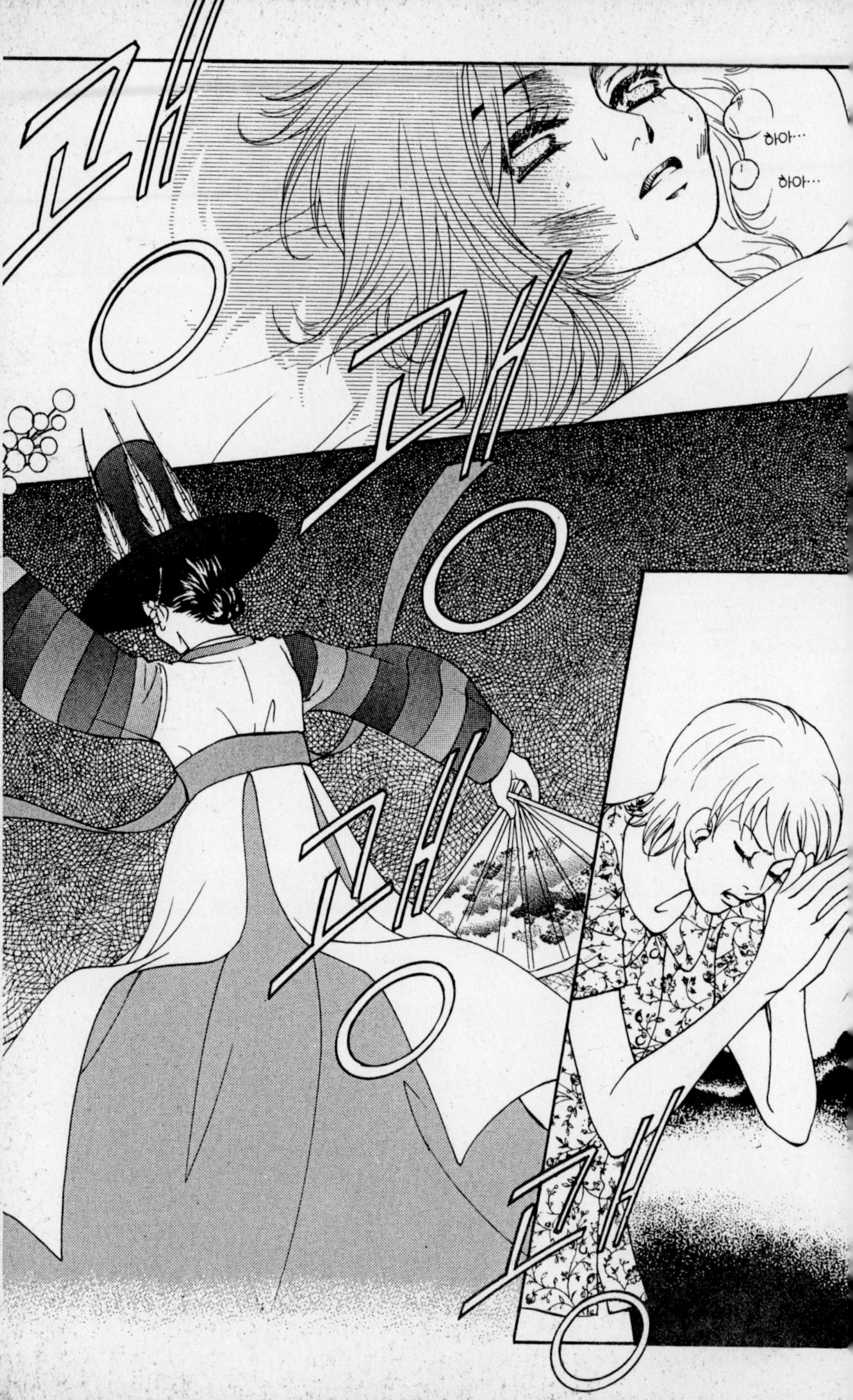
갱 갱 갱 갱
하아…
하아…

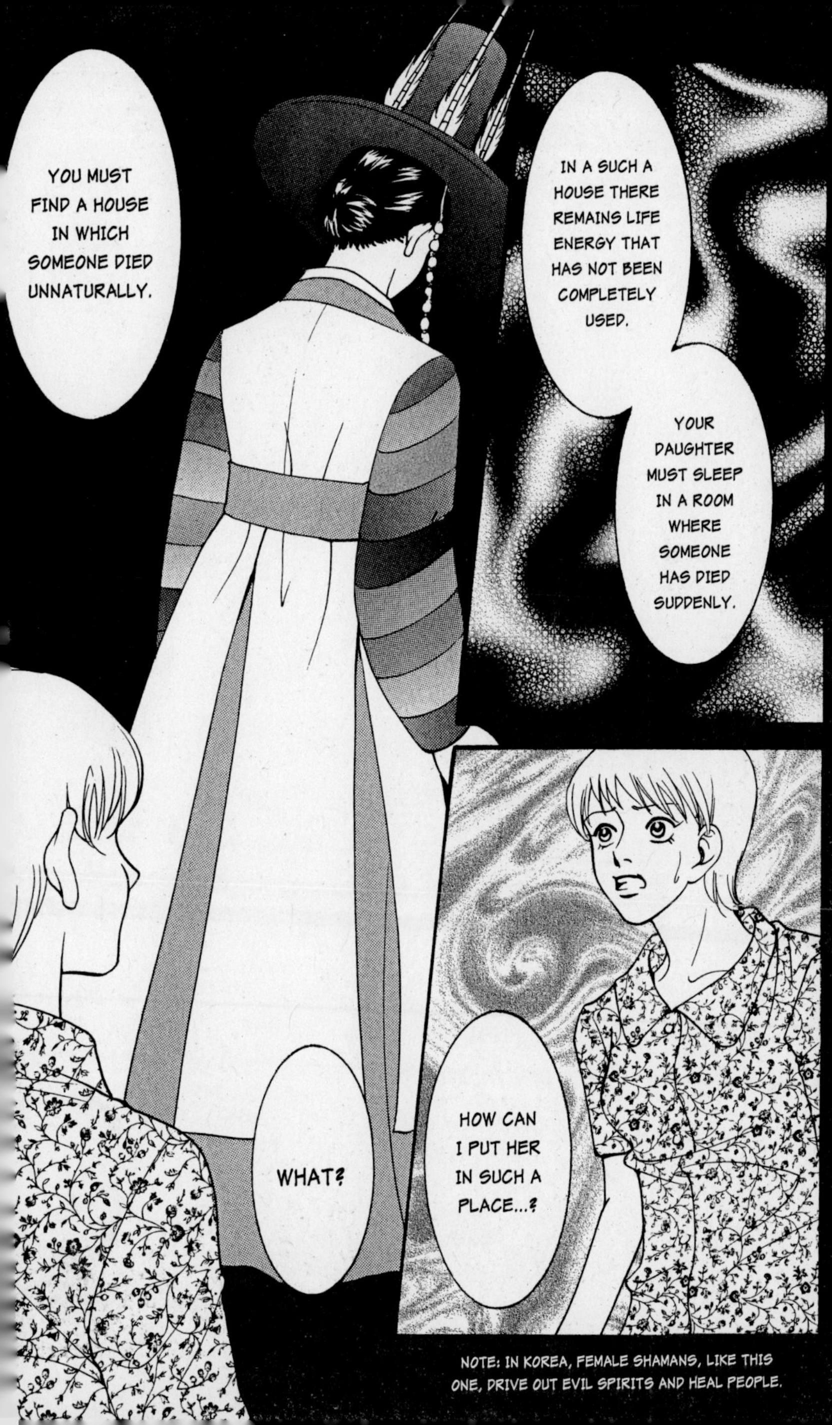

NOTE: IN KOREA, FEMALE SHAMANS, LIKE THIS ONE, DRIVE OUT EVIL SPIRITS AND HEAL PEOPLE.

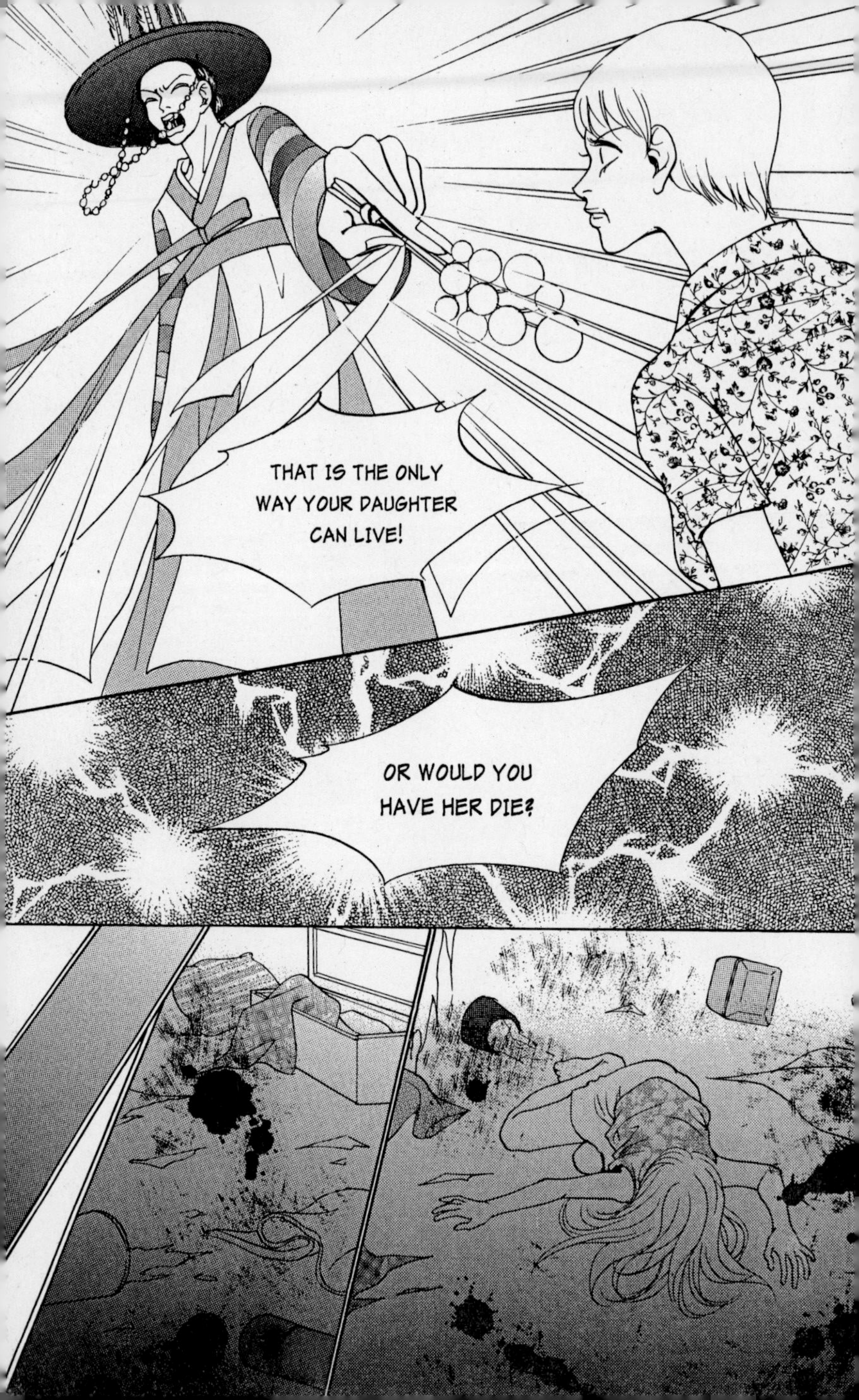
THAT IS THE ONLY WAY YOUR DAUGHTER CAN LIVE!
OR WOULD YOU HAVE HER DIE?

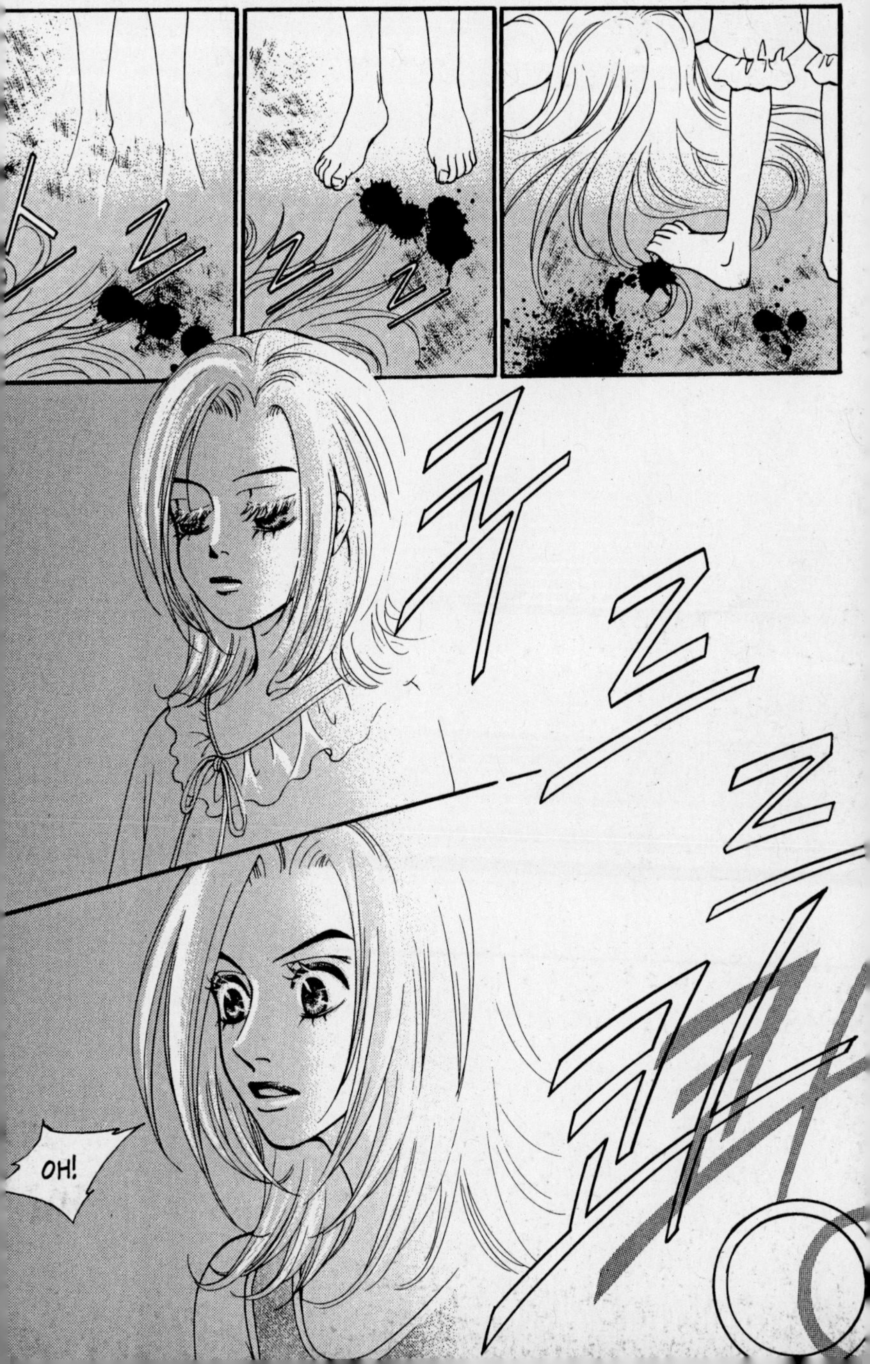
OH!

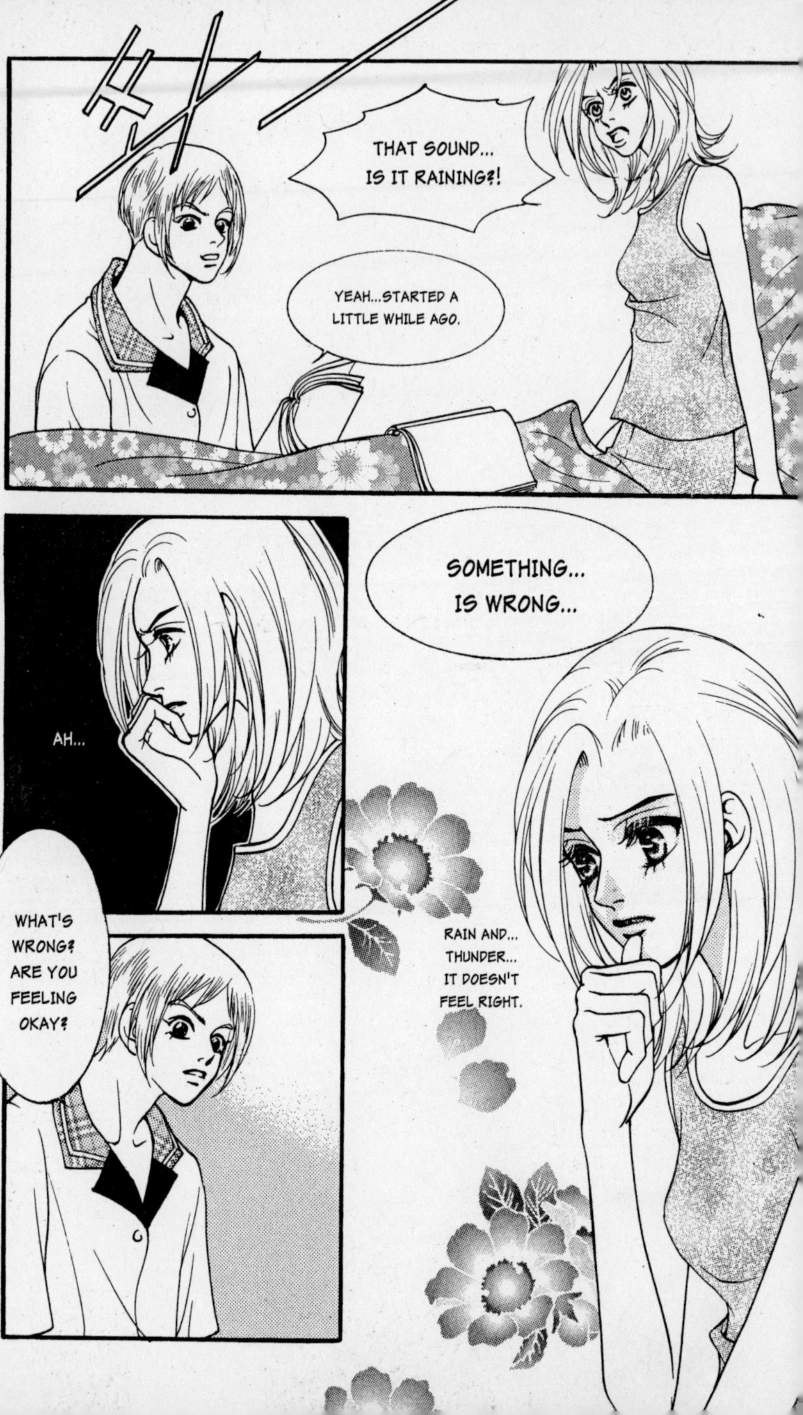
THAT SOUND... IS IT RAINING?!
YEAH...STARTED A LITTLE WHILE AGO.
AH...
WHAT'S WRONG? ARE YOU FEELING OKAY?
SOMETHING... IS WRONG...
RAIN AND... THUNDER... IT DOESN'T FEEL RIGHT.

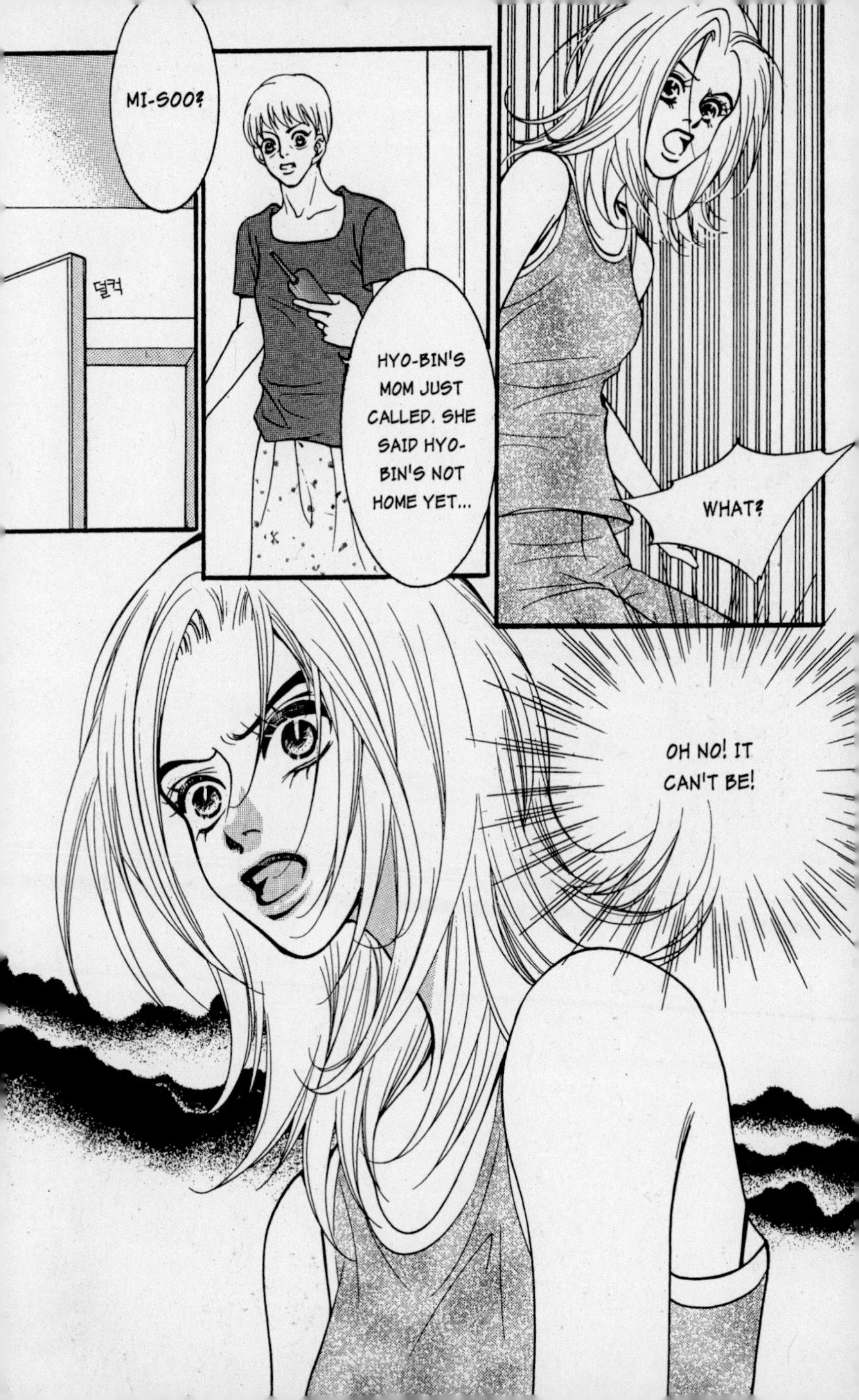
MI-SOO?
덜컥
HYO-BIN'S MOM JUST CALLED. SHE SAID HYO-BIN'S NOT HOME YET...
WHAT?
OH NO! IT CAN'T BE!

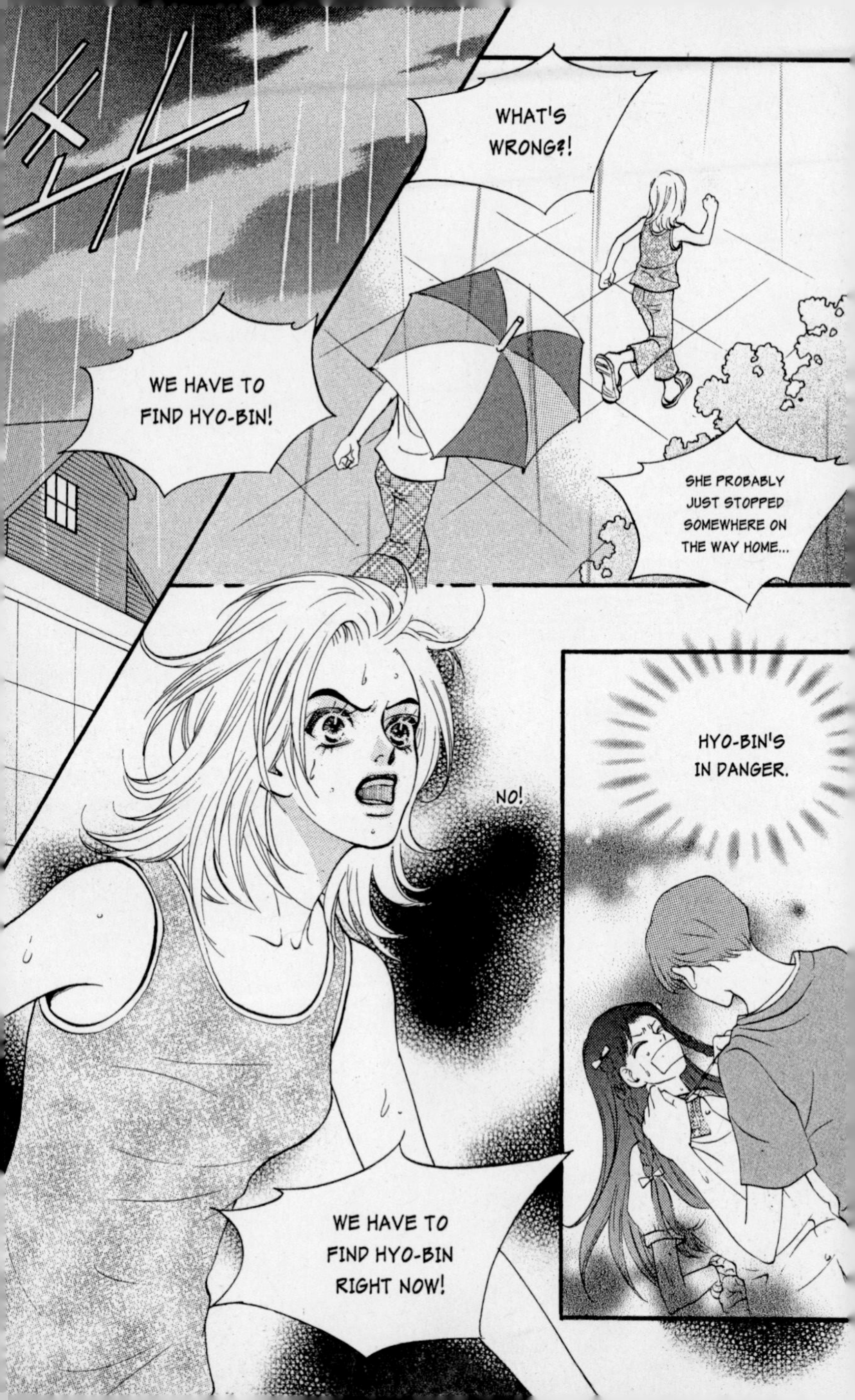
WE HAVE TO FIND HYO-BIN!
WHAT'S WRONG?!
SHE PROBABLY JUST STOPPED SOMEWHERE ON THE WAY HOME...
NO!
WE HAVE TO FIND HYO-BIN RIGHT NOW!
HYO-BIN'S IN DANGER.

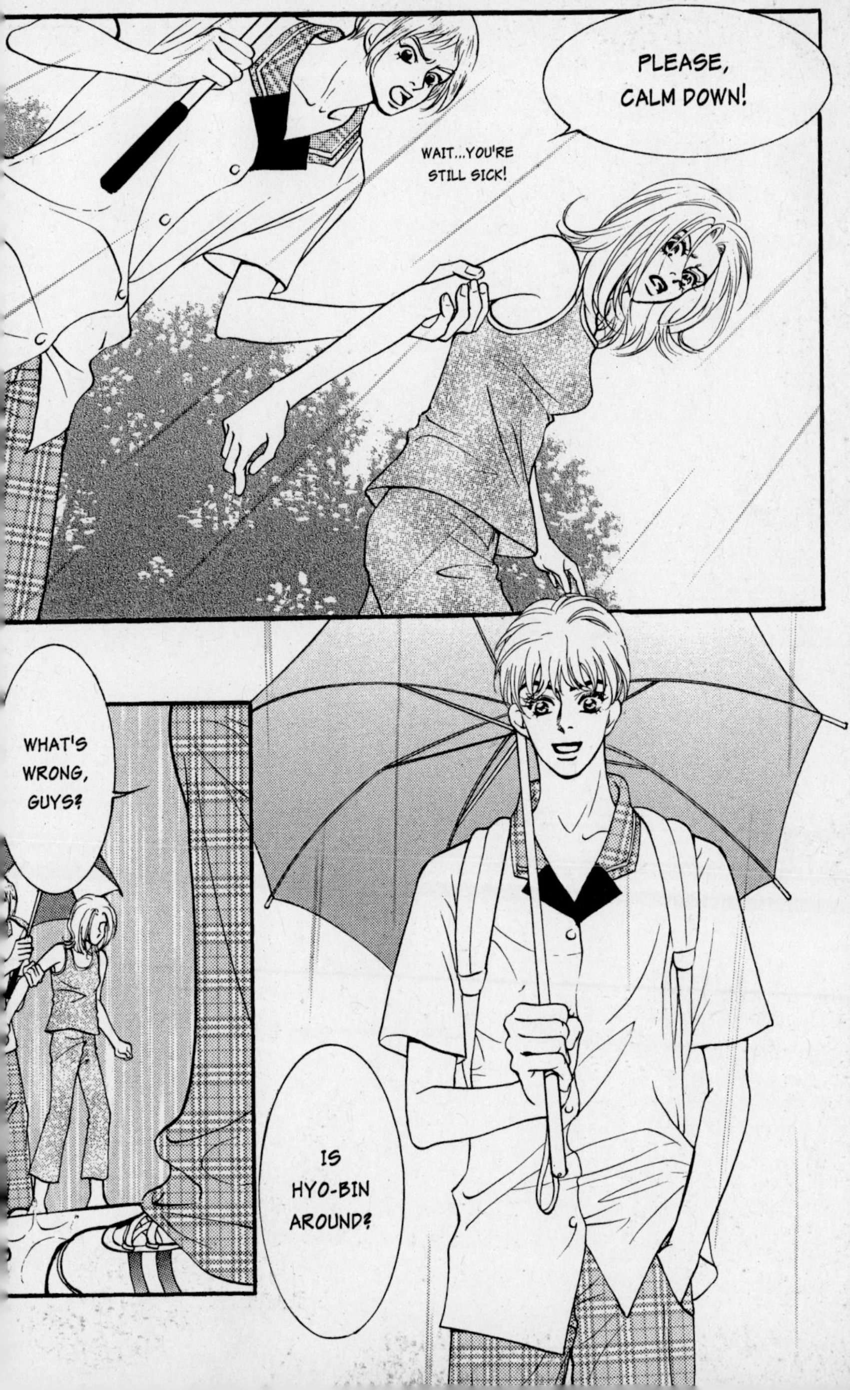
WAIT...YOU'RE STILL SICK!
PLEASE, CALM DOWN!
WHAT'S WRONG, GUYS?
IS HYO-BIN AROUND?

Grudge

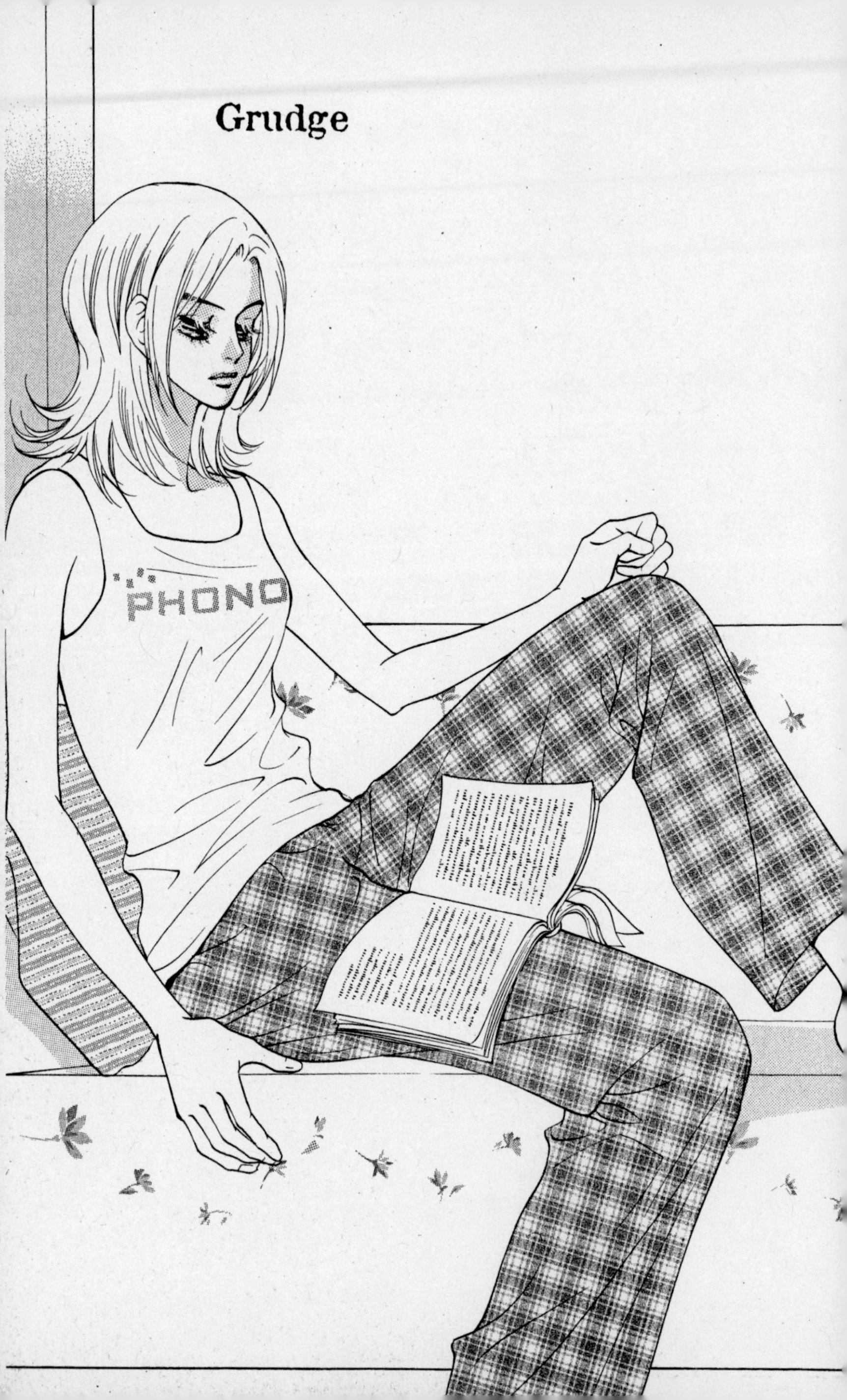
PHONO

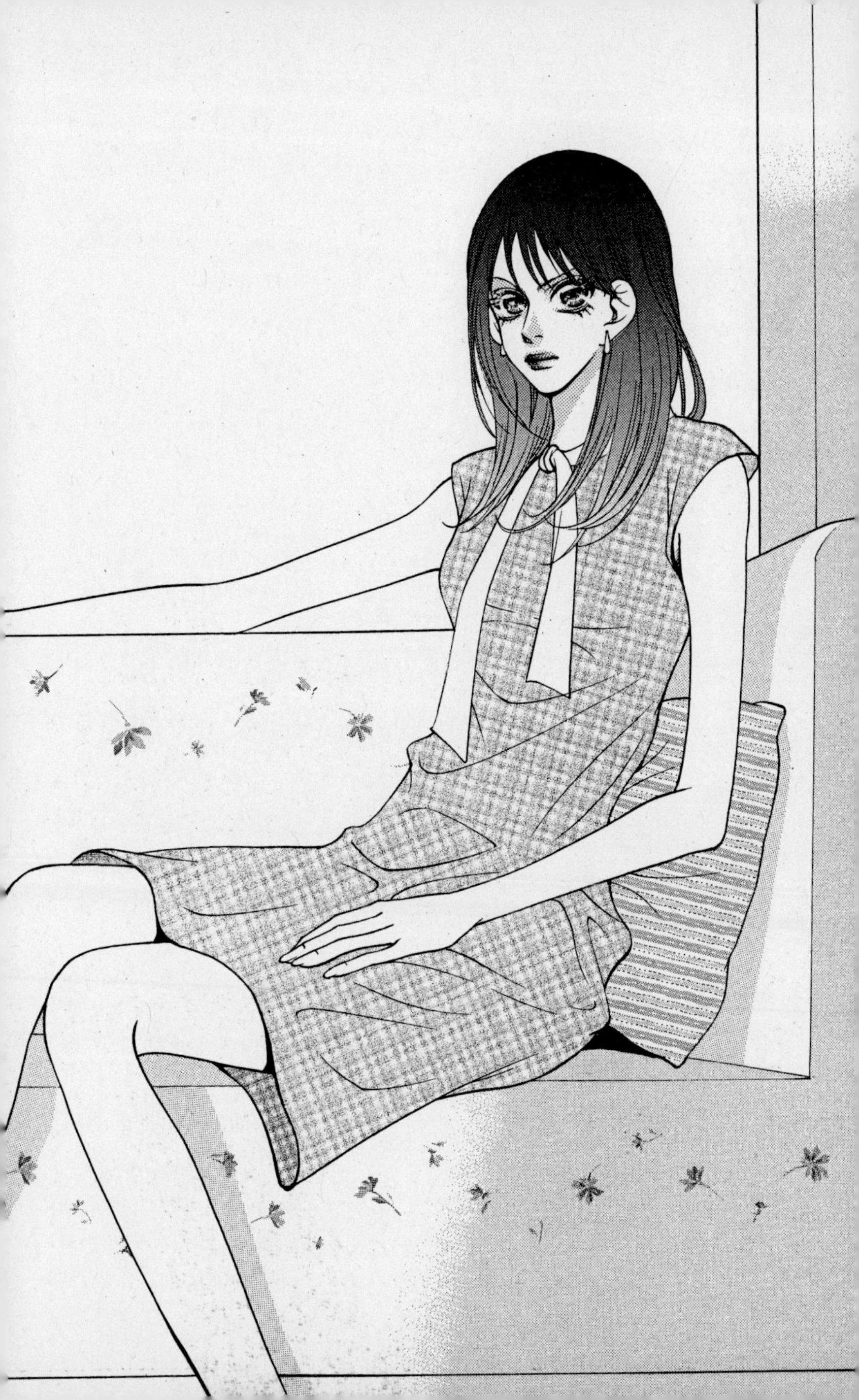

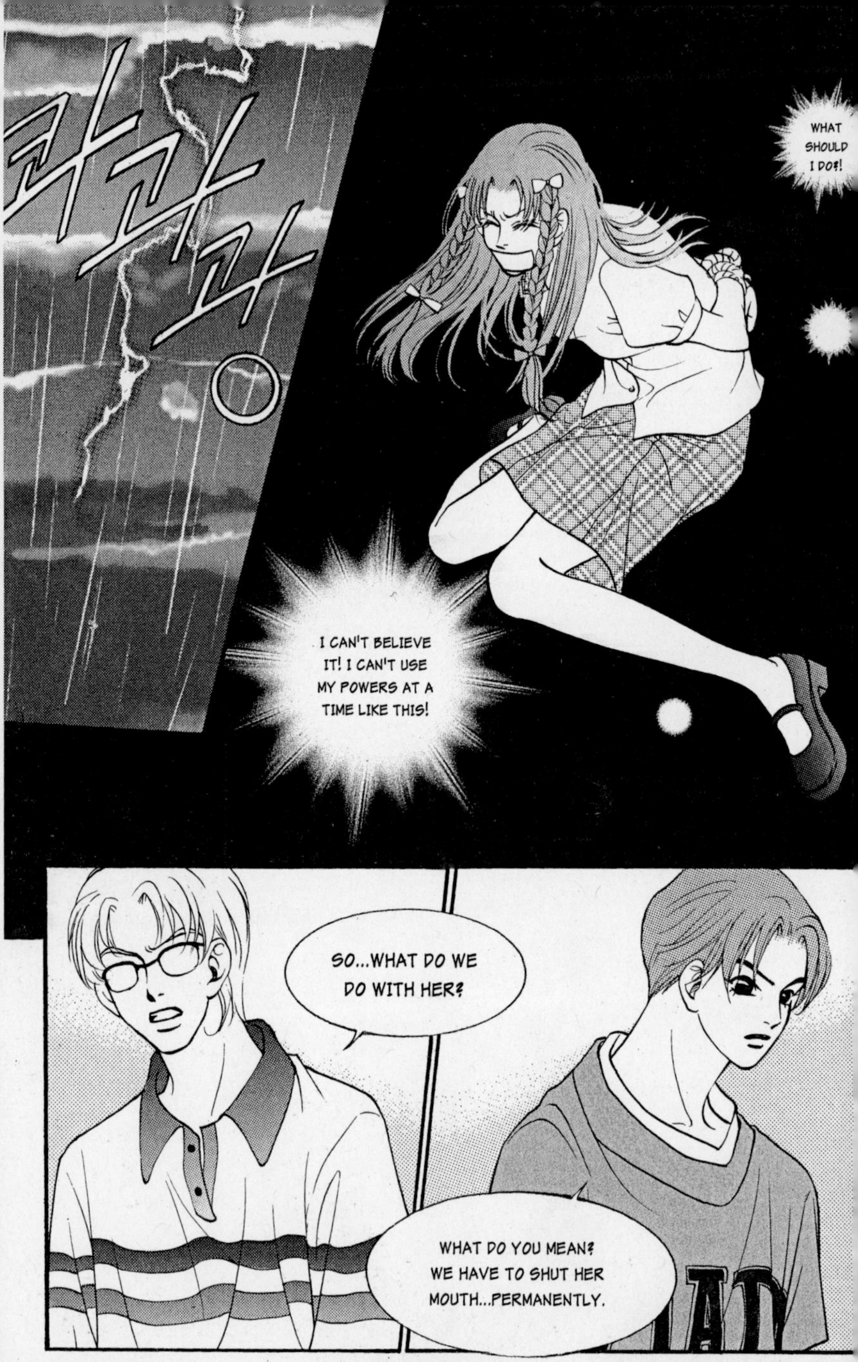
WHAT SHOULD I DO?!
I CAN'T BELIEVE IT! I CAN'T USE MY POWERS AT A TIME LIKE THIS!
SO...WHAT DO WE DO WITH HER?
WHAT DO YOU MEAN? WE HAVE TO SHUT HER MOUTH...PERMANENTLY.

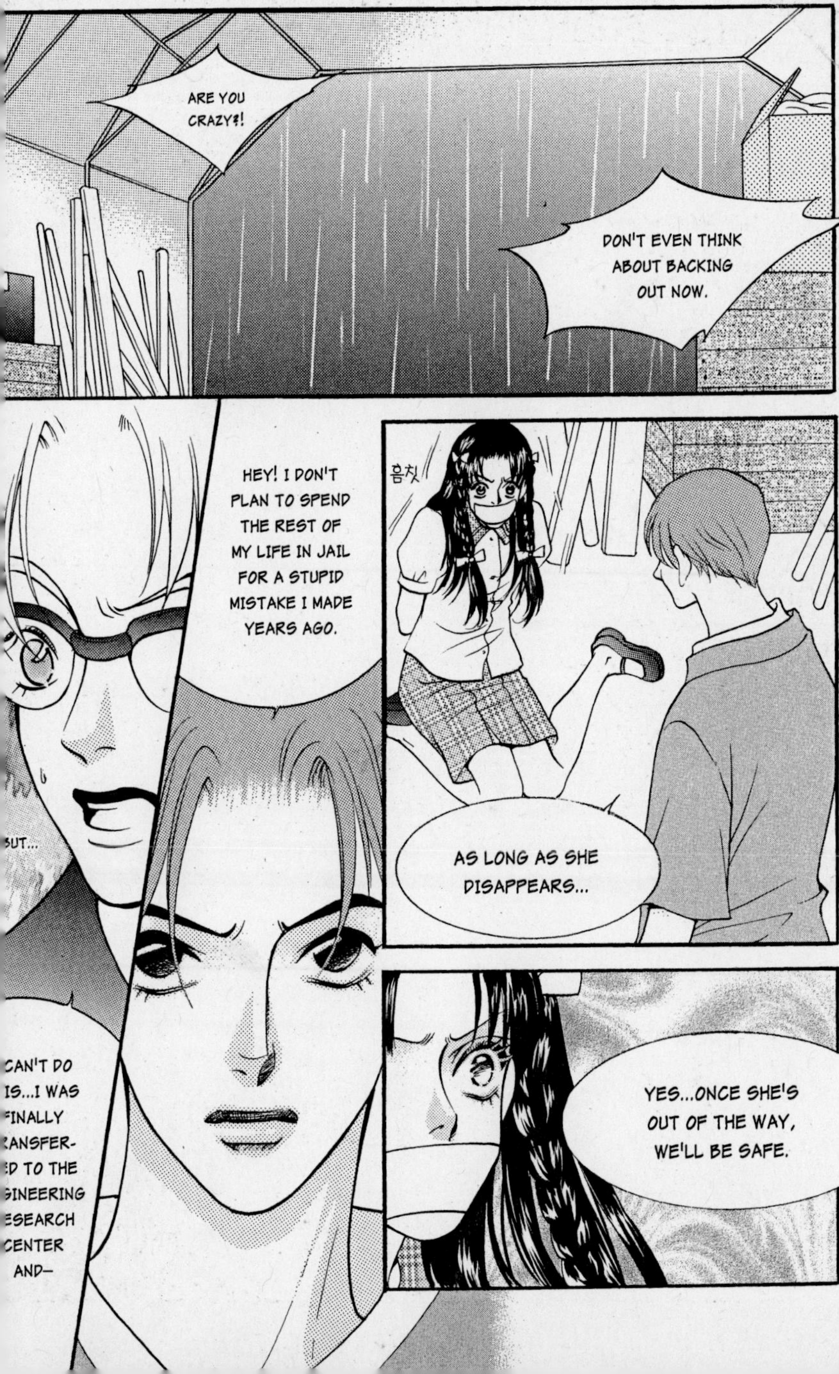
ARE YOU CRAZY?!
DON'T EVEN THINK ABOUT BACKING OUT NOW.
SUT...
CAN'T DO IS...I WAS FINALLY ANSFER-D TO THE GINEERING ESEARCH CENTER AND—
HEY! I DON'T PLAN TO SPEND THE REST OF MY LIFE IN JAIL FOR A STUPID MISTAKE I MADE YEARS AGO.
흠칫
AS LONG AS SHE DISAPPEARS...
YES...ONCE SHE'S OUT OF THE WAY, WE'LL BE SAFE.

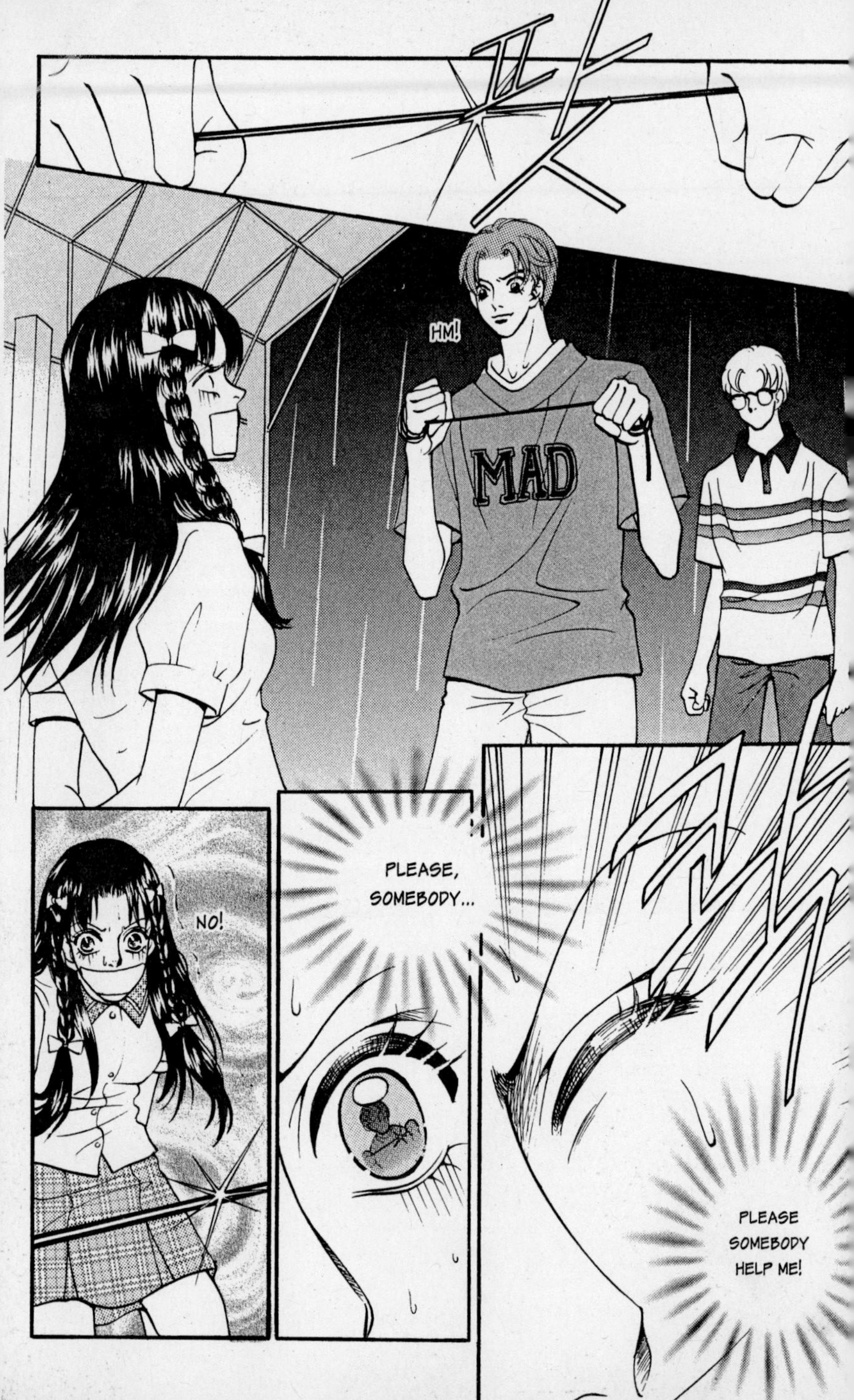
HM!
NO!
PLEASE, SOMEBODY...
PLEASE SOMEBODY HELP ME!

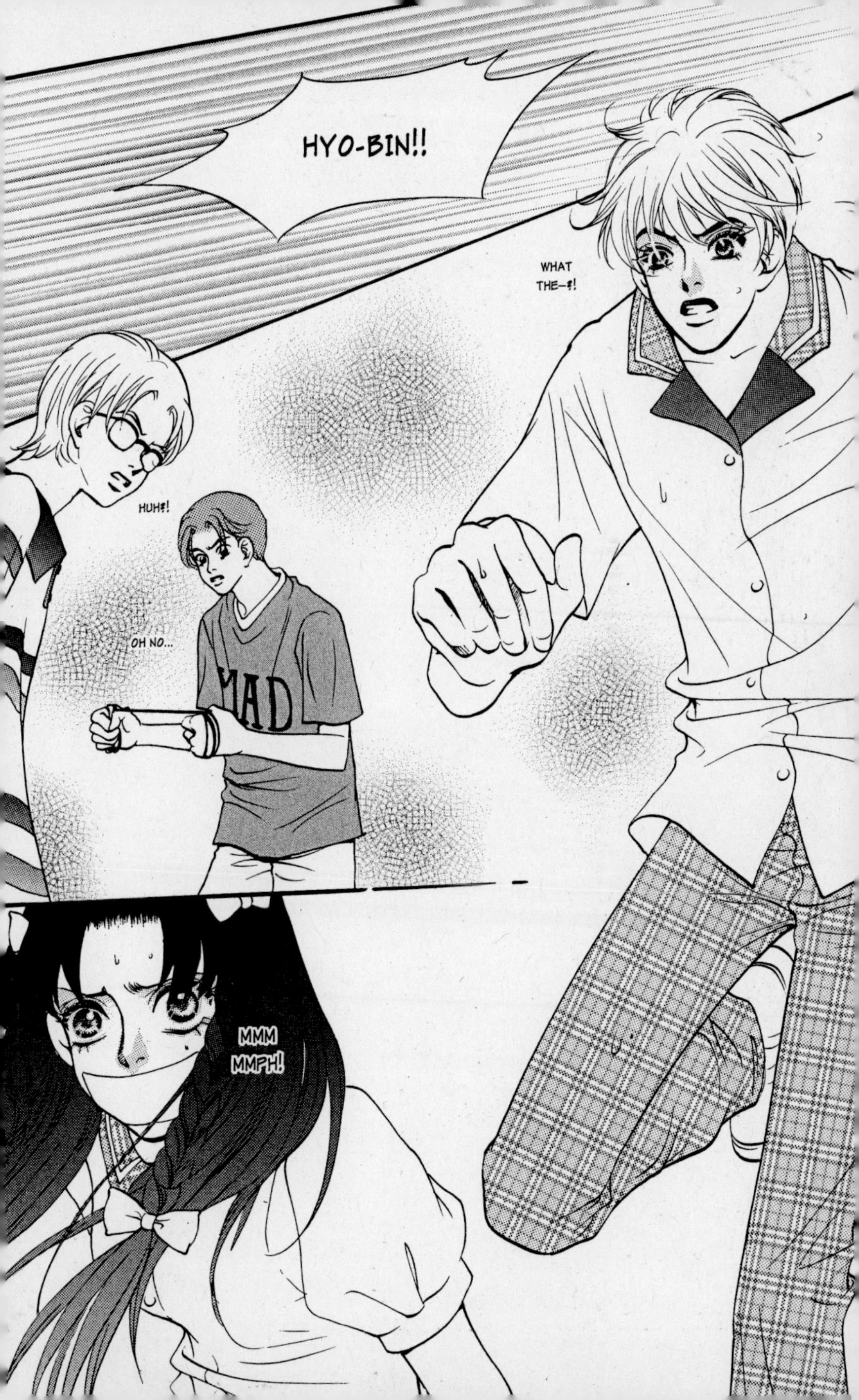
HYO-BIN!!
HUH?!
OH NO...
WHAT THE-?!
MMM MMPH!

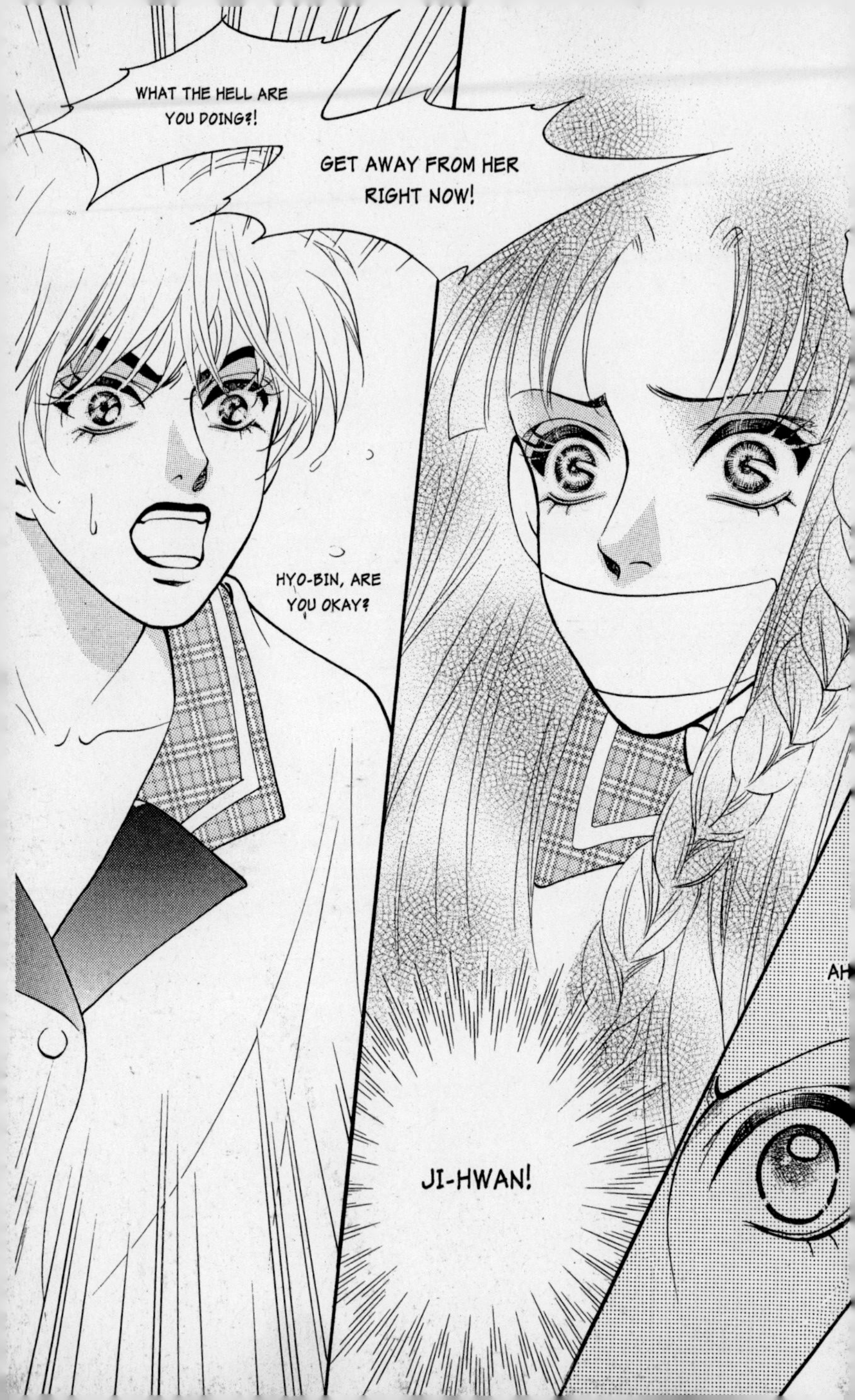
WHAT THE HELL ARE YOU DOING?!
GET AWAY FROM HER RIGHT NOW!
HYO-BIN, ARE YOU OKAY?
JI-HWAN!

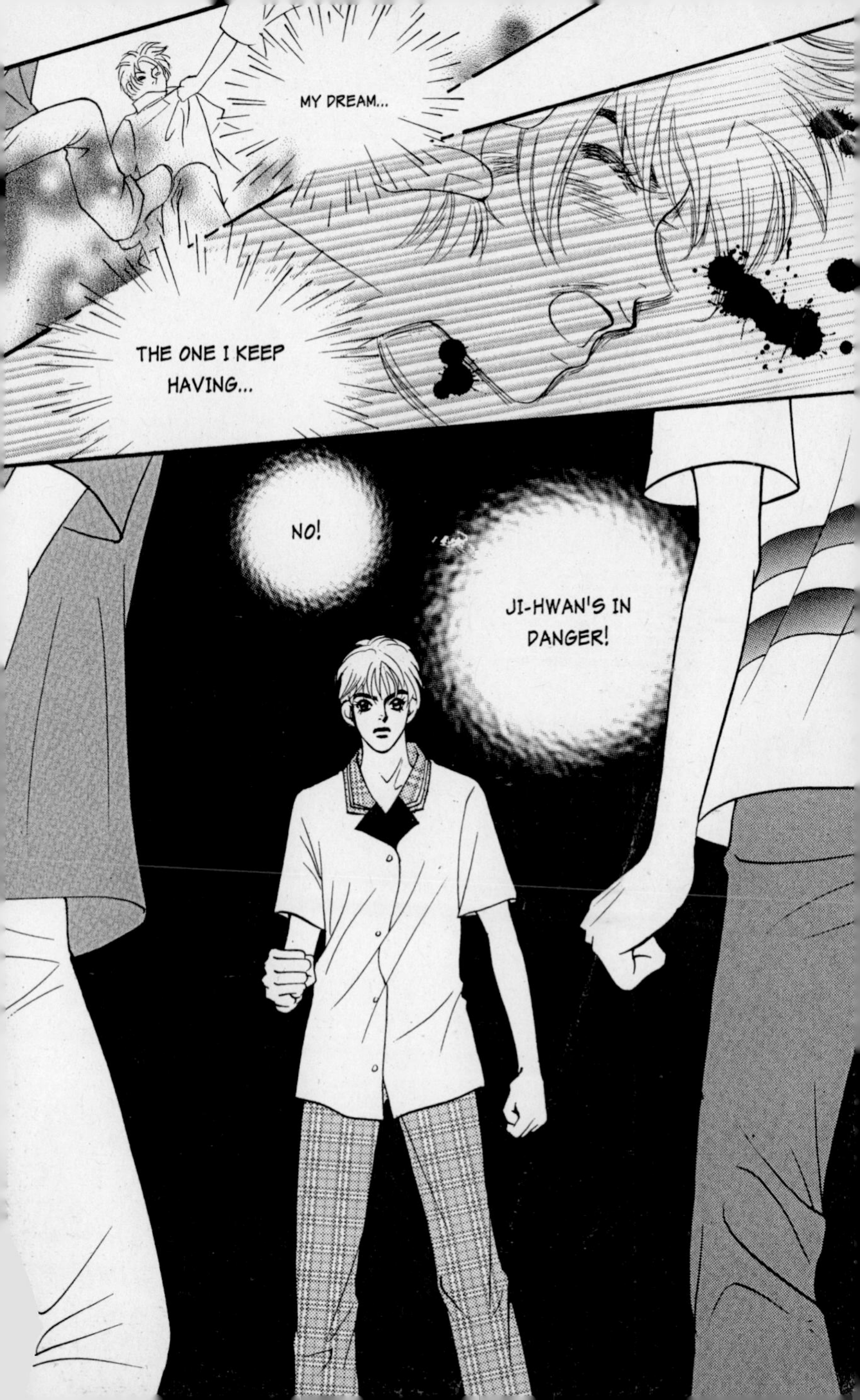
MY DREAM...
THE ONE I KEEP HAVING...
NO!
JI-HWAN'S IN DANGER!

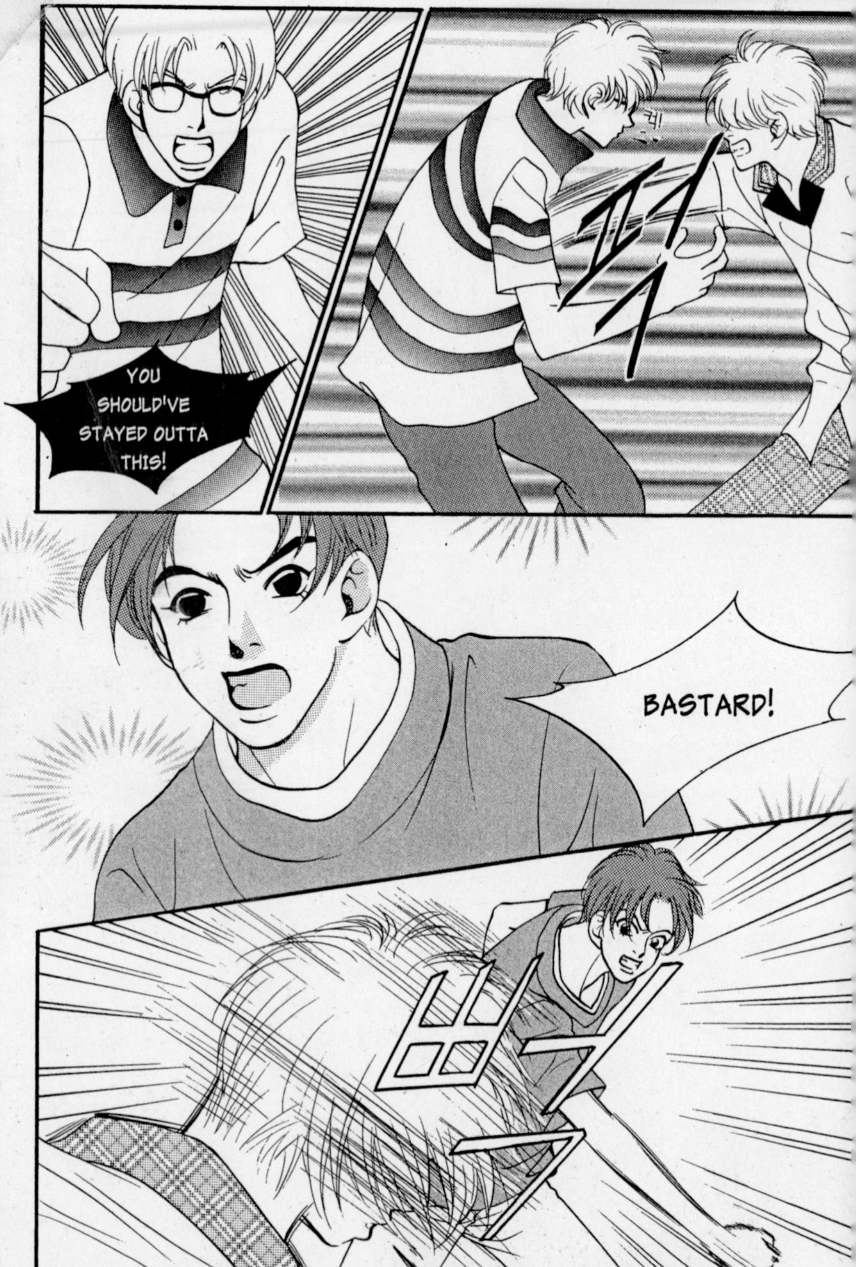
YOU SHOULD'VE STAYED OUTTA THIS!
BASTARD!

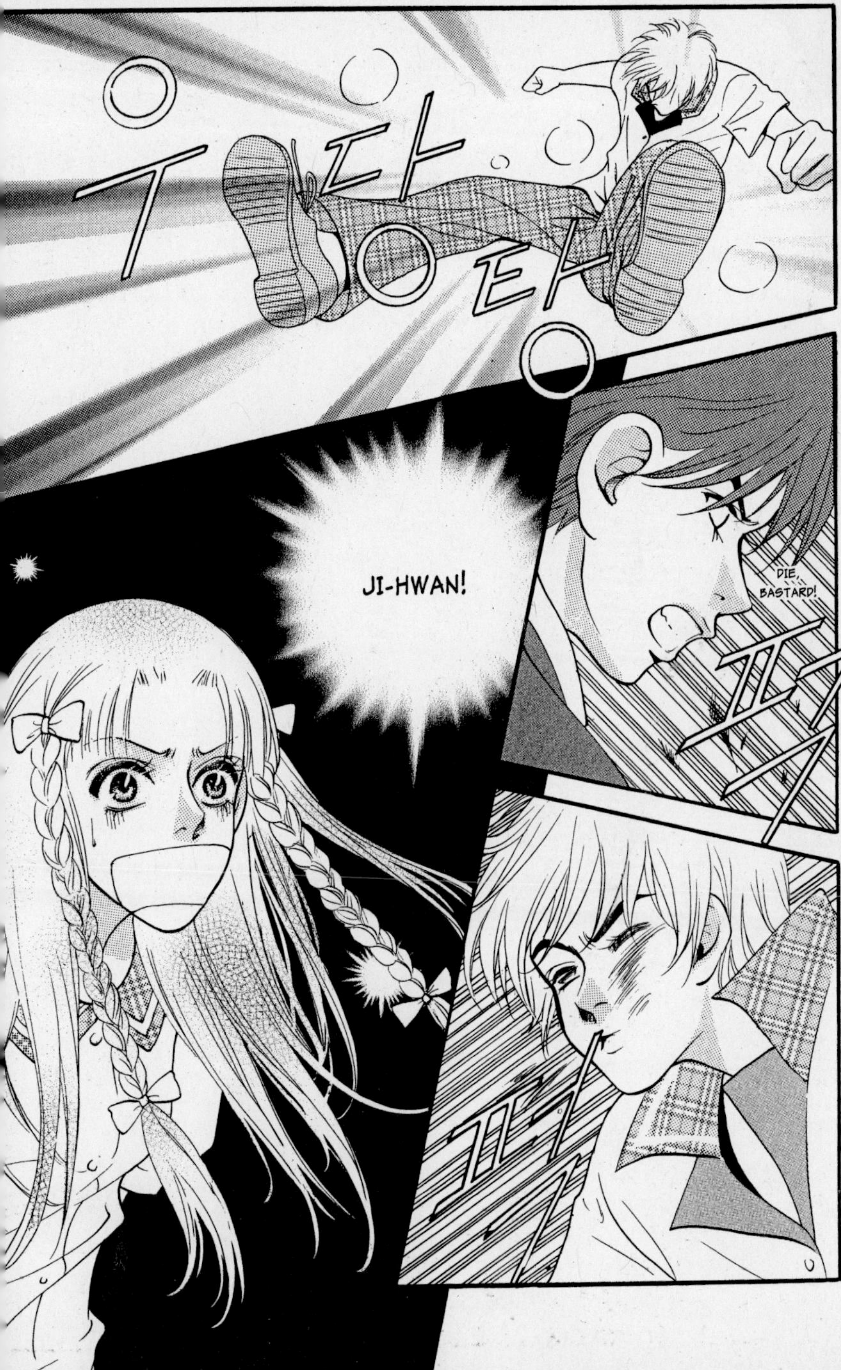
JI-HWAN!
DIE, BASTARD!

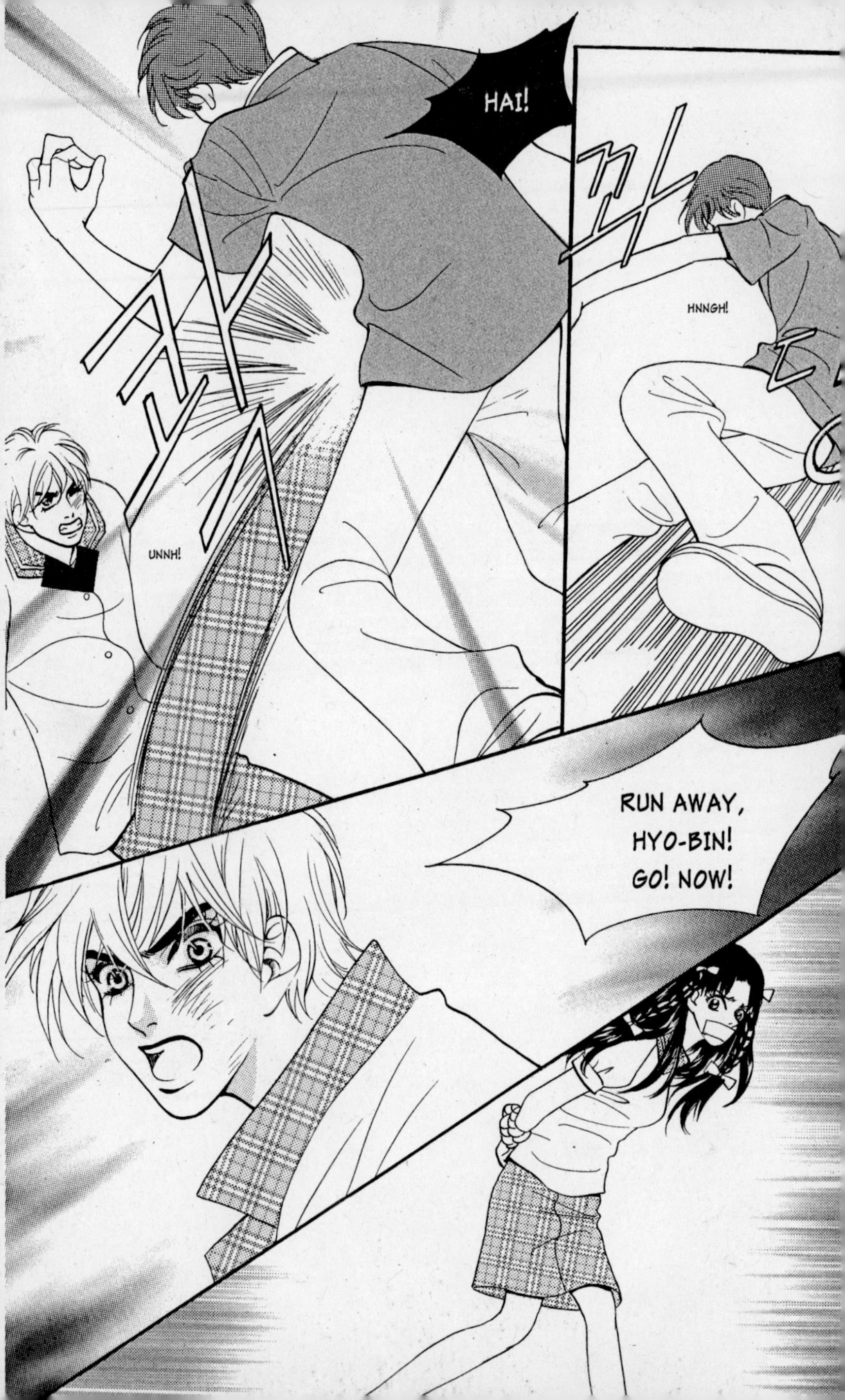
HAI!
UNNH!
HNNGH!
RUN AWAY, HYO-BIN! GO! NOW!

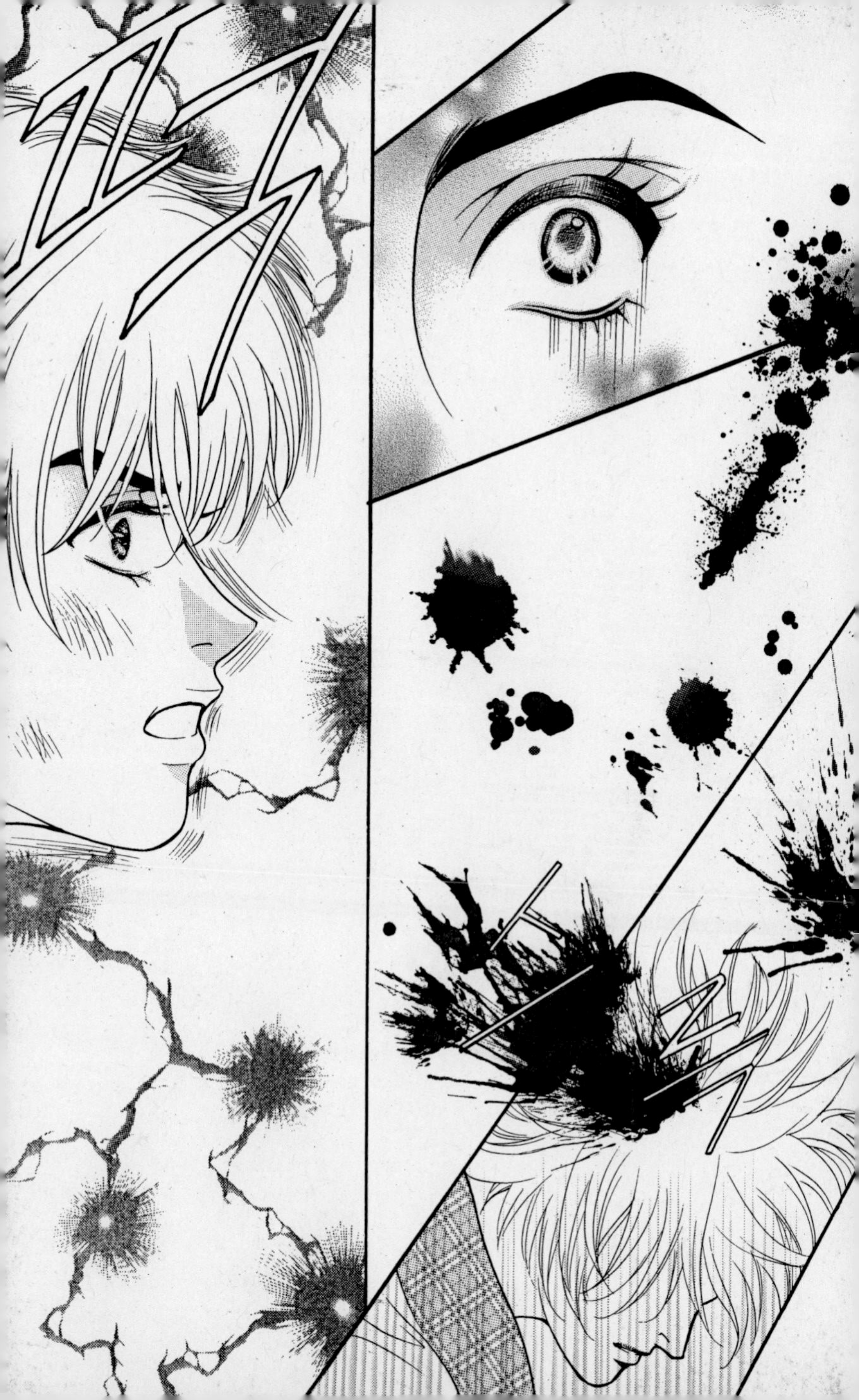

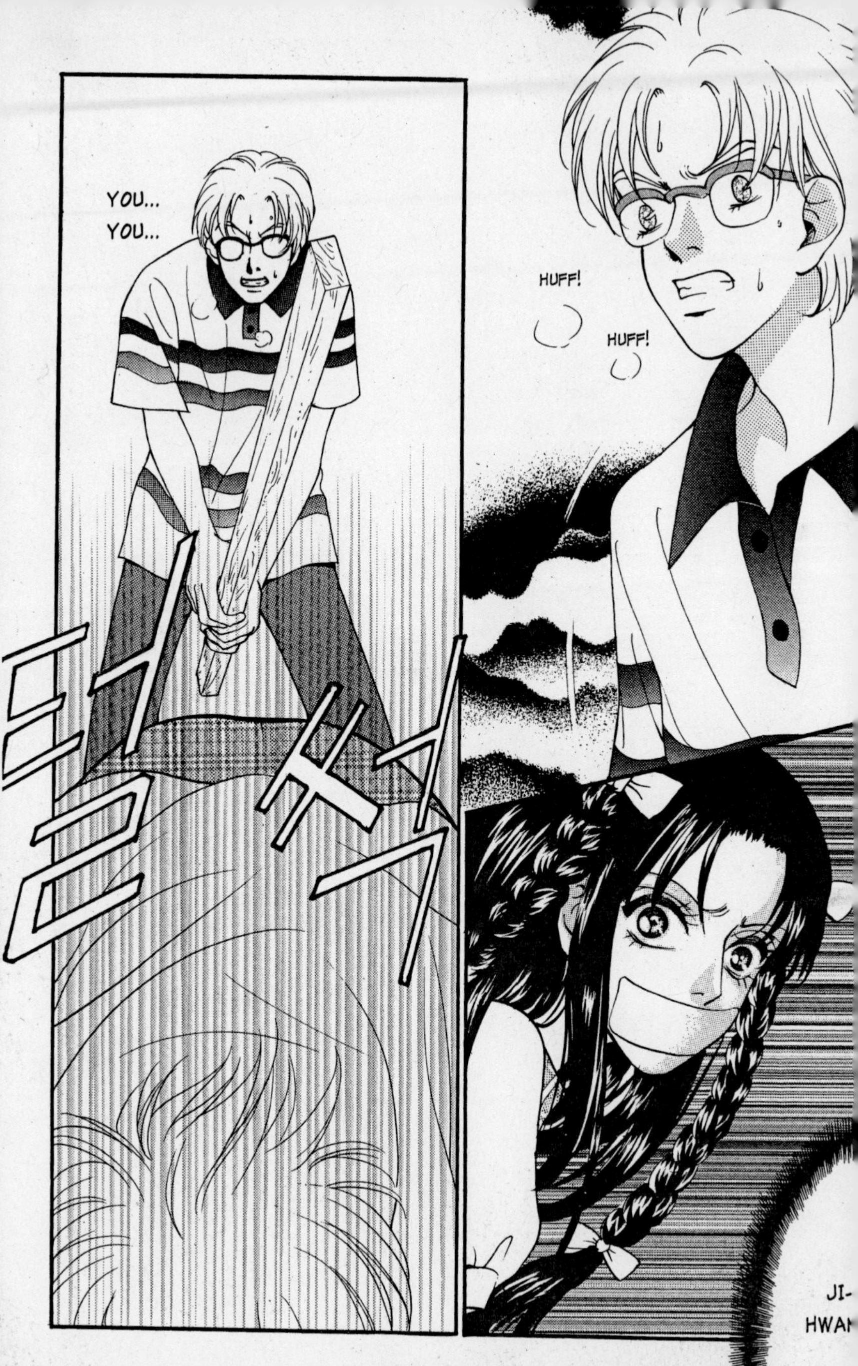
YOU...
YOU...
HUFF!
HUFF!
JI-
HWA

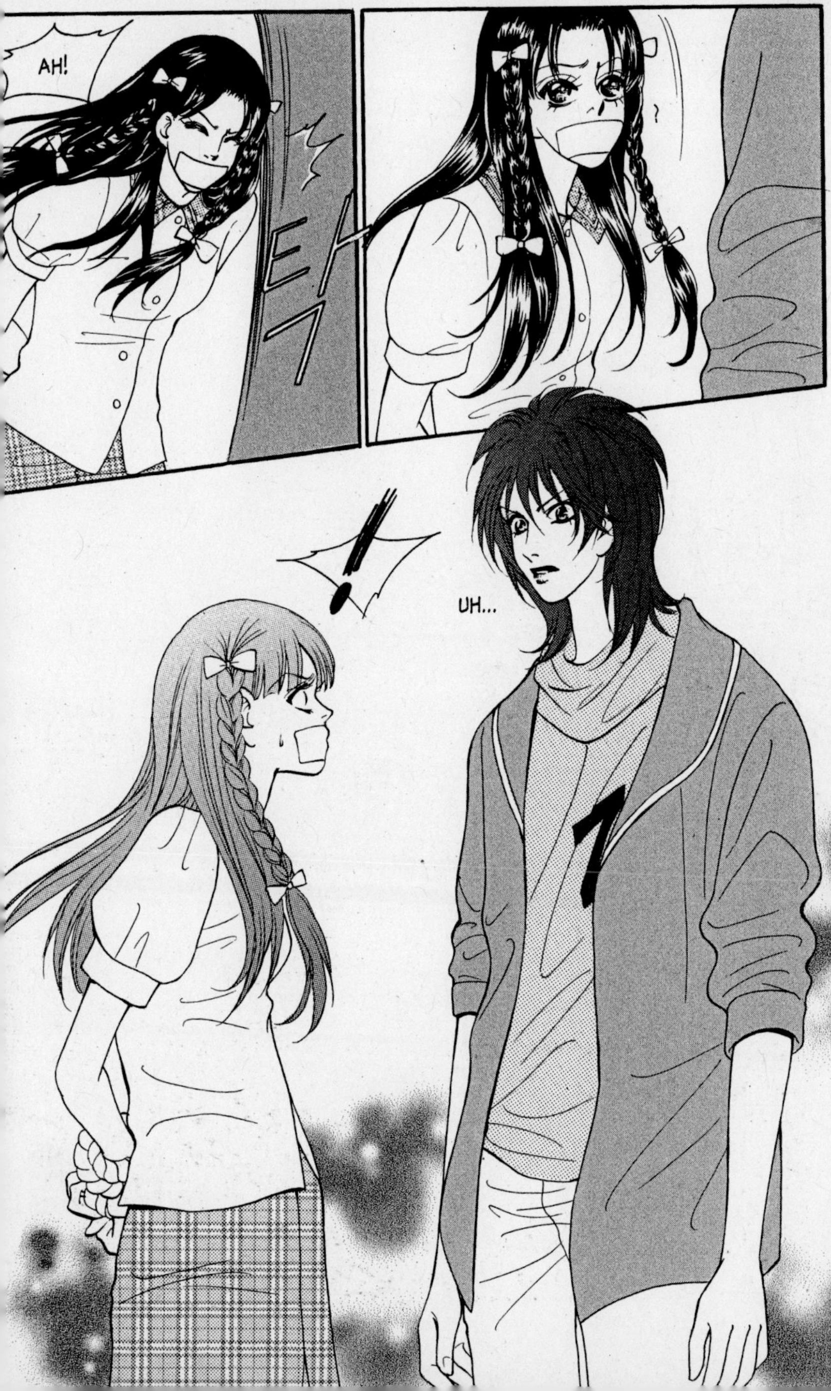
AH!
?
!
UH...

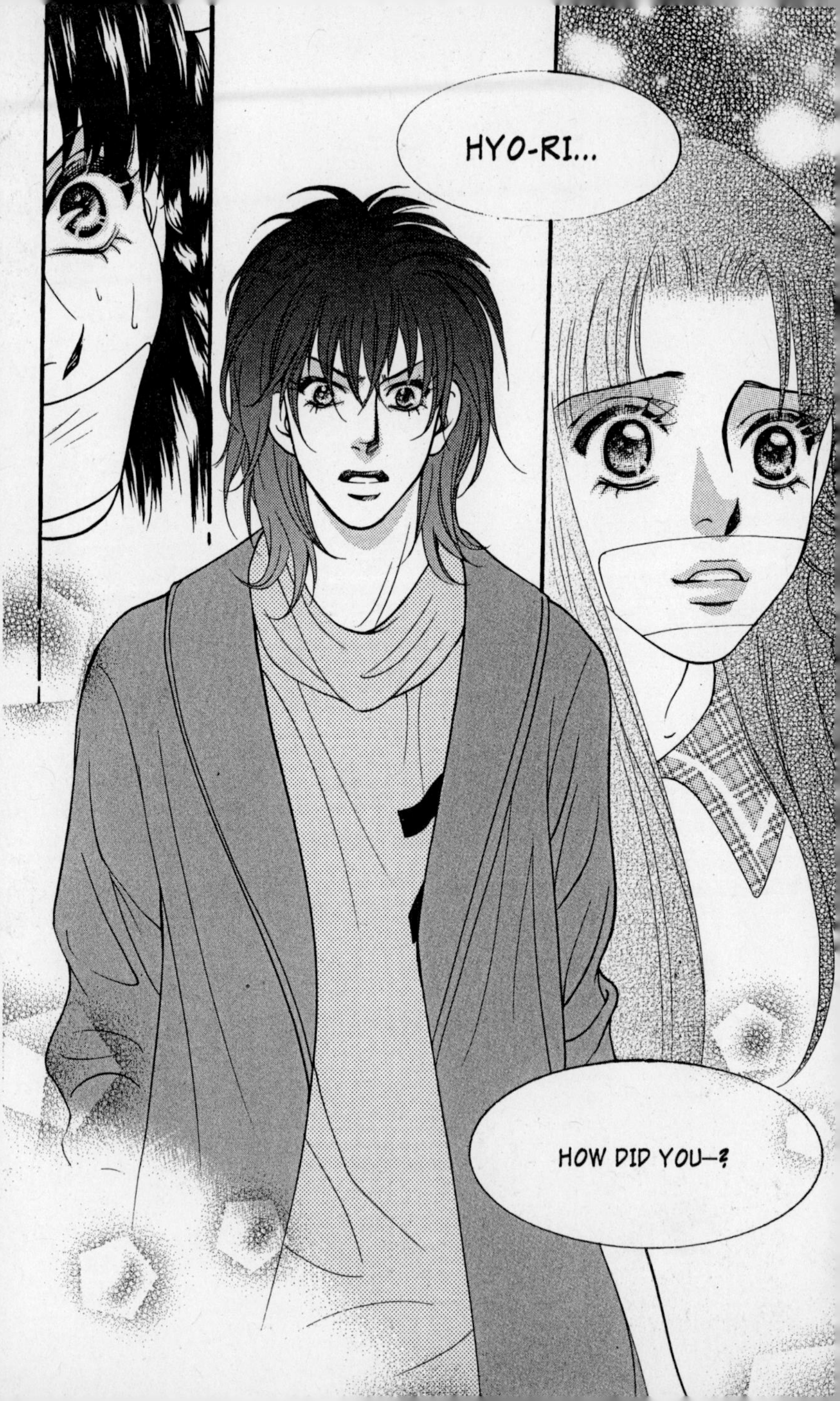
HYO-RI...
HOW DID YOU—?

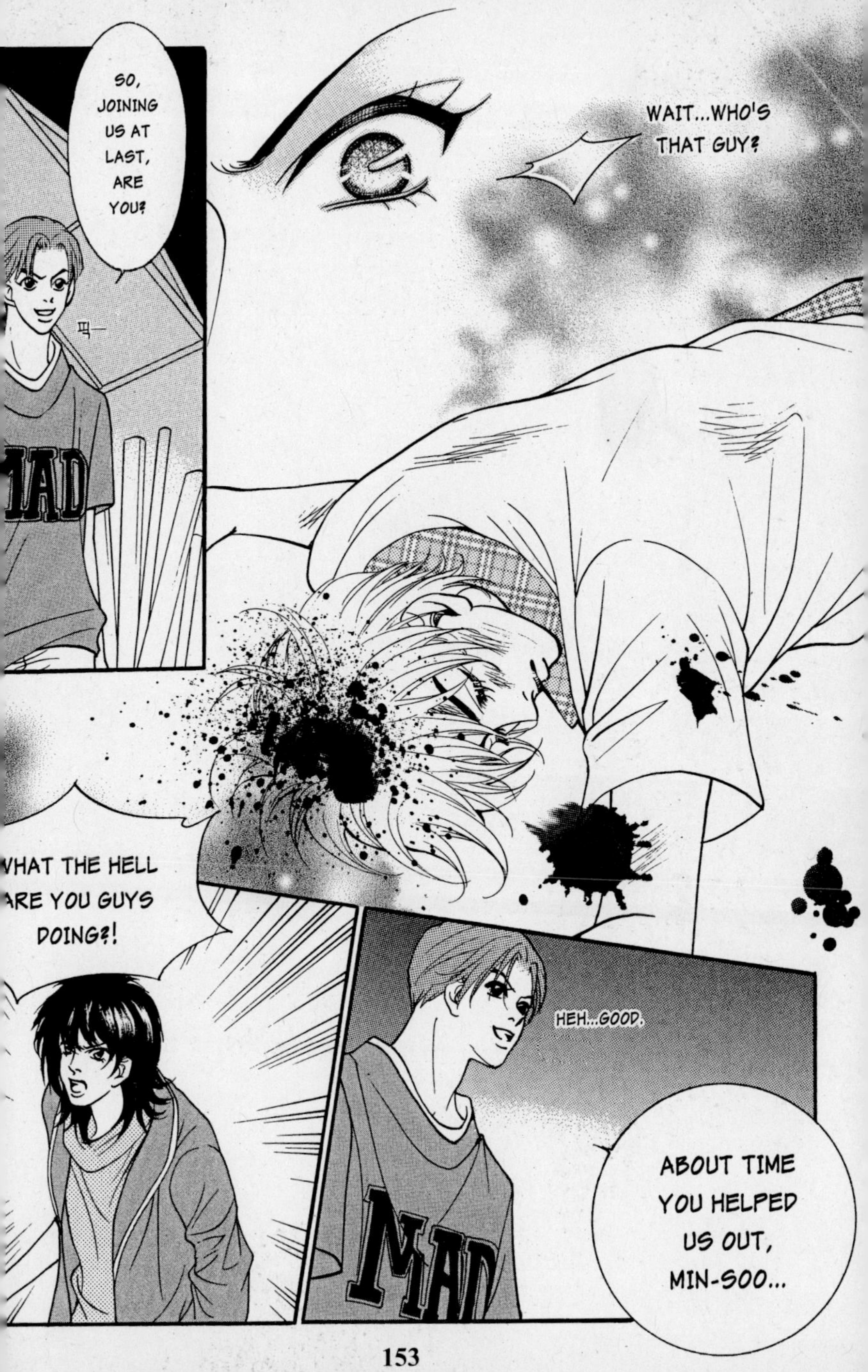
SO, JOINING US AT LAST, ARE YOU?
픽—
WAIT...WHO'S THAT GUY?
WHAT THE HELL ARE YOU GUYS DOING?!
HEH...GOOD.
ABOUT TIME YOU HELPED US OUT, MIN-SOO...

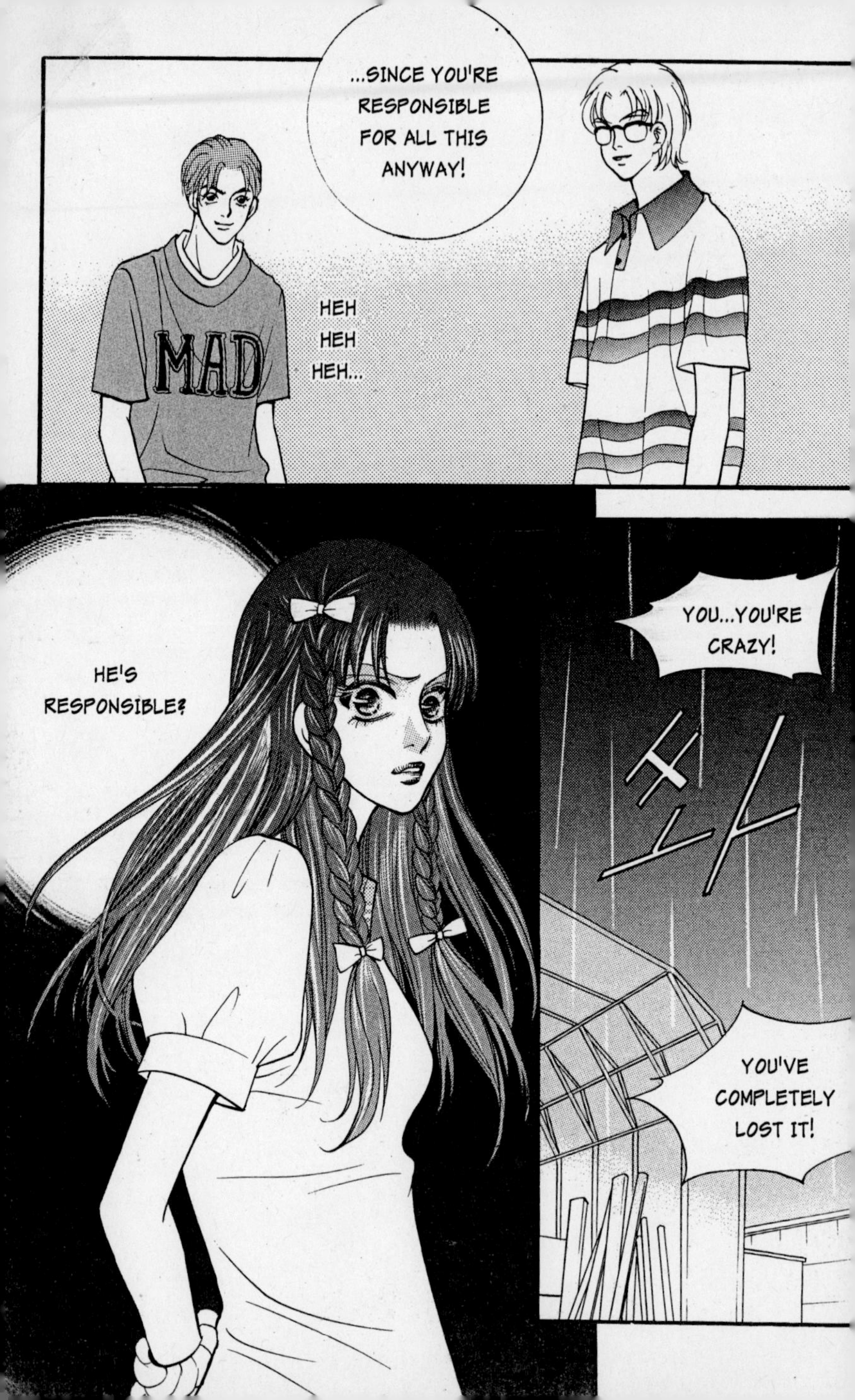
...SINCE YOU'RE RESPONSIBLE FOR ALL THIS ANYWAY!
HEH HEH HEH...
HE'S RESPONSIBLE?
YOU...YOU'RE CRAZY!
YOU'VE COMPLETELY LOST IT!

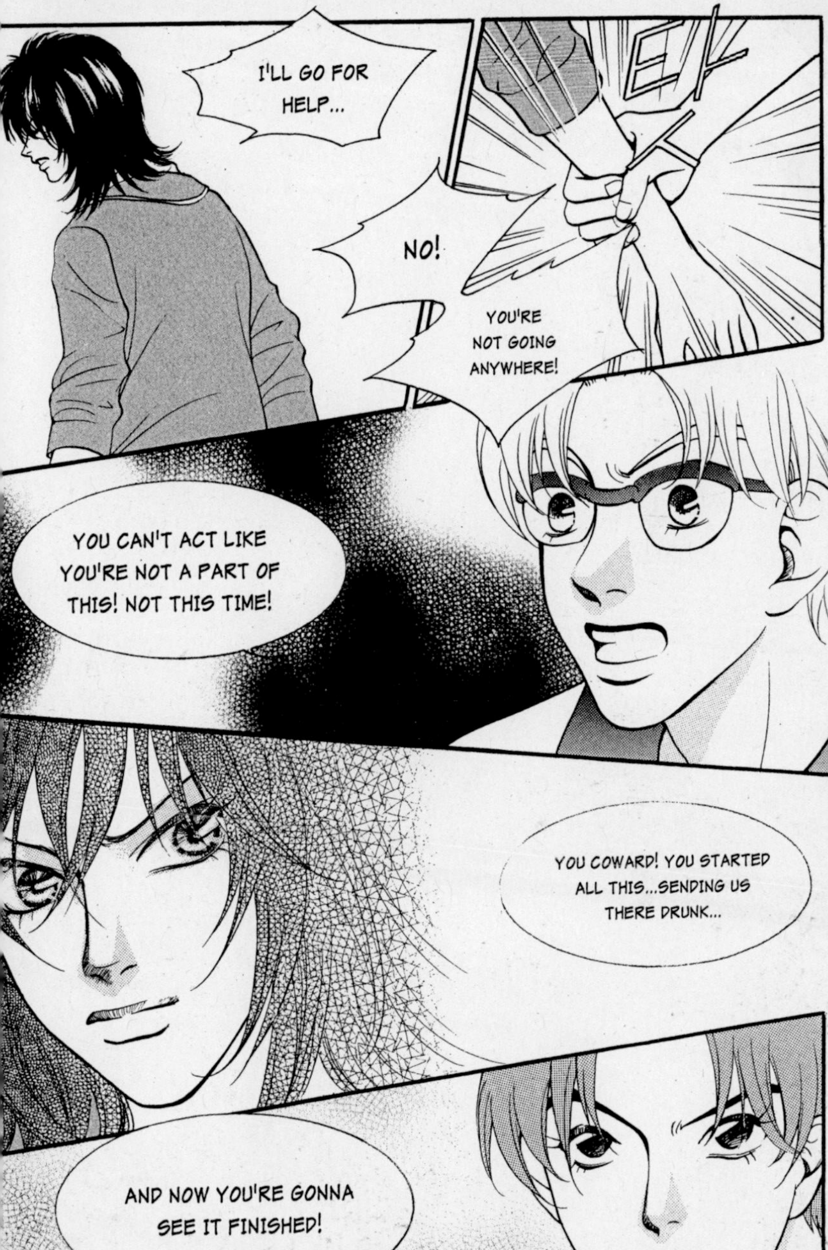
I'LL GO FOR HELP...
NO!
YOU'RE NOT GOING ANYWHERE!
YOU CAN'T ACT LIKE YOU'RE NOT A PART OF THIS! NOT THIS TIME!
YOU COWARD! YOU STARTED ALL THIS...SENDING US THERE DRUNK...
AND NOW YOU'RE GONNA SEE IT FINISHED!
SO THERE!

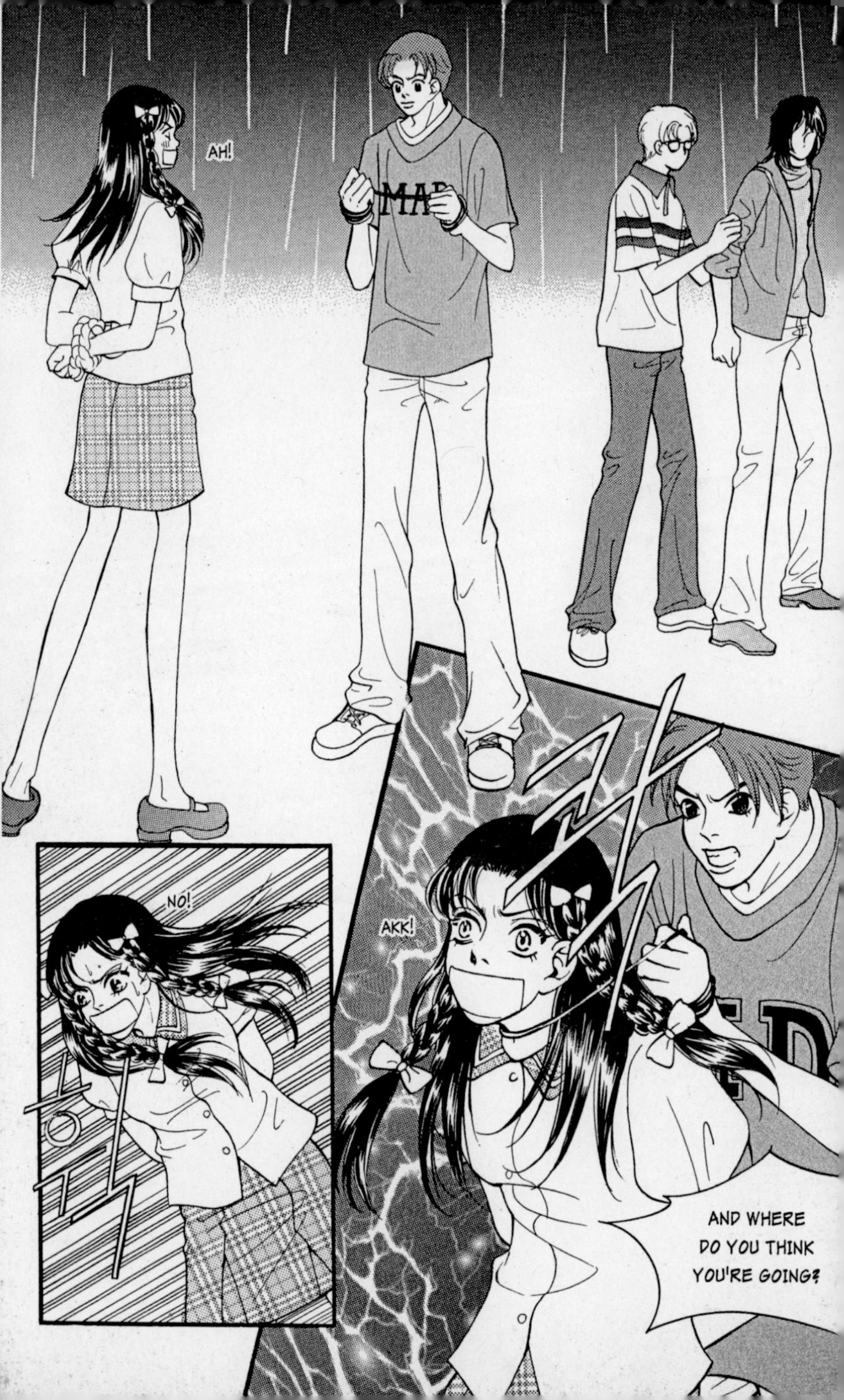
AH!
NO!
AKK!
AND WHERE DO YOU THINK YOU'RE GOING?

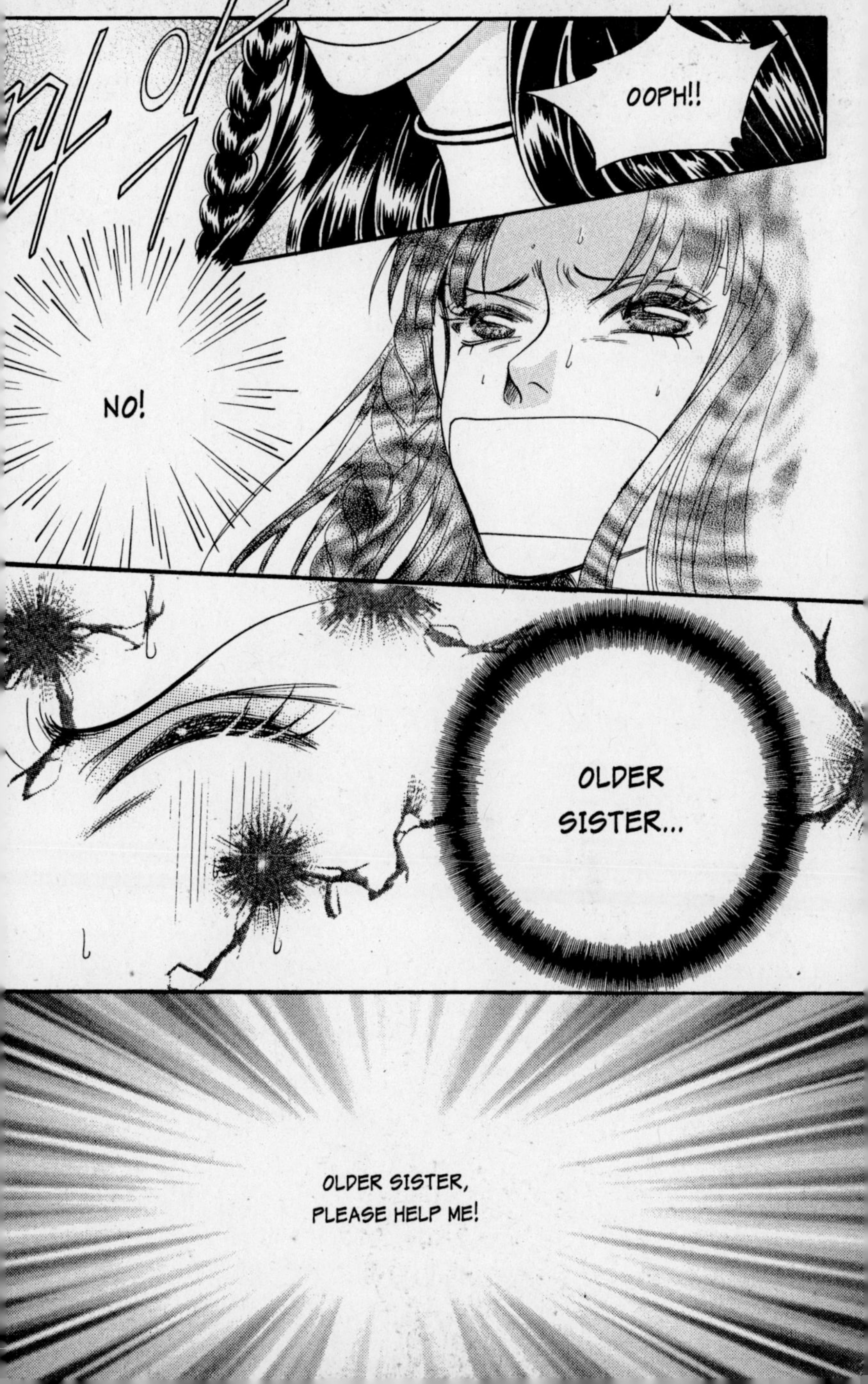
OOPH!!
NO!
OLDER SISTER...
OLDER SISTER, PLEASE HELP ME!

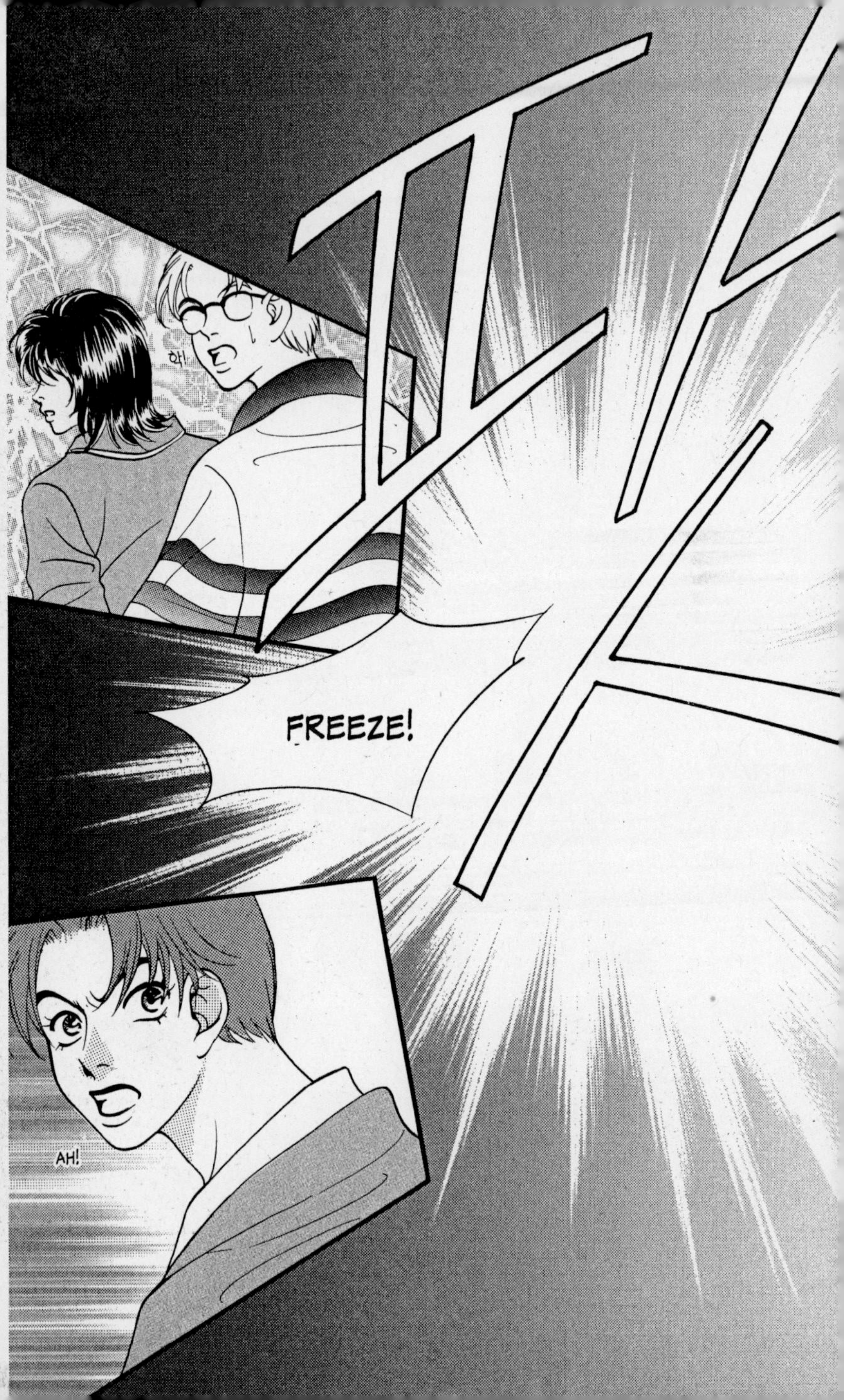
하!
FREEZE!
AH!

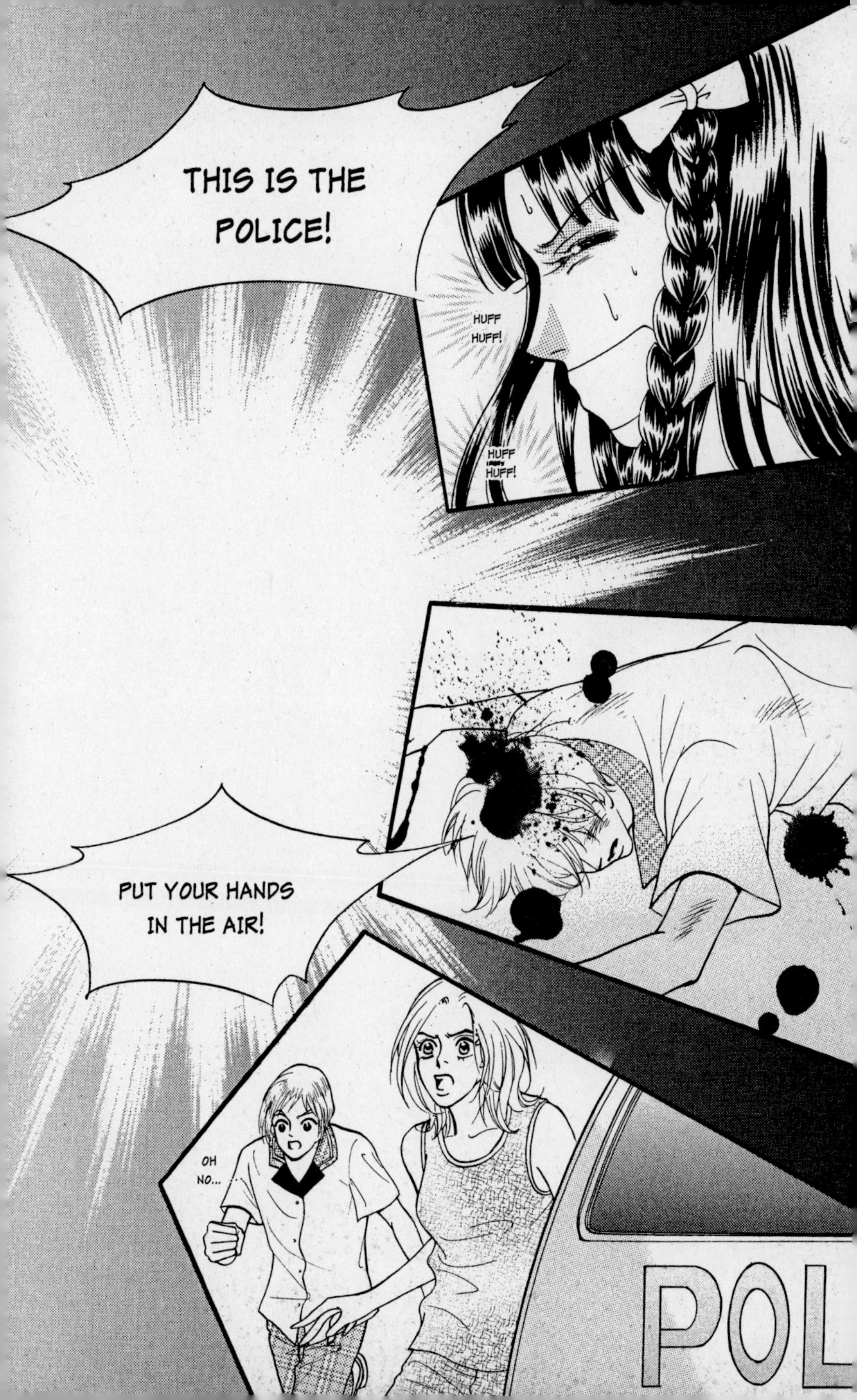
THIS IS THE POLICE!
HUFF HUFF!
HUFF HUFF!
PUT YOUR HANDS IN THE AIR!
OH NO...
POL

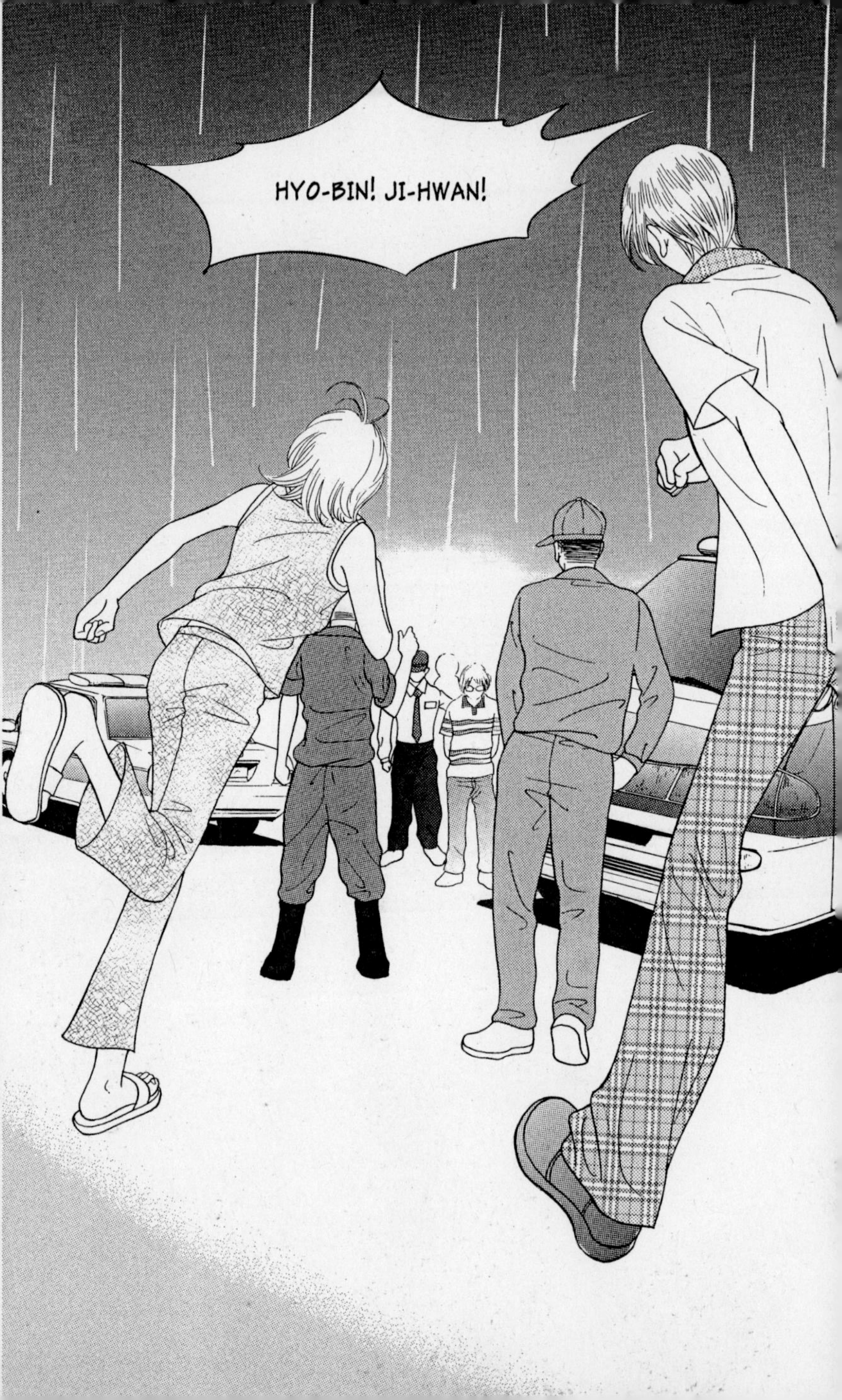
HYO-BIN! JI-HWAN!

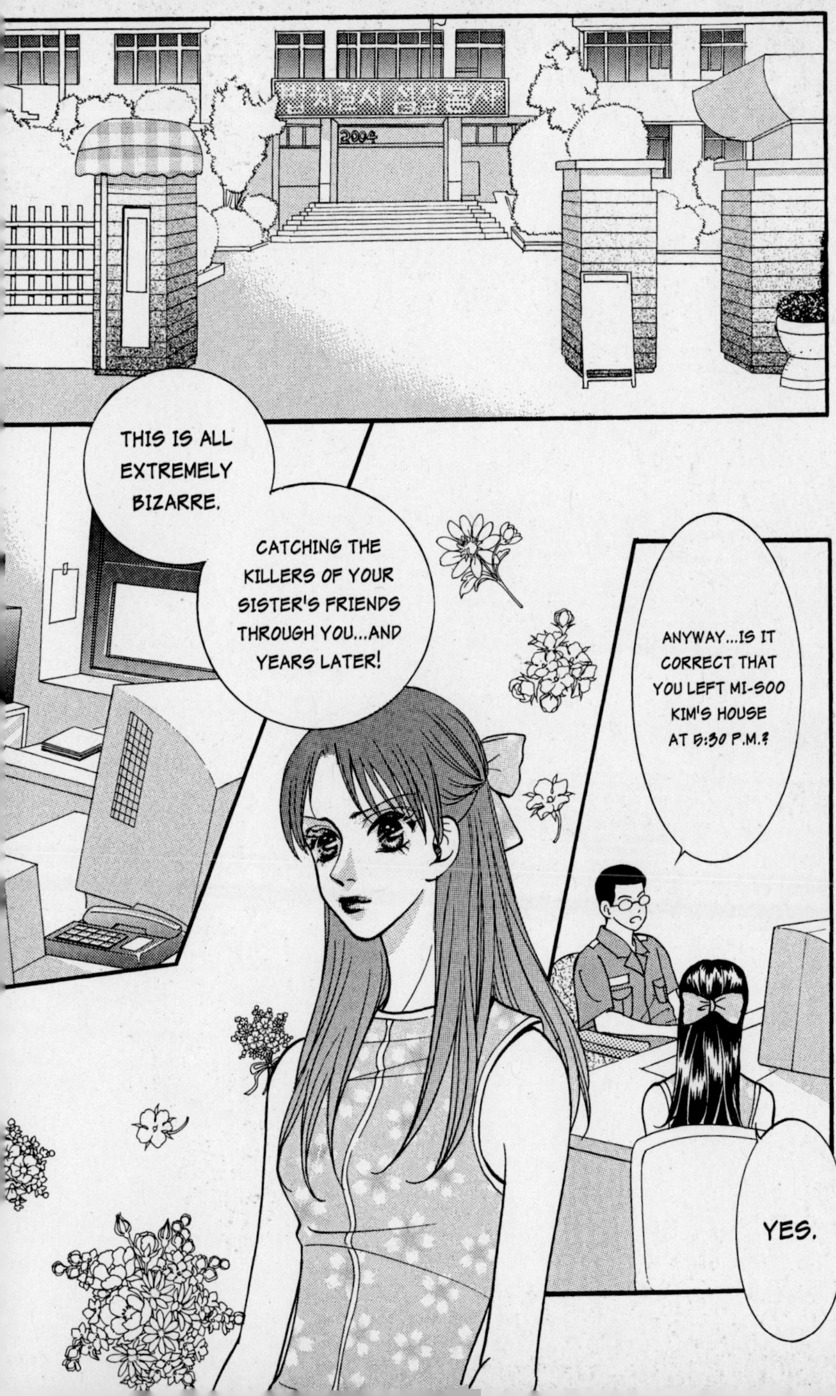

THIS IS ALL EXTREMELY BIZARRE.
CATCHING THE KILLERS OF YOUR SISTER'S FRIENDS THROUGH YOU...AND YEARS LATER!
ANYWAY...IS IT CORRECT THAT YOU LEFT MI-SOO KIM'S HOUSE AT 5:30 P.M.?
YES.

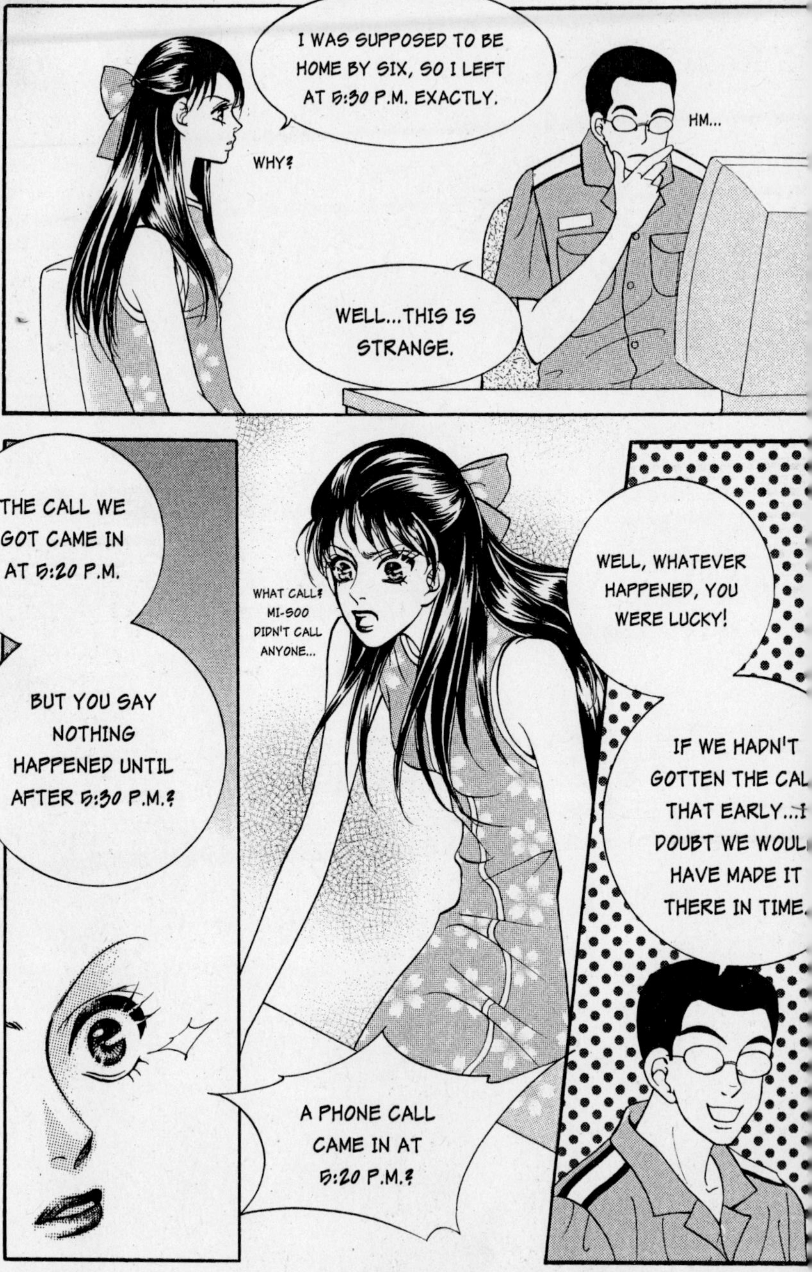
I WAS SUPPOSED TO BE HOME BY SIX, SO I LEFT AT 5:30 P.M. EXACTLY.
HM...
WHY?
WELL...THIS IS STRANGE.
THE CALL WE GOT CAME IN AT 5:20 P.M.
BUT YOU SAY NOTHING HAPPENED UNTIL AFTER 5:30 P.M.?
WHAT CALL? MI-SOO DIDN'T CALL ANYONE...
A PHONE CALL CAME IN AT 5:20 P.M.?
WELL, WHATEVER HAPPENED, YOU WERE LUCKY!
IF WE HADN'T GOTTEN THE CAL THAT EARLY...I DOUBT WE WOUL HAVE MADE IT THERE IN TIME.

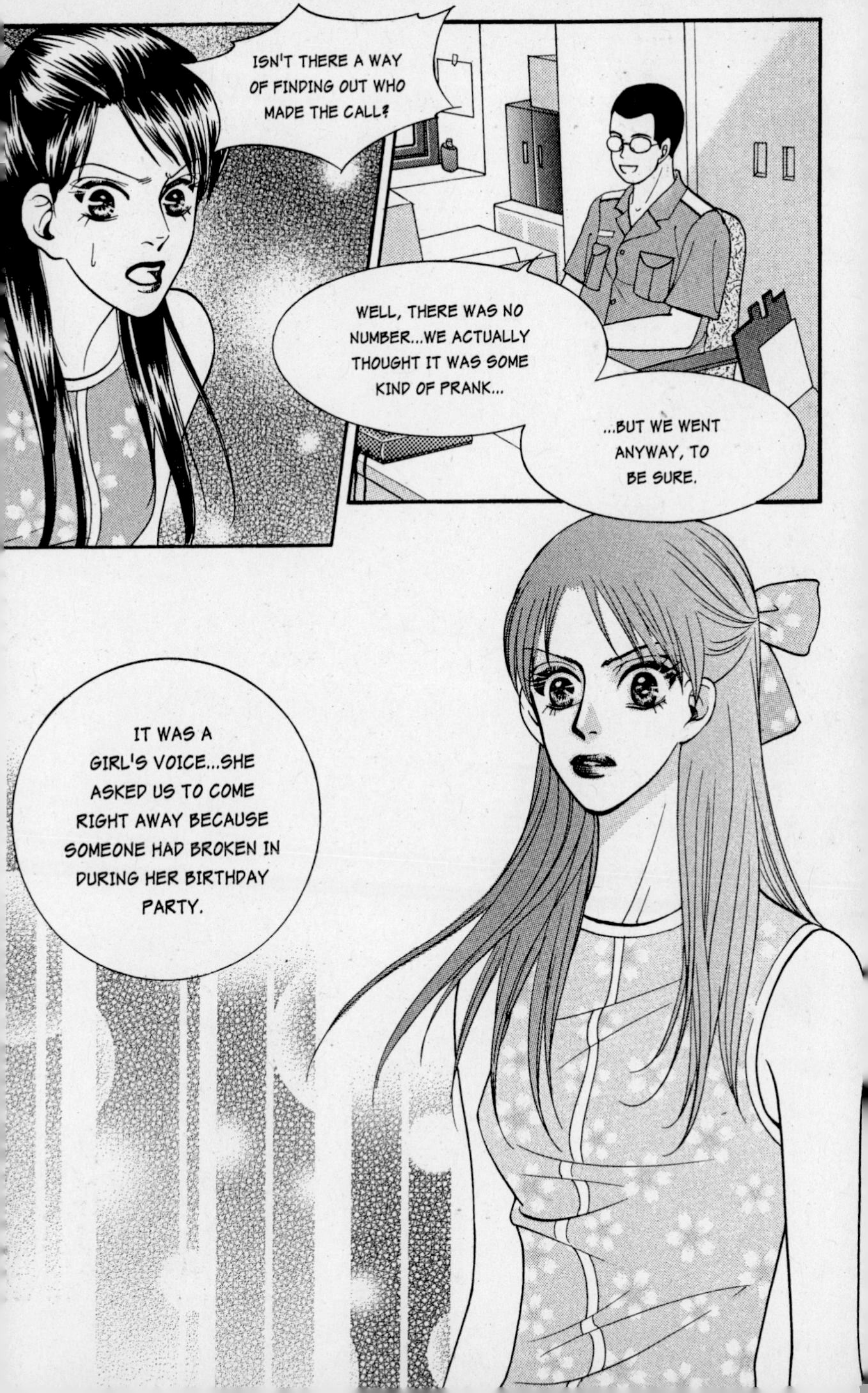
ISN'T THERE A WAY OF FINDING OUT WHO MADE THE CALL?
WELL, THERE WAS NO NUMBER...WE ACTUALLY THOUGHT IT WAS SOME KIND OF PRANK...
...BUT WE WENT ANYWAY, TO BE SURE.
IT WAS A GIRL'S VOICE...SHE ASKED US TO COME RIGHT AWAY BECAUSE SOMEONE HAD BROKEN IN DURING HER BIRTHDAY PARTY.

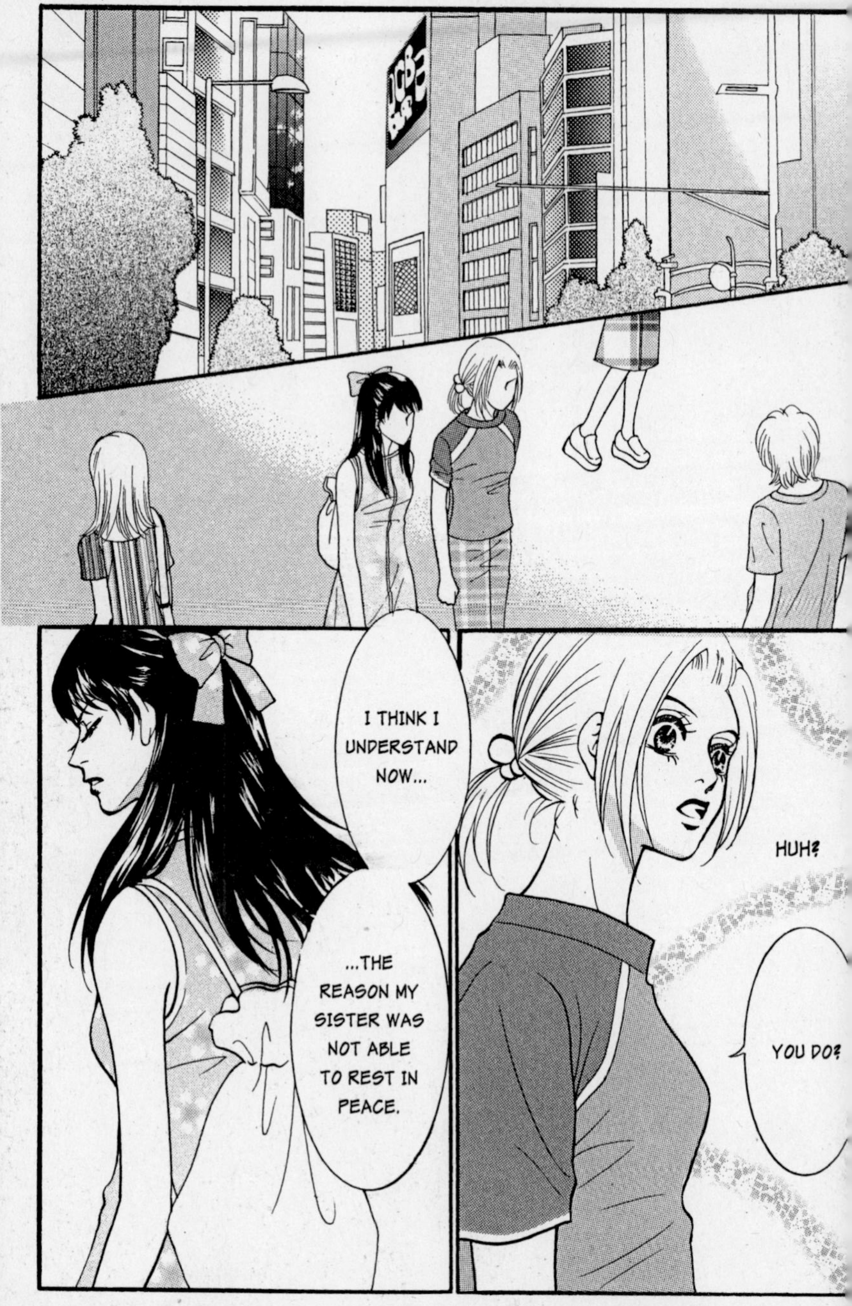
I THINK I UNDERSTAND NOW...
...THE REASON MY SISTER WAS NOT ABLE TO REST IN PEACE.
HUH?
YOU DO?

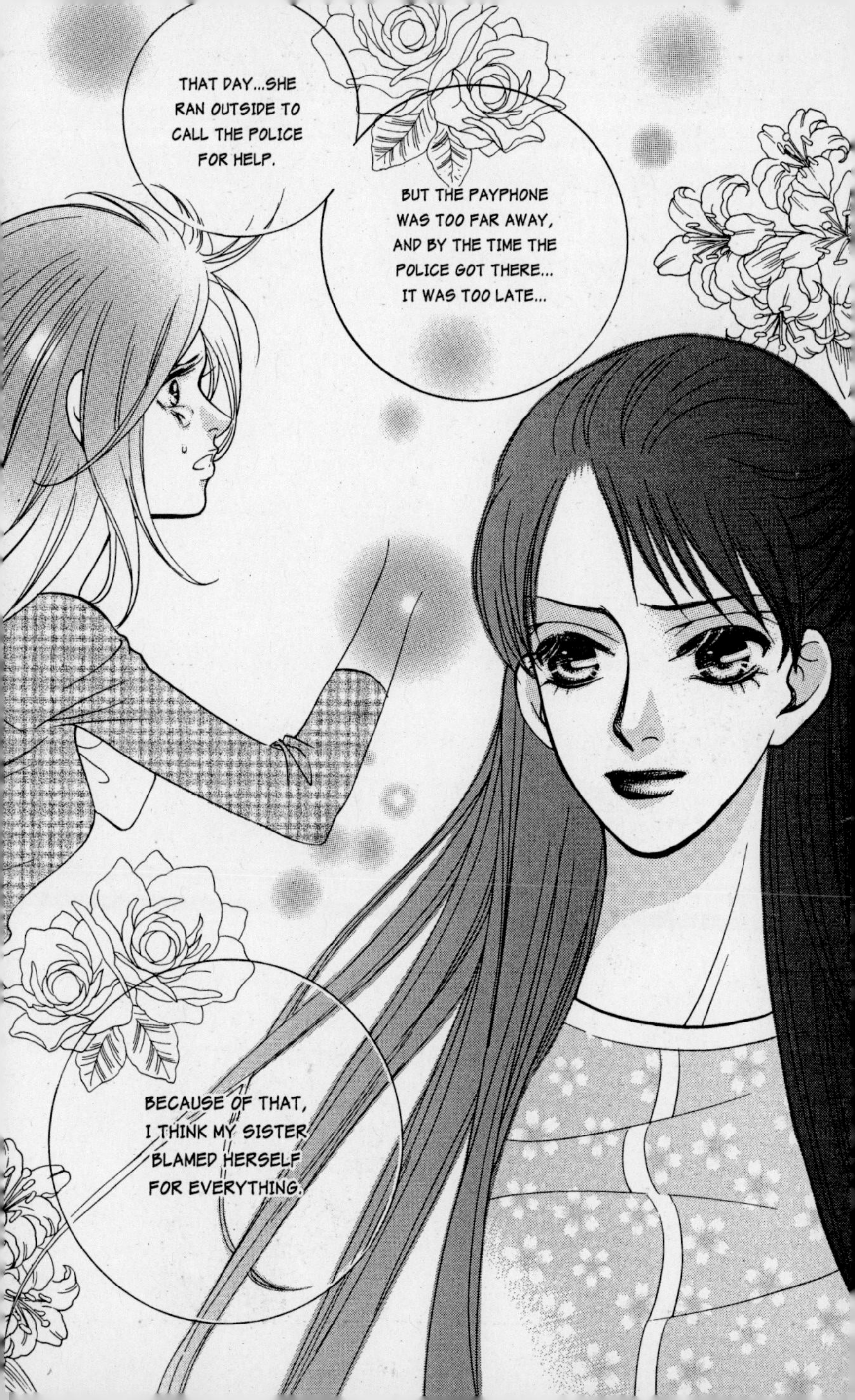
THAT DAY...SHE RAN OUTSIDE TO CALL THE POLICE FOR HELP.
BUT THE PAYPHONE WAS TOO FAR AWAY, AND BY THE TIME THE POLICE GOT THERE... IT WAS TOO LATE...
BECAUSE OF THAT, I THINK MY SISTER BLAMED HERSELF FOR EVERYTHING.

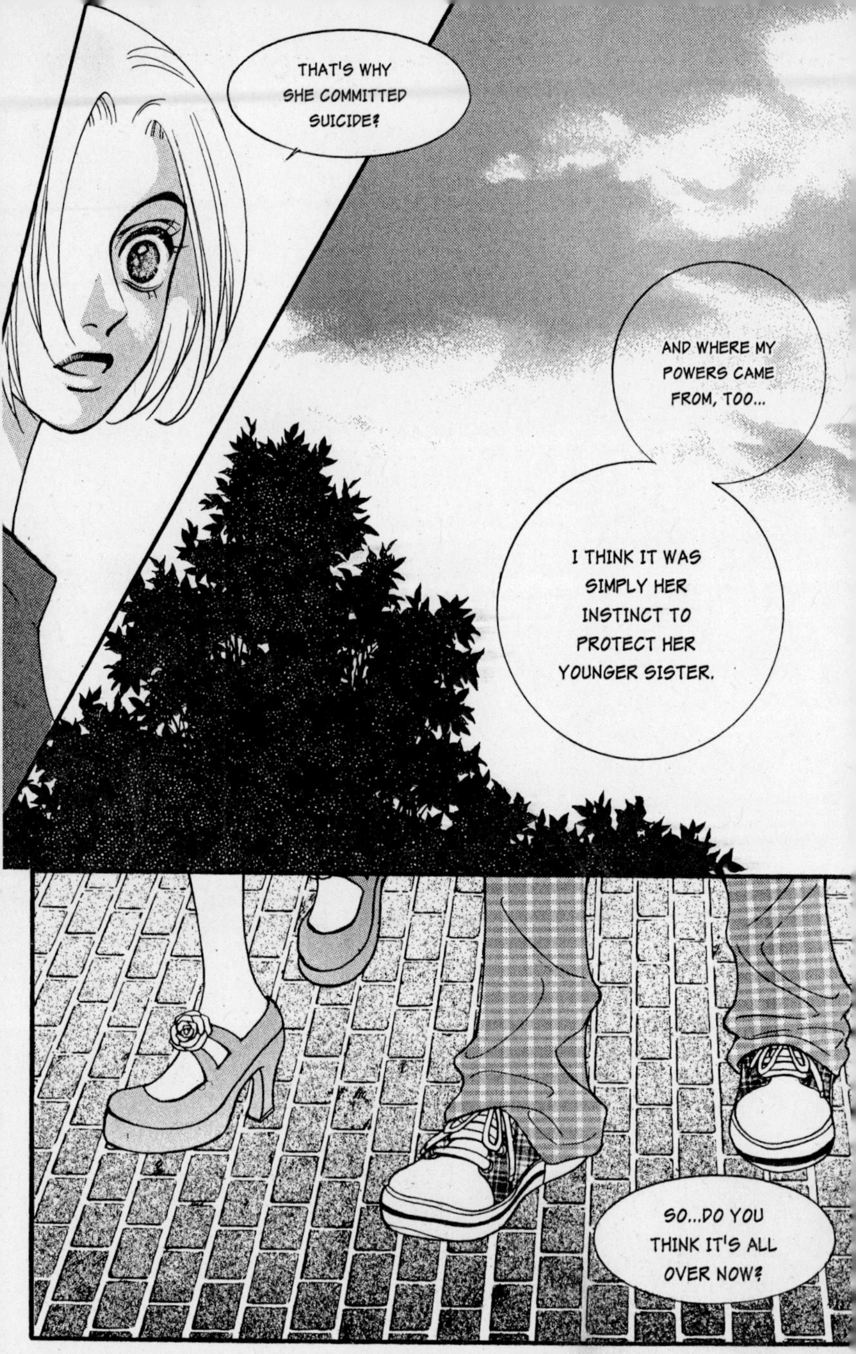
THAT'S WHY SHE COMMITTED SUICIDE?
AND WHERE MY POWERS CAME FROM, TOO...
I THINK IT WAS SIMPLY HER INSTINCT TO PROTECT HER YOUNGER SISTER.
SO...DO YOU THINK IT'S ALL OVER NOW?

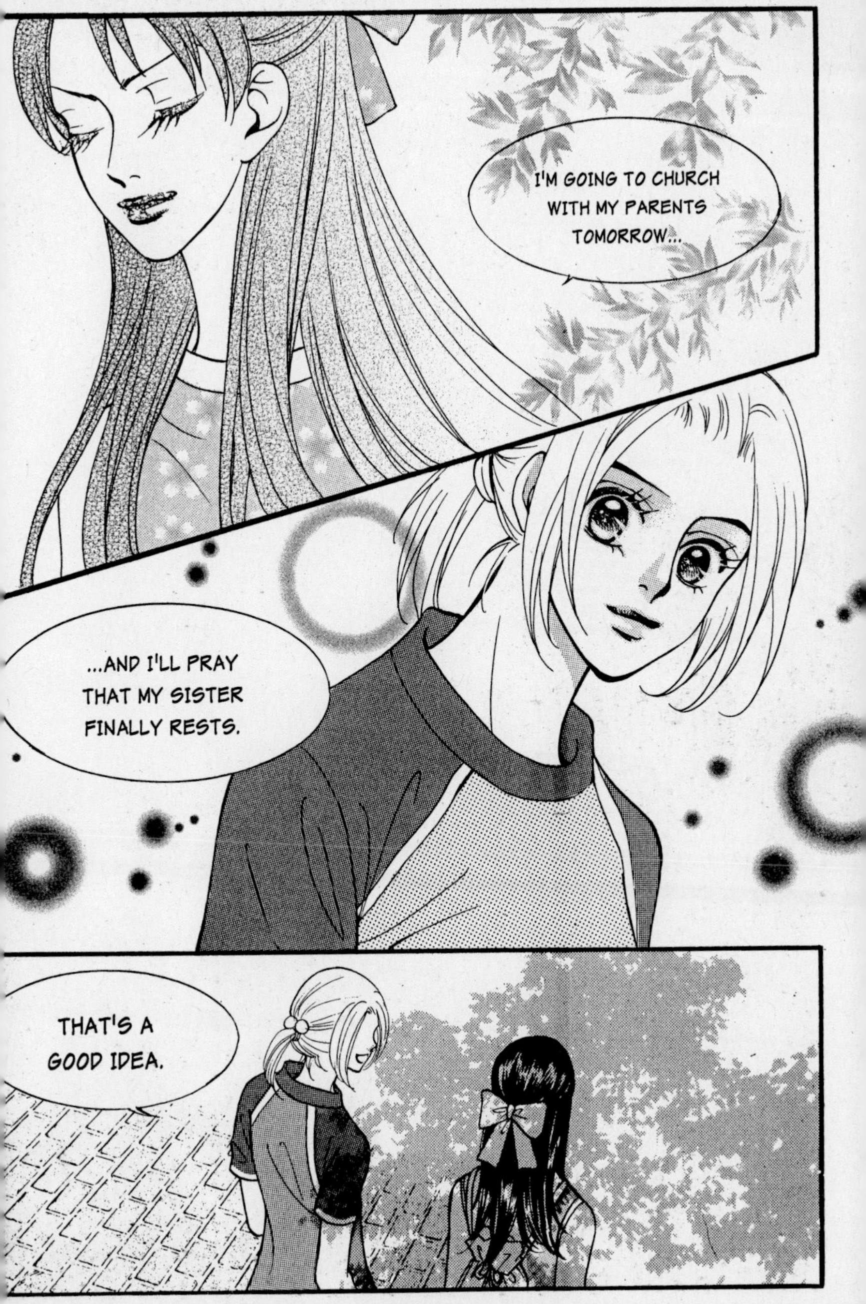
I'M GOING TO CHURCH WITH MY PARENTS TOMORROW...
...AND I'LL PRAY THAT MY SISTER FINALLY RESTS.
THAT'S A GOOD IDEA.

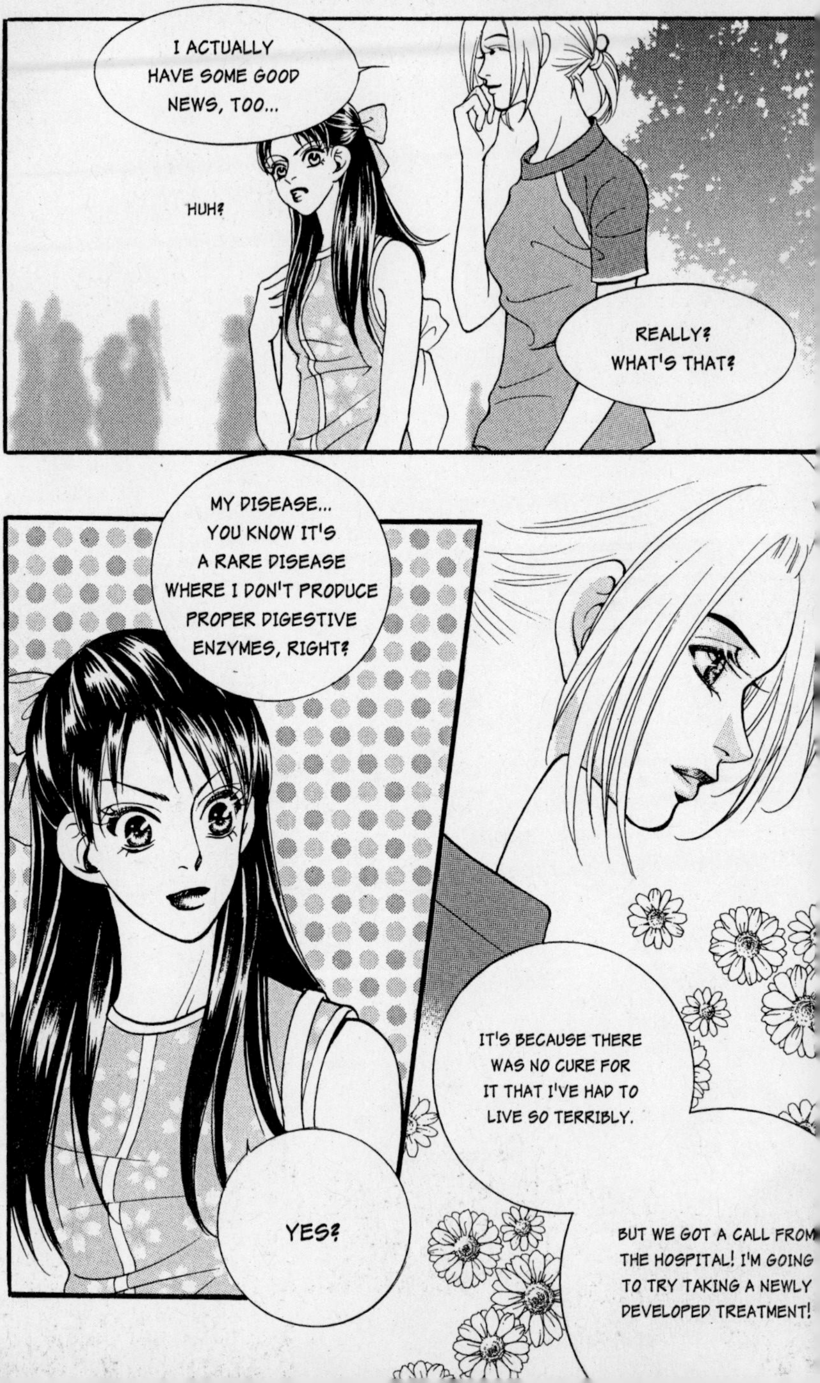
I ACTUALLY HAVE SOME GOOD NEWS, TOO...
HUH?
REALLY? WHAT'S THAT?
MY DISEASE... YOU KNOW IT'S A RARE DISEASE WHERE I DON'T PRODUCE PROPER DIGESTIVE ENZYMES, RIGHT?
YES?
IT'S BECAUSE THERE WAS NO CURE FOR IT THAT I'VE HAD TO LIVE SO TERRIBLY.
BUT WE GOT A CALL FROM THE HOSPITAL! I'M GOING TO TRY TAKING A NEWLY DEVELOPED TREATMENT!

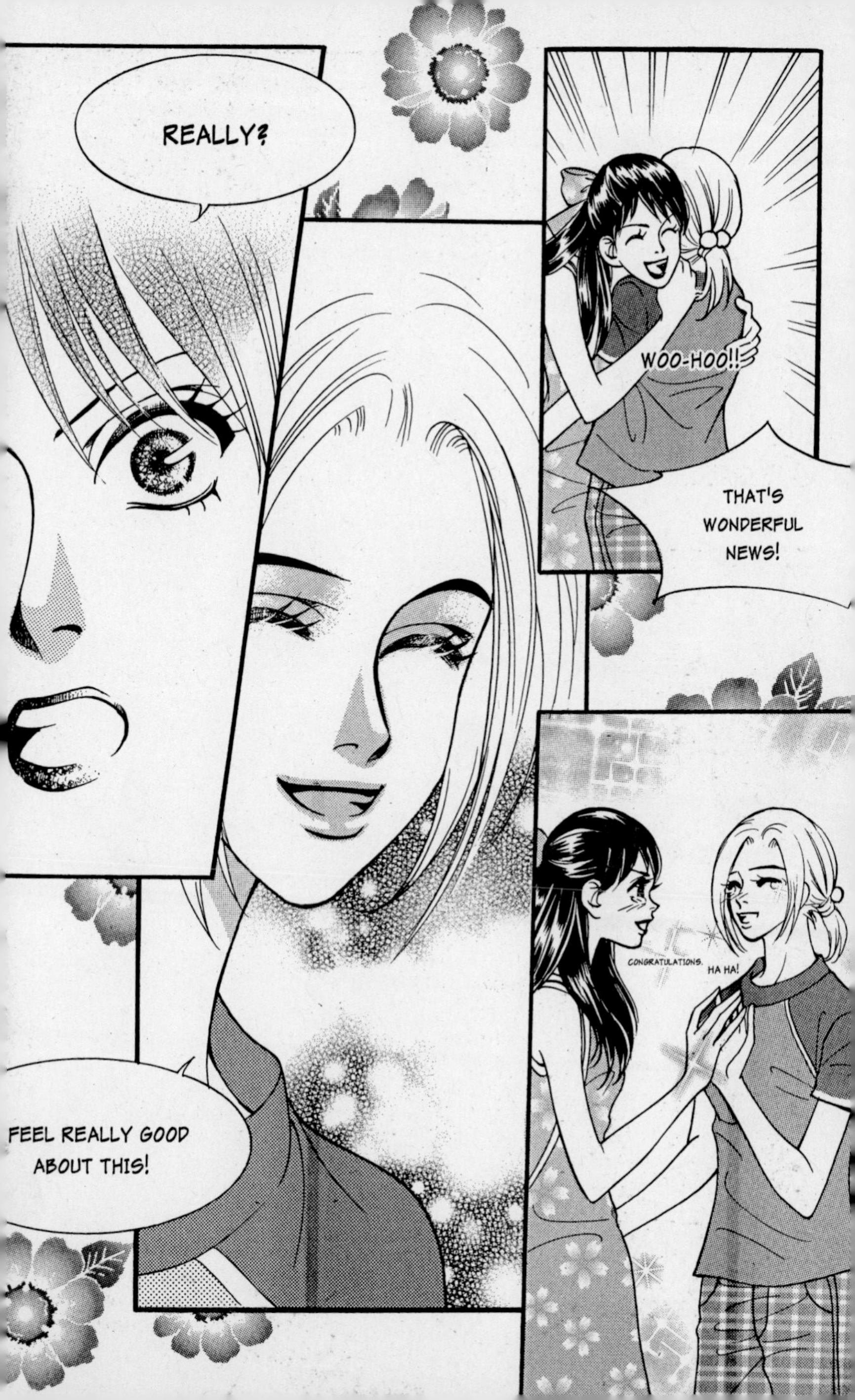
REALLY?
FEEL REALLY GOOD ABOUT THIS!
WOO-HOO!!
THAT'S WONDERFUL NEWS!
CONGRATULATIONS.
HA HA!

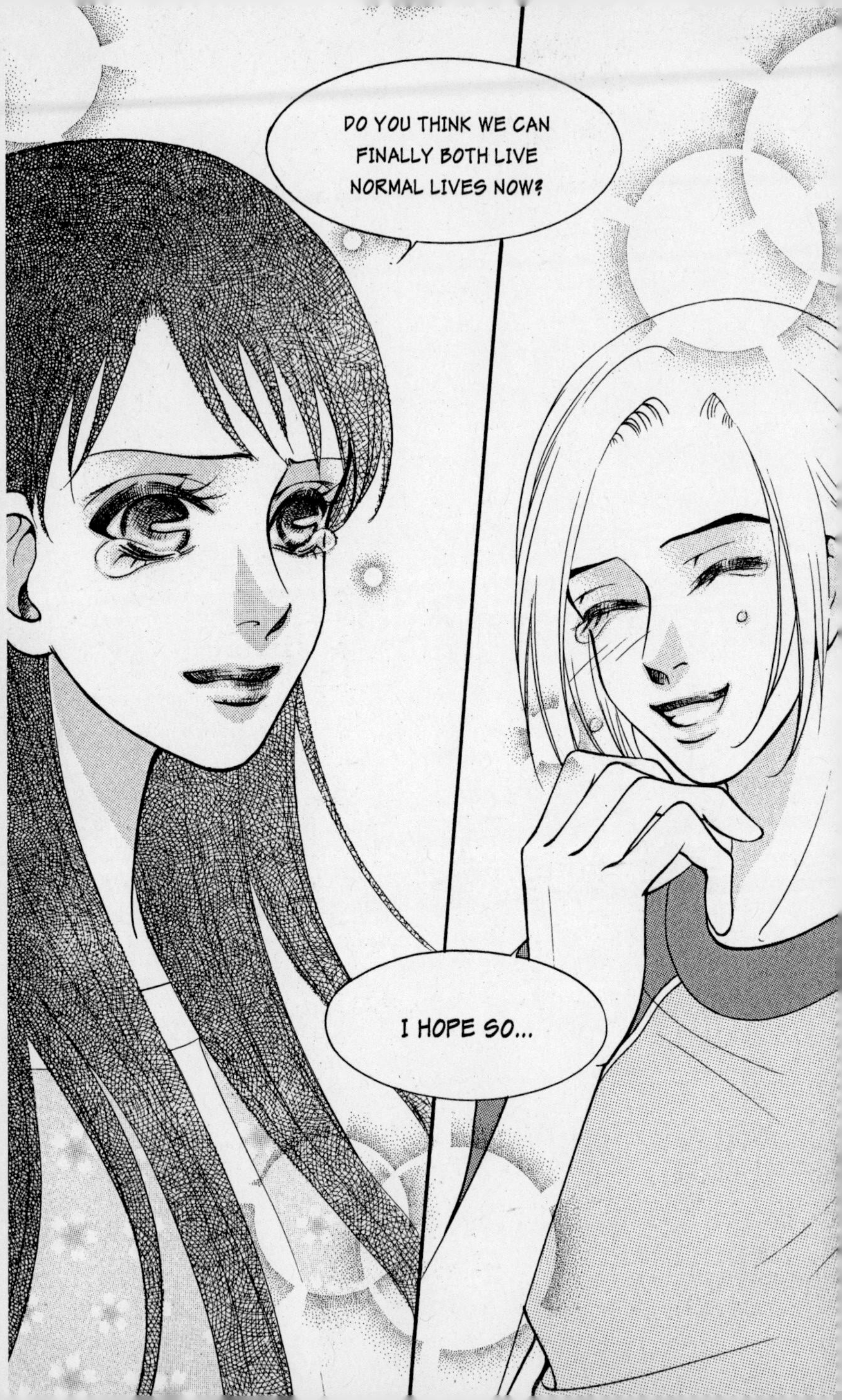
DO YOU THINK WE CAN FINALLY BOTH LIVE NORMAL LIVES NOW?
I HOPE SO...

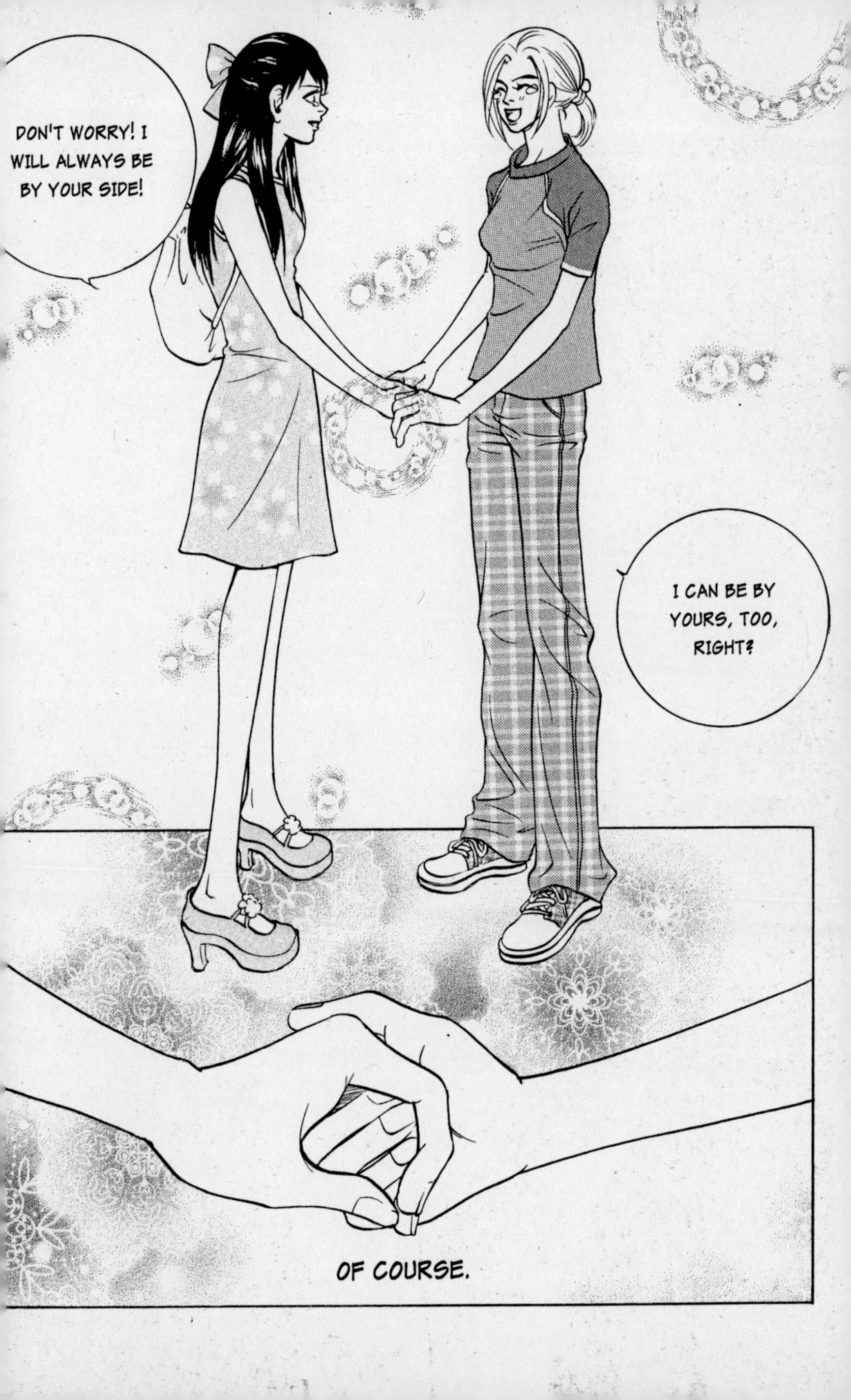
DON'T WORRY! I WILL ALWAYS BE BY YOUR SIDE!
I CAN BE BY YOURS, TOO, RIGHT?
OF COURSE.

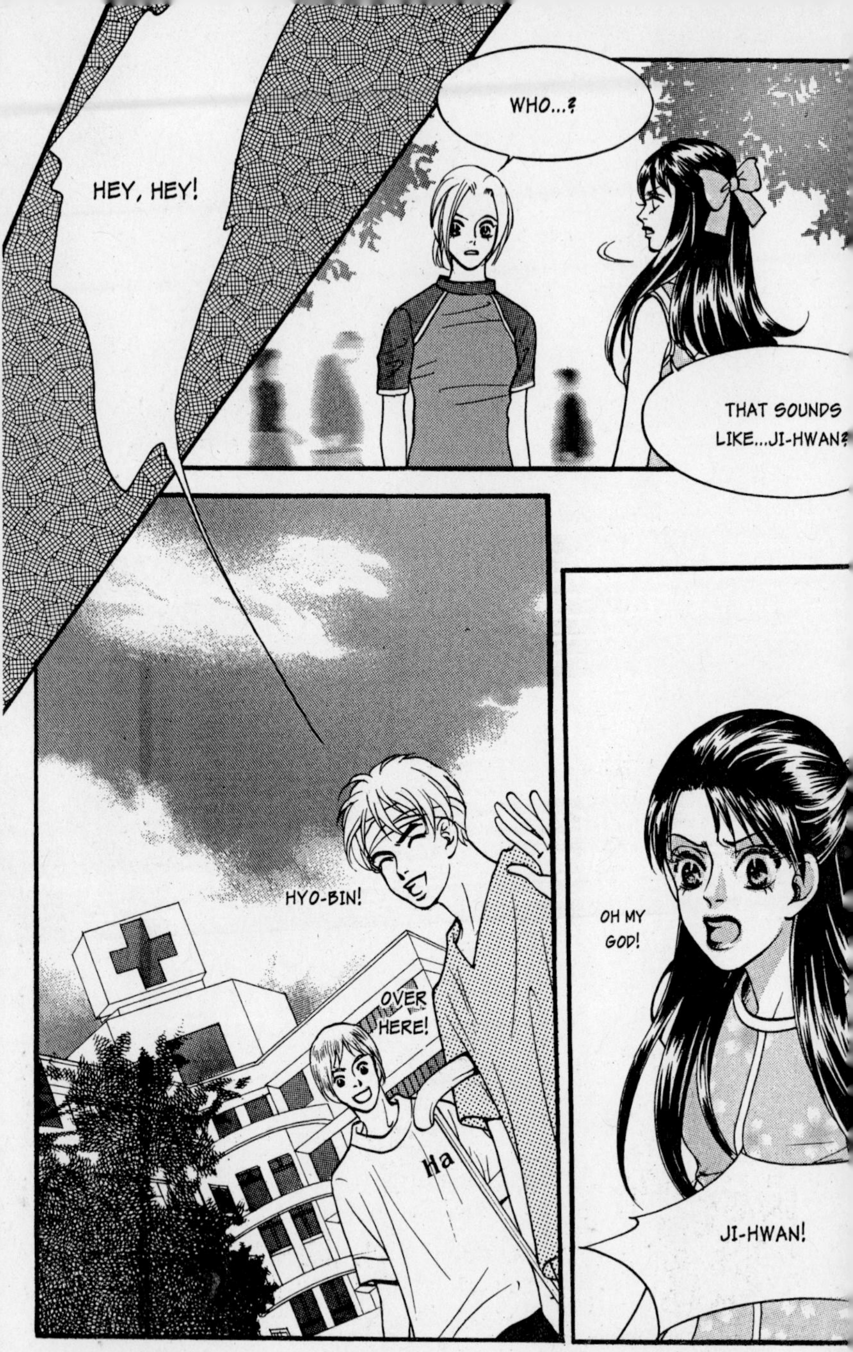
HEY, HEY!
WHO...?
THAT SOUNDS LIKE...JI-HWAN?
HYO-BIN!
OVER HERE!
Ha
OH MY GOD!
JI-HWAN!

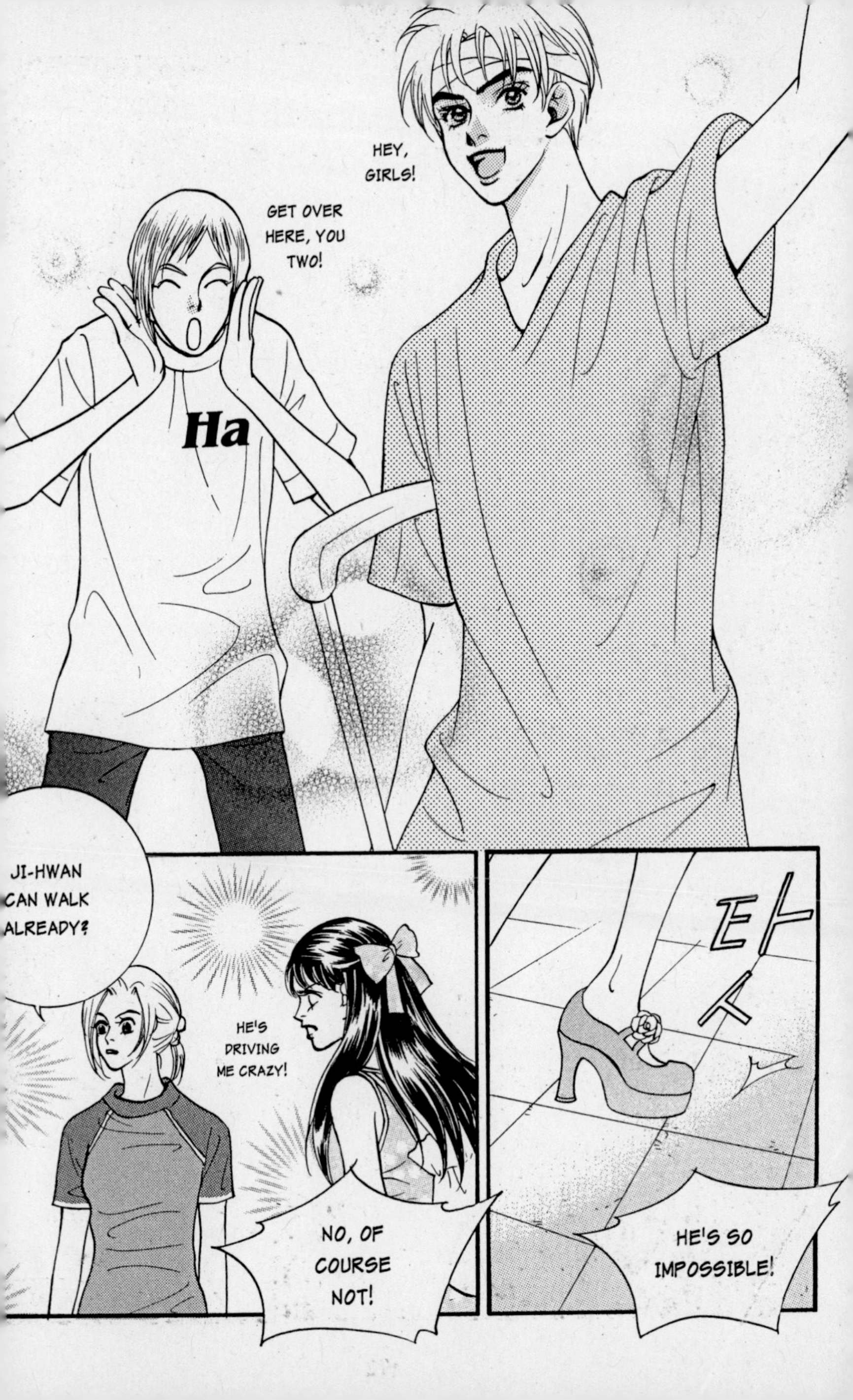
GET OVER HERE, YOU TWO!
HEY, GIRLS!
Ha
JI-HWAN CAN WALK ALREADY?
HE'S DRIVING ME CRAZY!
NO, OF COURSE NOT!
탁
HE'S SO IMPOSSIBLE!

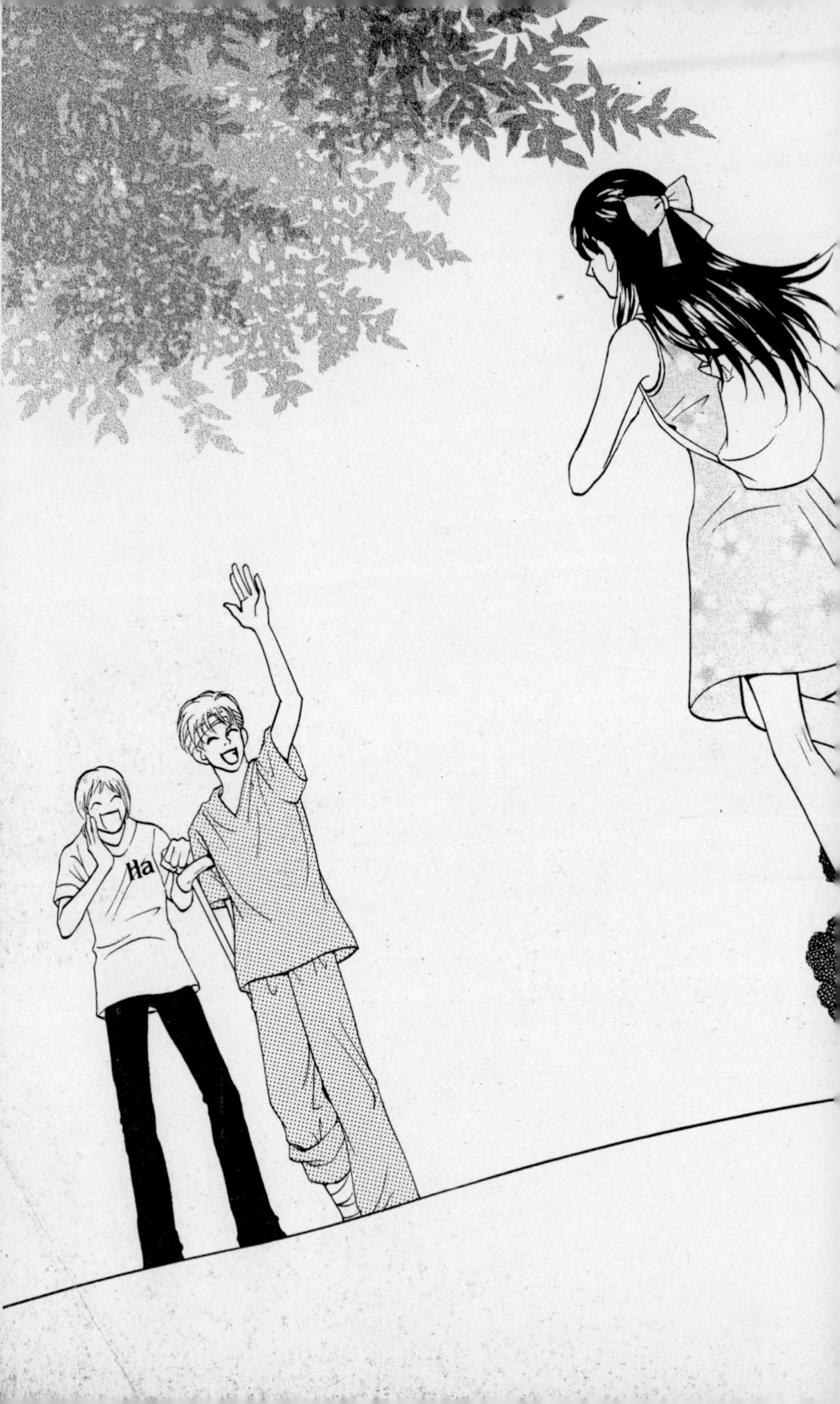
Ha

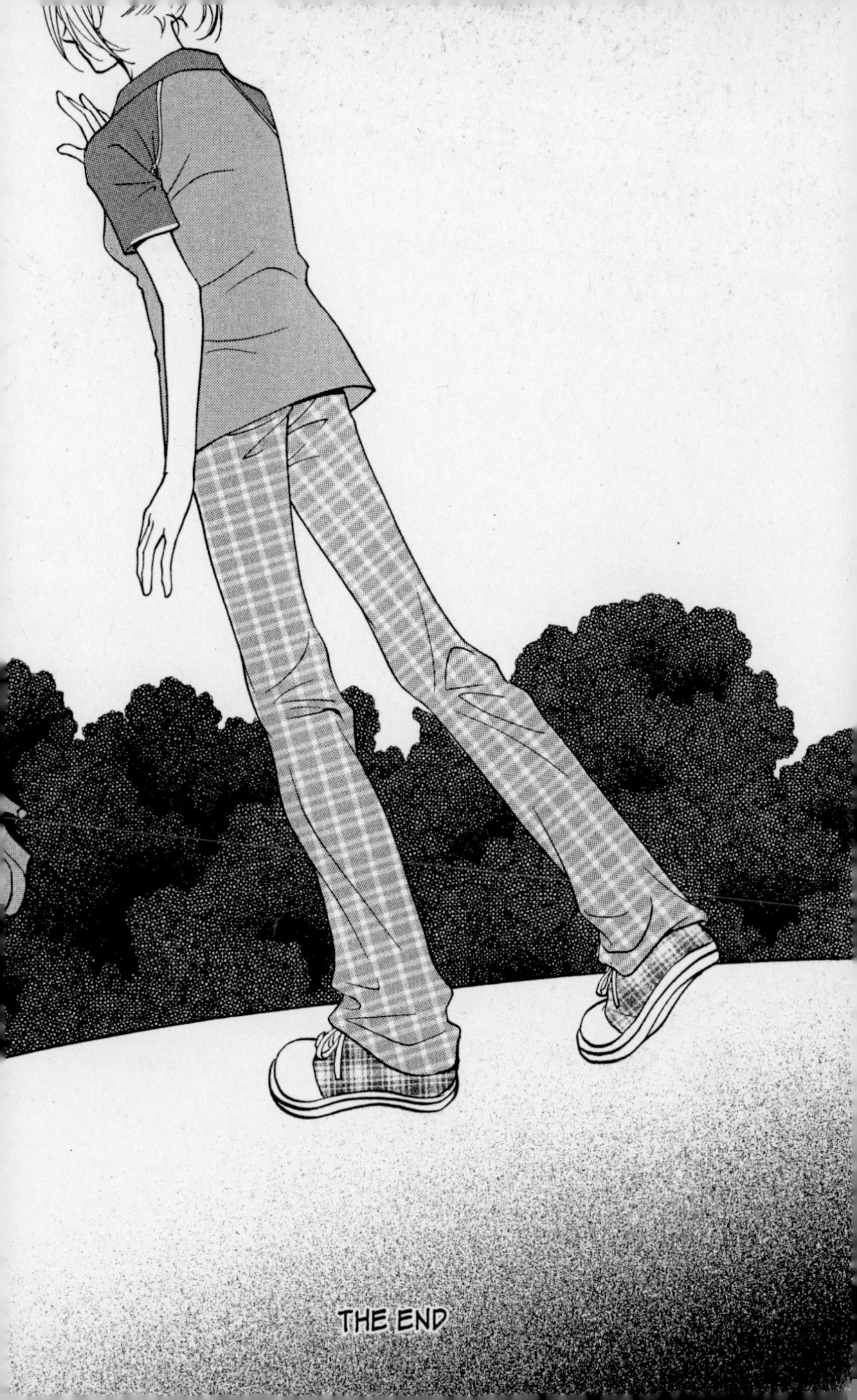
THE END

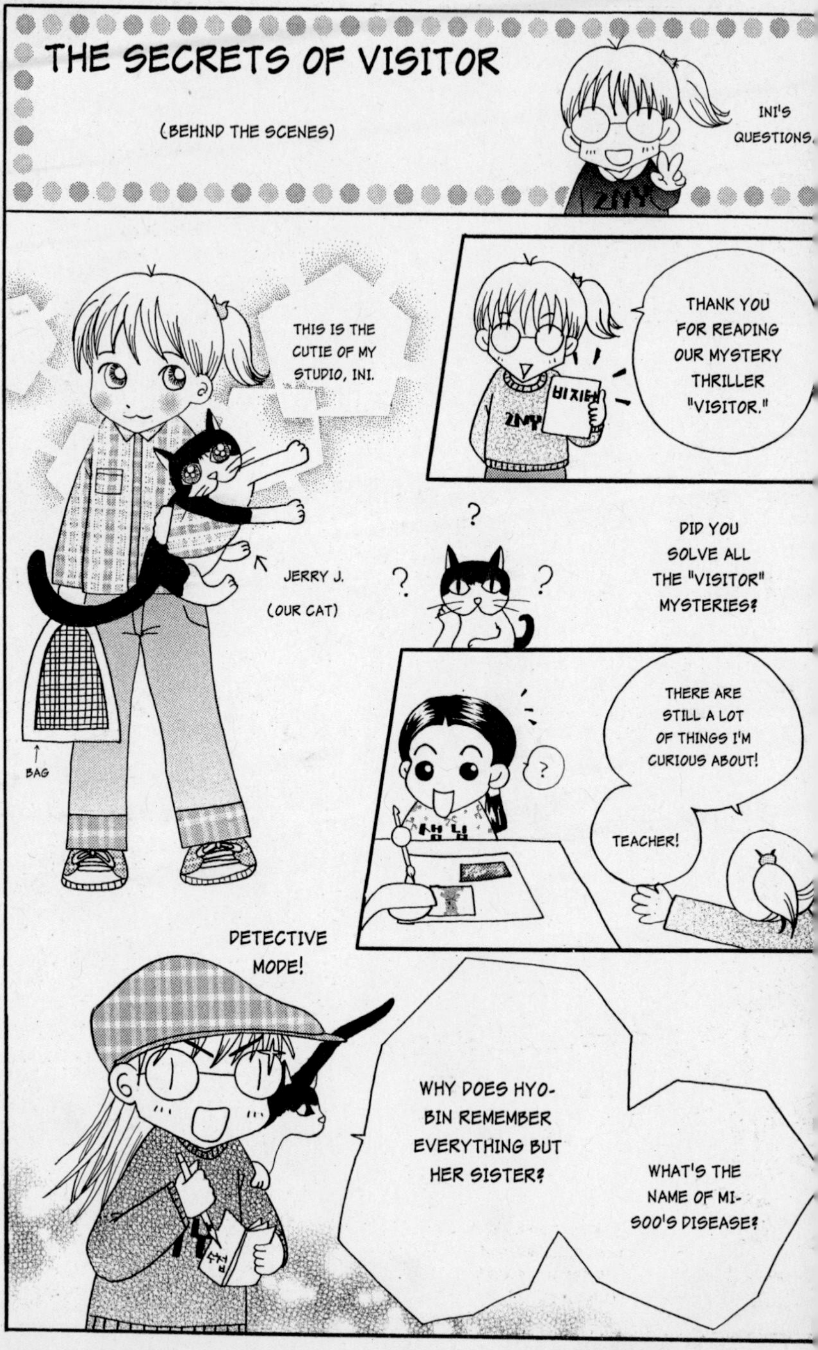
THE SECRETS OF VISITOR
(BEHIND THE SCENES)
INI'S QUESTIONS.
THIS IS THE CUTIE OF MY STUDIO, INI.
JERRY J.
(OUR CAT)
BAG
THANK YOU FOR READING OUR MYSTERY THRILLER "VISITOR."
비지터
DID YOU SOLVE ALL THE "VISITOR" MYSTERIES?
THERE ARE STILL A LOT OF THINGS I'M CURIOUS ABOUT!
TEACHER!
DETECTIVE MODE!
WHY DOES HYO-BIN REMEMBER EVERYTHING BUT HER SISTER?
WHAT'S THE NAME OF MI-SOO'S DISEASE?

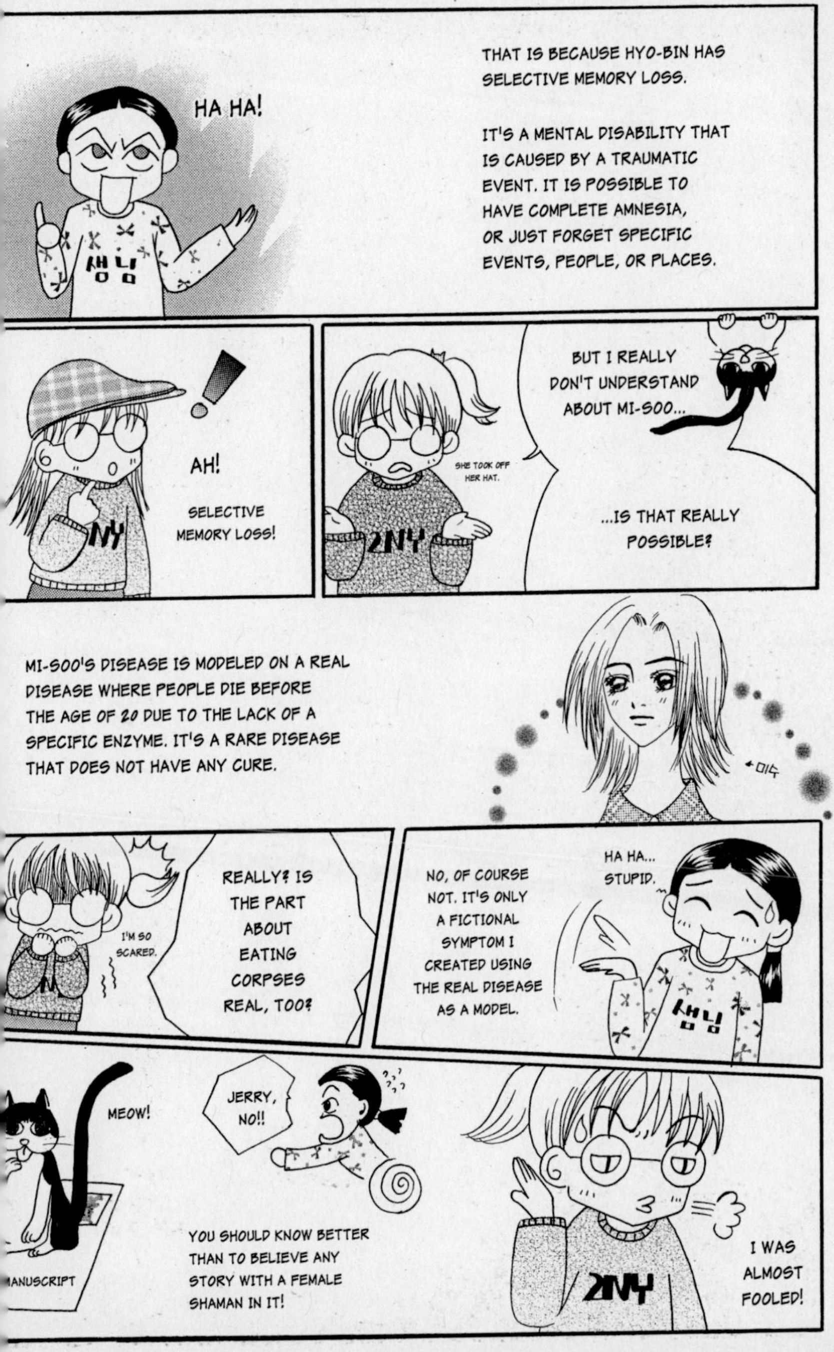
HA HA!
THAT IS BECAUSE HYO-BIN HAS SELECTIVE MEMORY LOSS.
IT'S A MENTAL DISABILITY THAT IS CAUSED BY A TRAUMATIC EVENT. IT IS POSSIBLE TO HAVE COMPLETE AMNESIA, OR JUST FORGET SPECIFIC EVENTS, PEOPLE, OR PLACES.
AH!
SELECTIVE MEMORY LOSS!
SHE TOOK OFF HER HAT.
BUT I REALLY DON'T UNDERSTAND ABOUT MI-SOO...
...IS THAT REALLY POSSIBLE?
MI-SOO'S DISEASE IS MODELED ON A REAL DISEASE WHERE PEOPLE DIE BEFORE THE AGE OF 20 DUE TO THE LACK OF A SPECIFIC ENZYME. IT'S A RARE DISEASE THAT DOES NOT HAVE ANY CURE.
←미수
I'M SO SCARED.
REALLY? IS THE PART ABOUT EATING CORPSES REAL, TOO?
NO, OF COURSE NOT. IT'S ONLY A FICTIONAL SYMPTOM I CREATED USING THE REAL DISEASE AS A MODEL.
HA HA... STUPID.
MEOW!
MANUSCRIPT
JERRY, NO!!
YOU SHOULD KNOW BETTER THAN TO BELIEVE ANY STORY WITH A FEMALE SHAMAN IN IT!
I WAS ALMOST FOOLED!

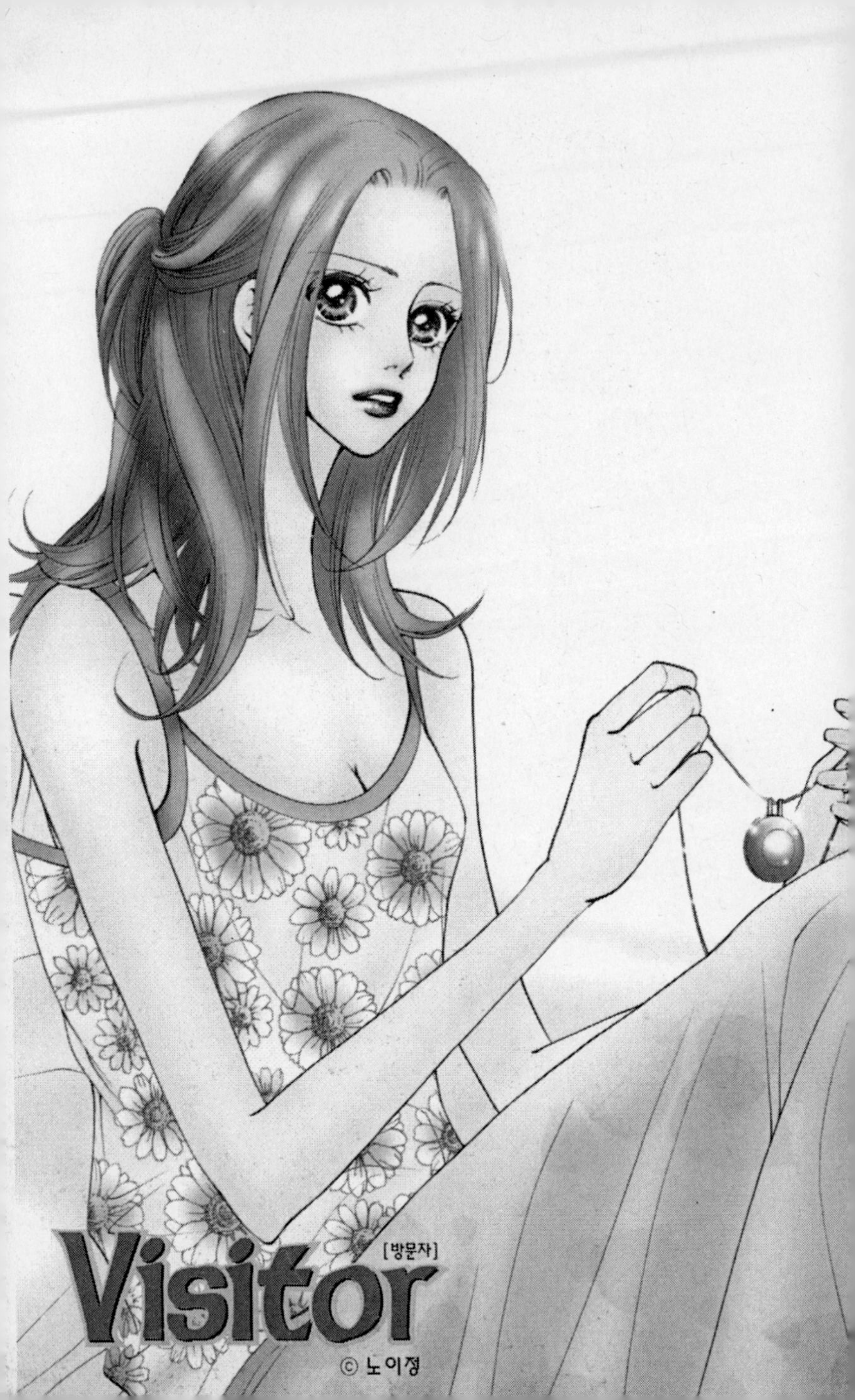

[방문자]
Visitor
© 노이정

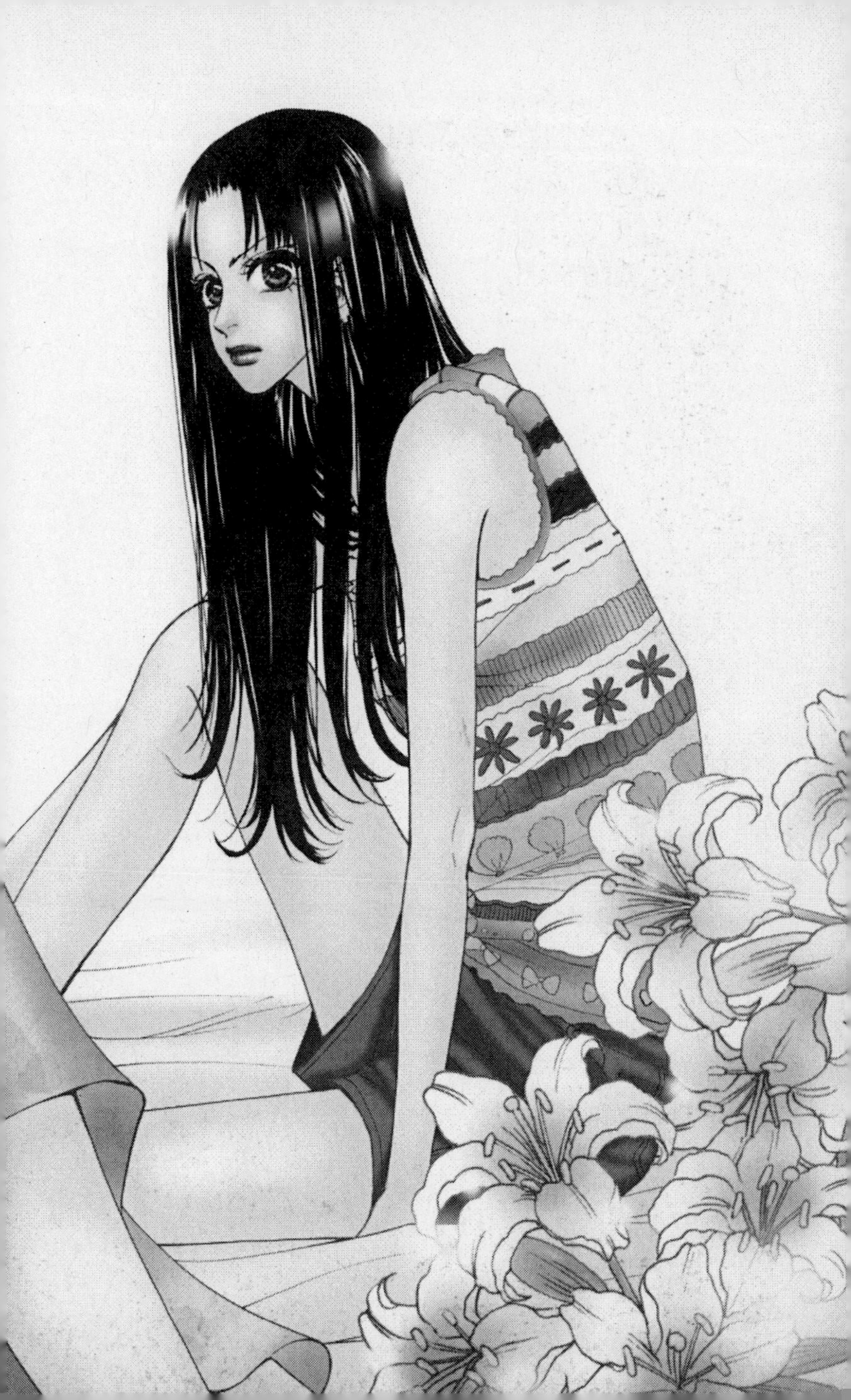

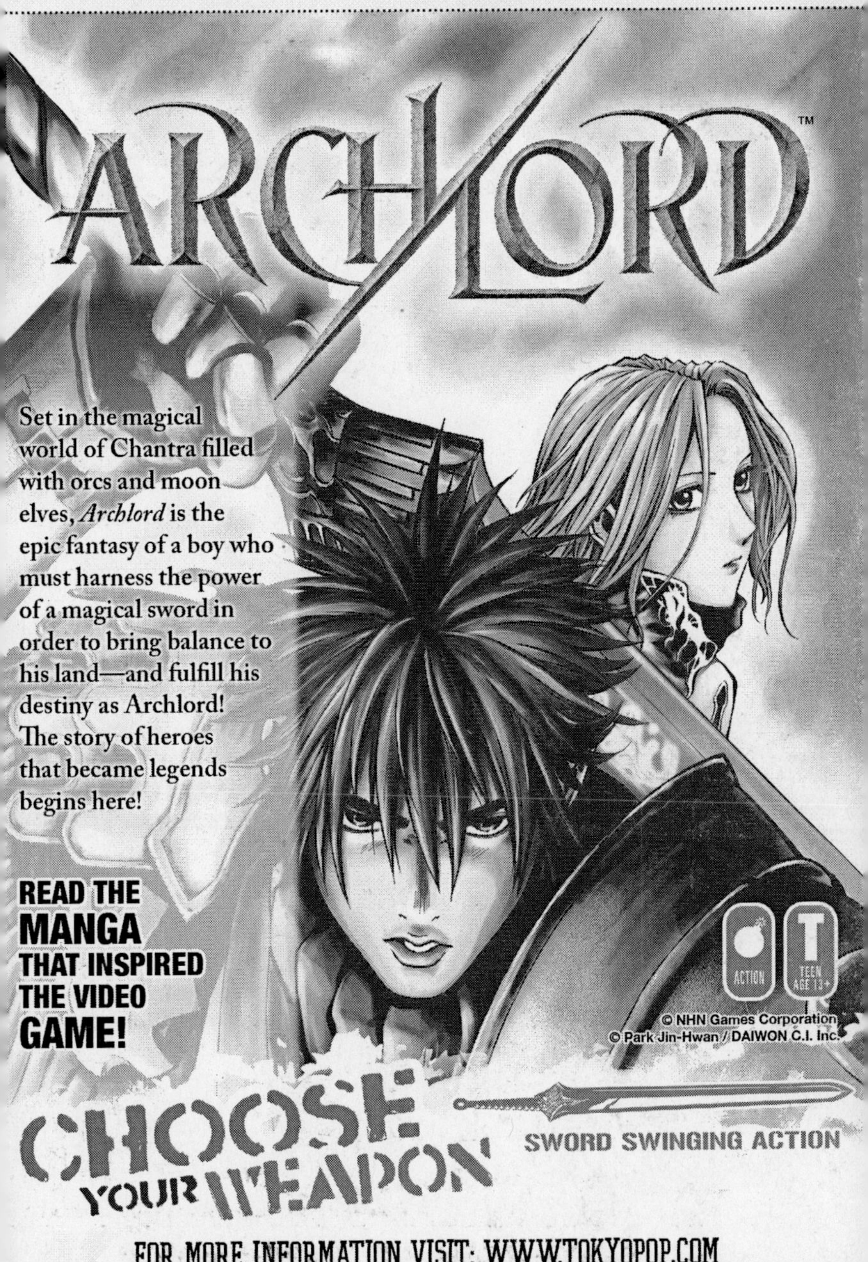
ARCHLORD™
Set in the magical world of Chantra filled with orcs and moon elves, *Archlord* is the epic fantasy of a boy who must harness the power of a magical sword in order to bring balance to his land—and fulfill his destiny as Archlord! The story of heroes that became legends begins here!
READ THE MANGA THAT INSPIRED THE VIDEO GAME!
ACTION
T
TEEN AGE 13+
© NHN Games Corporation
© Park Jin-Hwan / DAIWON C.I. Inc.
CHOOSE YOUR WEAPON
SWORD SWINGING ACTION
FOR MORE INFORMATION VISIT: WWW.TOKYOPOP.COM

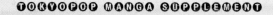